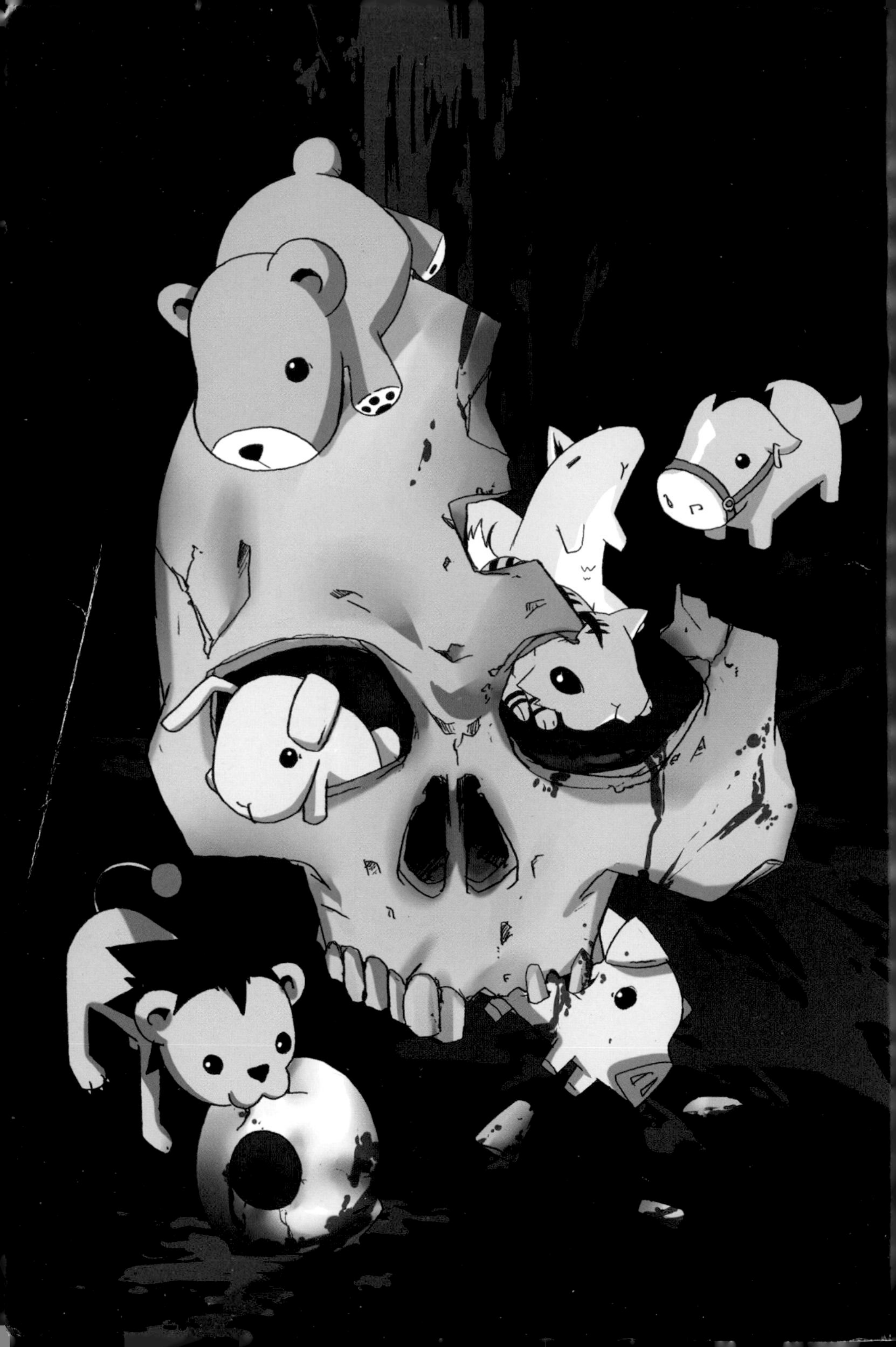

JUDGE

YOSHIKI TONOGAI

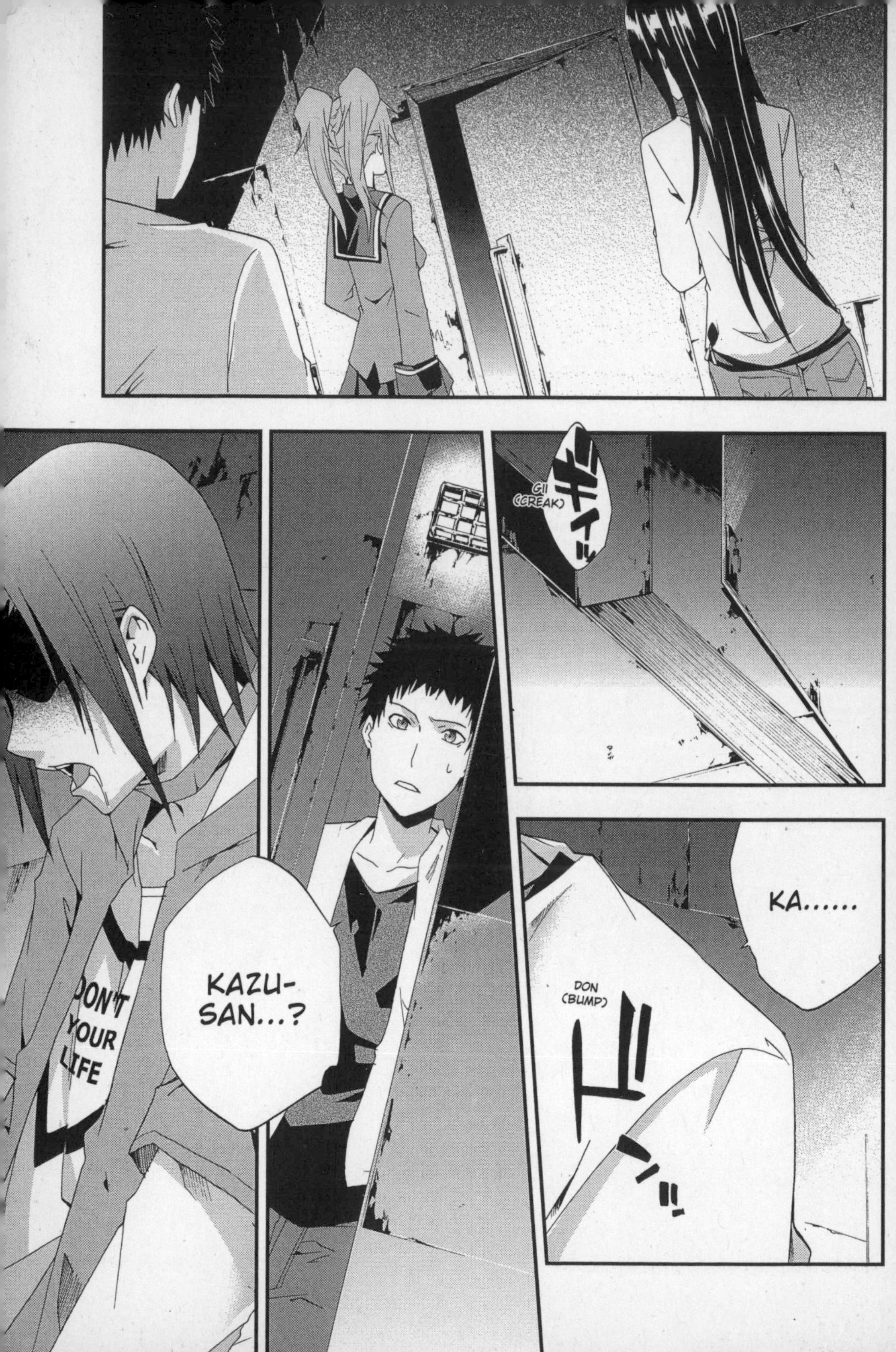
GII (CREAK)
KA......
DON (BUMP)
KAZU-SAN...?
DON'T YOUR LIFE

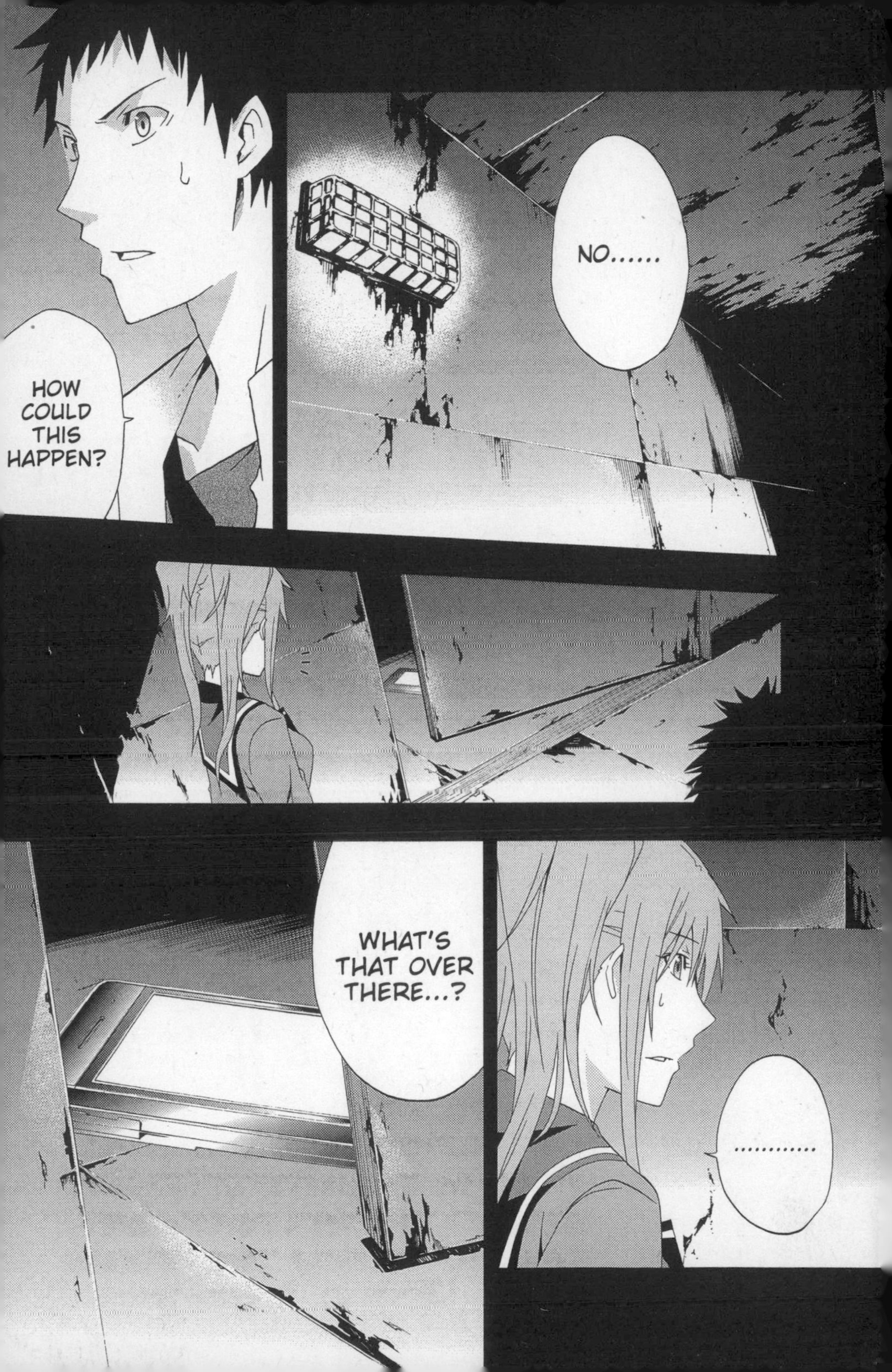
NO......
HOW COULD THIS HAPPEN?
....
WHAT'S THAT OVER THERE...?

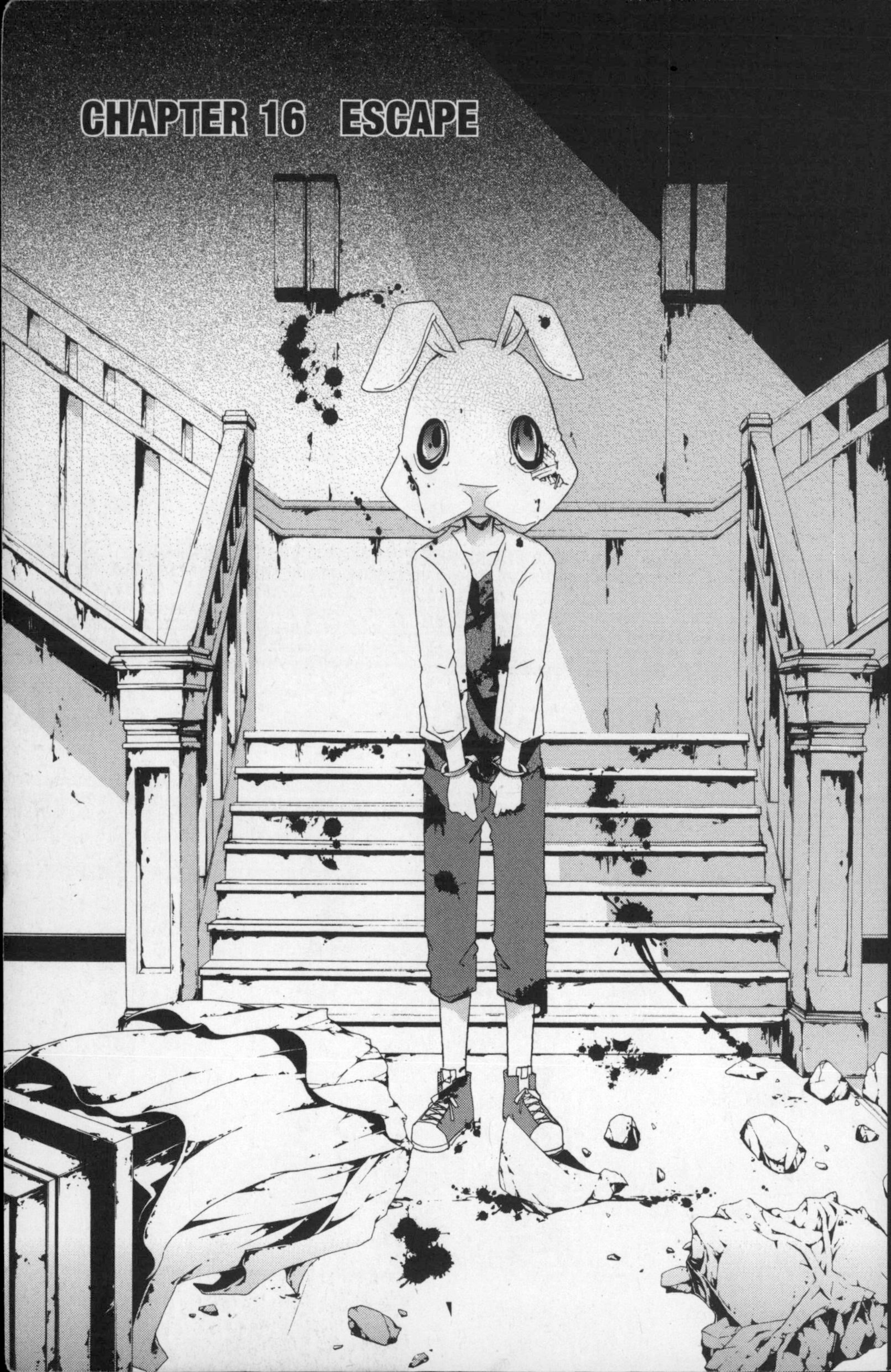
CHAPTER 16 ESCAPE

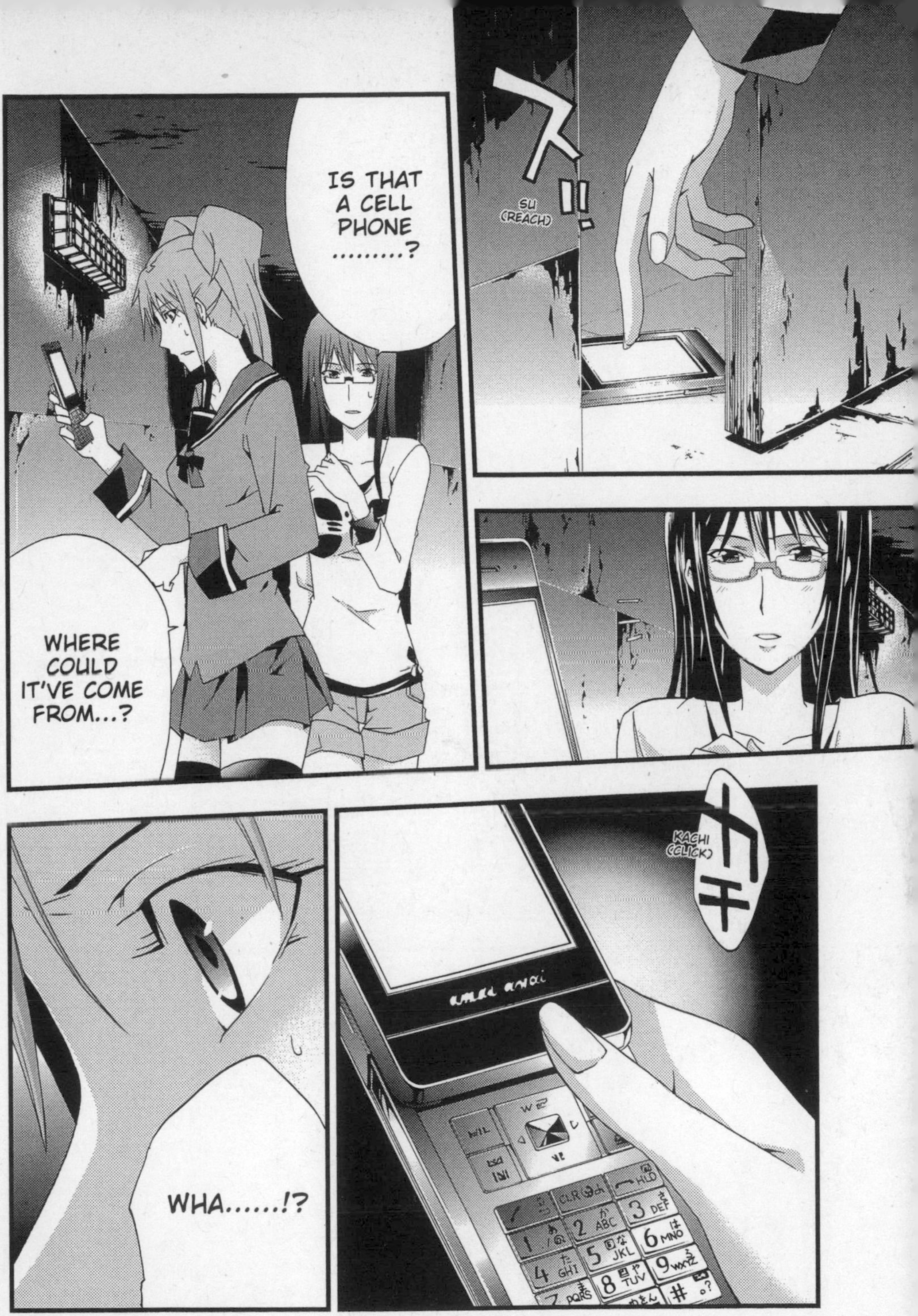

SU (REACH)
IS THAT A CELL PHONE ....?
WHERE COULD IT'VE COME FROM...?
KACHI (CLICK)
WHA......!?

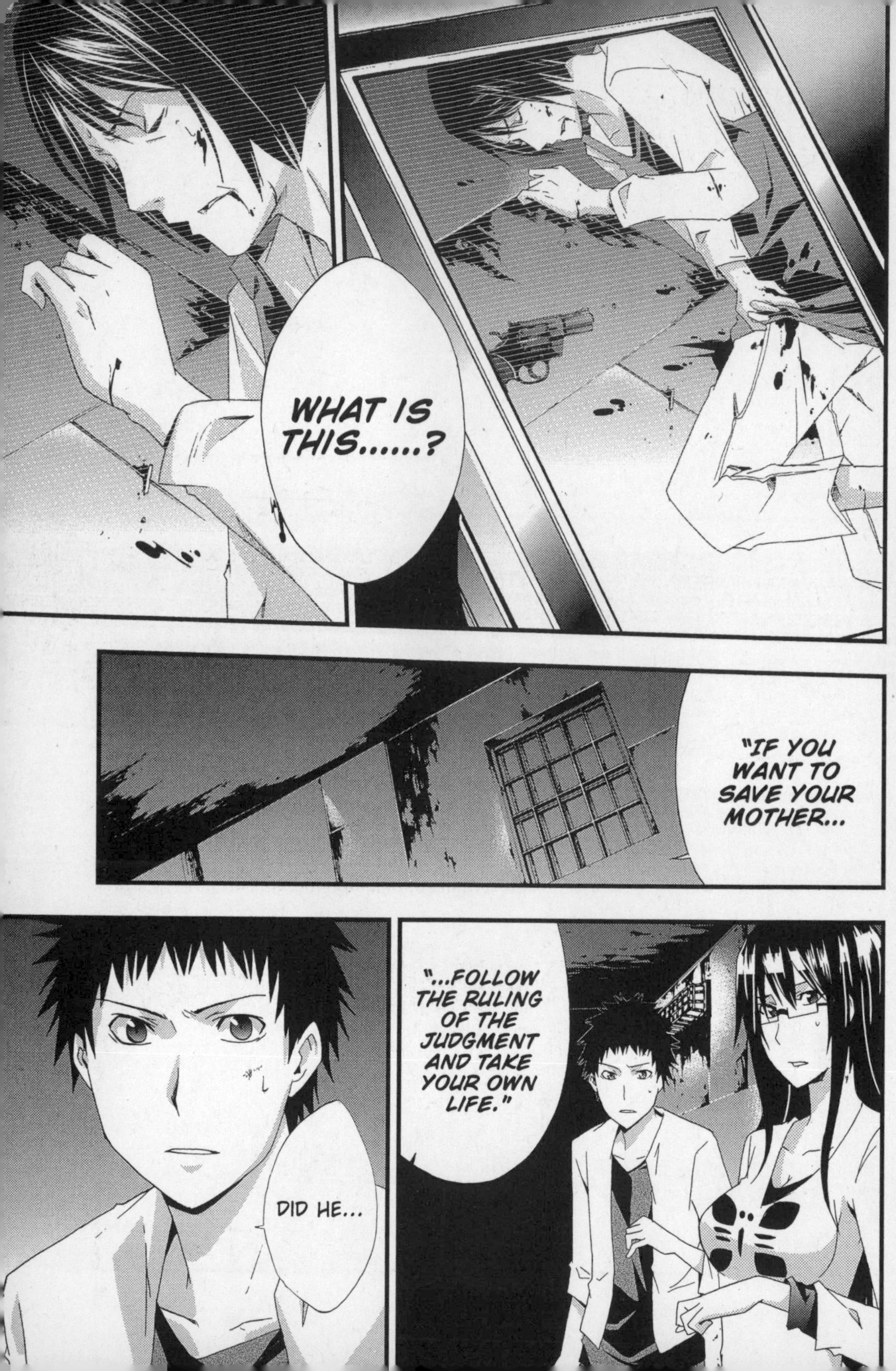
WHAT IS THIS......?
"IF YOU WANT TO SAVE YOUR MOTHER...
"...FOLLOW THE RULING OF THE JUDGMENT AND TAKE YOUR OWN LIFE."
DID HE...

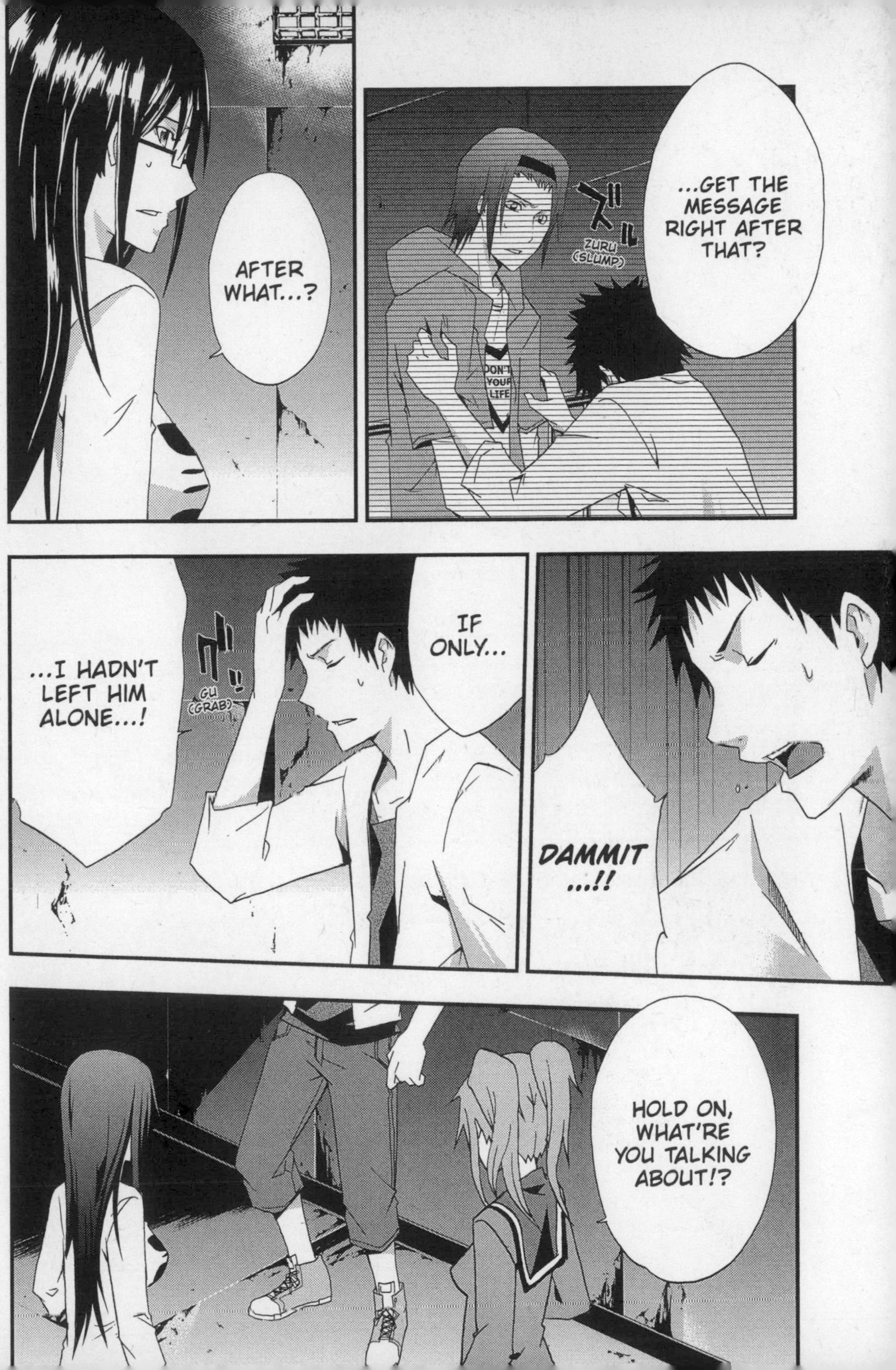
...GET THE MESSAGE RIGHT AFTER THAT?
ZURU (SLUMP)
AFTER WHAT...?
DAMMIT ...!!
IF ONLY...
GU (GRAB)
...I HADN'T LEFT HIM ALONE...!
HOLD ON, WHAT'RE YOU TALKING ABOUT!?

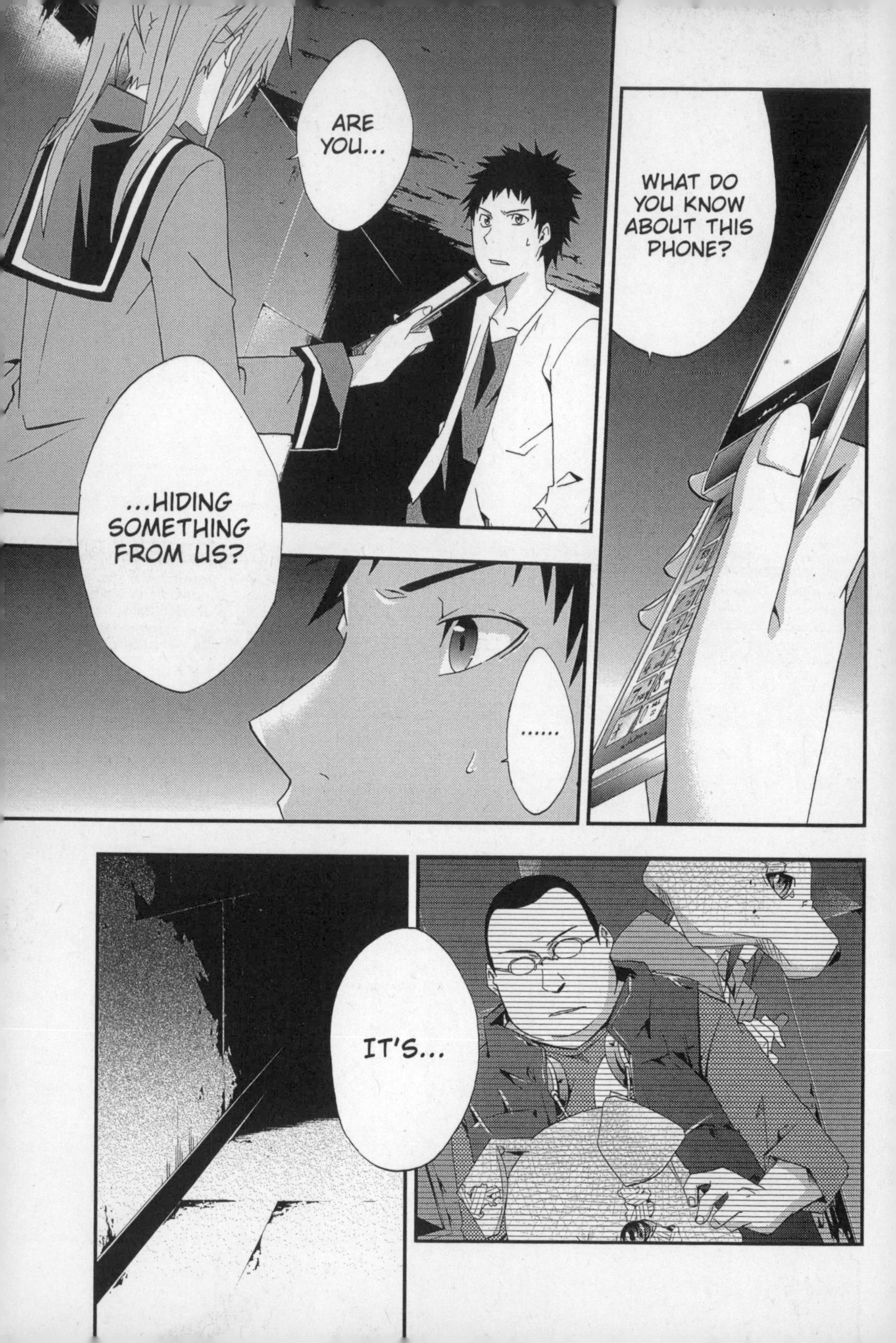
WHAT DO YOU KNOW ABOUT THIS PHONE?
ARE YOU...
...HIDING SOMETHING FROM US?
......
IT'S...

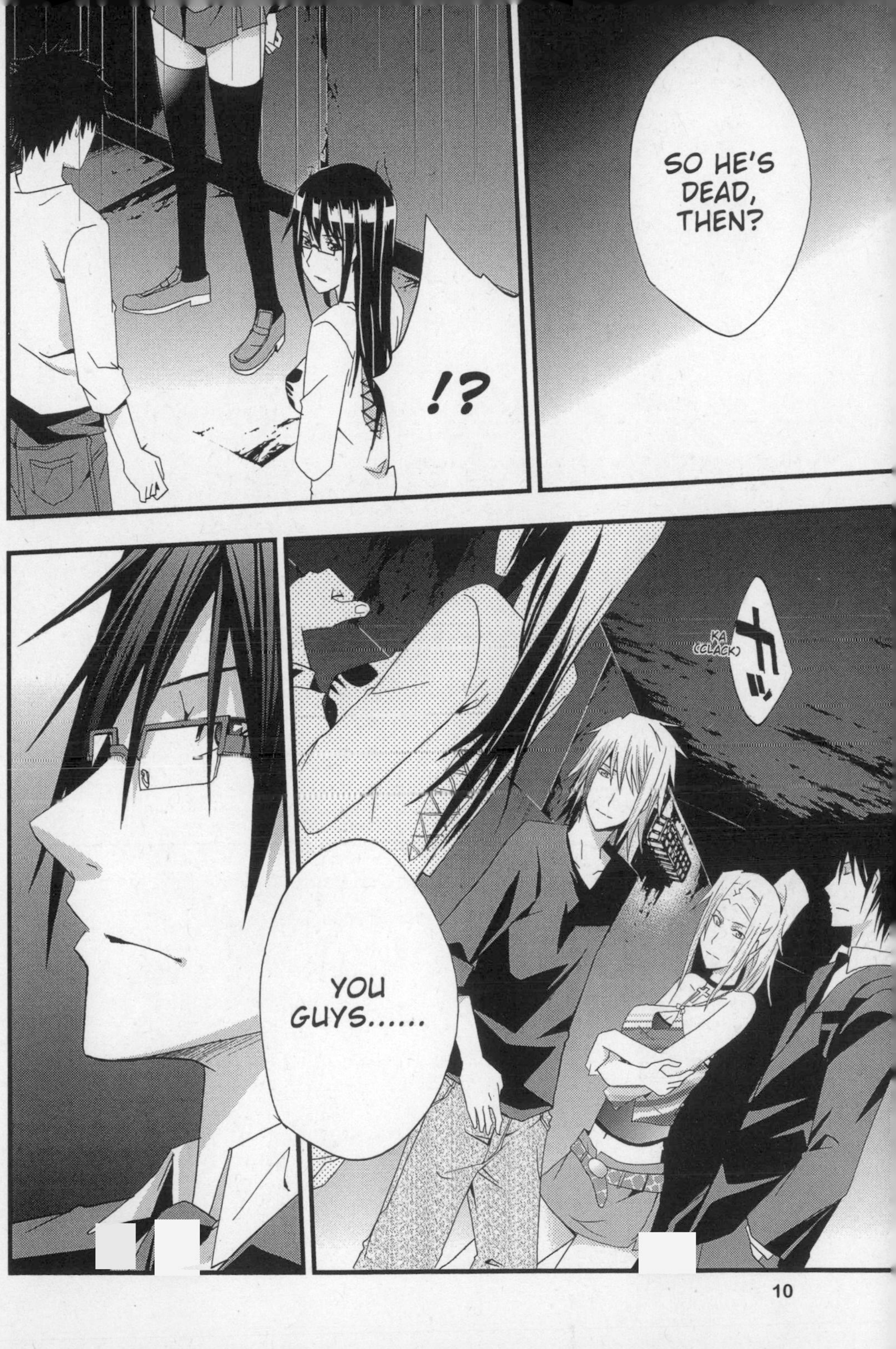
SO HE'S DEAD, THEN?
!?
KA (CLACK)
YOU GUYS......

......?

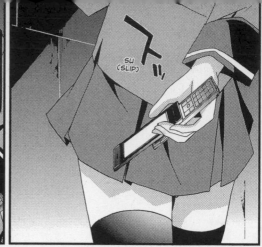

SU
(SLIP)

KA

KA

....

WELL,
THAT'S A
LETDOWN.

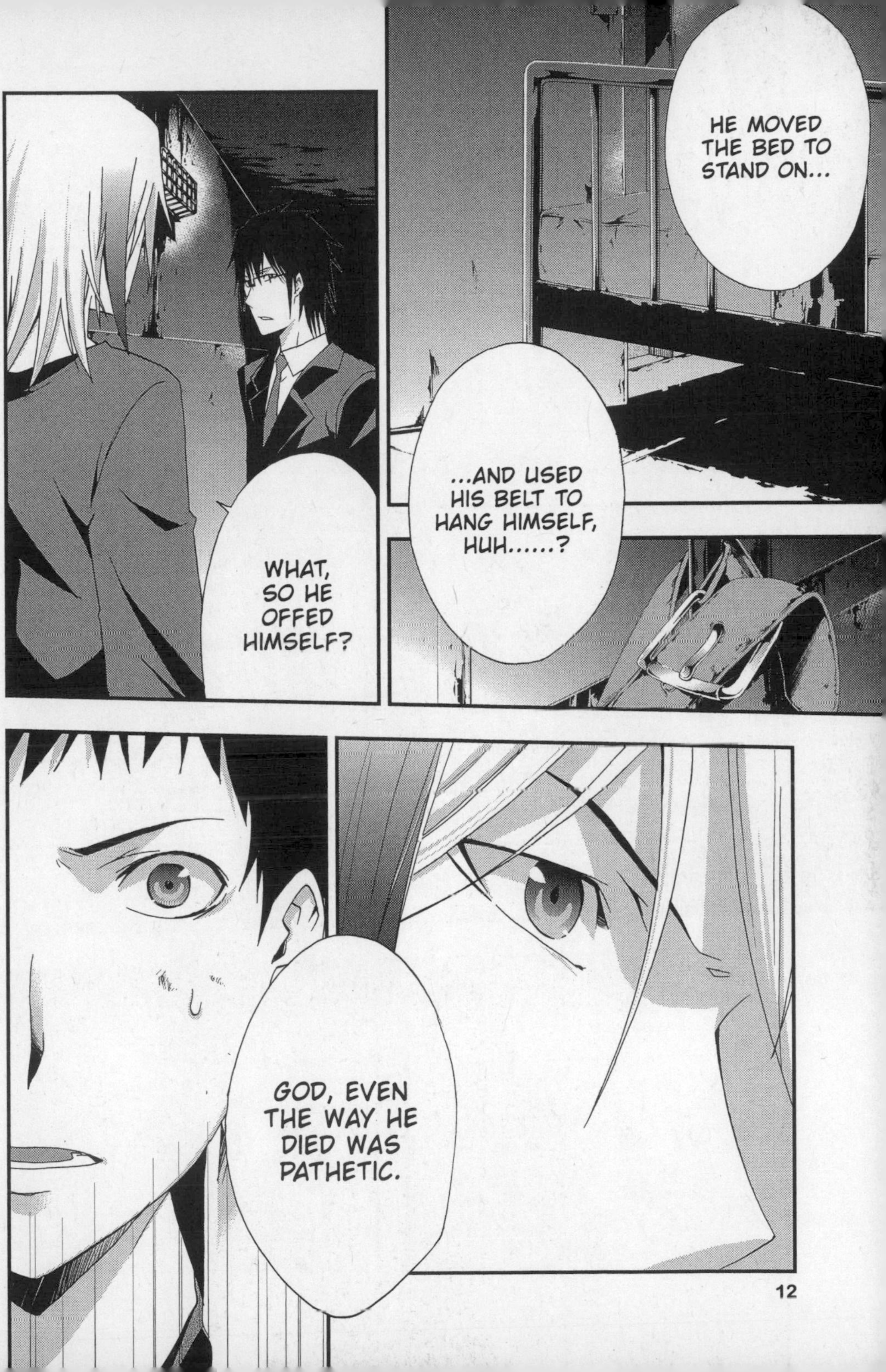
HE MOVED THE BED TO STAND ON...
...AND USED HIS BELT TO HANG HIMSELF, HUH......?
WHAT, SO HE OFFED HIMSELF?
GOD, EVEN THE WAY HE DIED WAS PATHETIC.

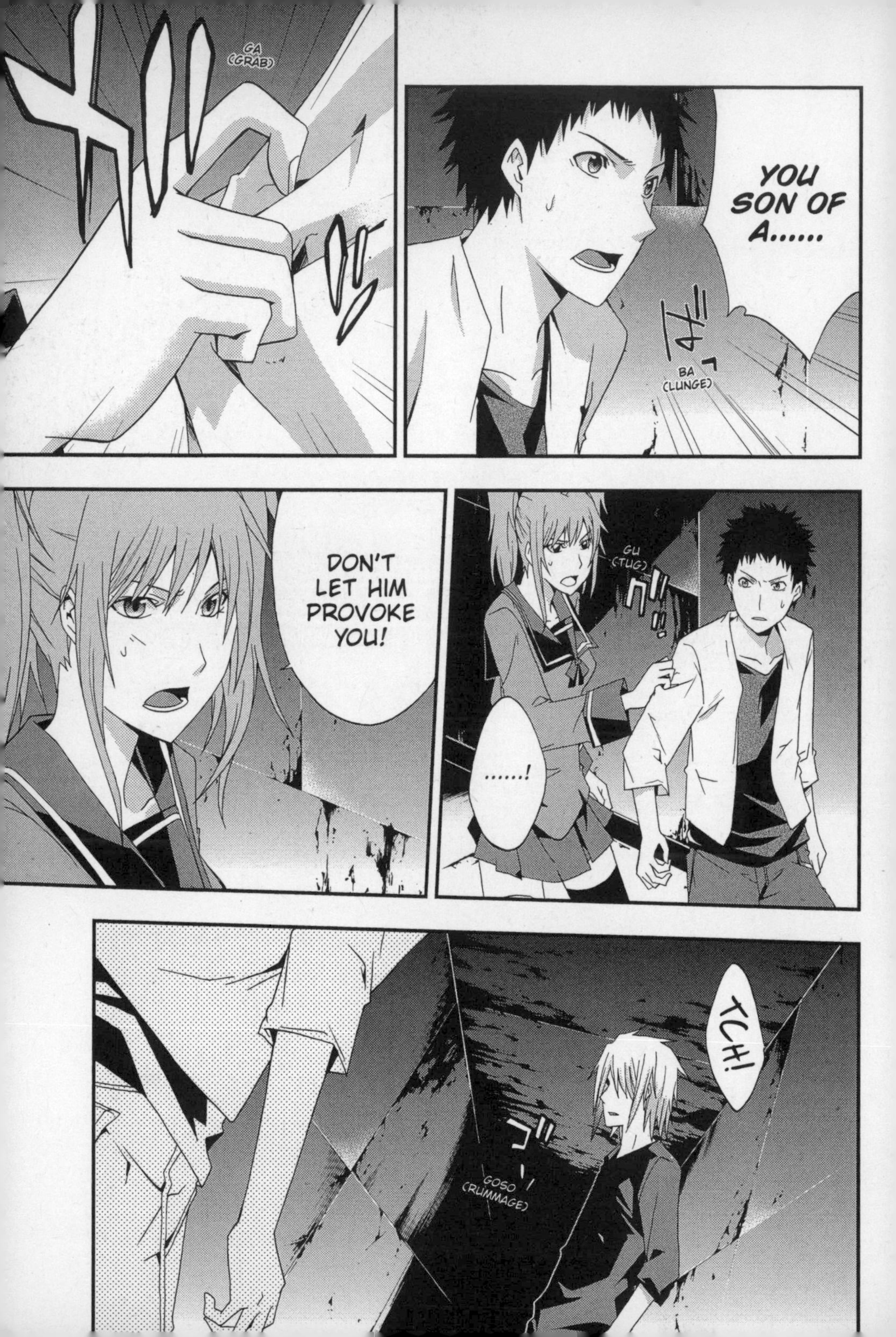
YOU SON OF A......
BA (LUNGE)
GA (GRAB)
GU (TUG)
......!
DON'T LET HIM PROVOKE YOU!
TCH!
GOSO (RUMMAGE)

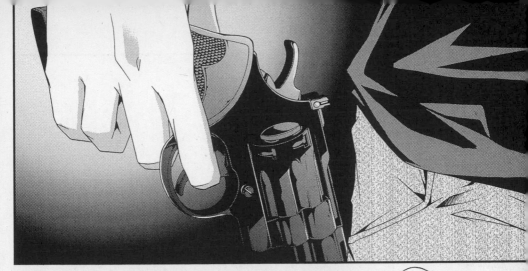

AND HERE I THOUGHT...

...I'D FINALLY GET TO TRY SHOOTING THIS THING.

I'M NOT GOING TO USE IT...

...WHICH MEANS I'M GIVING YOU A CHANCE TO LIVE.

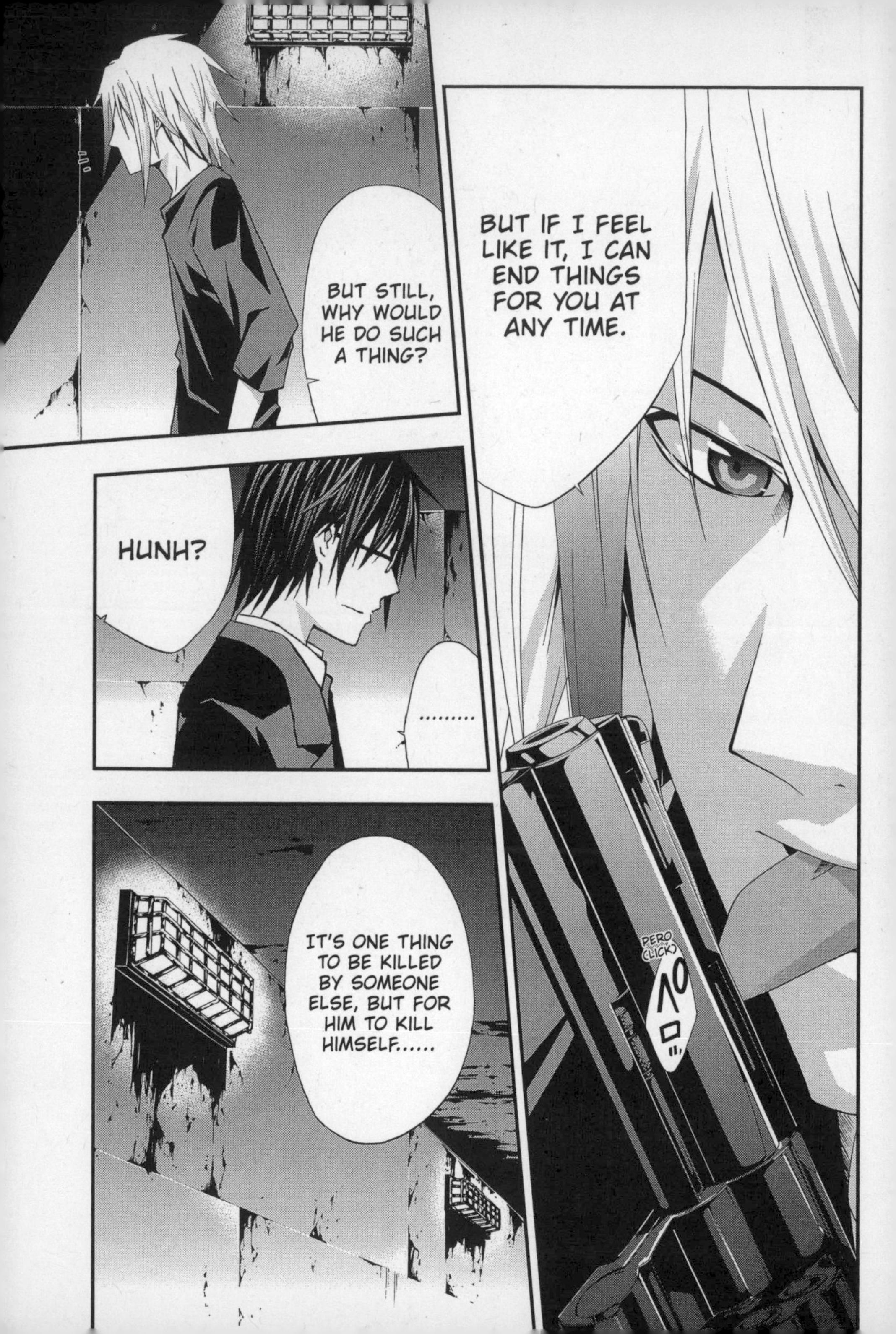
BUT IF I FEEL LIKE IT, I CAN END THINGS FOR YOU AT ANY TIME.
PERO (CLICK)
BUT STILL, WHY WOULD HE DO SUCH A THING?
HUNH?
....
IT'S ONE THING TO BE KILLED BY SOMEONE ELSE, BUT FOR HIM TO KILL HIMSELF......

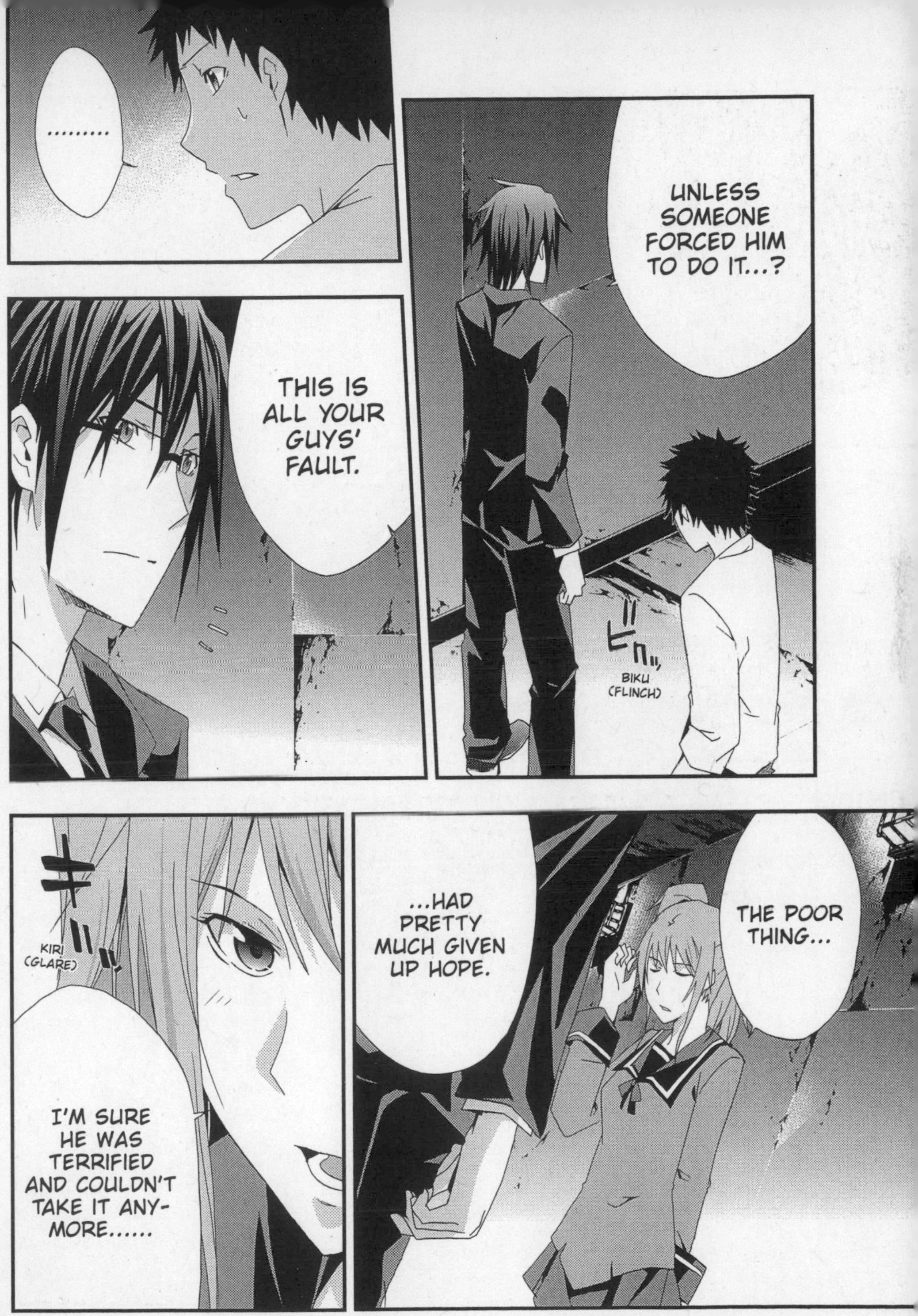
UNLESS SOMEONE FORCED HIM TO DO IT...?
BIKU (FLINCH)
....
THIS IS ALL YOUR GUYS' FAULT.
THE POOR THING...
...HAD PRETTY MUCH GIVEN UP HOPE.
KIRI (GLARE)
I'M SURE HE WAS TERRIFIED AND COULDN'T TAKE IT ANY-MORE......

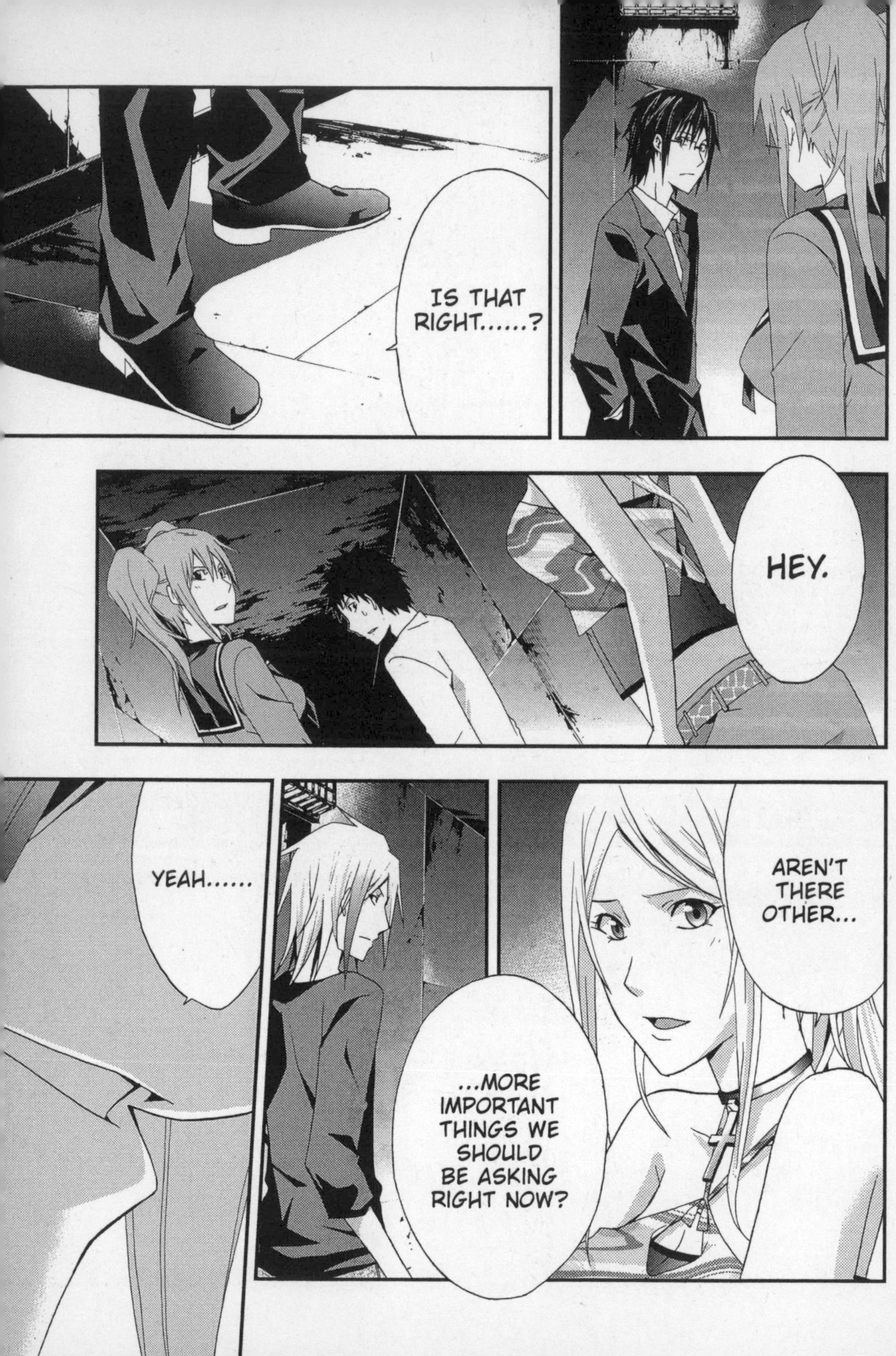
IS THAT RIGHT......?
HEY.
AREN'T THERE OTHER...
...MORE IMPORTANT THINGS WE SHOULD BE ASKING RIGHT NOW?
YEAH......

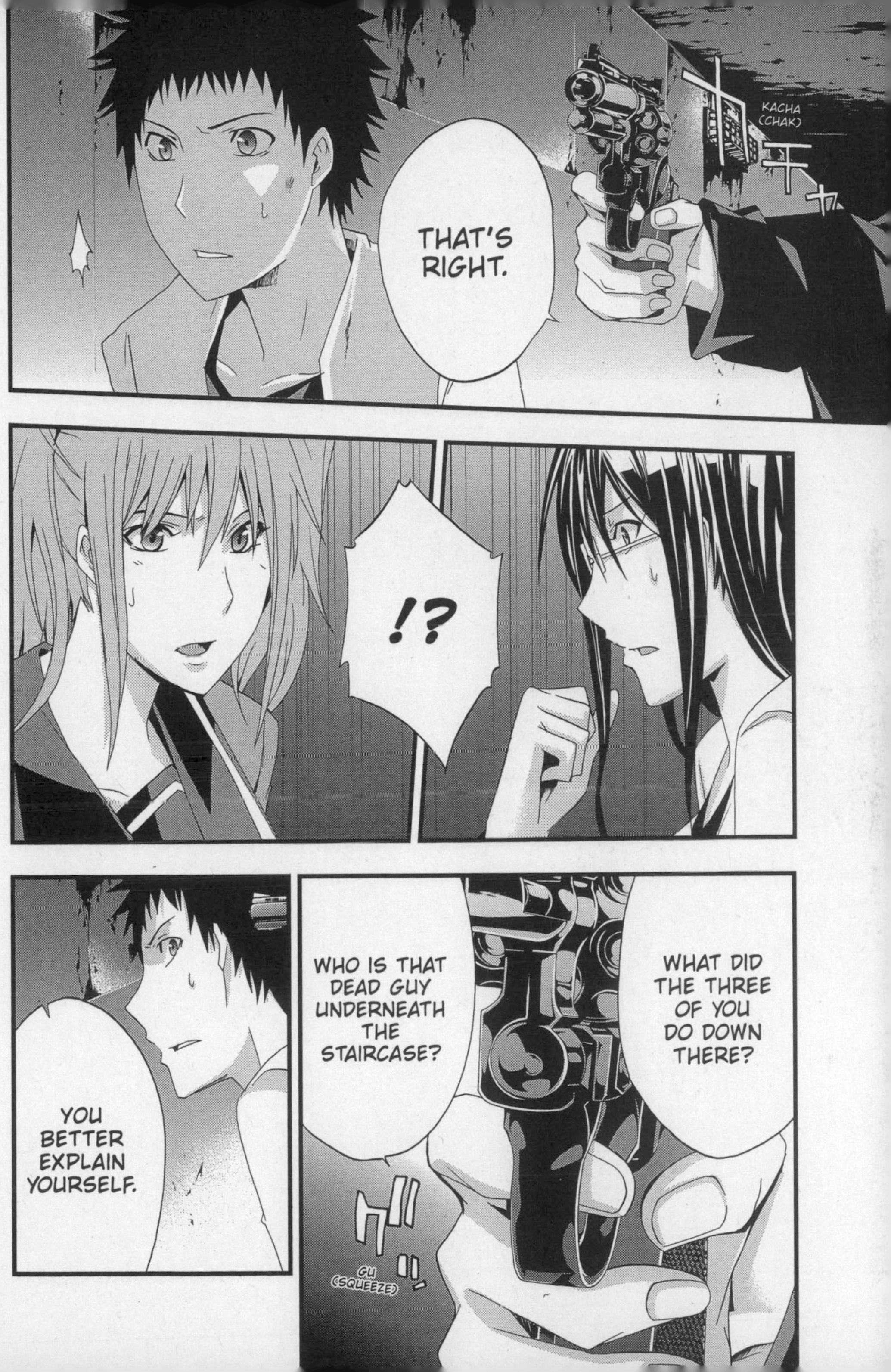
KACHA (CHAK)
THAT'S RIGHT.
!?
WHAT DID THE THREE OF YOU DO DOWN THERE?
WHO IS THAT DEAD GUY UNDERNEATH THE STAIRCASE?
GU (SQUEEZE)
YOU BETTER EXPLAIN YOURSELF.

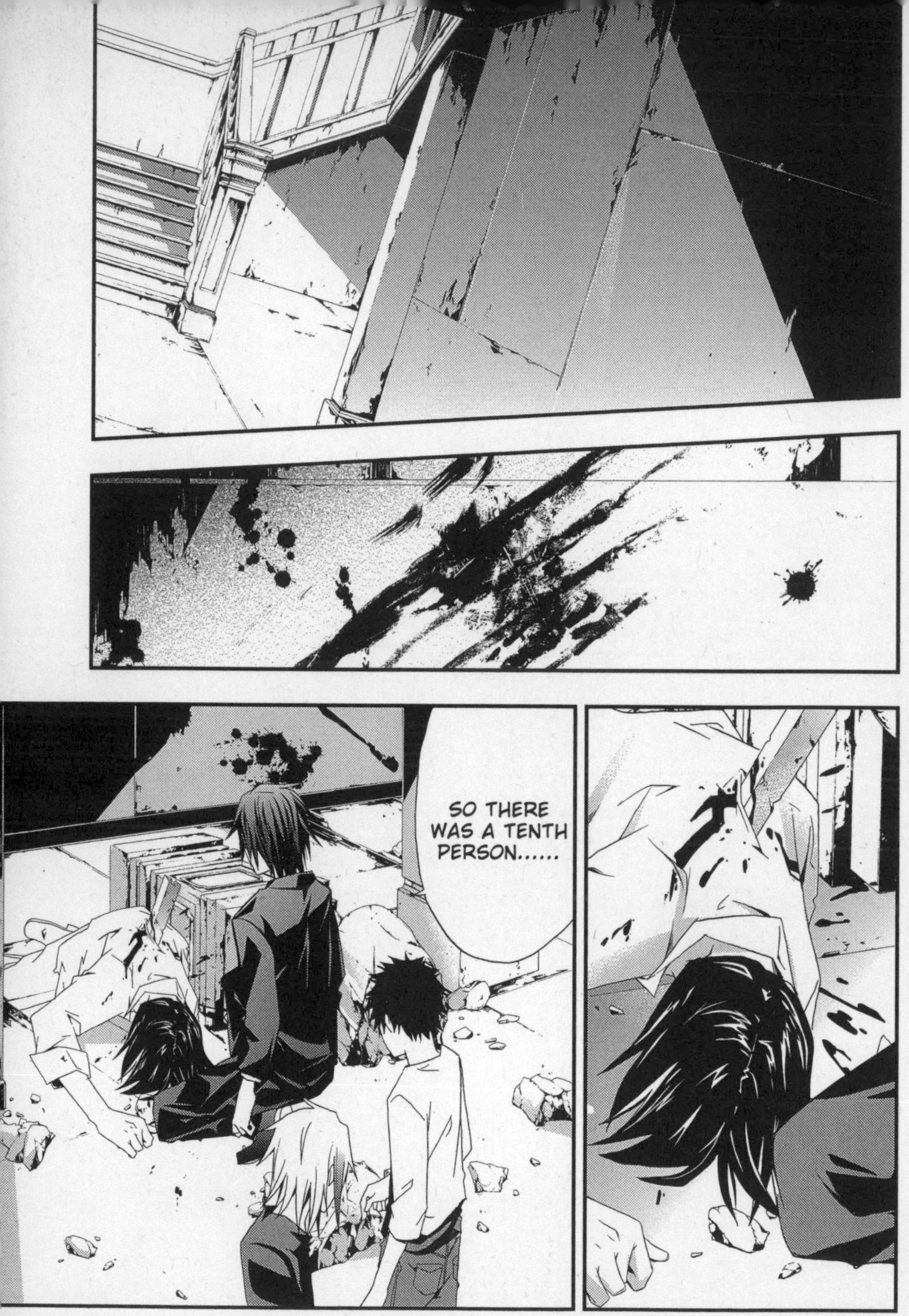
SO THERE WAS A TENTH PERSON......

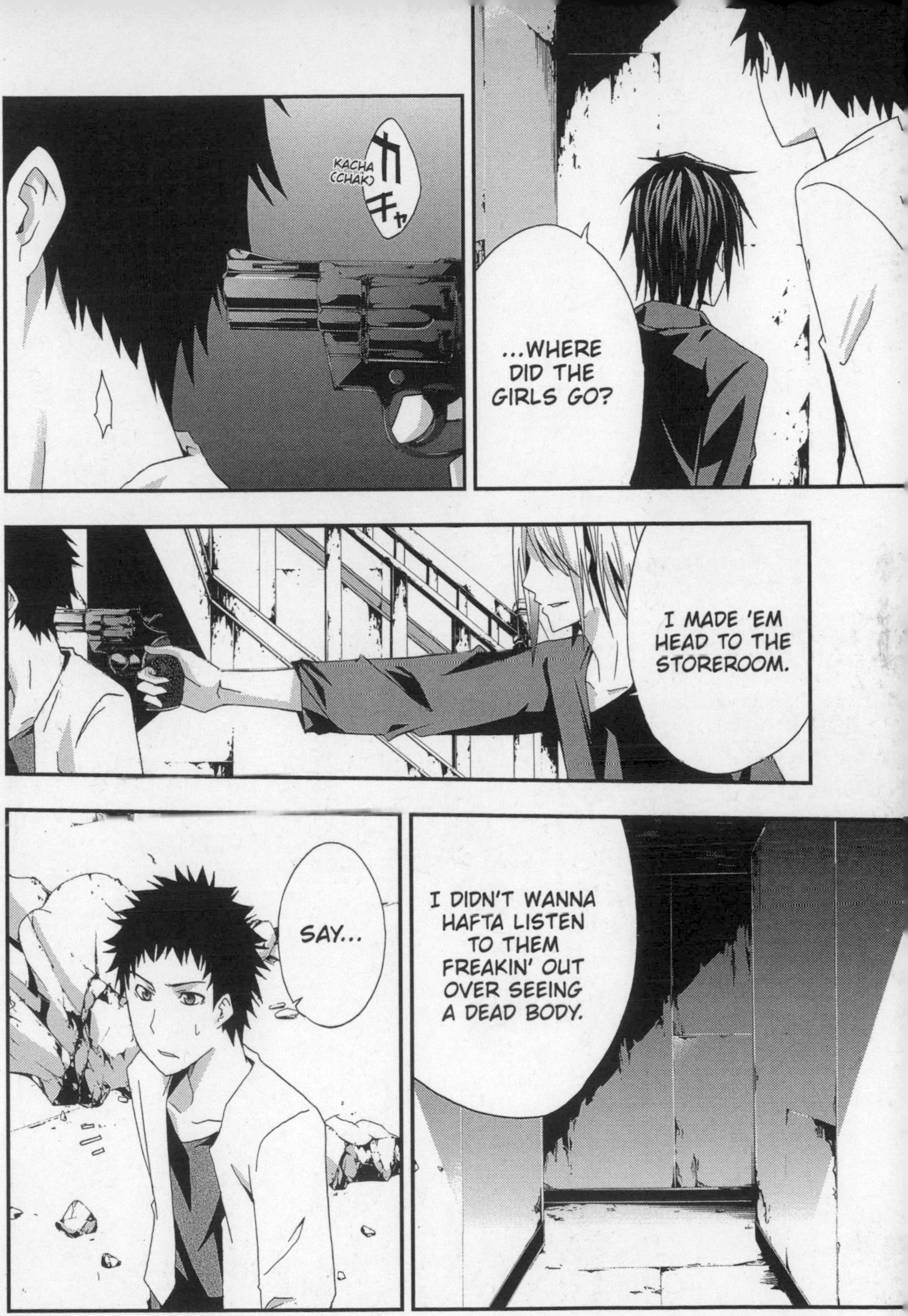
...WHERE DID THE GIRLS GO?
カチャ
KACHA (CHAK)
I MADE 'EM HEAD TO THE STOREROOM.
I DIDN'T WANNA HAFTA LISTEN TO THEM FREAKIN' OUT OVER SEEING A DEAD BODY.
SAY...

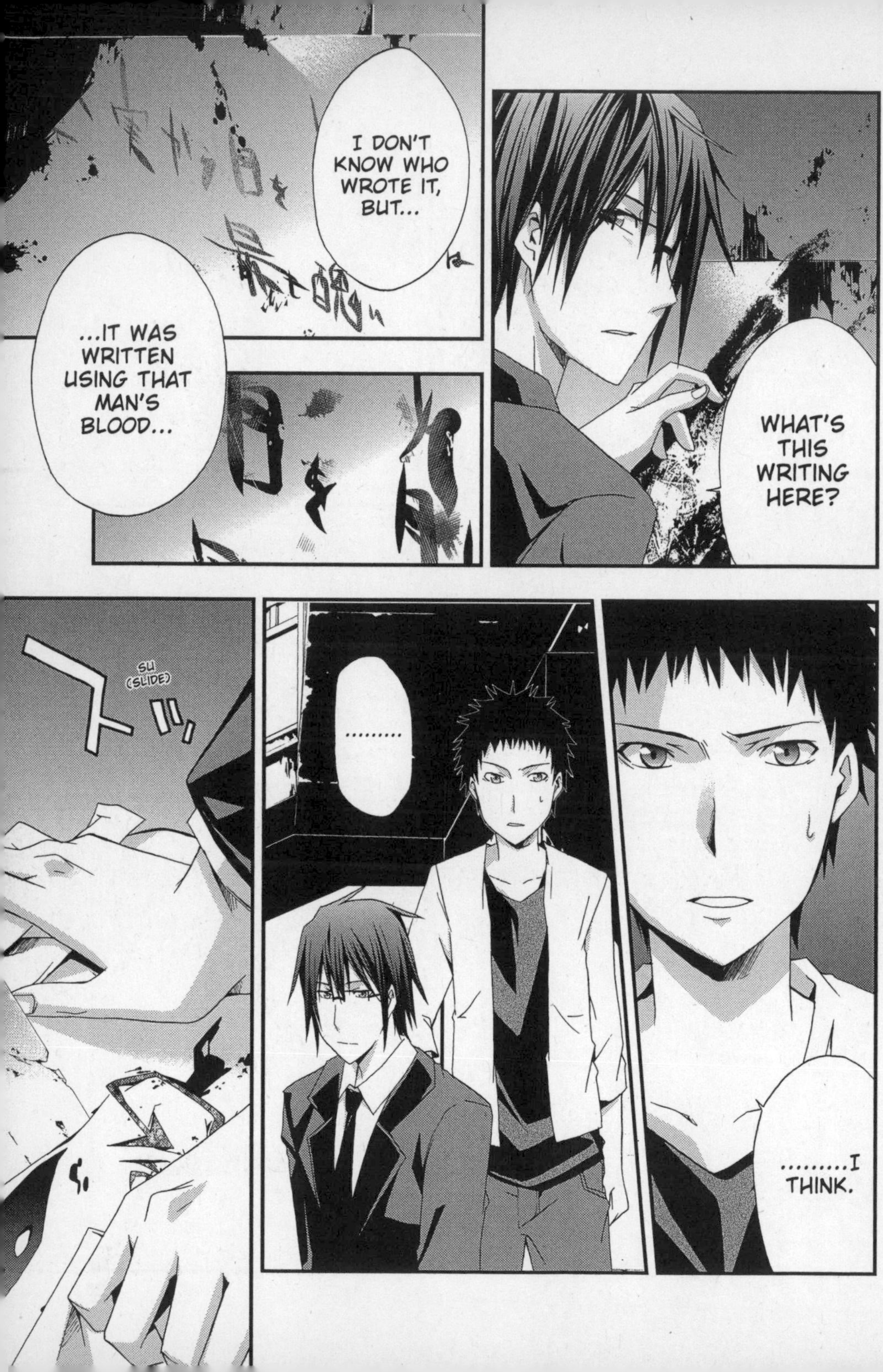
WHAT'S THIS WRITING HERE?
I DON'T KNOW WHO WROTE IT, BUT...
...IT WAS WRITTEN USING THAT MAN'S BLOOD...
.........I THINK.
....
SU (SLIDE)

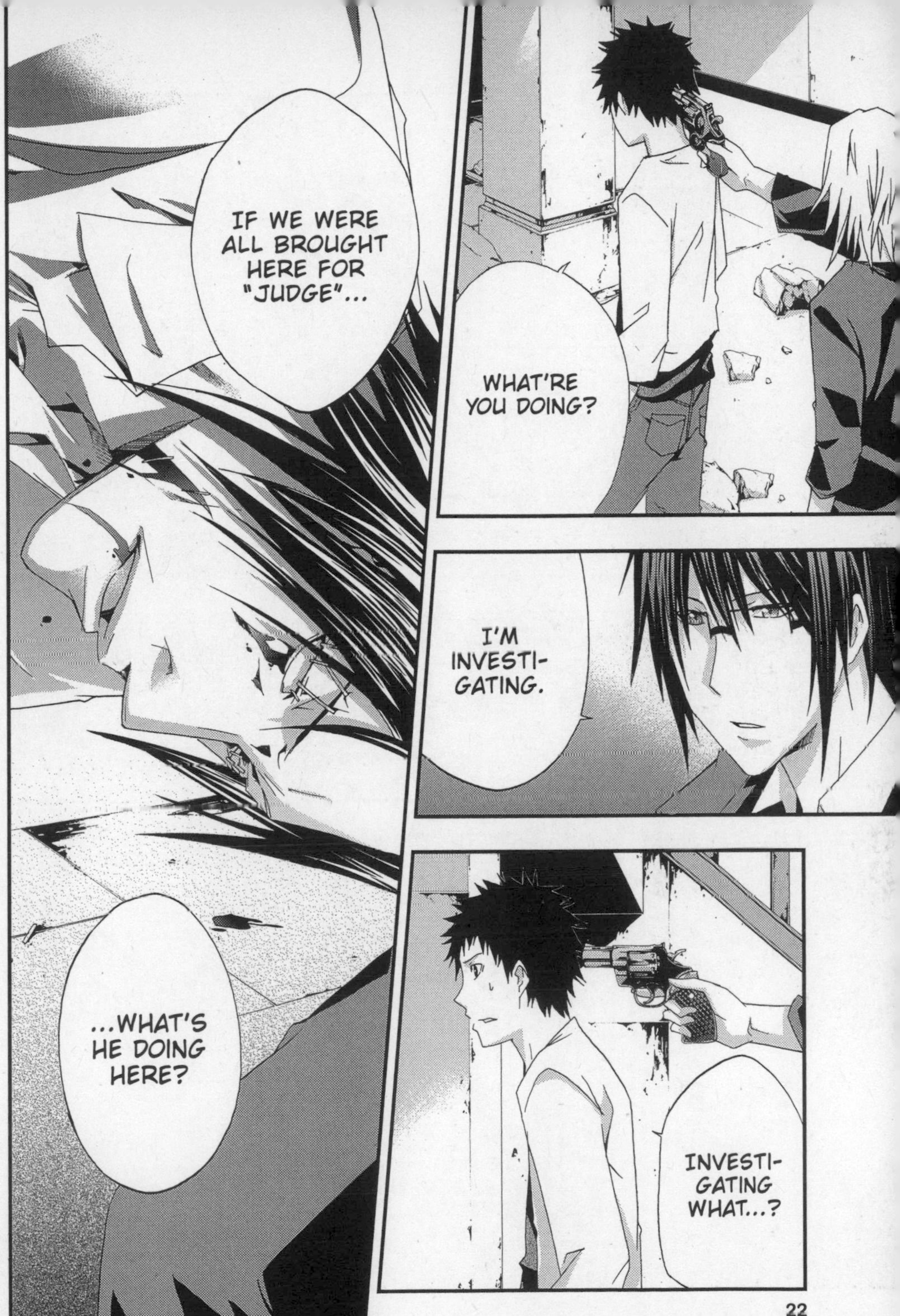
WHAT'RE YOU DOING?
I'M INVESTI-GATING.
INVESTI-GATING WHAT...?
IF WE WERE ALL BROUGHT HERE FOR "JUDGE"...
...WHAT'S HE DOING HERE?

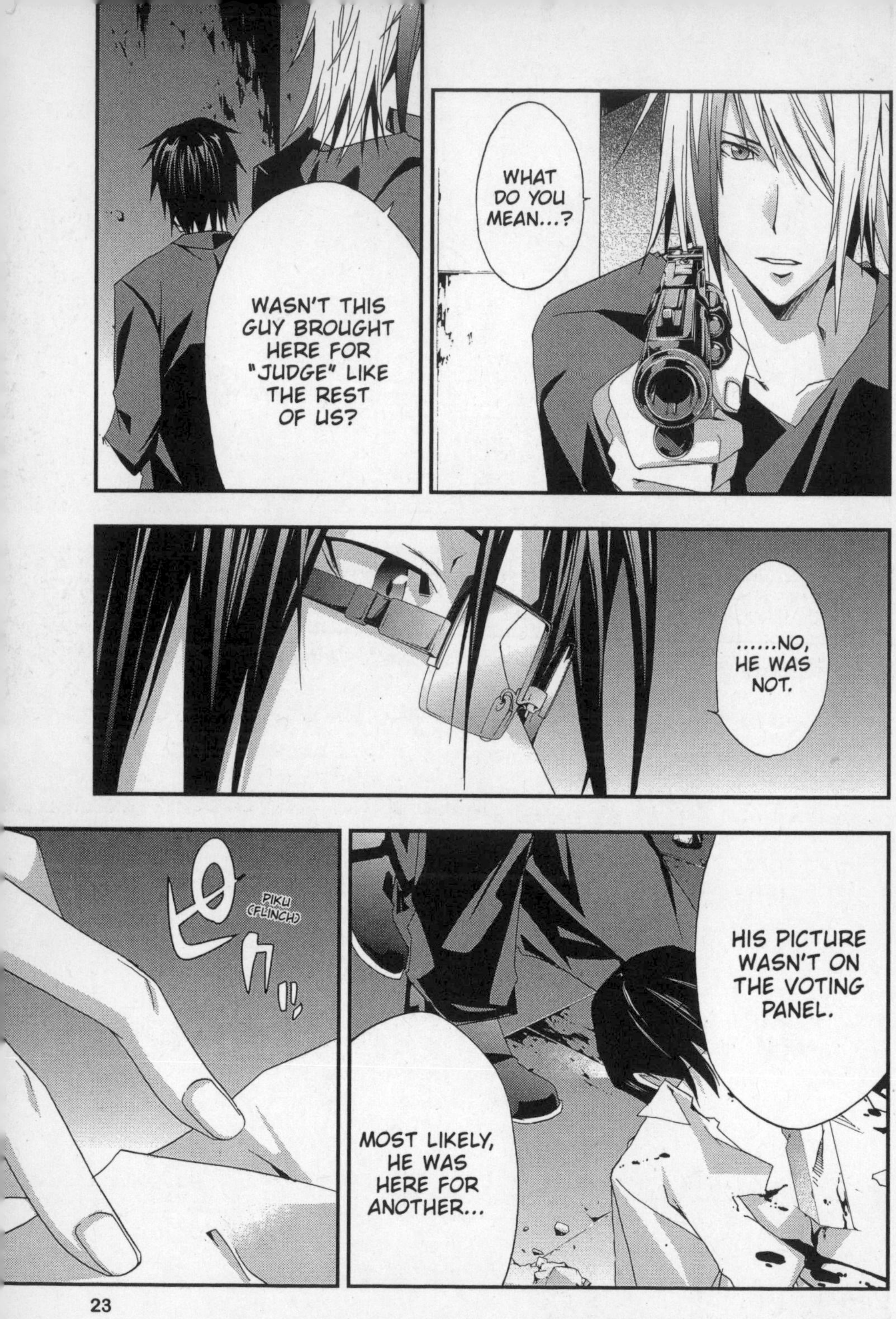
WHAT DO YOU MEAN...?
WASN'T THIS GUY BROUGHT HERE FOR "JUDGE" LIKE THE REST OF US?
......NO, HE WAS NOT.
HIS PICTURE WASN'T ON THE VOTING PANEL.
MOST LIKELY, HE WAS HERE FOR ANOTHER...
PIKU (FLINCH)

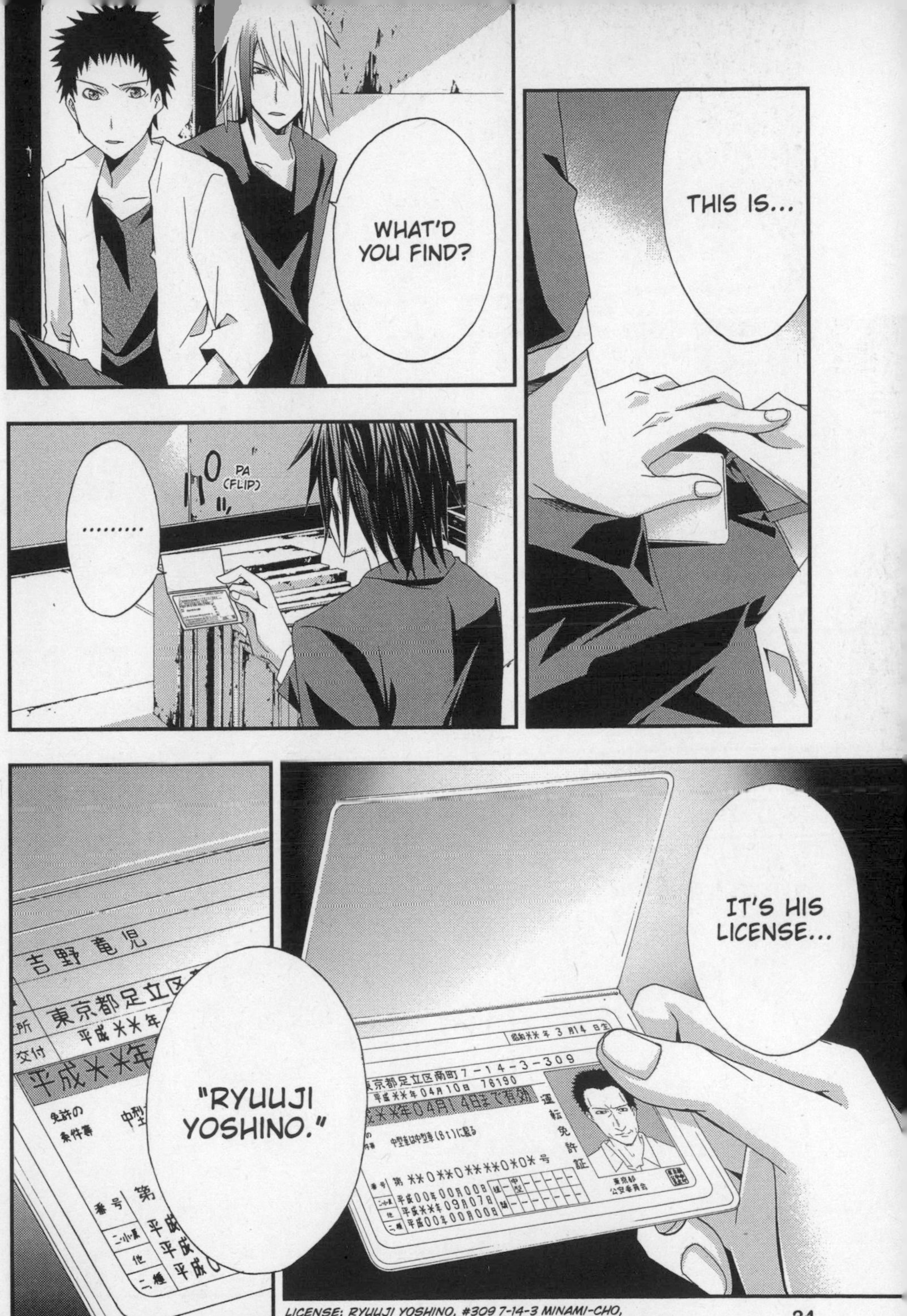
THIS IS...
WHAT'D YOU FIND?
PA (FLIP)
....
IT'S HIS LICENSE...
"RYUUJI YOSHINO."

LICENSE: RYUUJI YOSHINO, #309 7-14-3 MINAMI-CHO, ADACHI-KU, TOKYO, VALID UNTIL 04-14-XX, DRIVER'S LICENSE

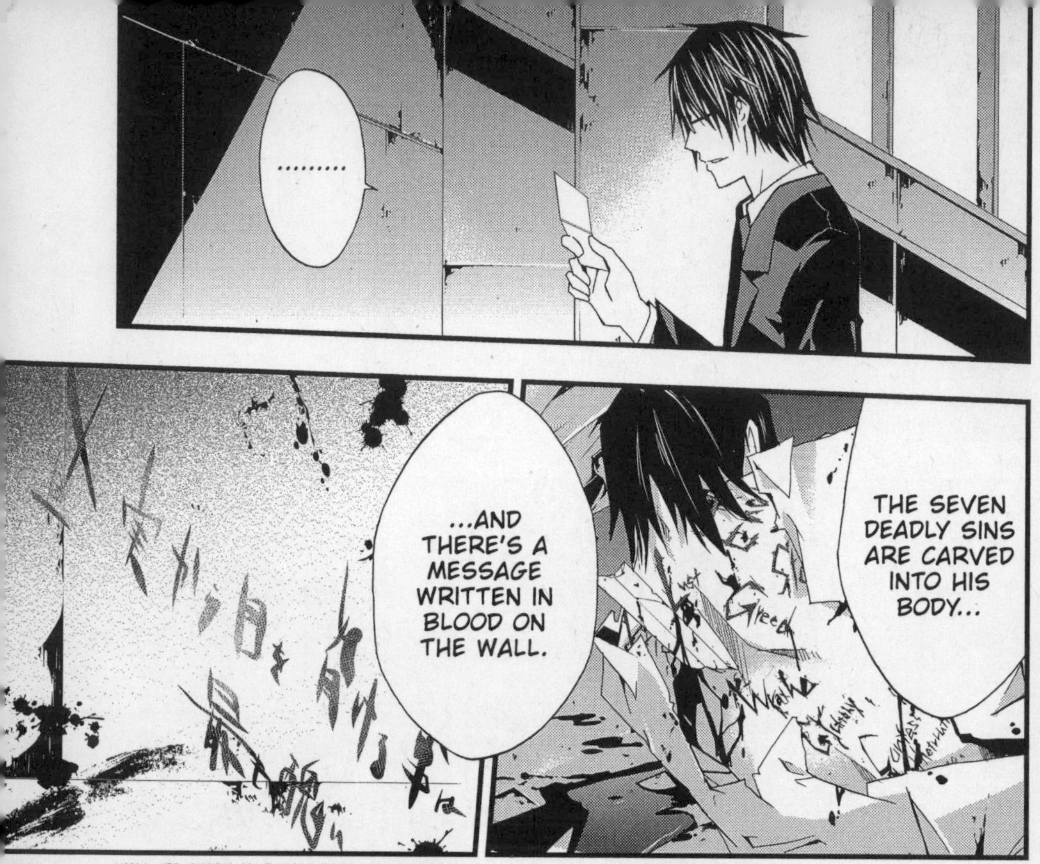
....
THE SEVEN DEADLY SINS ARE CARVED INTO HIS BODY...
...AND THERE'S A MESSAGE WRITTEN IN BLOOD ON THE WALL.

WALL: TO AVERT YOUR EYES FROM THE TRUTH IS THE MOST UNSIGHTLY THING ONE CAN DO.

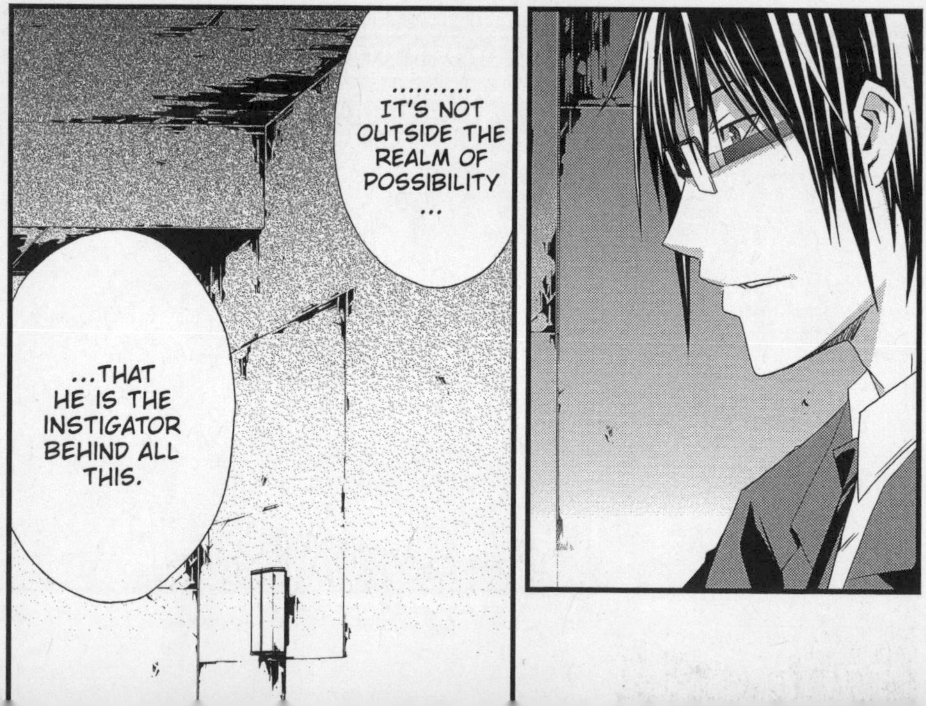
.... IT'S NOT OUTSIDE THE REALM OF POSSIBILITY ...
...THAT HE IS THE INSTIGATOR BEHIND ALL THIS.

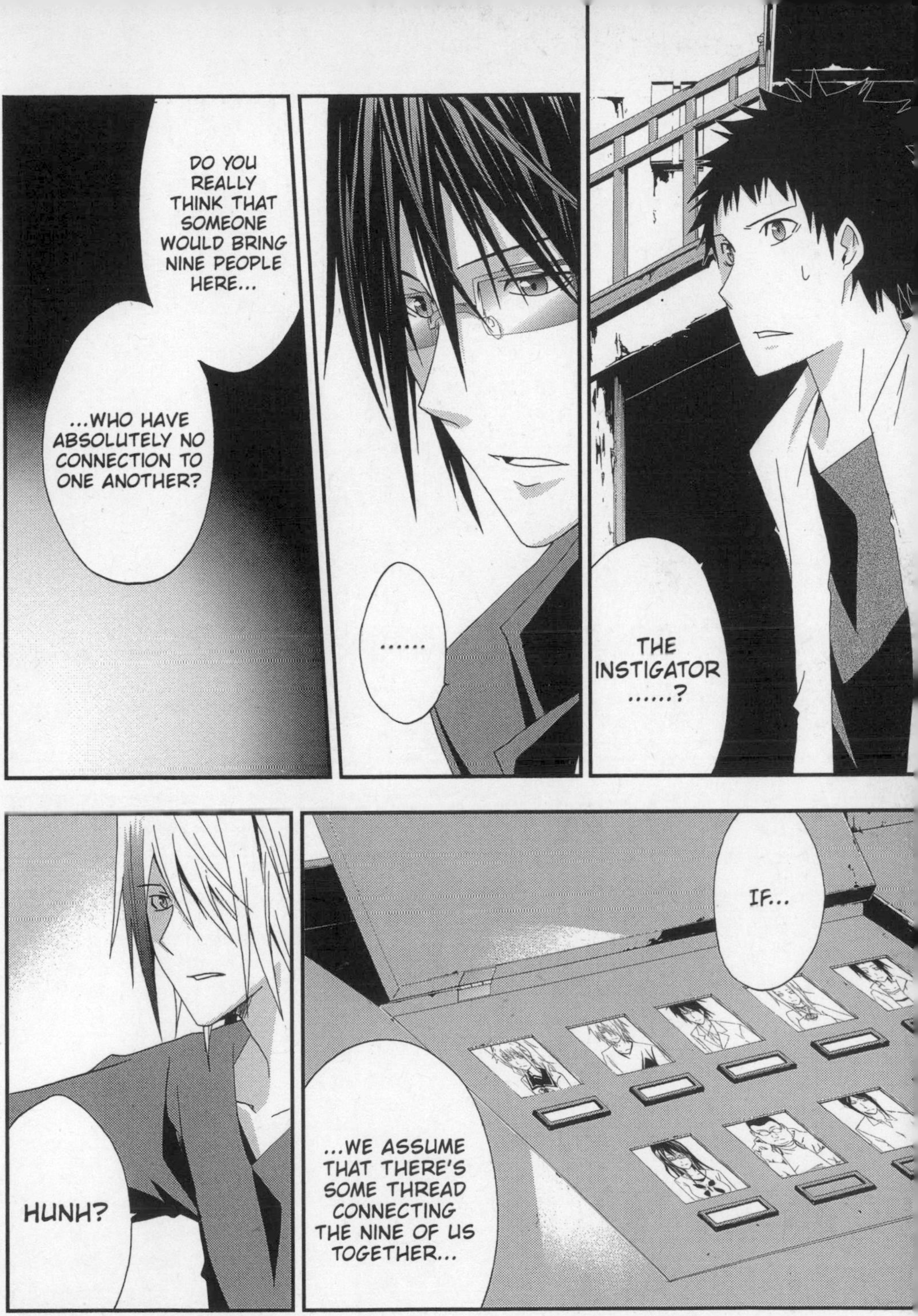
THE INSTIGATOR ......?
......
DO YOU REALLY THINK THAT SOMEONE WOULD BRING NINE PEOPLE HERE...
...WHO HAVE ABSOLUTELY NO CONNECTION TO ONE ANOTHER?
IF...
...WE ASSUME THAT THERE'S SOME THREAD CONNECTING THE NINE OF US TOGETHER...
HUNH?

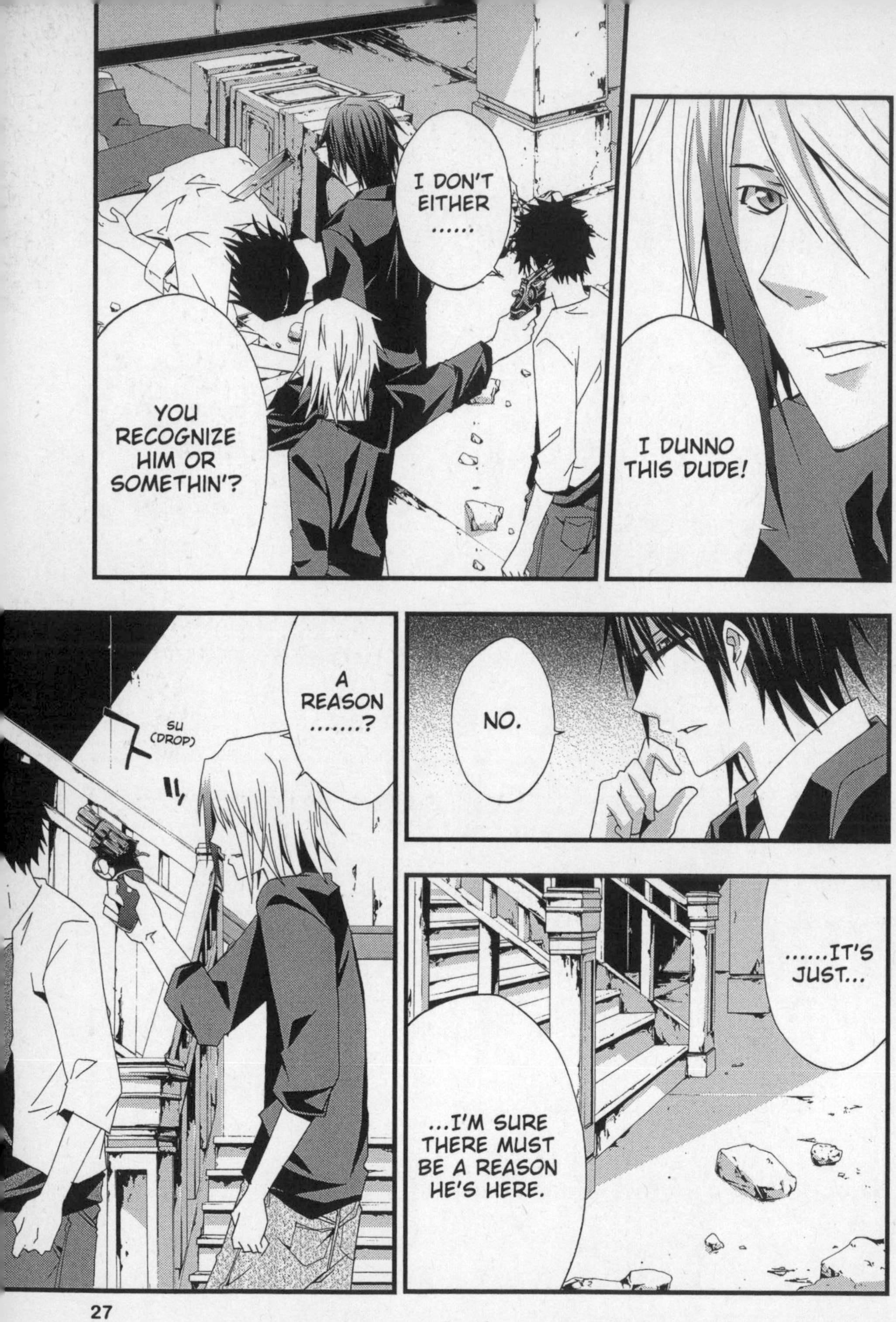

I DUNNO THIS DUDE!
I DON'T EITHER ......
YOU RECOGNIZE HIM OR SOMETHIN'?
NO.
......IT'S JUST...
...I'M SURE THERE MUST BE A REASON HE'S HERE.
A REASON ....?
SU (DROP)

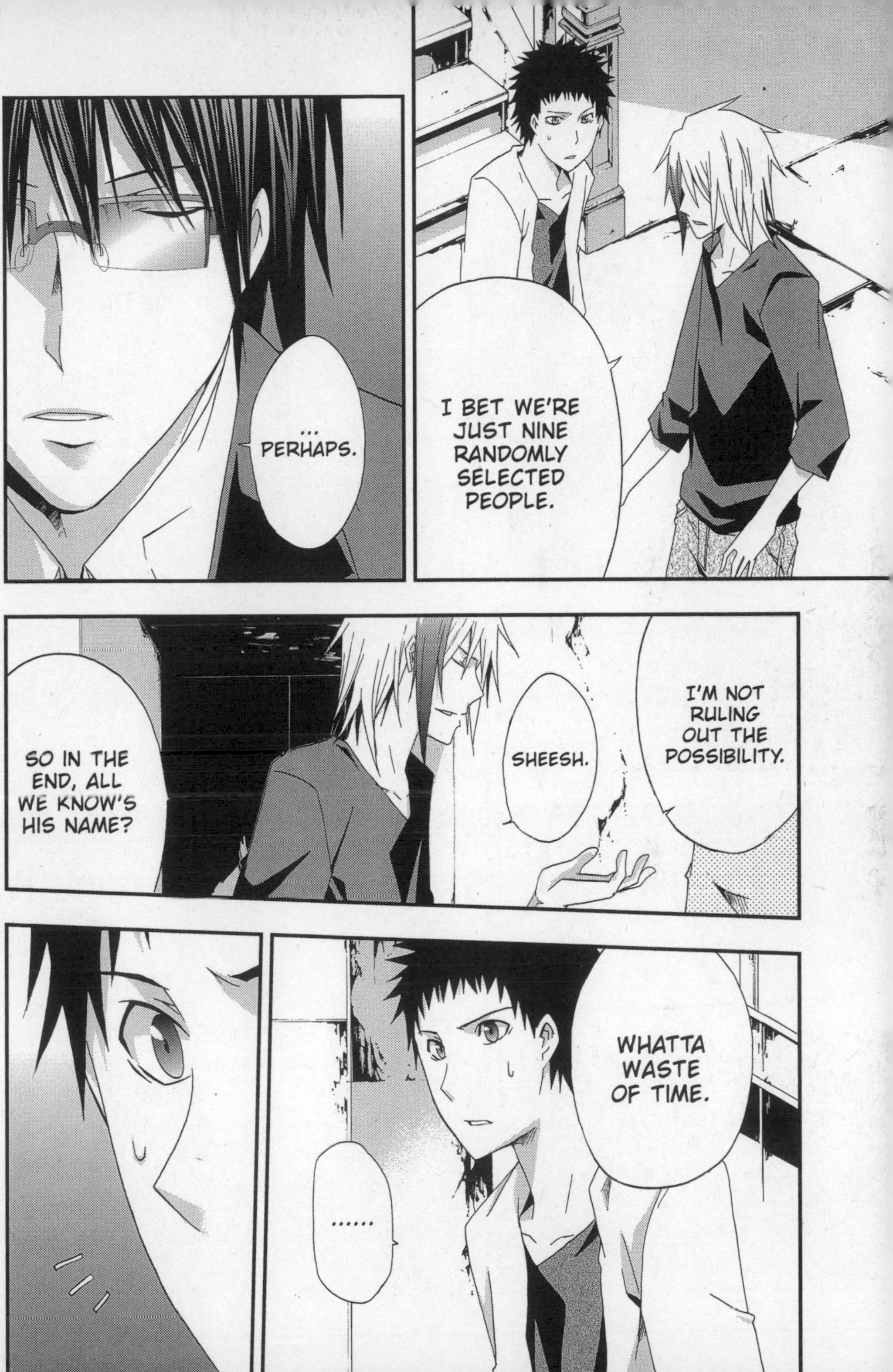
I BET WE'RE JUST NINE RANDOMLY SELECTED PEOPLE.
... PERHAPS.
I'M NOT RULING OUT THE POSSIBILITY.
SHEESH.
SO IN THE END, ALL WE KNOW'S HIS NAME?
WHATTA WASTE OF TIME.
......

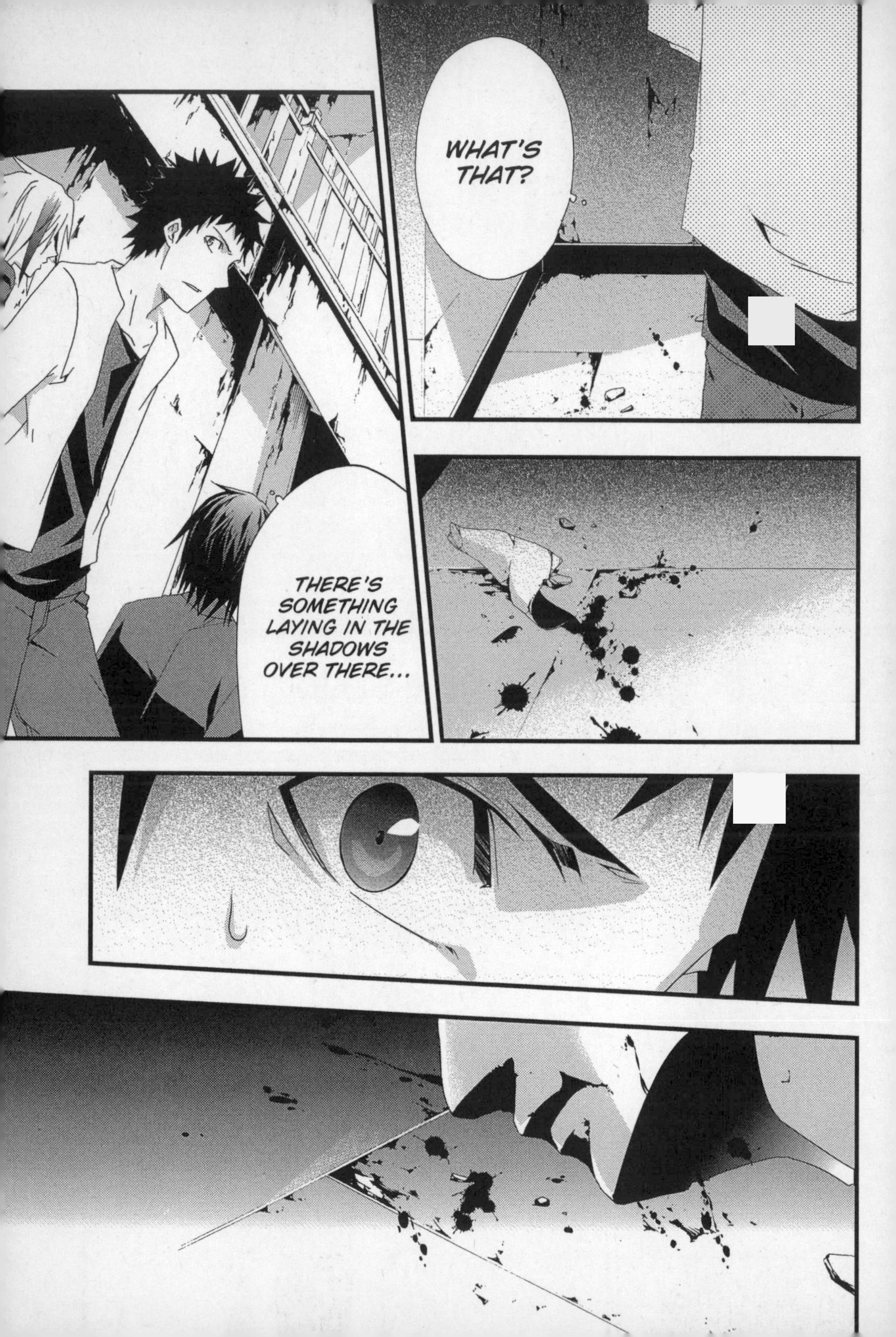
WHAT'S THAT?
THERE'S SOMETHING LAYING IN THE SHADOWS OVER THERE...

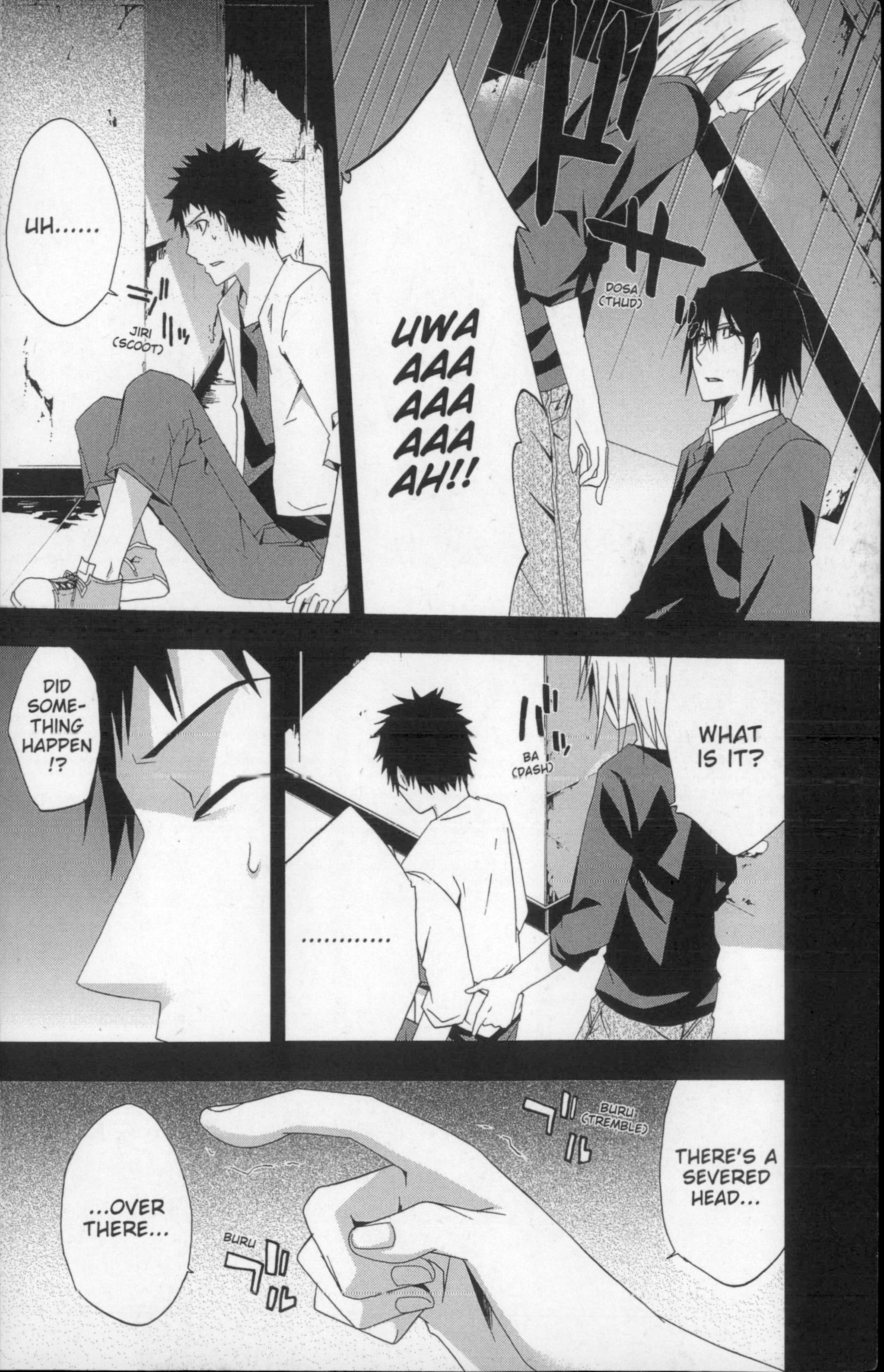
DOSA (THUD)
UWAAAAAAAAAAAAAAH!!
UH......
JIRI (SCOOT)
WHAT IS IT?
BA (DASH)
....
DID SOMETHING-HAPPEN !?
THERE'S A SEVERED HEAD...
BURU (TREMBLE)
...OVER THERE...
BURU

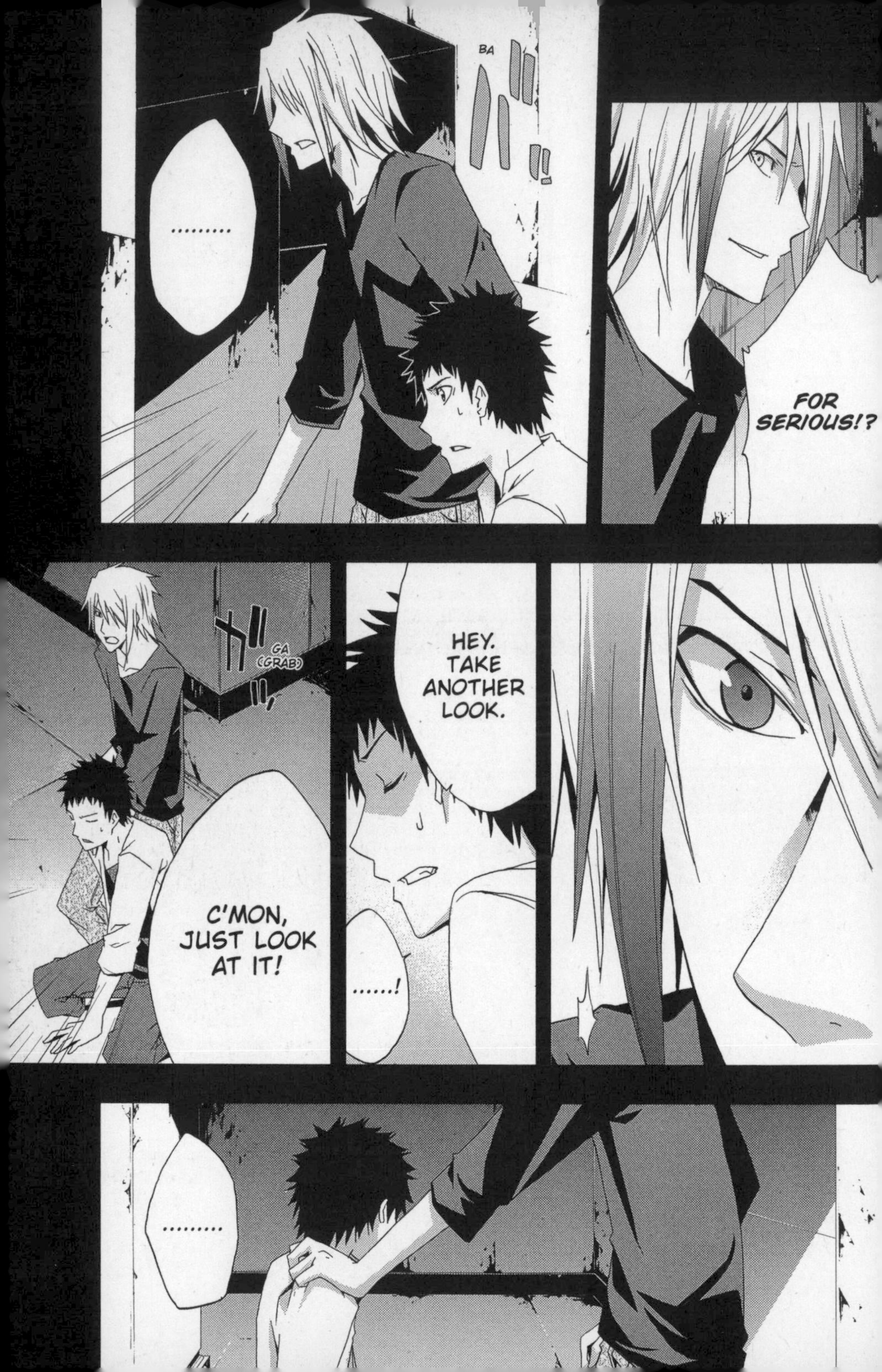
FOR SERIOUS!?
BA
....
HEY. TAKE ANOTHER LOOK.
......!
GA (GRAB)
C'MON, JUST LOOK AT IT!
....

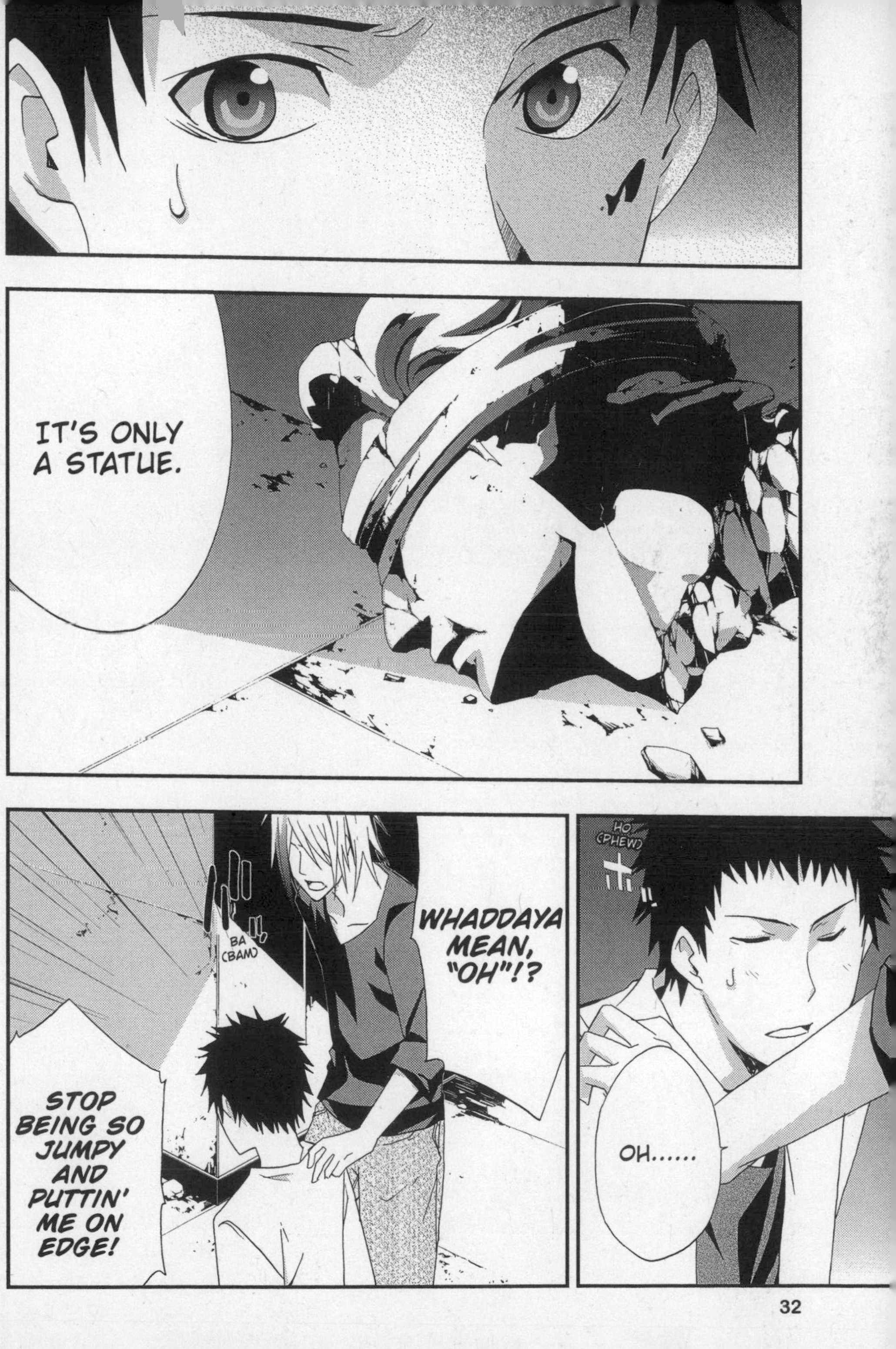
IT'S ONLY A STATUE.
HO (PHEW)
OH......
WHADDAYA MEAN, "OH"!?
BA (BAM)
STOP BEING SO JUMPY AND PUTTIN' ME ON EDGE!

DO IT AGAIN AND I'LL BLOW YOUR BRAINS OUT!!

....

SHARI
(JANGLE)

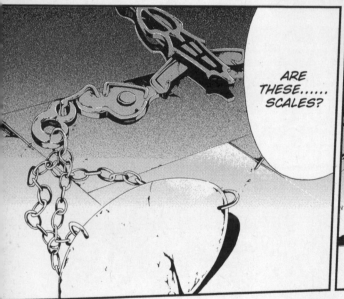

ARE THESE...... SCALES?

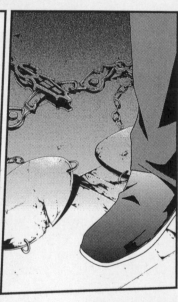

....

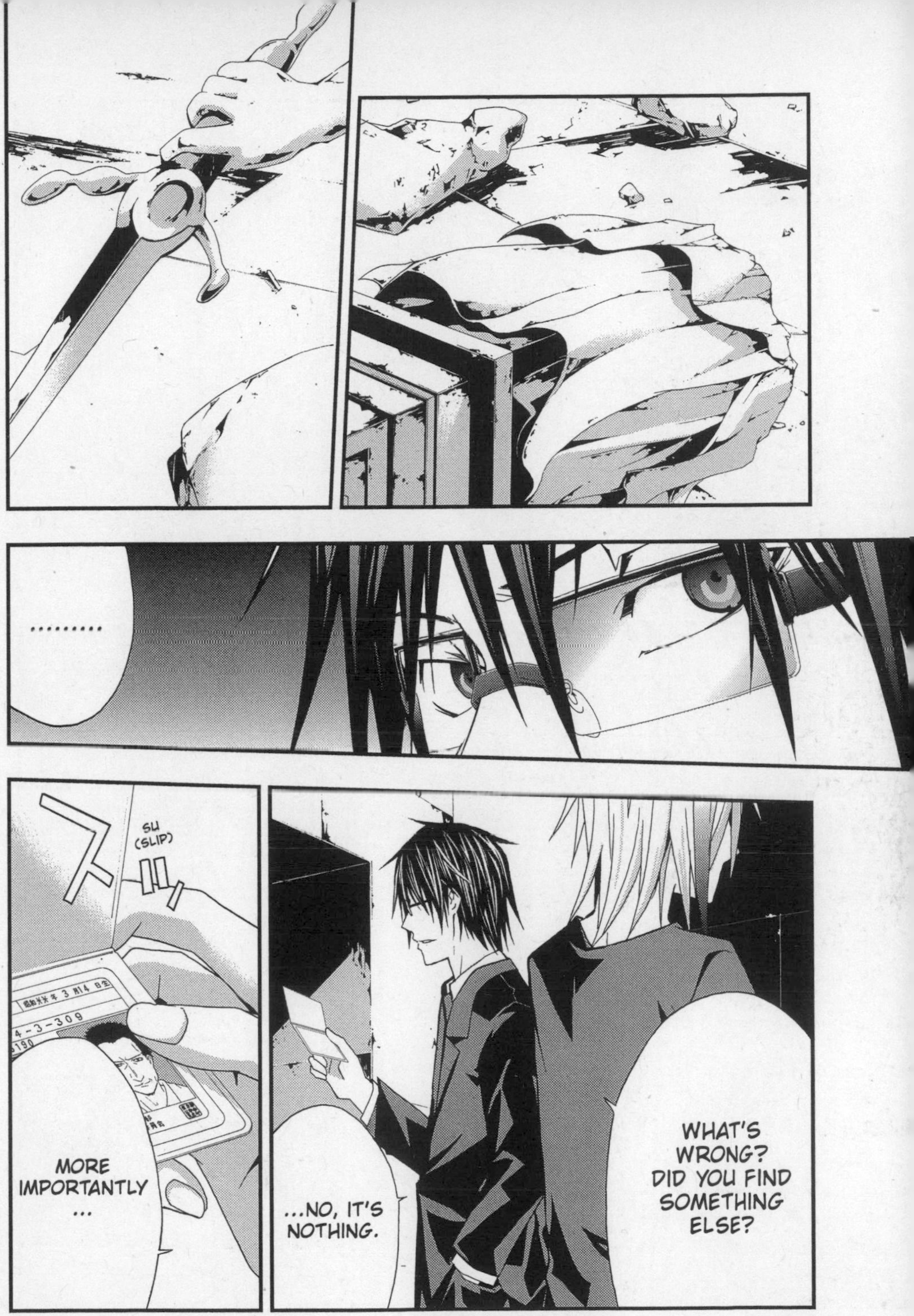
....
WHAT'S WRONG? DID YOU FIND SOMETHING ELSE?
...NO, IT'S NOTHING.
SU (SLIP)
MORE IMPORTANTLY ...

...LOOK WHAT WE HAVE HERE.

A MEMORY CARD!?

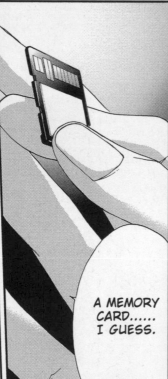

A MEMORY CARD...... I GUESS.

WHAT'S THAT?

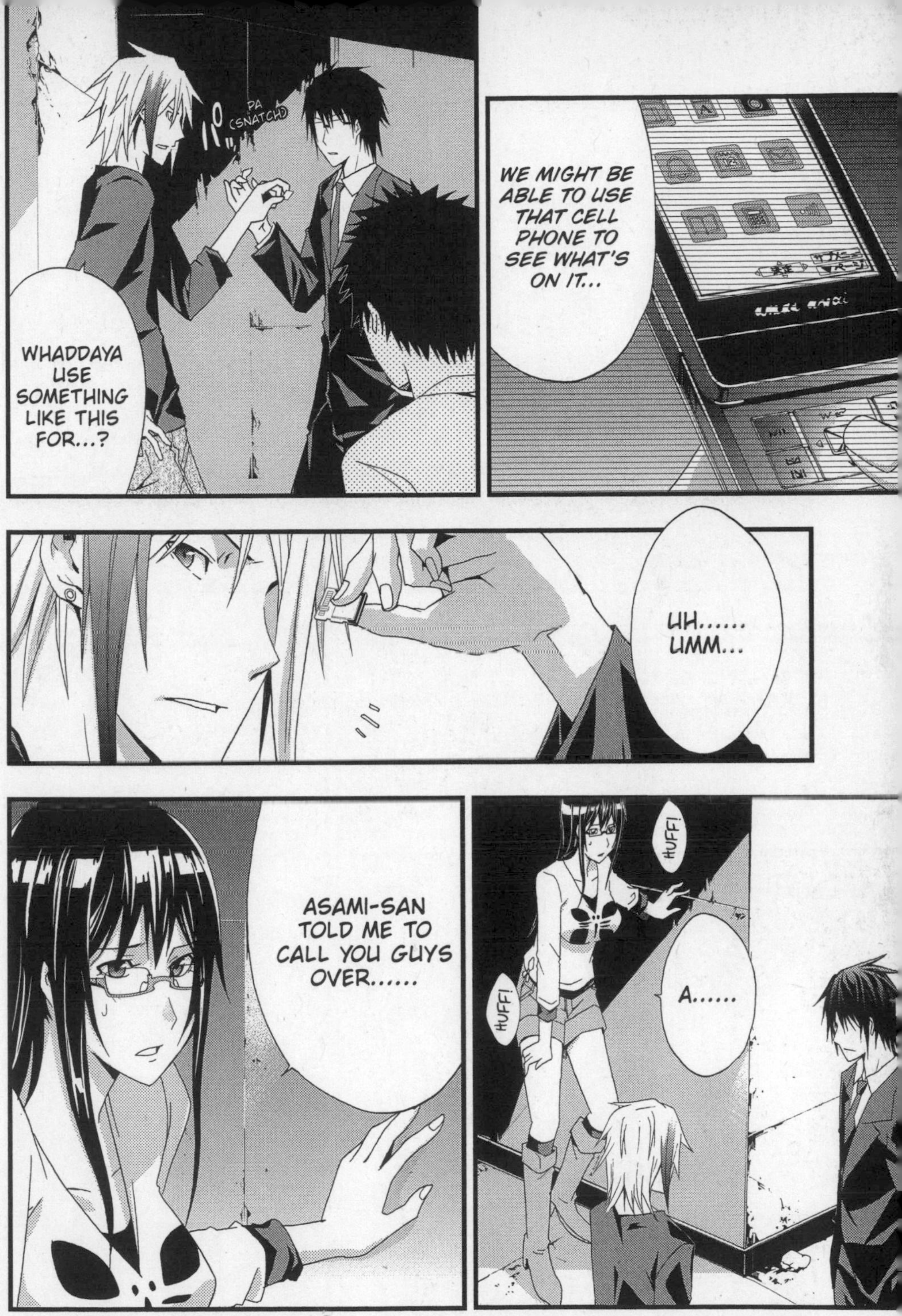
WE MIGHT BE ABLE TO USE THAT CELL PHONE TO SEE WHAT'S ON IT...
PA (SNATCH)
WHADDAYA USE SOMETHING LIKE THIS FOR...?
UH...... UMM...
HUFF!
A......
HUFF!
ASAMI-SAN TOLD ME TO CALL YOU GUYS OVER......

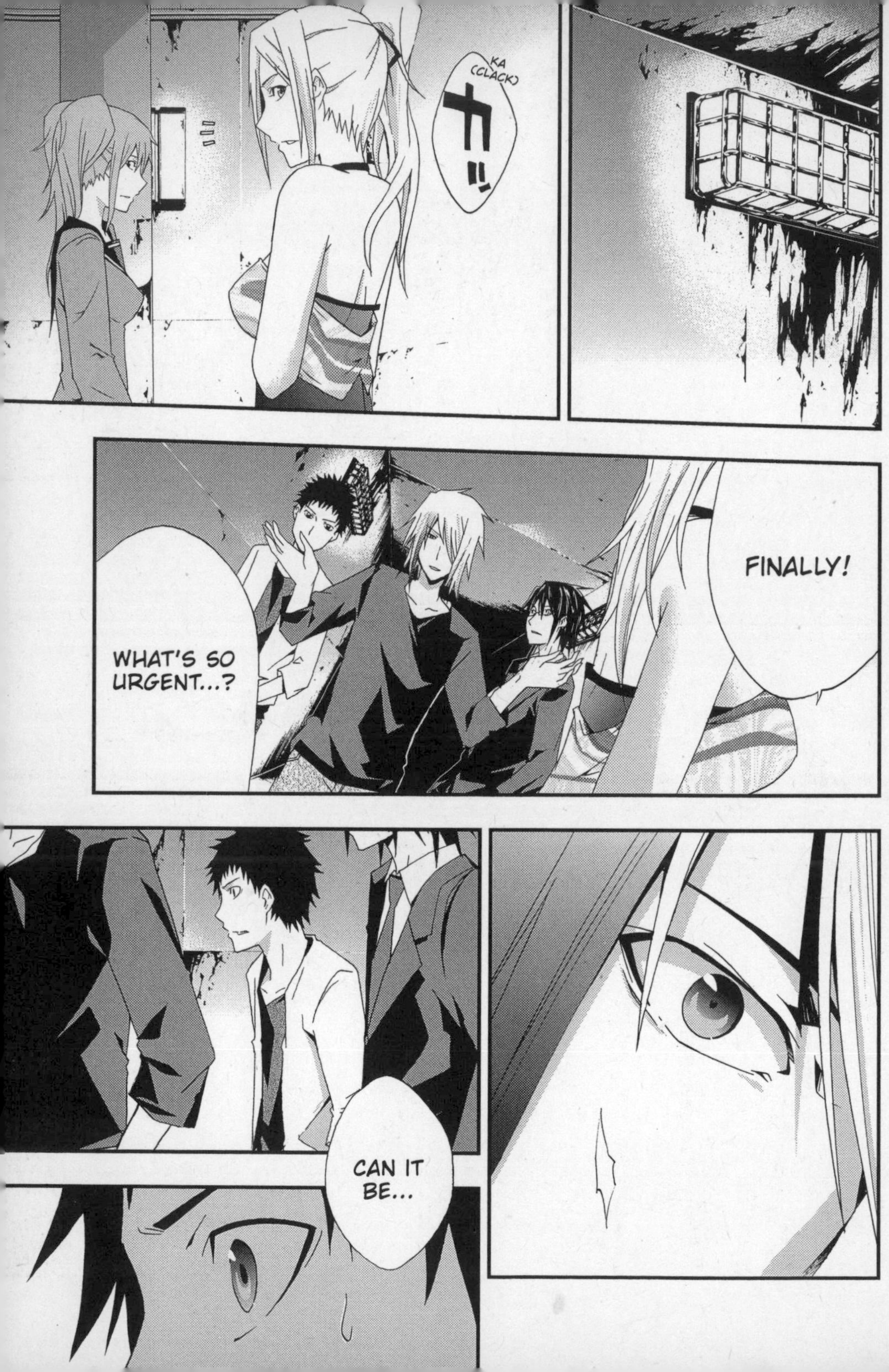
KA (CLACK)
カッ
FINALLY!
WHAT'S SO URGENT...?
CAN IT BE...

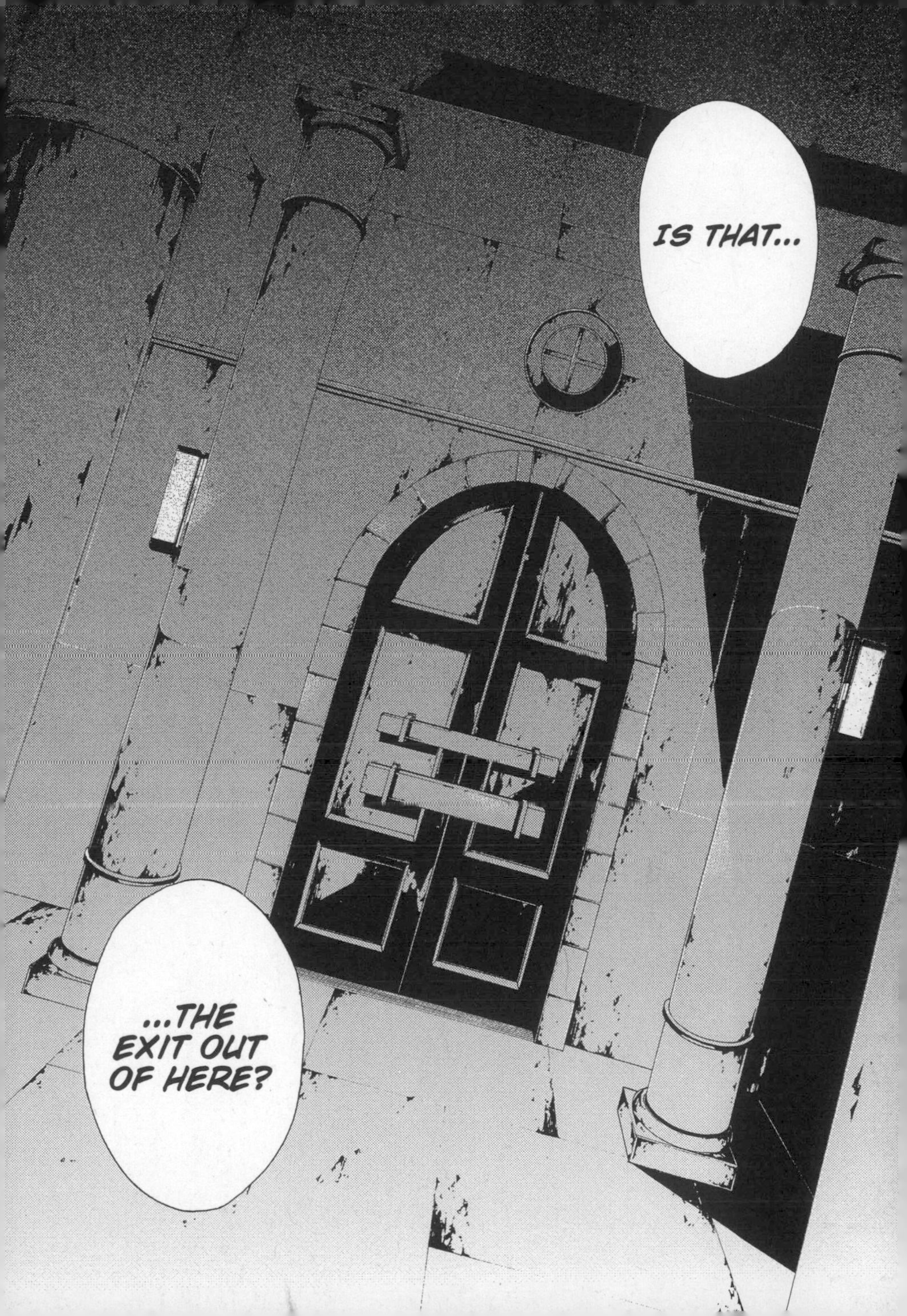
IS THAT...
...THE EXIT OUT OF HERE?

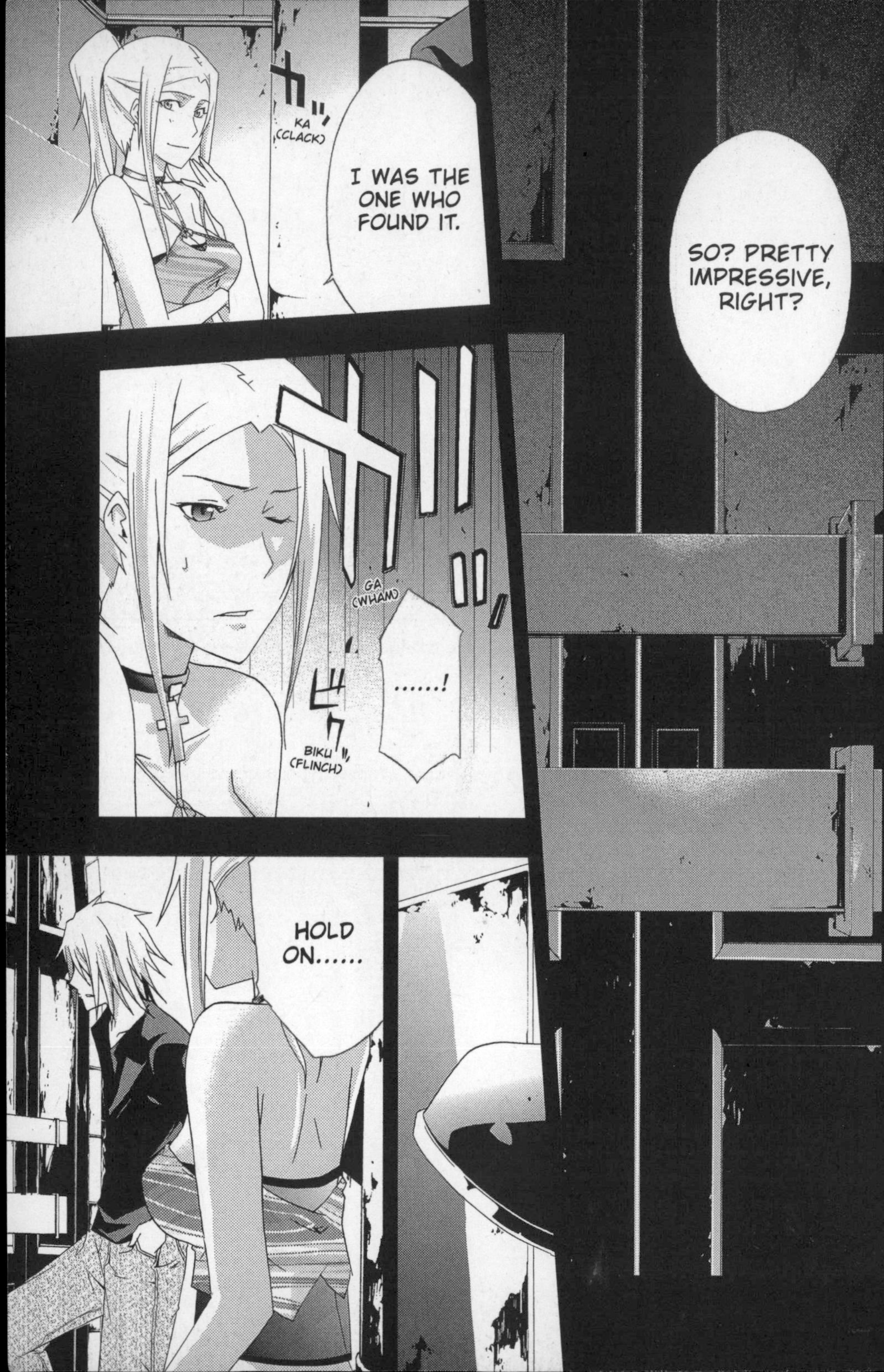
SO? PRETTY IMPRESSIVE, RIGHT?
KA (CLACK)
I WAS THE ONE WHO FOUND IT.
GA (WHAM)
......!
BIKU (FLINCH)
HOLD ON......

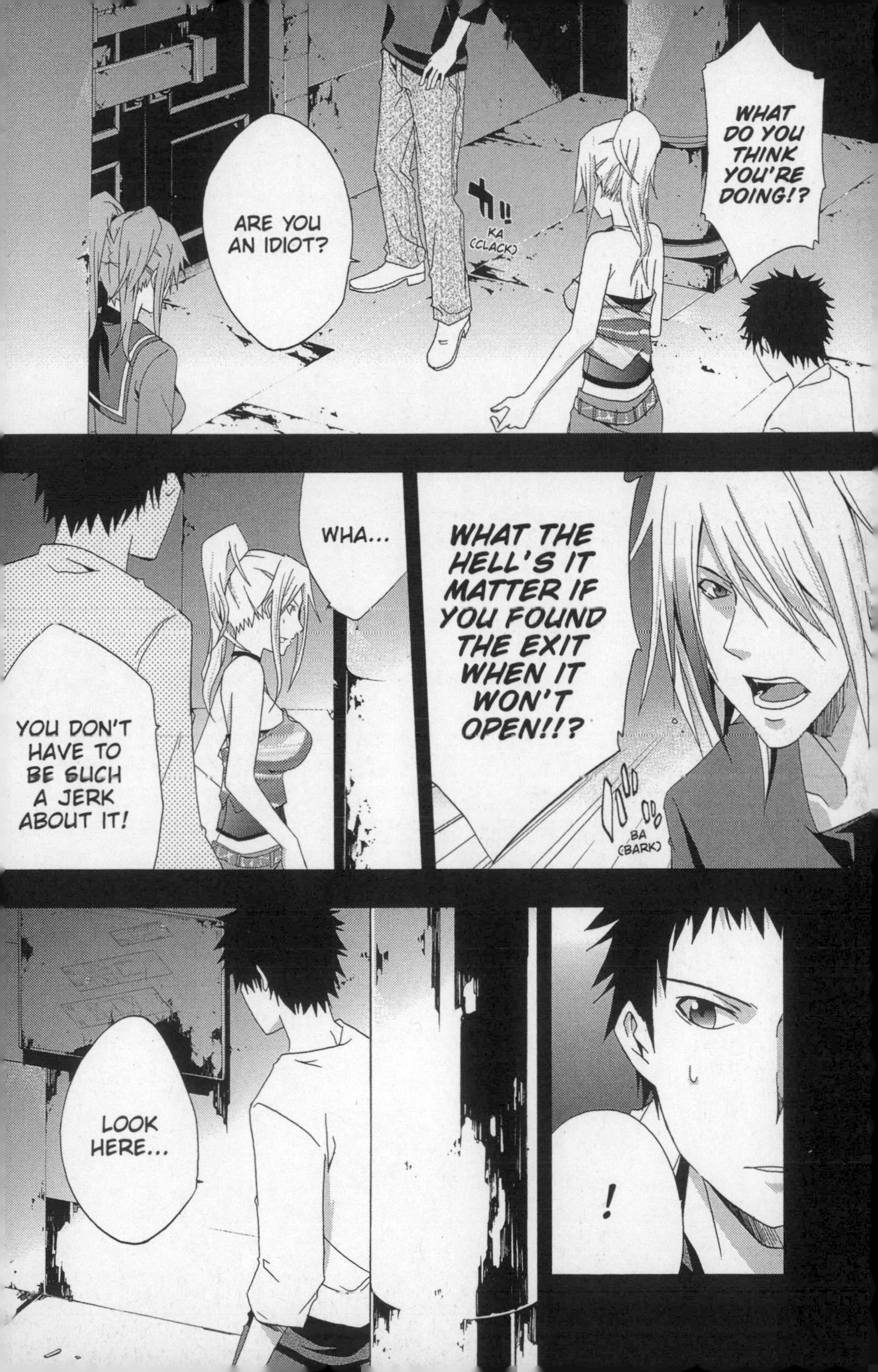
WHAT DO YOU THINK YOU'RE DOING!?
KA (CLACK)
ARE YOU AN IDIOT?
WHAT THE HELL'S IT MATTER IF YOU FOUND THE EXIT WHEN IT WON'T OPEN!!?
BA (BARK)
WHA...
YOU DON'T HAVE TO BE SUCH A JERK ABOUT IT!
!
LOOK HERE...

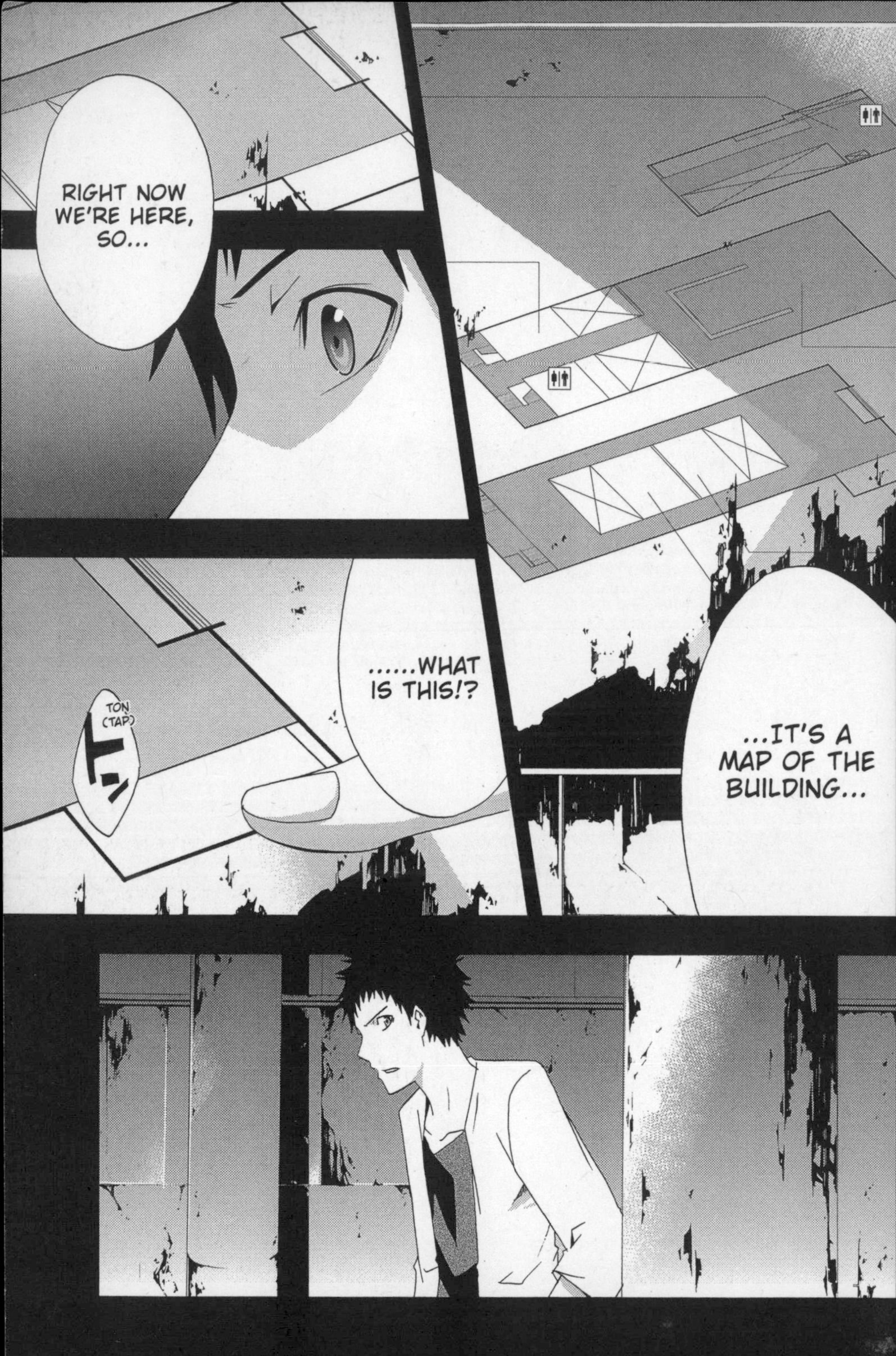

...IT'S A MAP OF THE BUILDING...
RIGHT NOW WE'RE HERE, SO...
......WHAT IS THIS!?
TON (TAP)

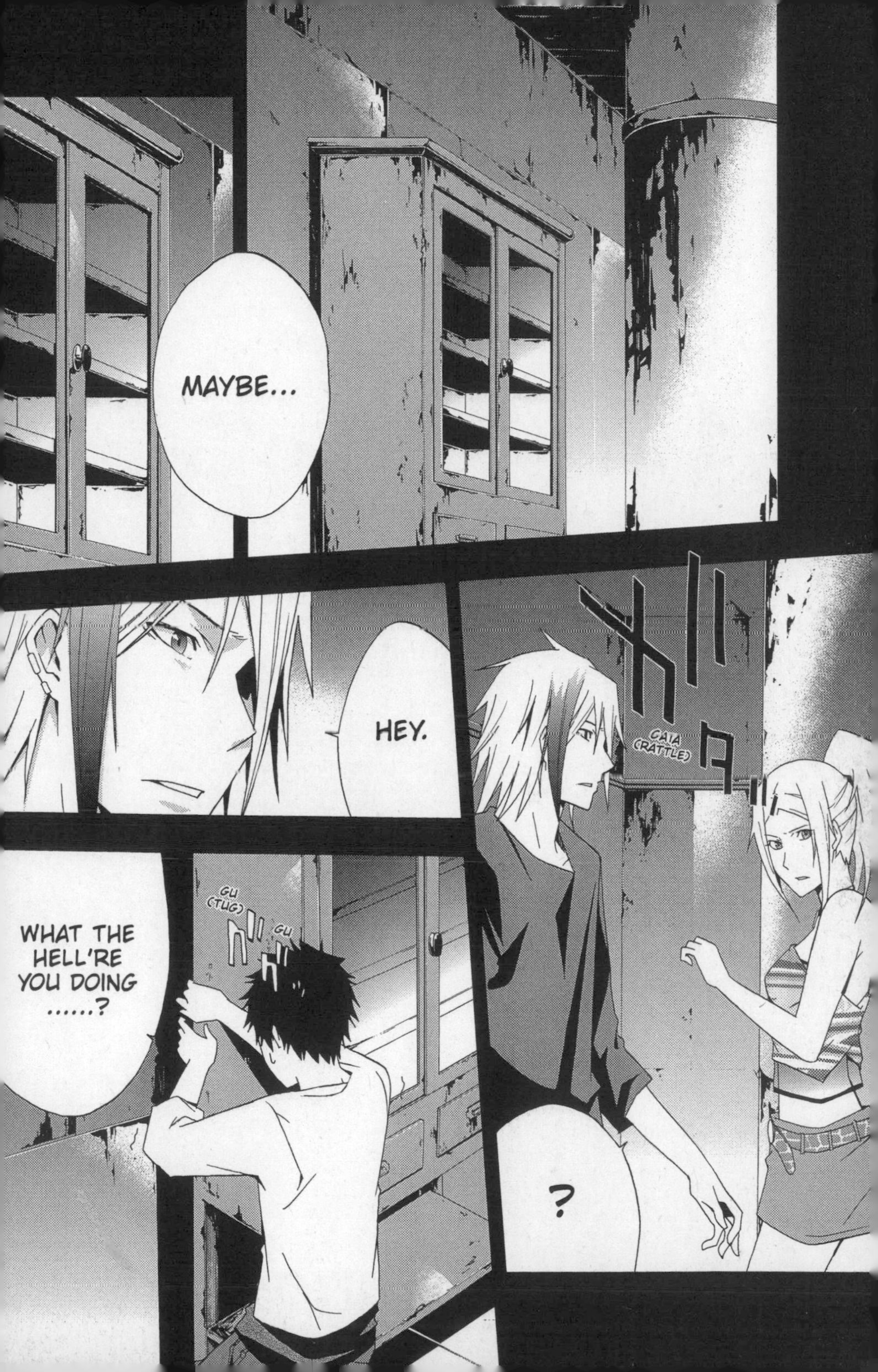
MAYBE...
GAIA (RATTLE)
?
HEY.
GU (TUG)
GU
WHAT THE HELL'RE YOU DOING ......?

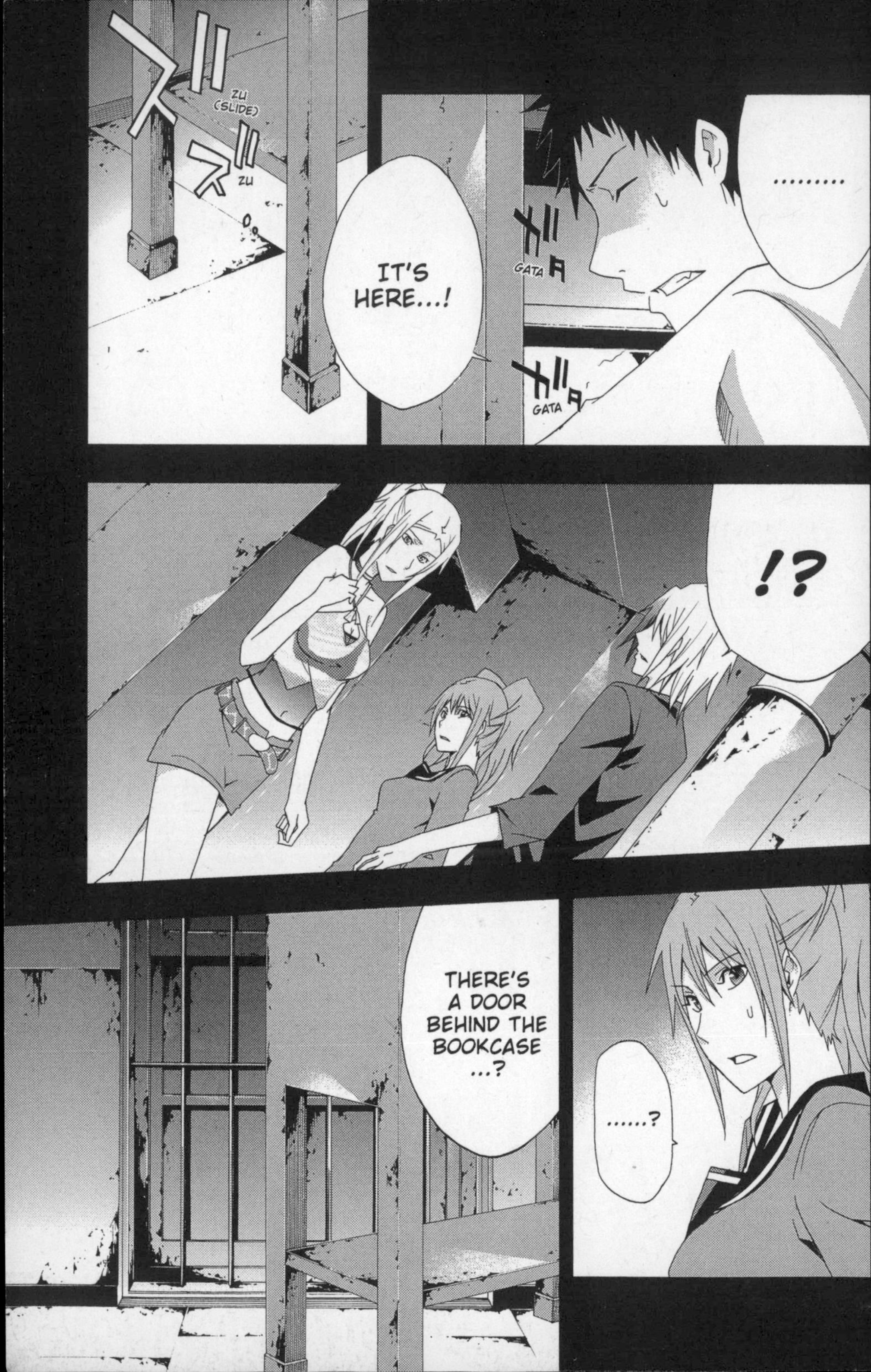
....
GATA
GATA
IT'S HERE...!
ZU (SLIDE)
ZU
!?
......?
THERE'S A DOOR BEHIND THE BOOKCASE ...?

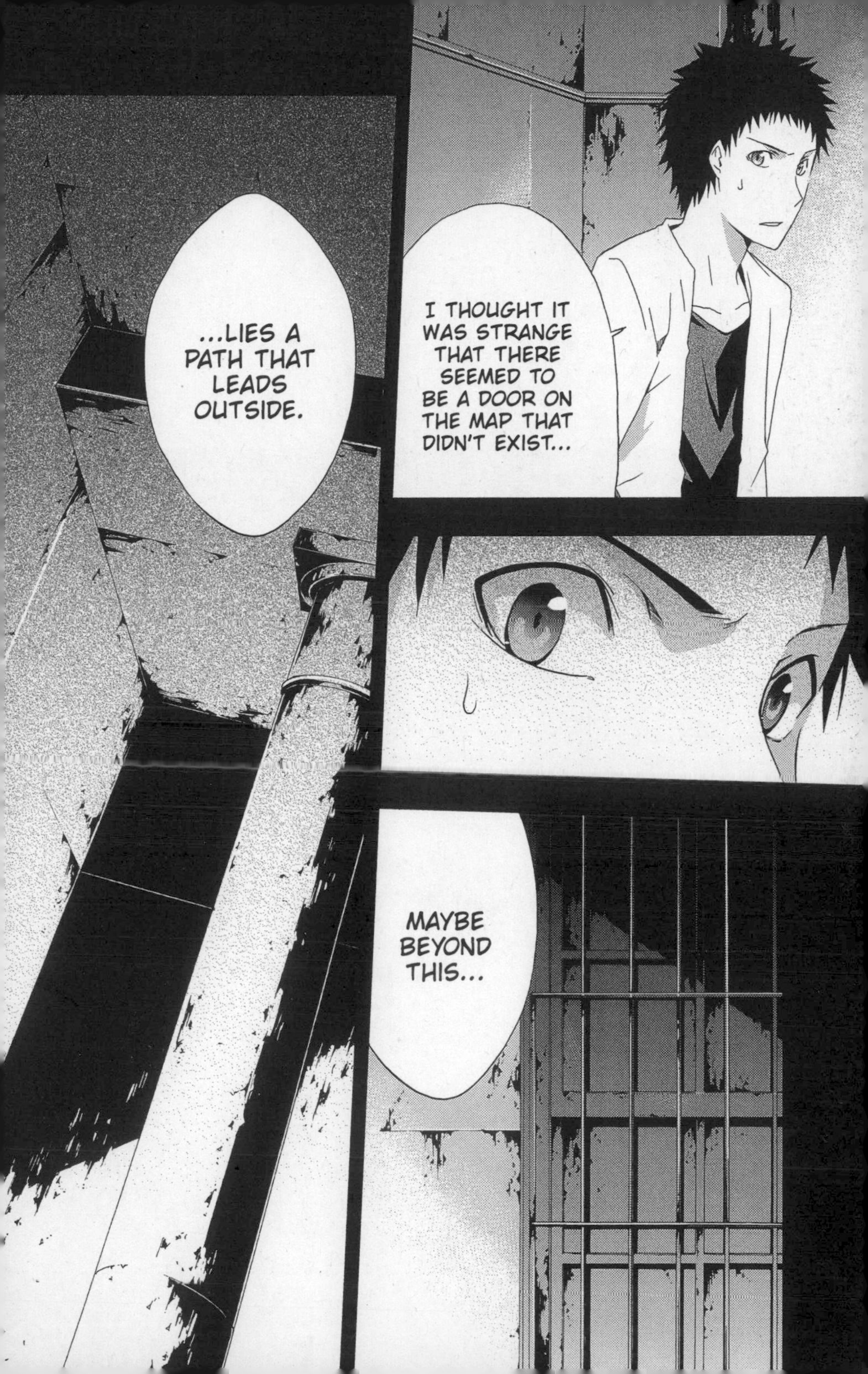
I THOUGHT IT WAS STRANGE THAT THERE SEEMED TO BE A DOOR ON THE MAP THAT DIDN'T EXIST...
MAYBE BEYOND THIS...
...LIES A PATH THAT LEADS OUTSIDE.

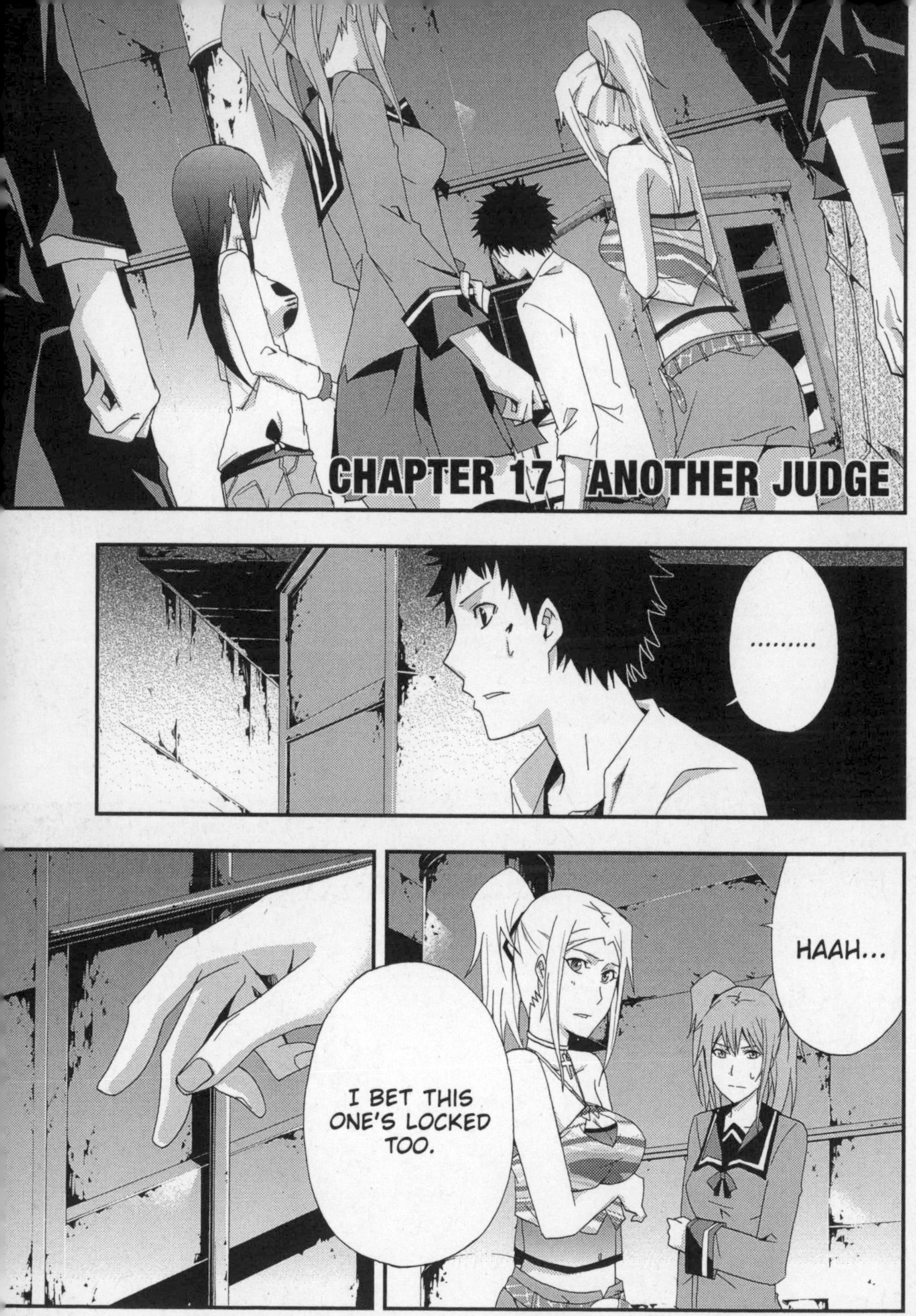
CHAPTER 17 ANOTHER JUDGE
....
HAAH...
I BET THIS ONE'S LOCKED TOO.

GACHA
(CLACK)

IT OPENED
...!?

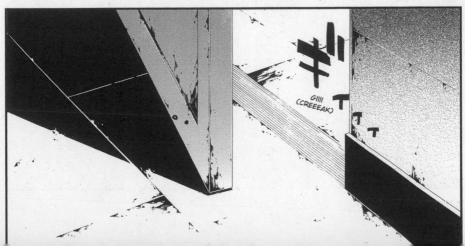

GIII
(CREEEAK)

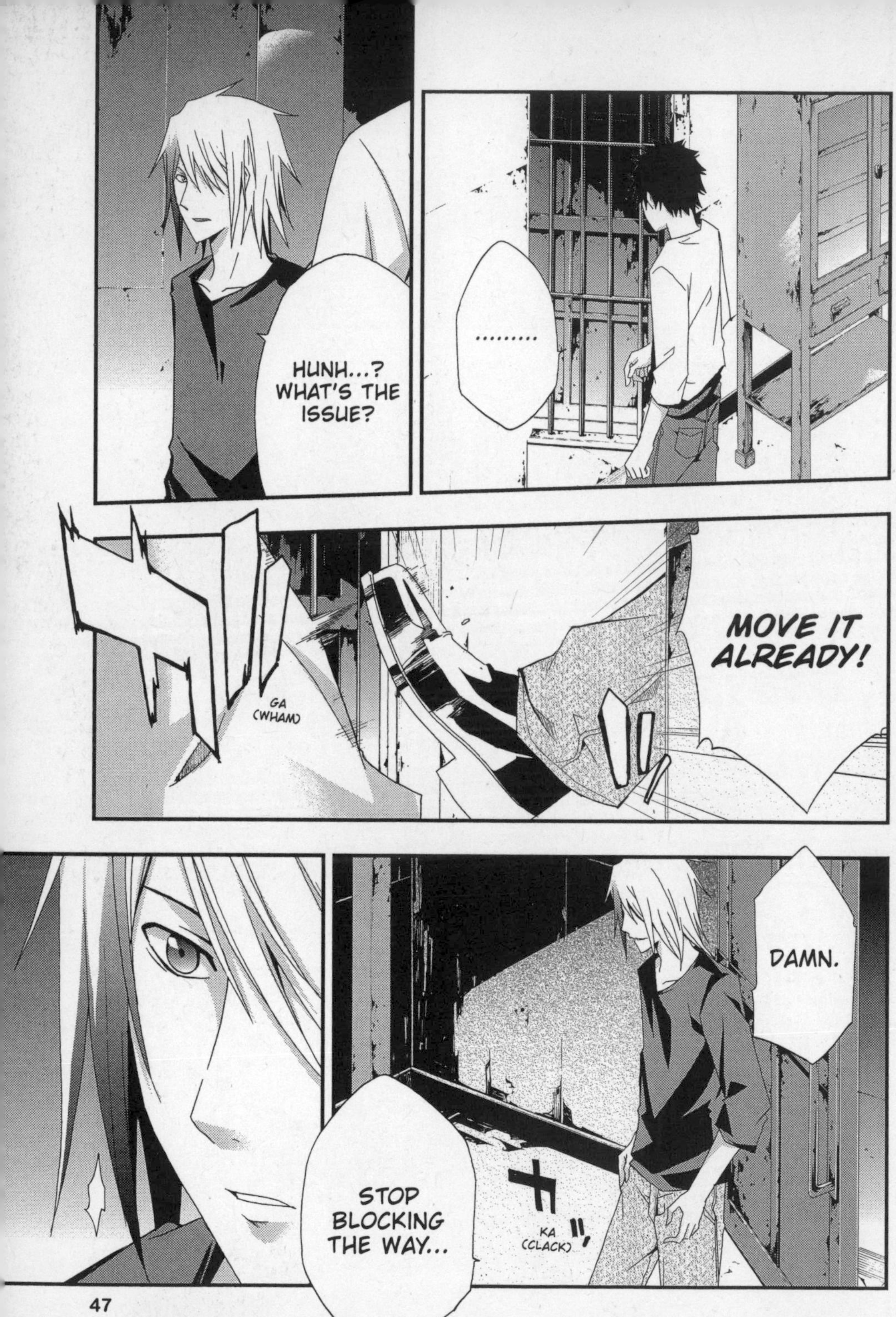
....
HUNH...? WHAT'S THE ISSUE?
MOVE IT ALREADY!
GA (WHAM)
DAMN.
KA (CLACK)
STOP BLOCKING THE WAY...

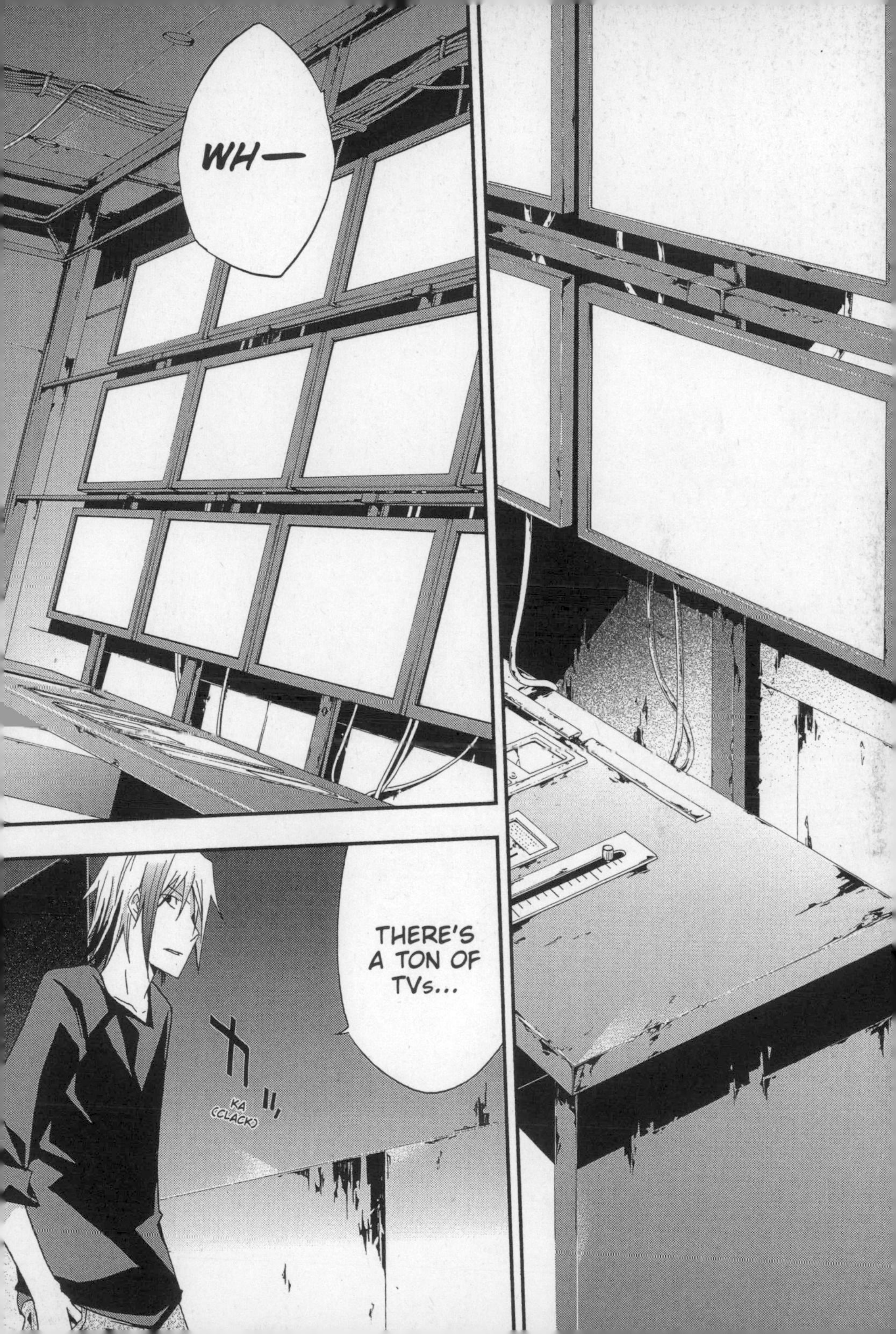
WH—
THERE'S A TON OF TVs...
KA (CLACK)

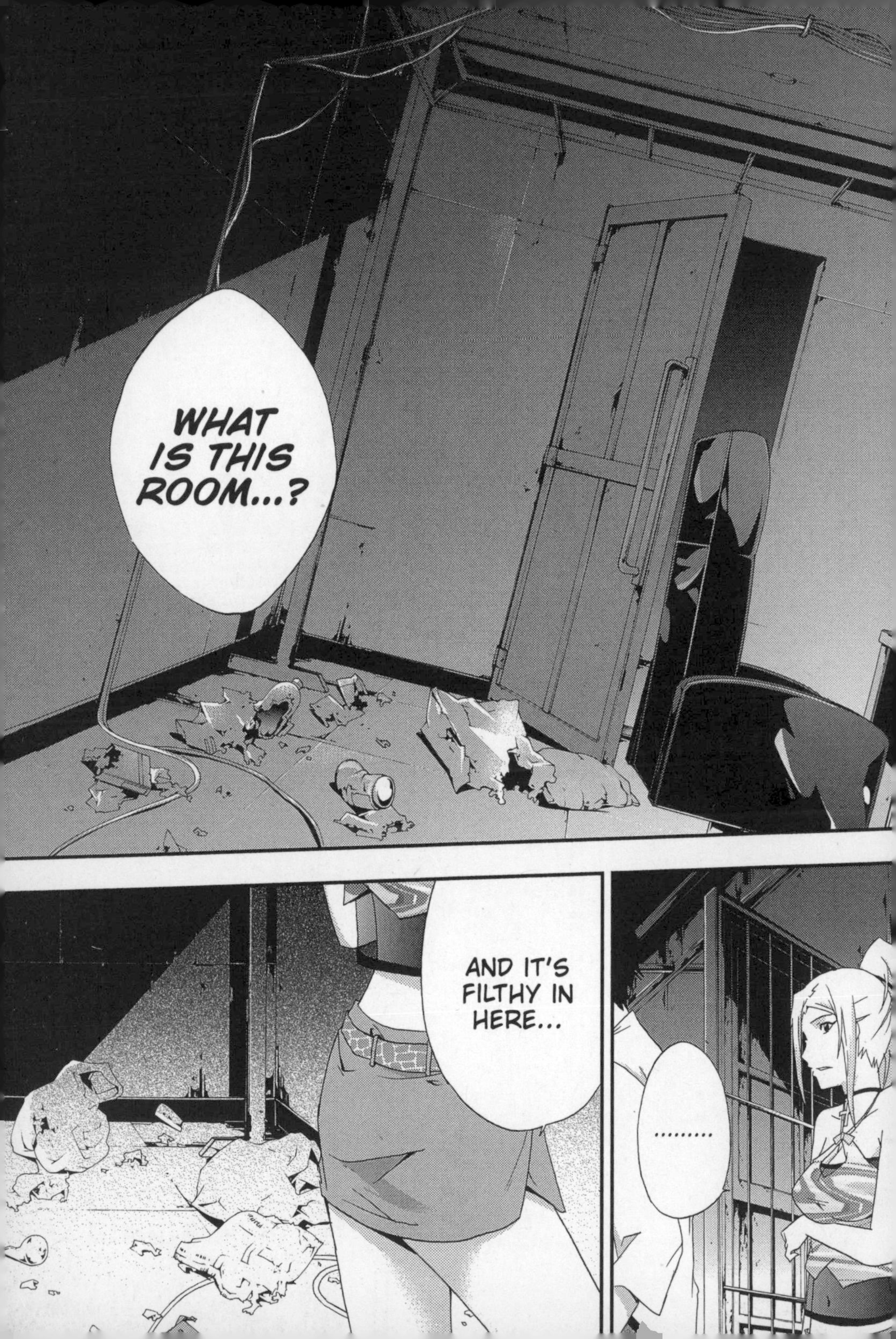
WHAT IS THIS ROOM...?
....
AND IT'S FILTHY IN HERE...

THIS IS DISGUSTING.

WHO JUST TOSSES TRASH ON THE FLOOR LIKE THIS...?

グシャ GUSHA (CRUSH)

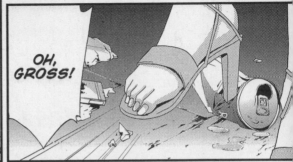

OH, GROSS!

WHAT WERE THEY WATCHING...

...WITH THIS MANY SCREENS?

....

50

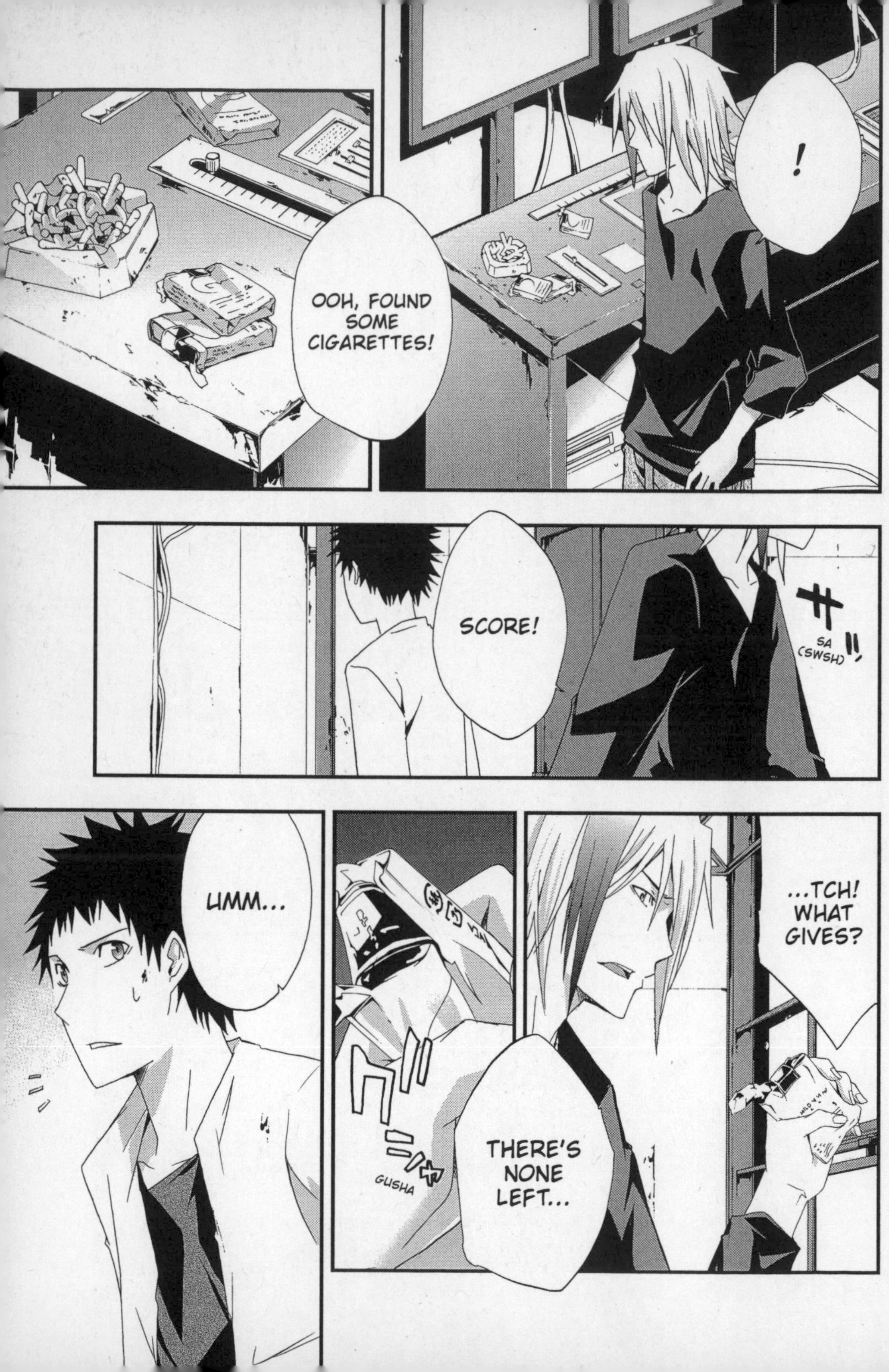
!
OOH, FOUND SOME CIGARETTES!
SCORE!
SA (SWSH)
...TCH! WHAT GIVES?
THERE'S NONE LEFT...
GUSHA
UMM...

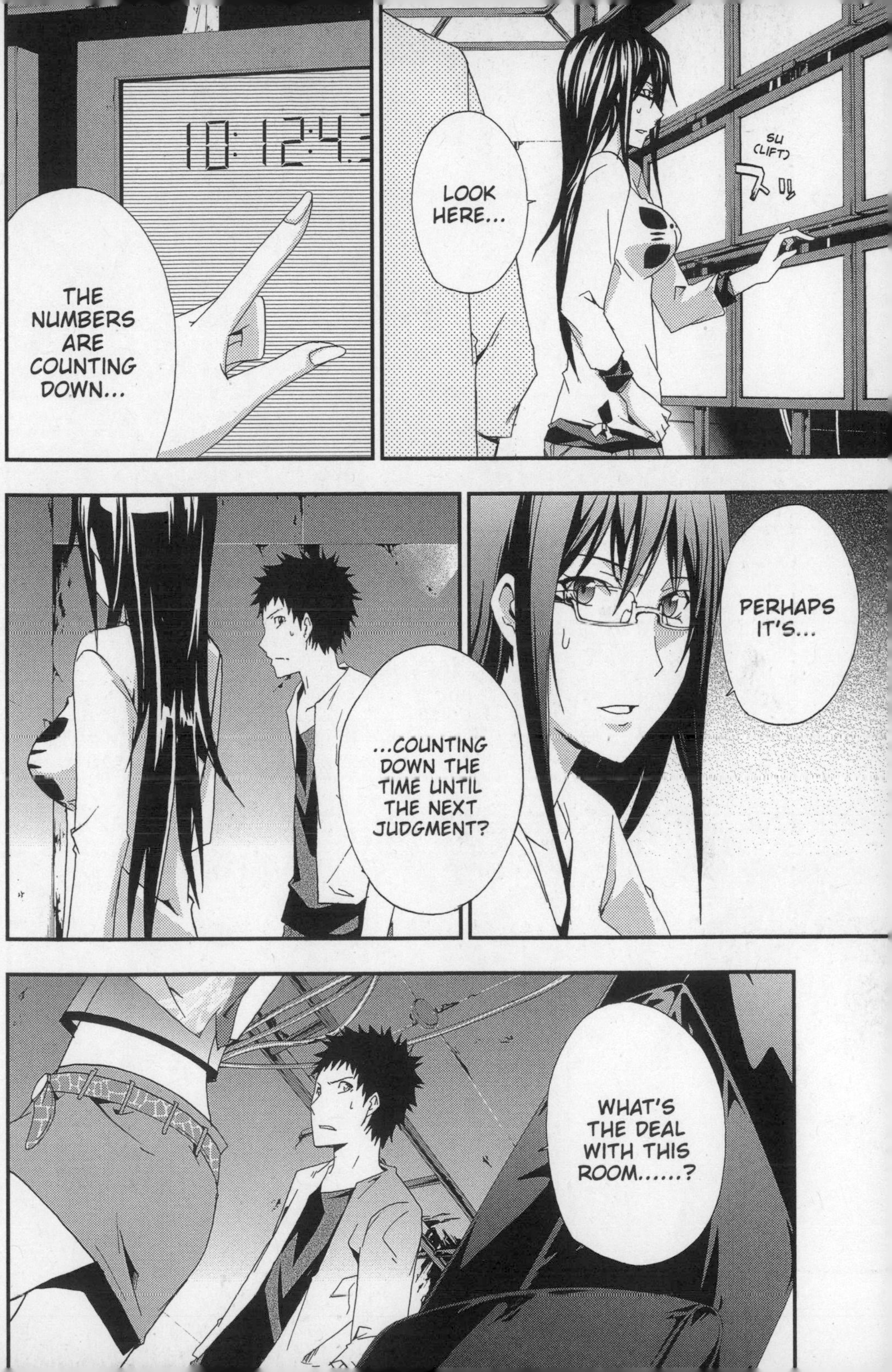
SU (LIFT)
LOOK HERE...
THE NUMBERS ARE COUNTING DOWN...
PERHAPS IT'S...
...COUNTING DOWN THE TIME UNTIL THE NEXT JUDGMENT?
WHAT'S THE DEAL WITH THIS ROOM......?

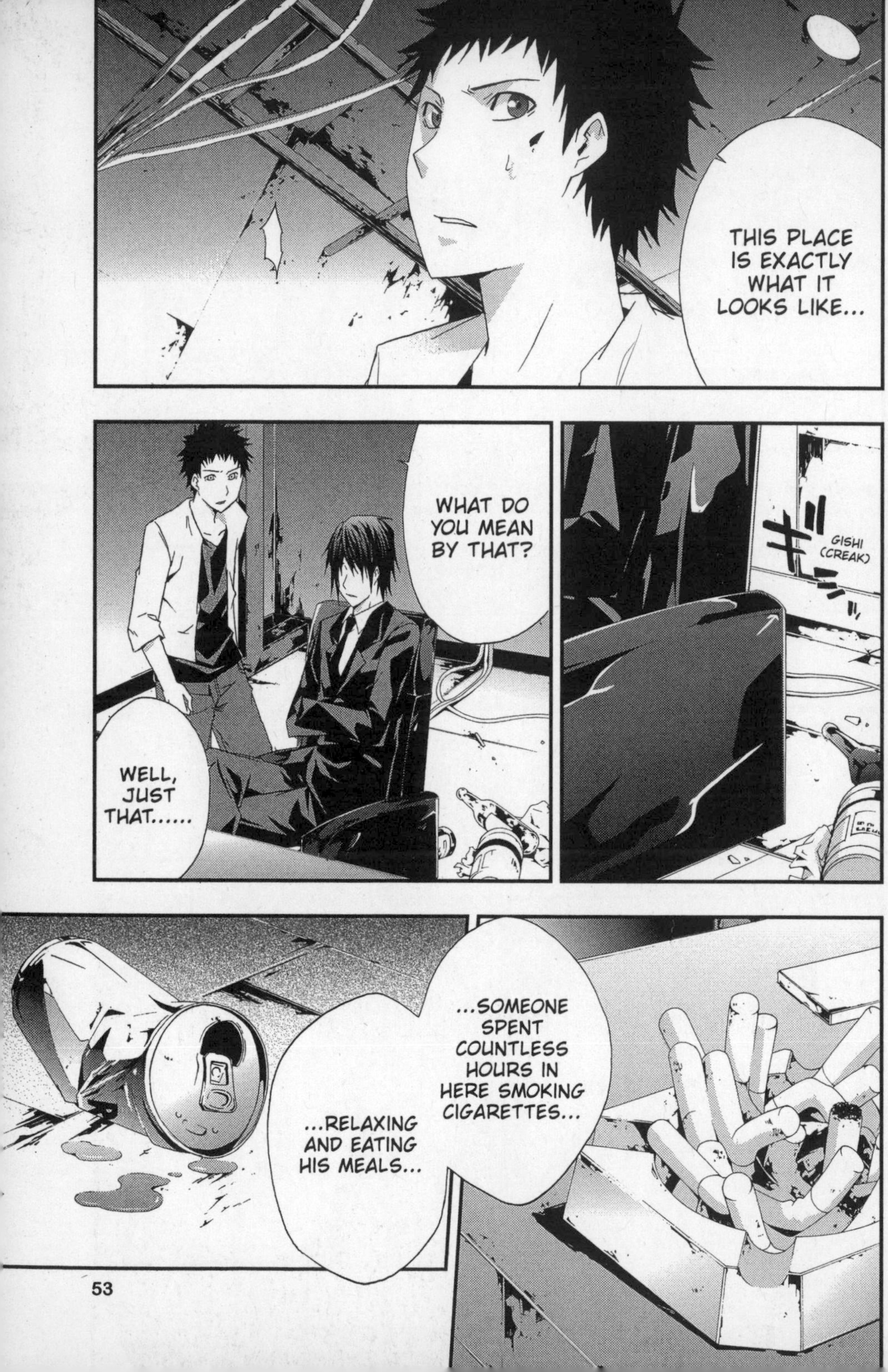
THIS PLACE IS EXACTLY WHAT IT LOOKS LIKE...
GISHI (CREAK)
WHAT DO YOU MEAN BY THAT?
WELL, JUST THAT......
...SOMEONE SPENT COUNTLESS HOURS IN HERE SMOKING CIGARETTES...
...RELAXING AND EATING HIS MEALS...

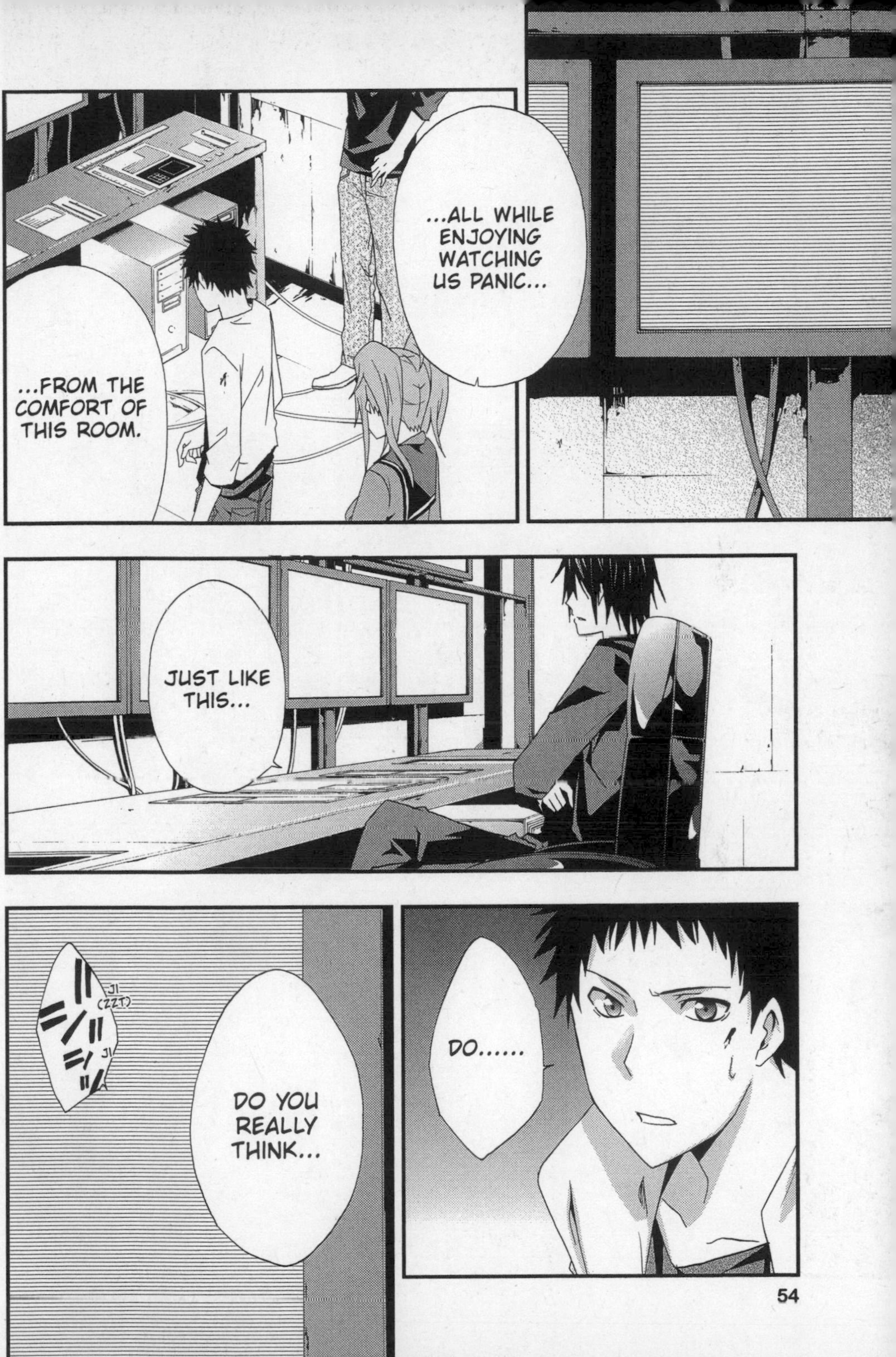
...ALL WHILE ENJOYING WATCHING US PANIC...
...FROM THE COMFORT OF THIS ROOM.
JUST LIKE THIS...
DO......
JI (ZZT) JI
DO YOU REALLY THINK...

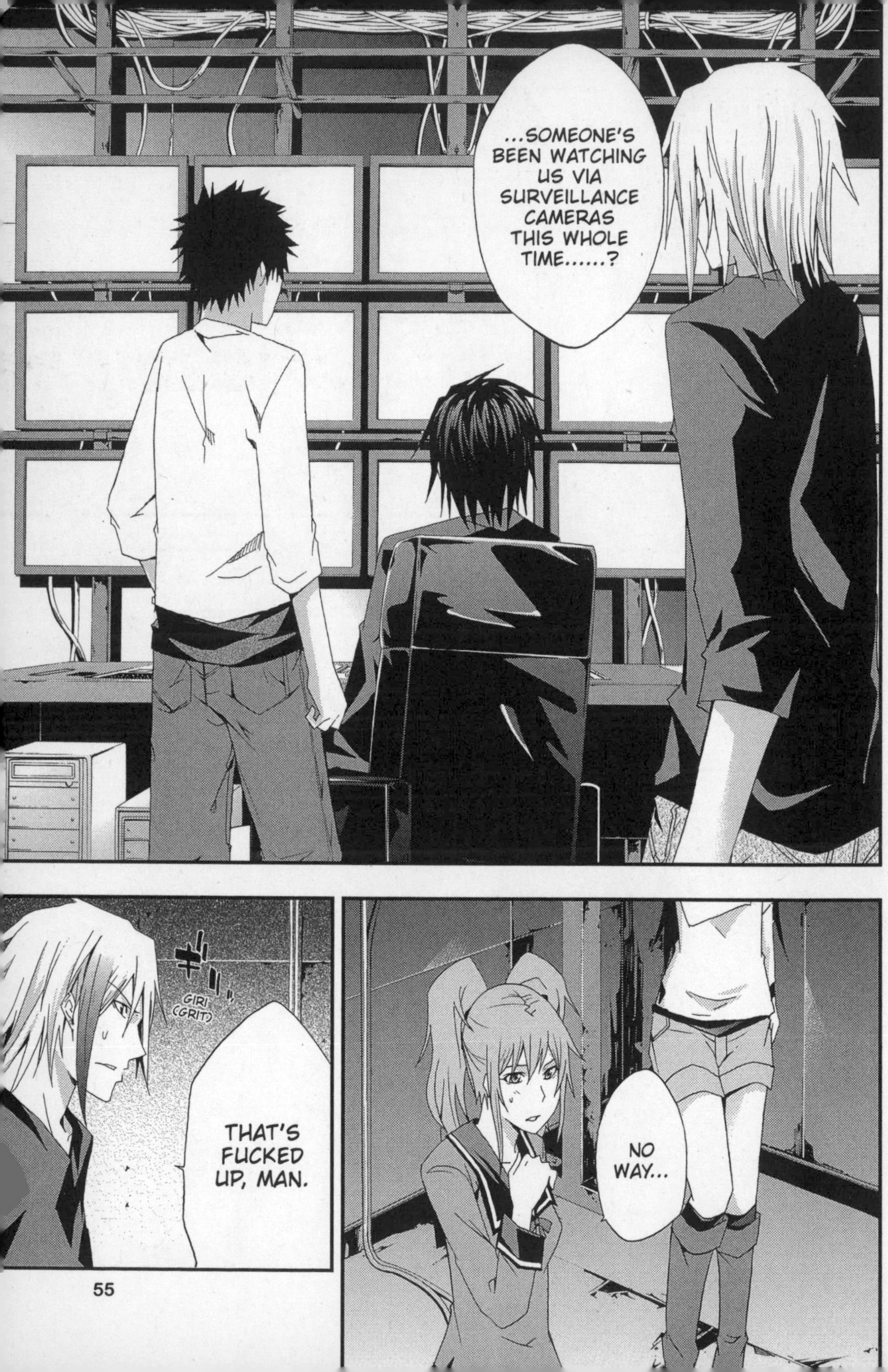
...SOMEONE'S BEEN WATCHING US VIA SURVEILLANCE CAMERAS THIS WHOLE TIME......?
NO WAY...
GIRI (GRIT)
THAT'S FUCKED UP, MAN.

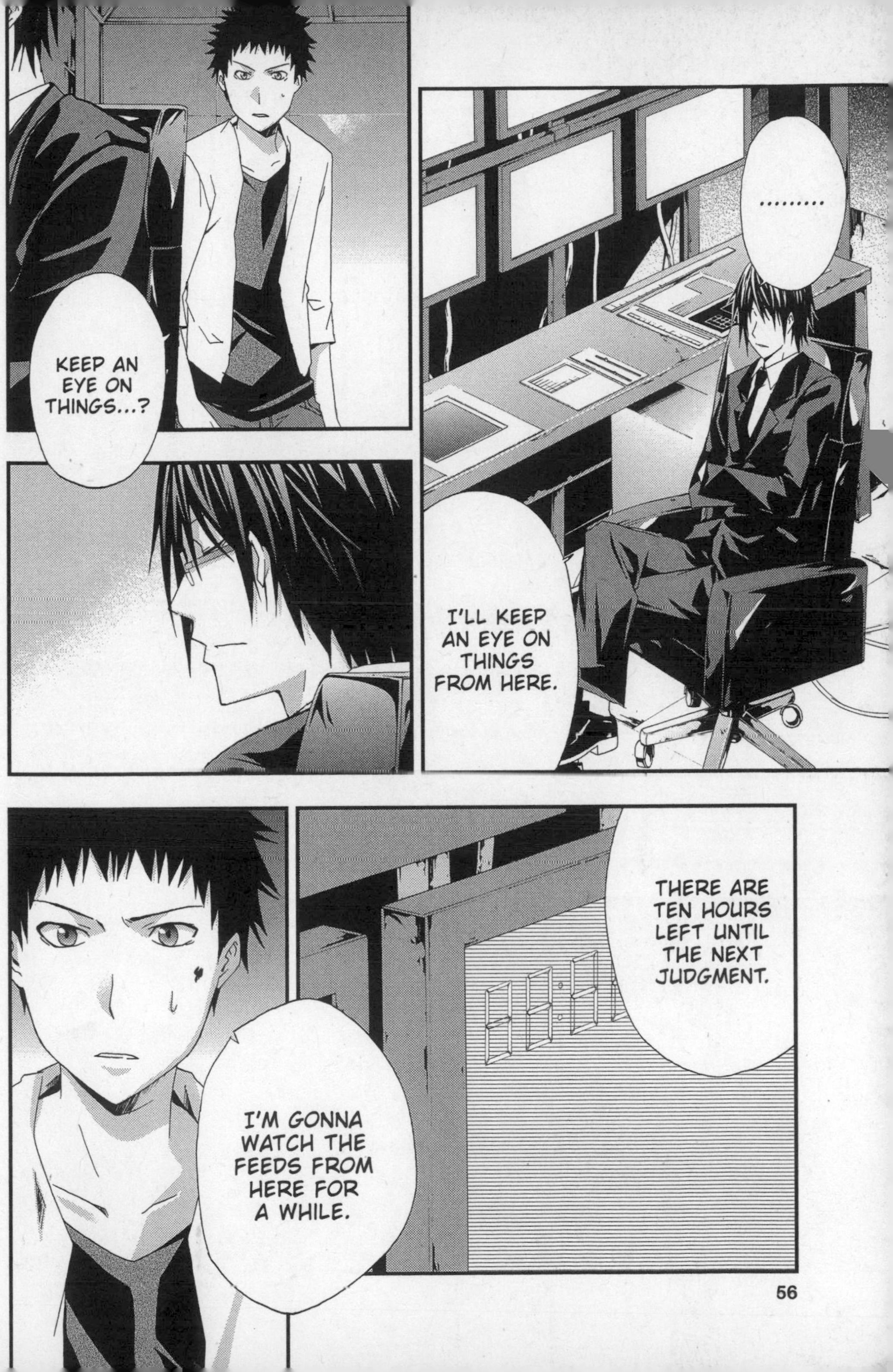
....
I'LL KEEP AN EYE ON THINGS FROM HERE.
KEEP AN EYE ON THINGS...?
THERE ARE TEN HOURS LEFT UNTIL THE NEXT JUDGMENT.
I'M GONNA WATCH THE FEEDS FROM HERE FOR A WHILE.

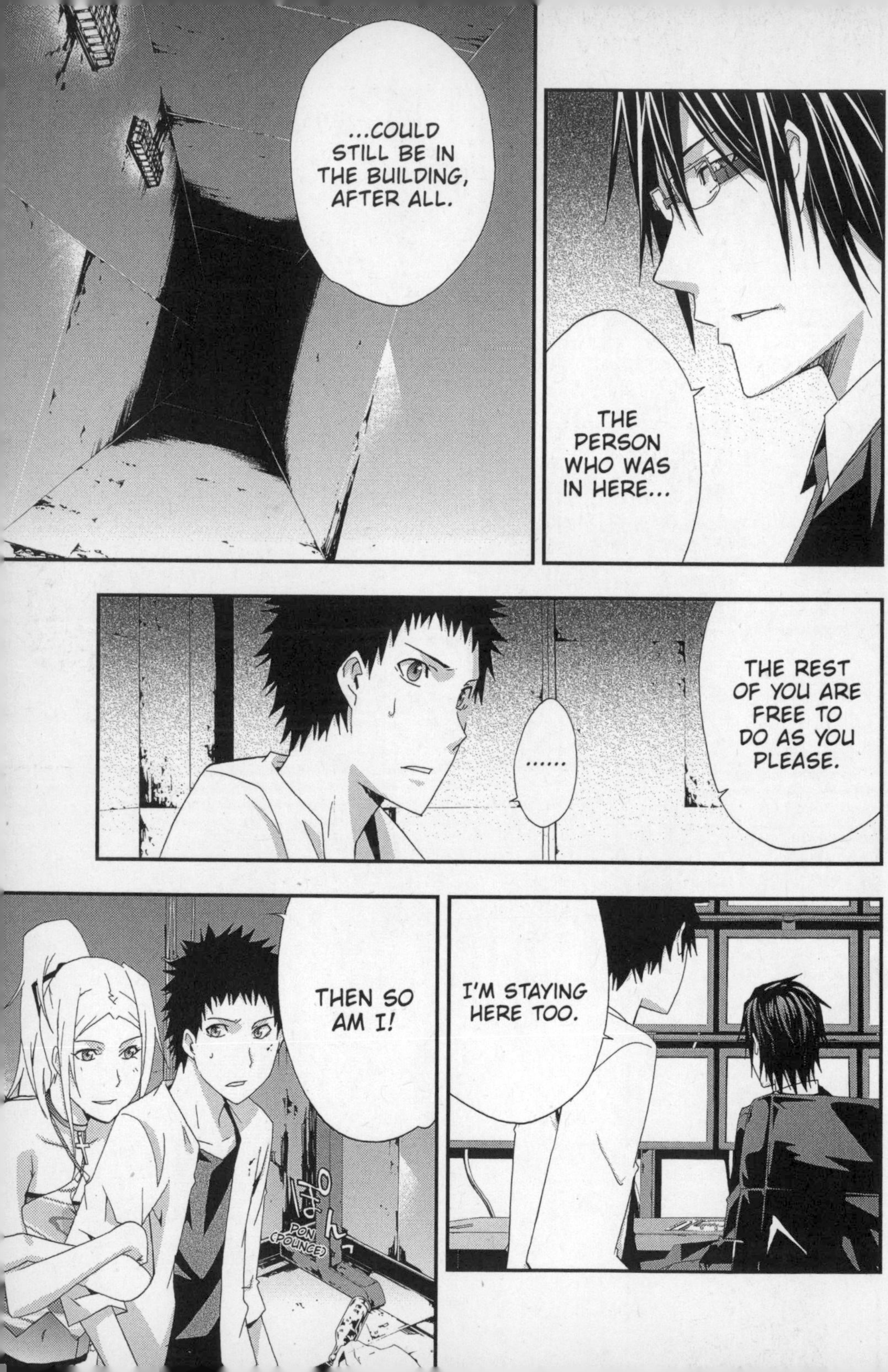
THE PERSON WHO WAS IN HERE...
...COULD STILL BE IN THE BUILDING, AFTER ALL.
THE REST OF YOU ARE FREE TO DO AS YOU PLEASE.
......
I'M STAYING HERE TOO.
THEN SO AM I!
PON (POUNCE)

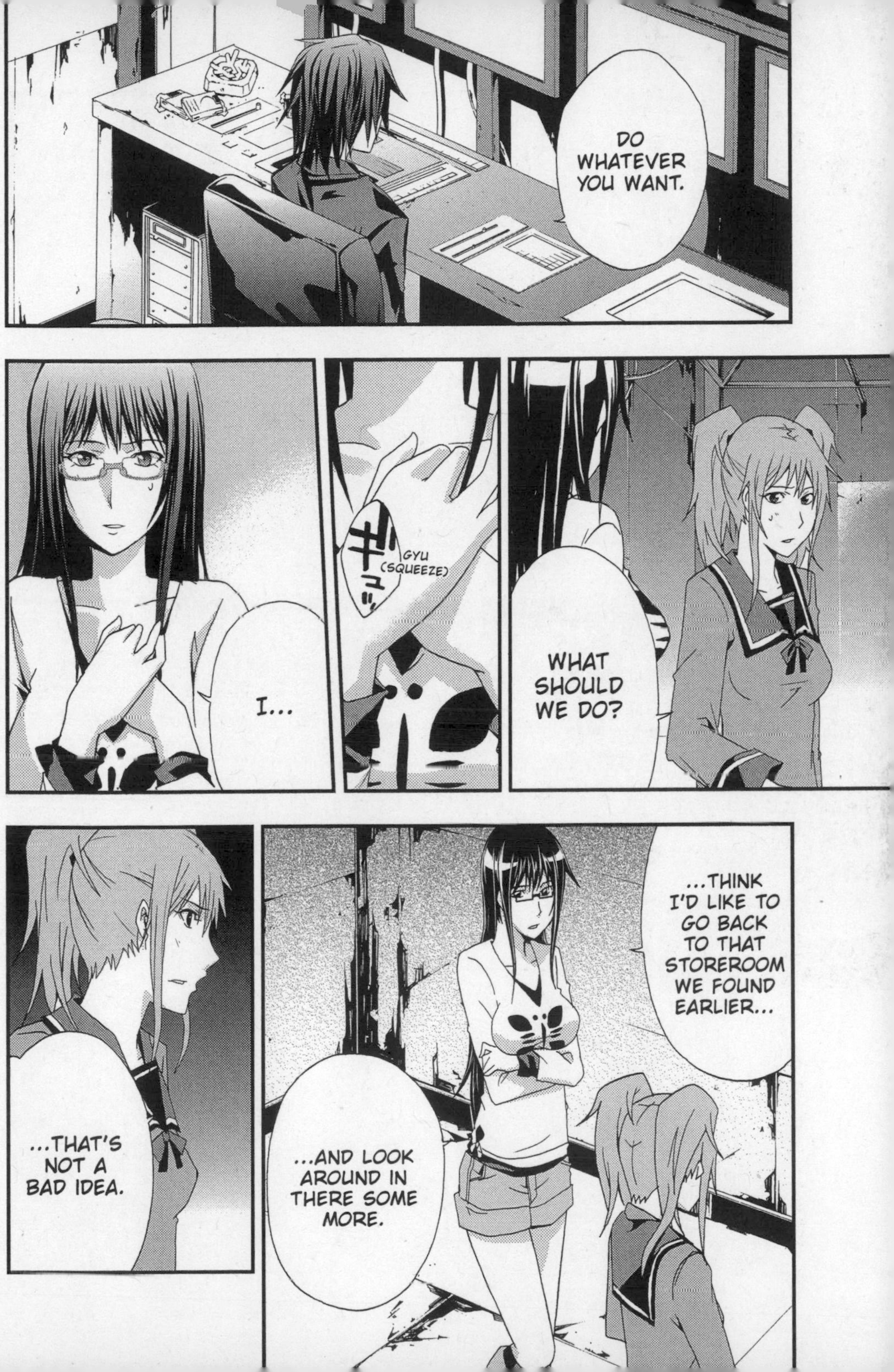
DO WHATEVER YOU WANT.
WHAT SHOULD WE DO?
GYU (SQUEEZE)
I...
...THINK I'D LIKE TO GO BACK TO THAT STOREROOM WE FOUND EARLIER...
...AND LOOK AROUND IN THERE SOME MORE.
...THAT'S NOT A BAD IDEA.

......

AS LONG AS WE ALL MEET BACK IN THAT ROOM ONCE IT'S TIME, IT DOESN'T MATTER.

IN THAT CASE, I'LL DO WHATEVER I WANT TOO...

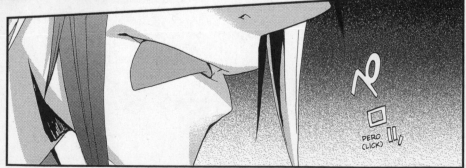

PERO (CLICK)

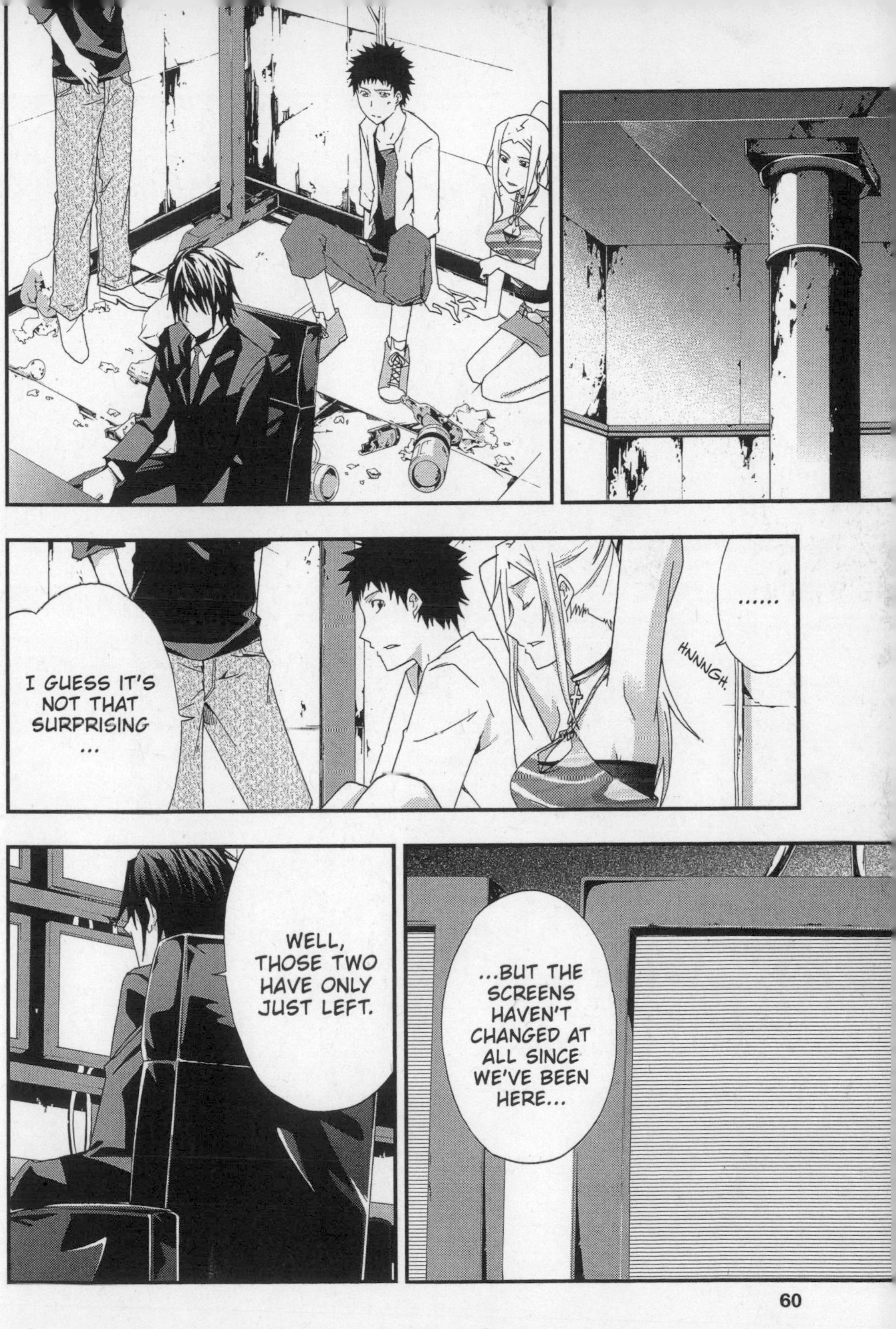
......
HNNNGH.
I GUESS IT'S NOT THAT SURPRISING ...
...BUT THE SCREENS HAVEN'T CHANGED AT ALL SINCE WE'VE BEEN HERE...
WELL, THOSE TWO HAVE ONLY JUST LEFT.

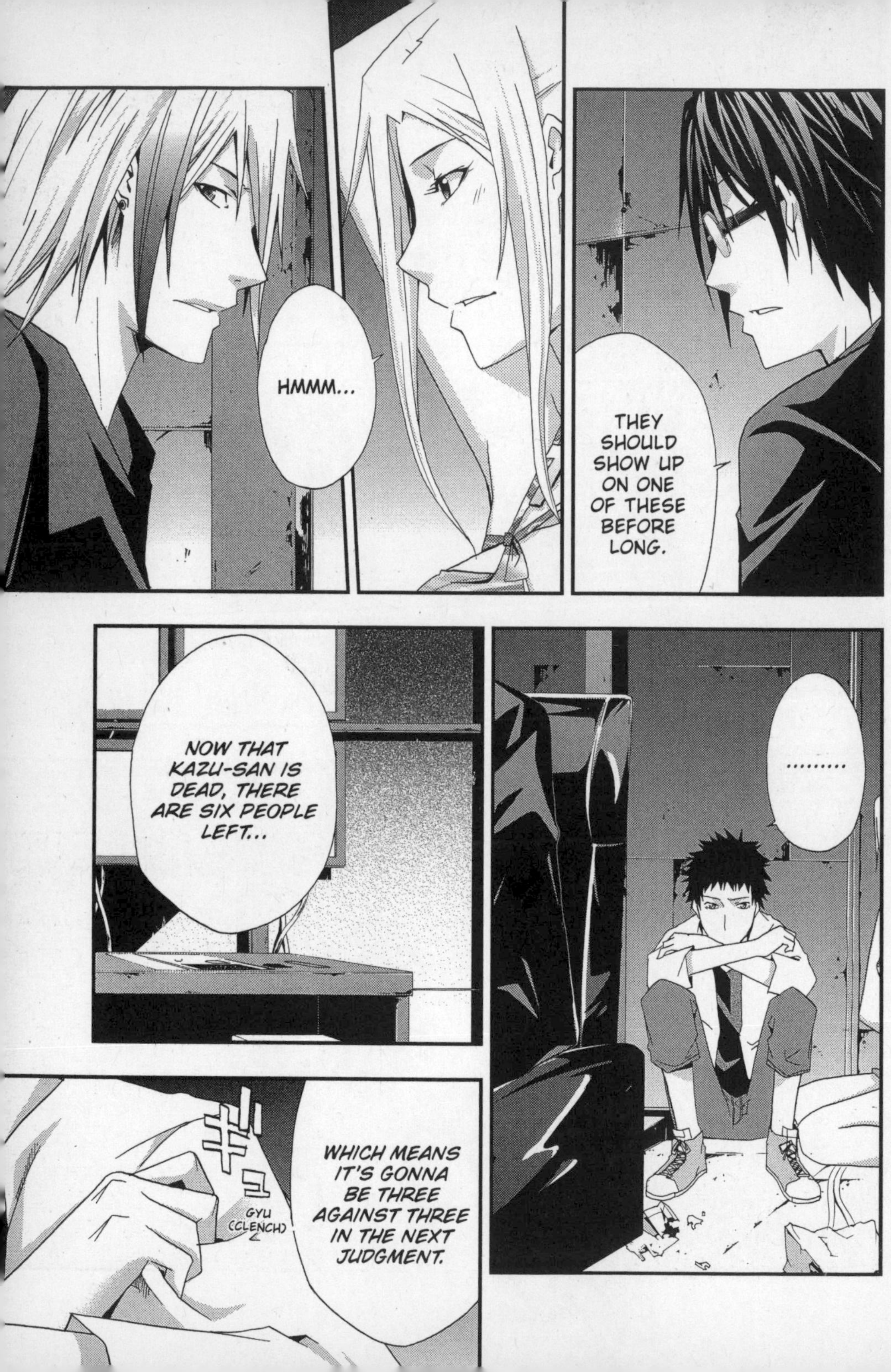
THEY SHOULD SHOW UP ON ONE OF THESE BEFORE LONG.
HMMM...
....
NOW THAT KAZU-SAN IS DEAD, THERE ARE SIX PEOPLE LEFT...
ギュ
GYU (CLENCH)
WHICH MEANS IT'S GONNA BE THREE AGAINST THREE IN THE NEXT JUDGMENT.

WHO DO WE VOTE FOR IN THE NEXT ONE.........?

AND IF THE VOTE ENDS IN A TIE, WHAT HAPPENS THEN?

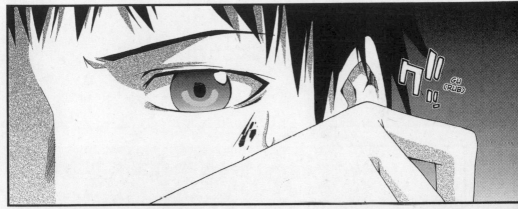

GU (RUB)

DON YOUR LIFE

KAZU-SAN...

62

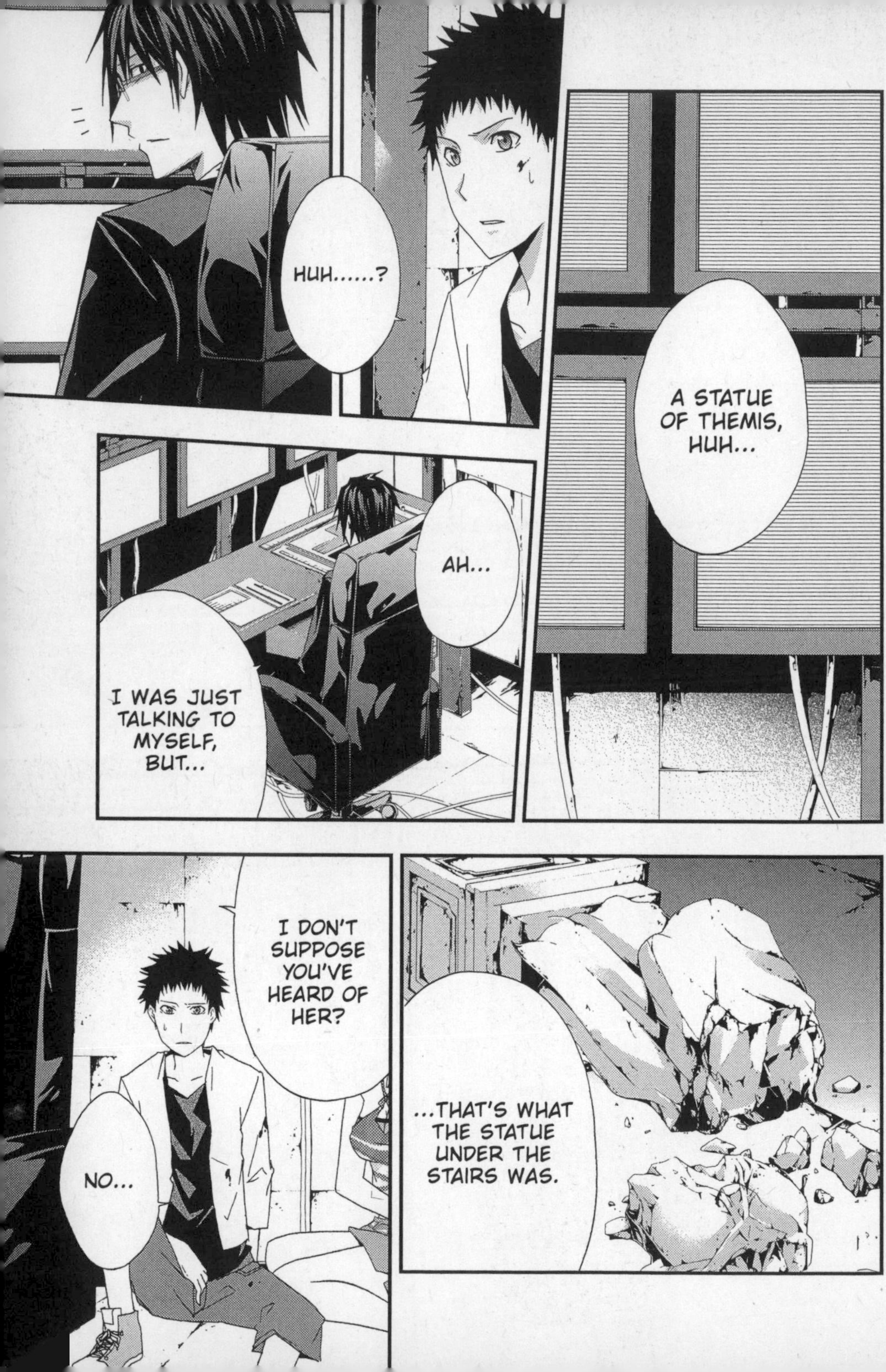
A STATUE OF THEMIS, HUH...
HUH......?
AH...
I WAS JUST TALKING TO MYSELF, BUT...
...THAT'S WHAT THE STATUE UNDER THE STAIRS WAS.
I DON'T SUPPOSE YOU'VE HEARD OF HER?
NO...

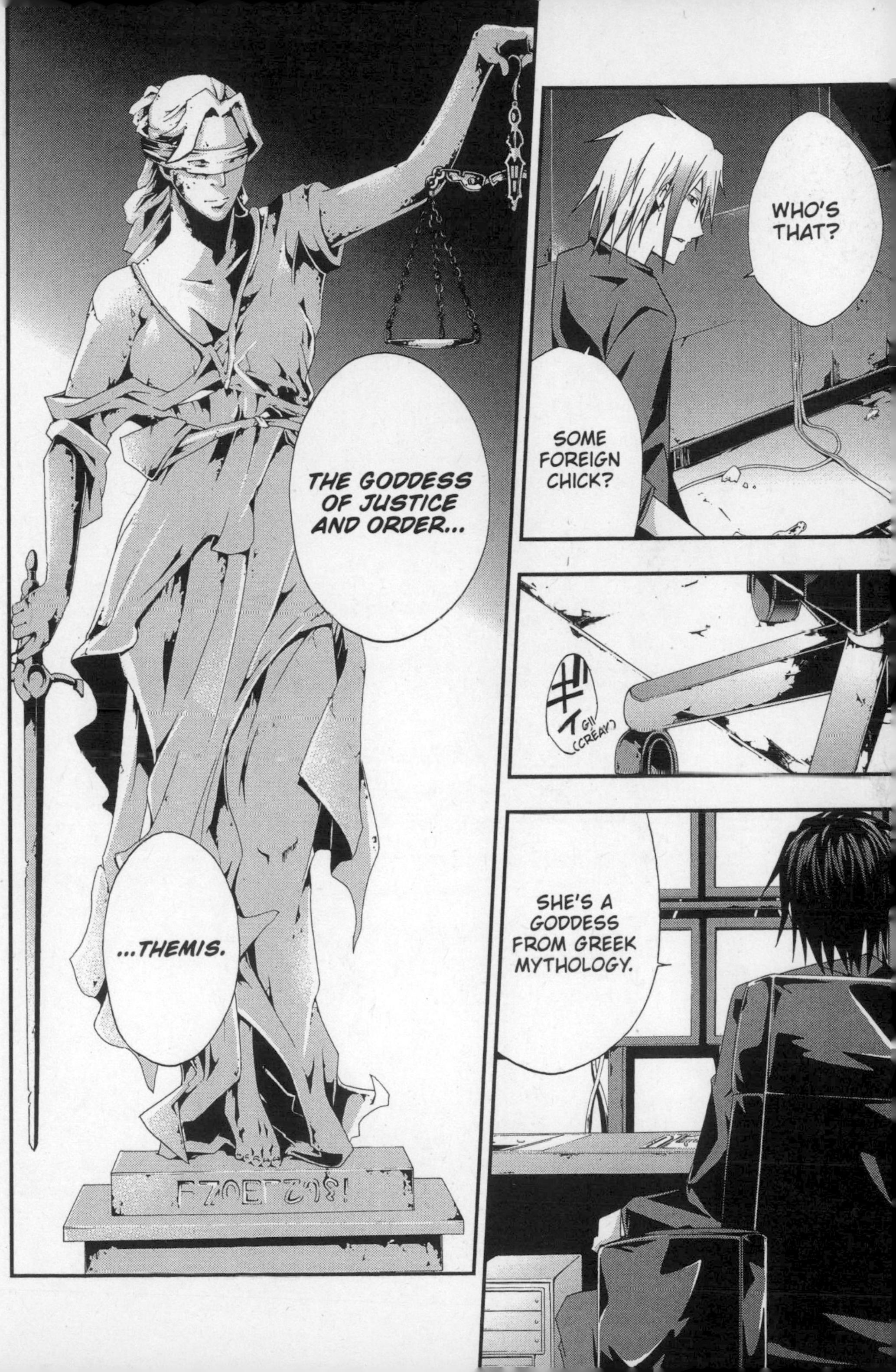
WHO'S THAT?
SOME FOREIGN CHICK?
ギイ
GII (CREAK)
SHE'S A GODDESS FROM GREEK MYTHOLOGY.
THE GODDESS OF JUSTICE AND ORDER...
...THEMIS.

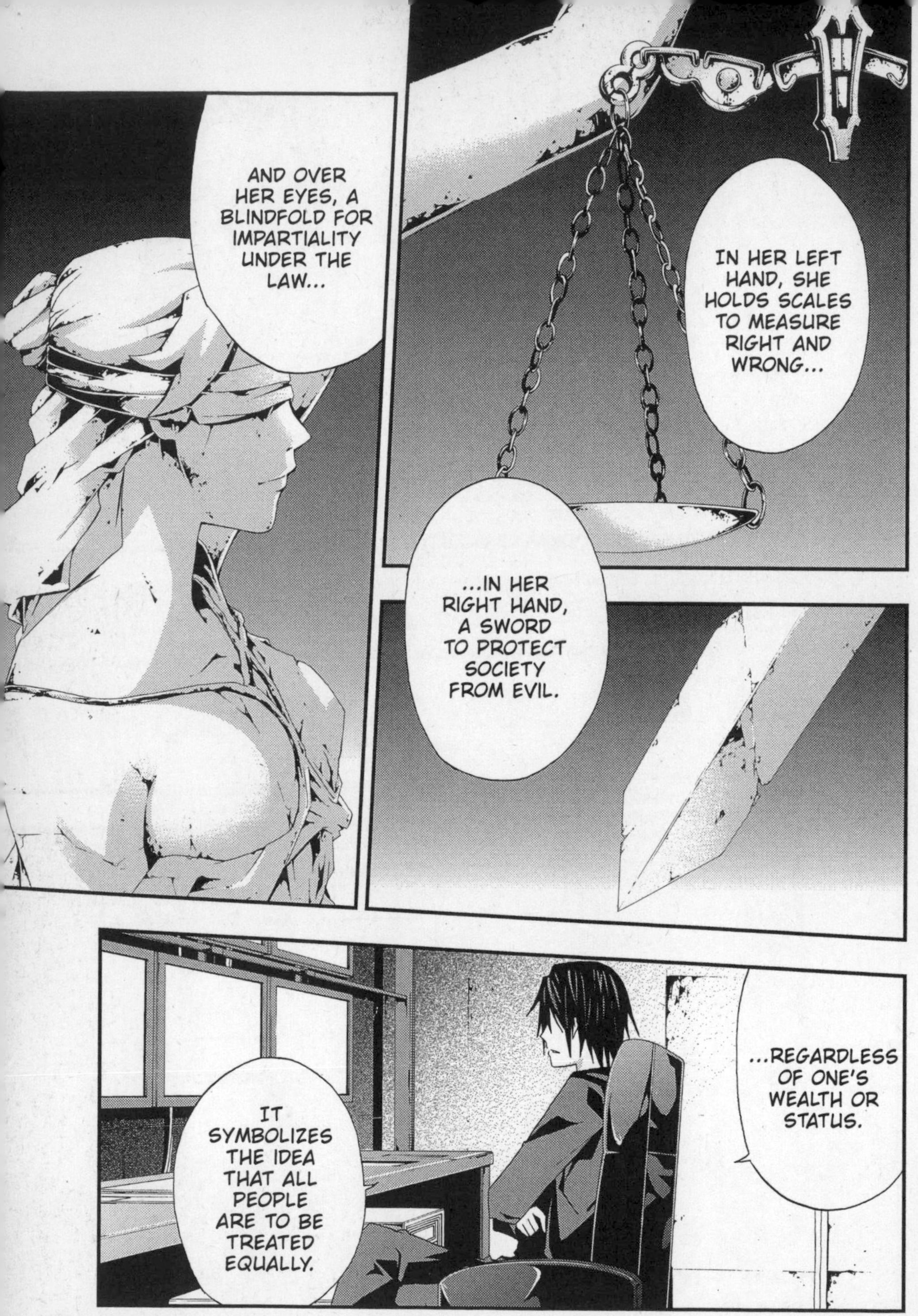
IN HER LEFT HAND, SHE HOLDS SCALES TO MEASURE RIGHT AND WRONG...
...IN HER RIGHT HAND, A SWORD TO PROTECT SOCIETY FROM EVIL.
AND OVER HER EYES, A BLINDFOLD FOR IMPARTIALITY UNDER THE LAW...
...REGARDLESS OF ONE'S WEALTH OR STATUS.
IT SYMBOLIZES THE IDEA THAT ALL PEOPLE ARE TO BE TREATED EQUALLY.

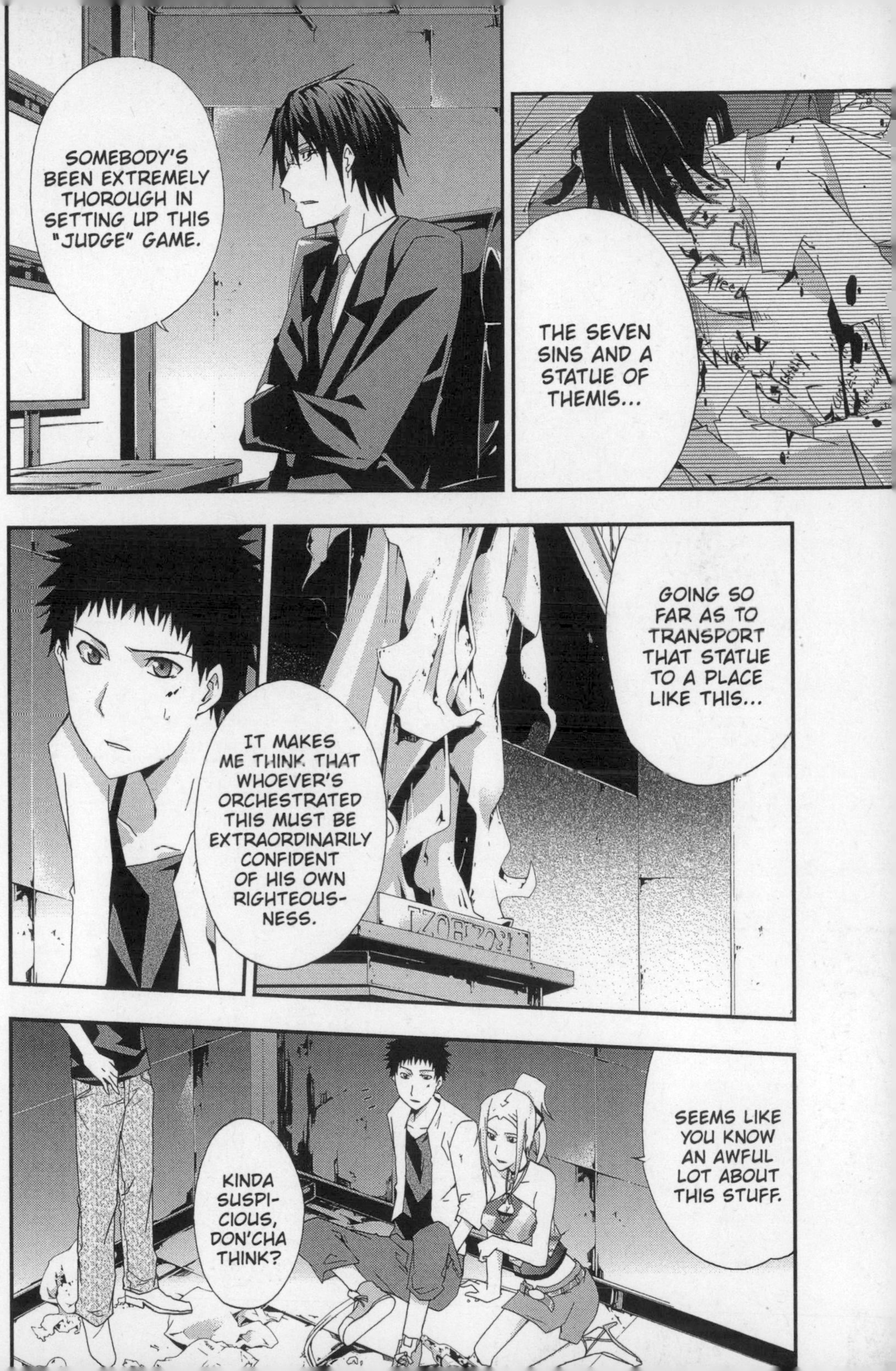
THE SEVEN SINS AND A STATUE OF THEMIS...
SOMEBODY'S BEEN EXTREMELY THOROUGH IN SETTING UP THIS "JUDGE" GAME.
GOING SO FAR AS TO TRANSPORT THAT STATUE TO A PLACE LIKE THIS...
IT MAKES ME THINK THAT WHOEVER'S ORCHESTRATED THIS MUST BE EXTRAORDINARILY CONFIDENT OF HIS OWN RIGHTEOUS-NESS.
SEEMS LIKE YOU KNOW AN AWFUL LOT ABOUT THIS STUFF.
KINDA SUSPI-CIOUS, DON'CHA THINK?

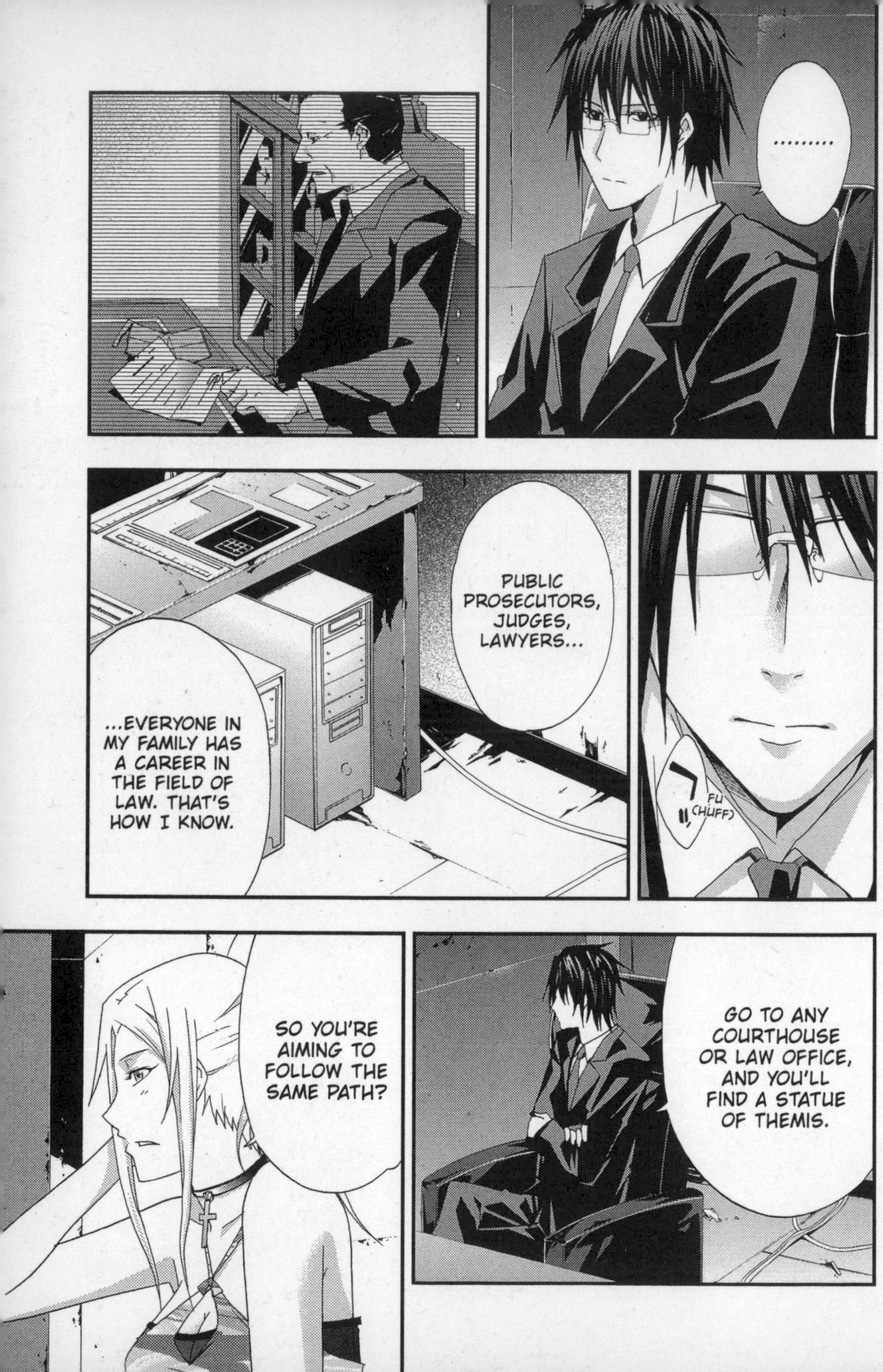
....
FU (HUFF)
PUBLIC PROSECUTORS, JUDGES, LAWYERS...
...EVERYONE IN MY FAMILY HAS A CAREER IN THE FIELD OF LAW. THAT'S HOW I KNOW.
GO TO ANY COURTHOUSE OR LAW OFFICE, AND YOU'LL FIND A STATUE OF THEMIS.
SO YOU'RE AIMING TO FOLLOW THE SAME PATH?

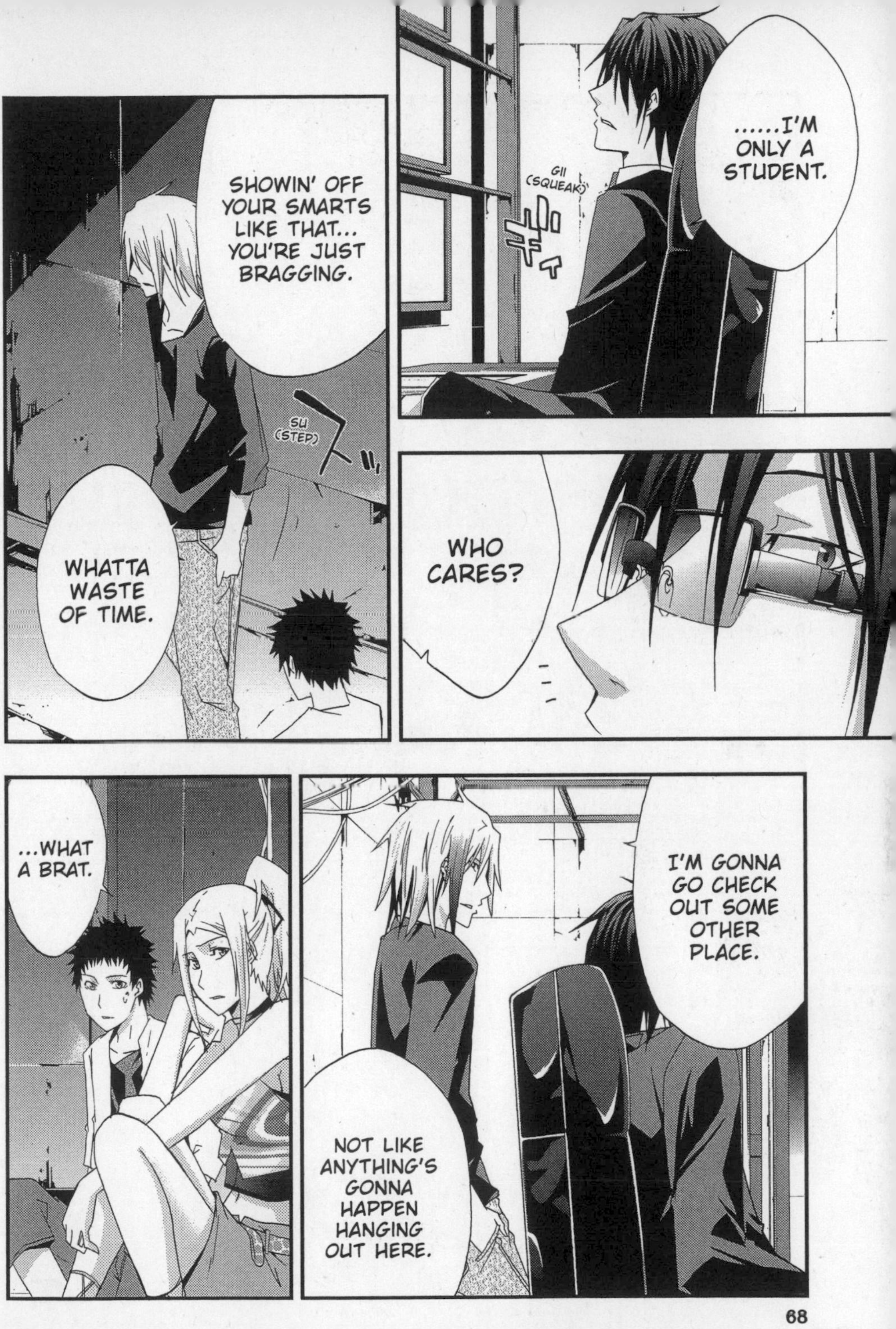
......I'M ONLY A STUDENT.
GII (SQUEAK)
WHO CARES?
SHOWIN' OFF YOUR SMARTS LIKE THAT... YOU'RE JUST BRAGGING.
SU (STEP)
WHATTA WASTE OF TIME.
I'M GONNA GO CHECK OUT SOME OTHER PLACE.
NOT LIKE ANYTHING'S GONNA HAPPEN HANGING OUT HERE.
...WHAT A BRAT.

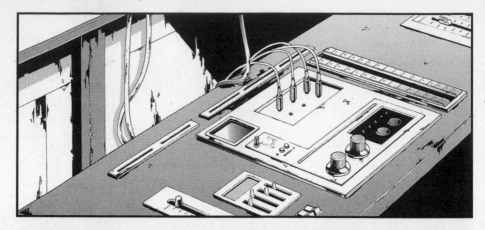

TON
(BUMP)

!?

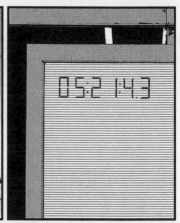

05:2 14.3

ASAMI-
SAN...?

UH!

SUU
(ZZZ)

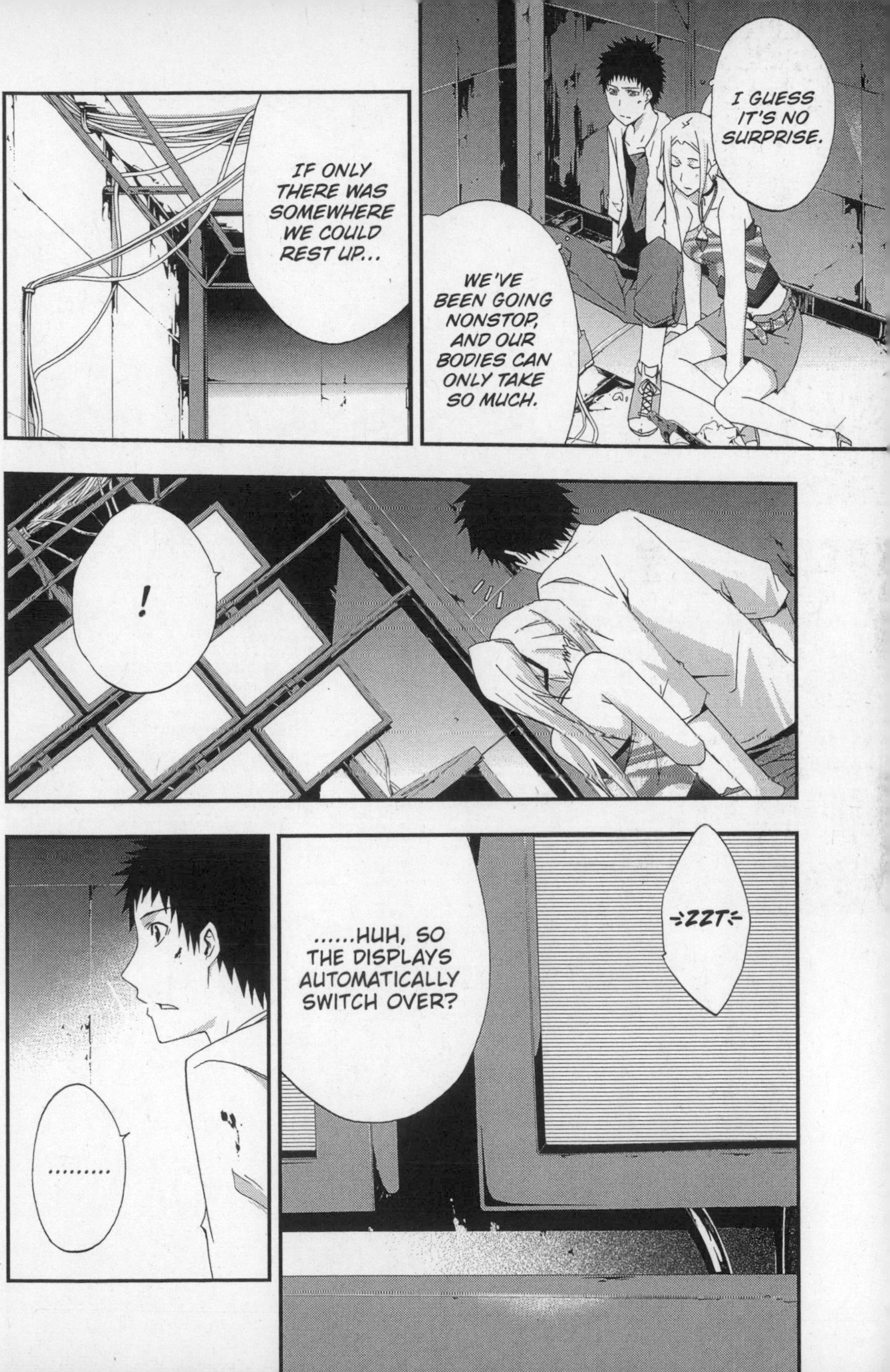

I GUESS IT'S NO SURPRISE.
WE'VE BEEN GOING NONSTOP, AND OUR BODIES CAN ONLY TAKE SO MUCH.
IF ONLY THERE WAS SOMEWHERE WE COULD REST UP...
!
ZZZT
......HUH, SO THE DISPLAYS AUTOMATICALLY SWITCH OVER?
....

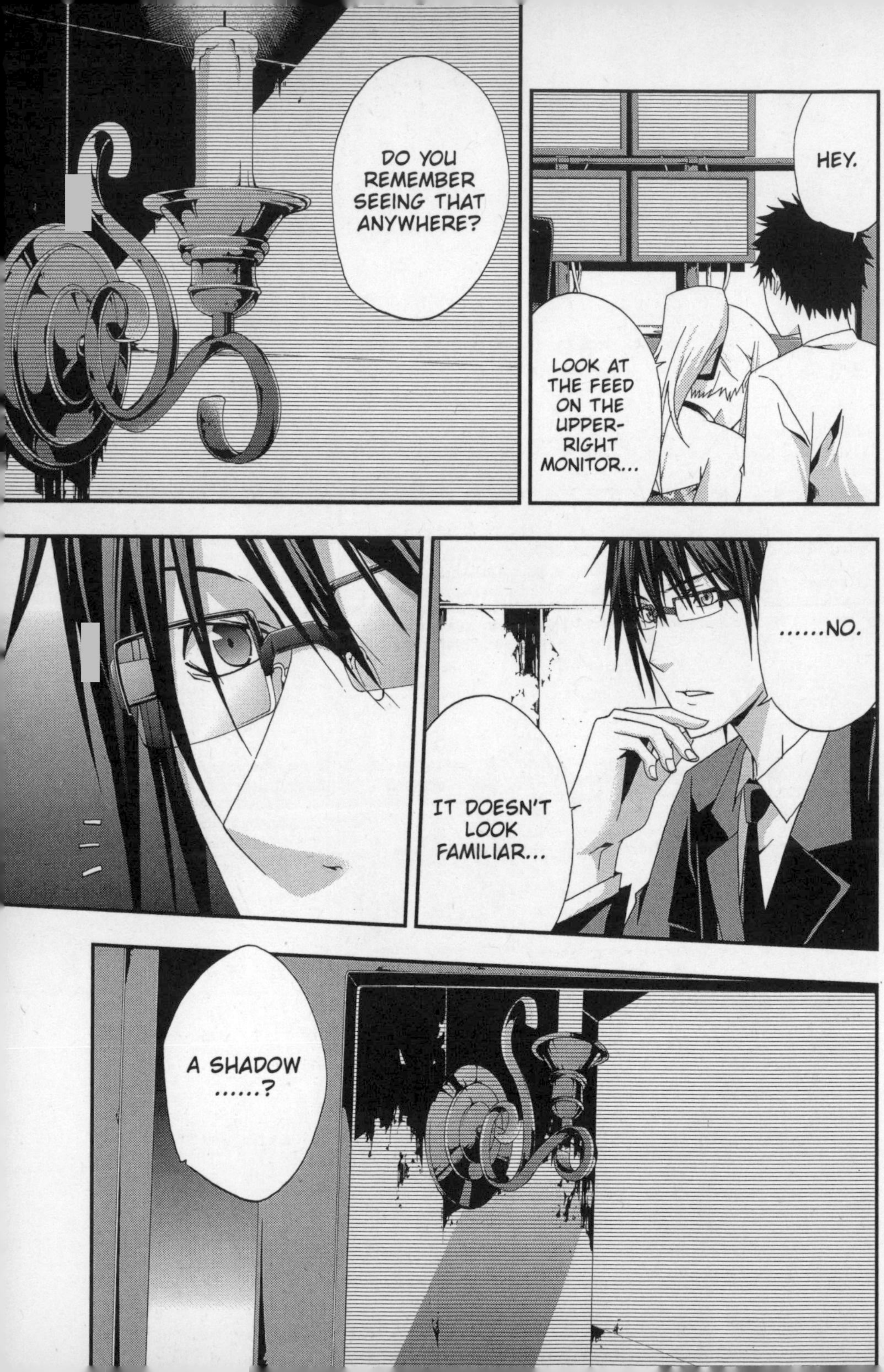
HEY.
LOOK AT THE FEED ON THE UPPER-RIGHT MONITOR...
DO YOU REMEMBER SEEING THAT ANYWHERE?
......NO.
IT DOESN'T LOOK FAMILIAR...
A SHADOW ......?

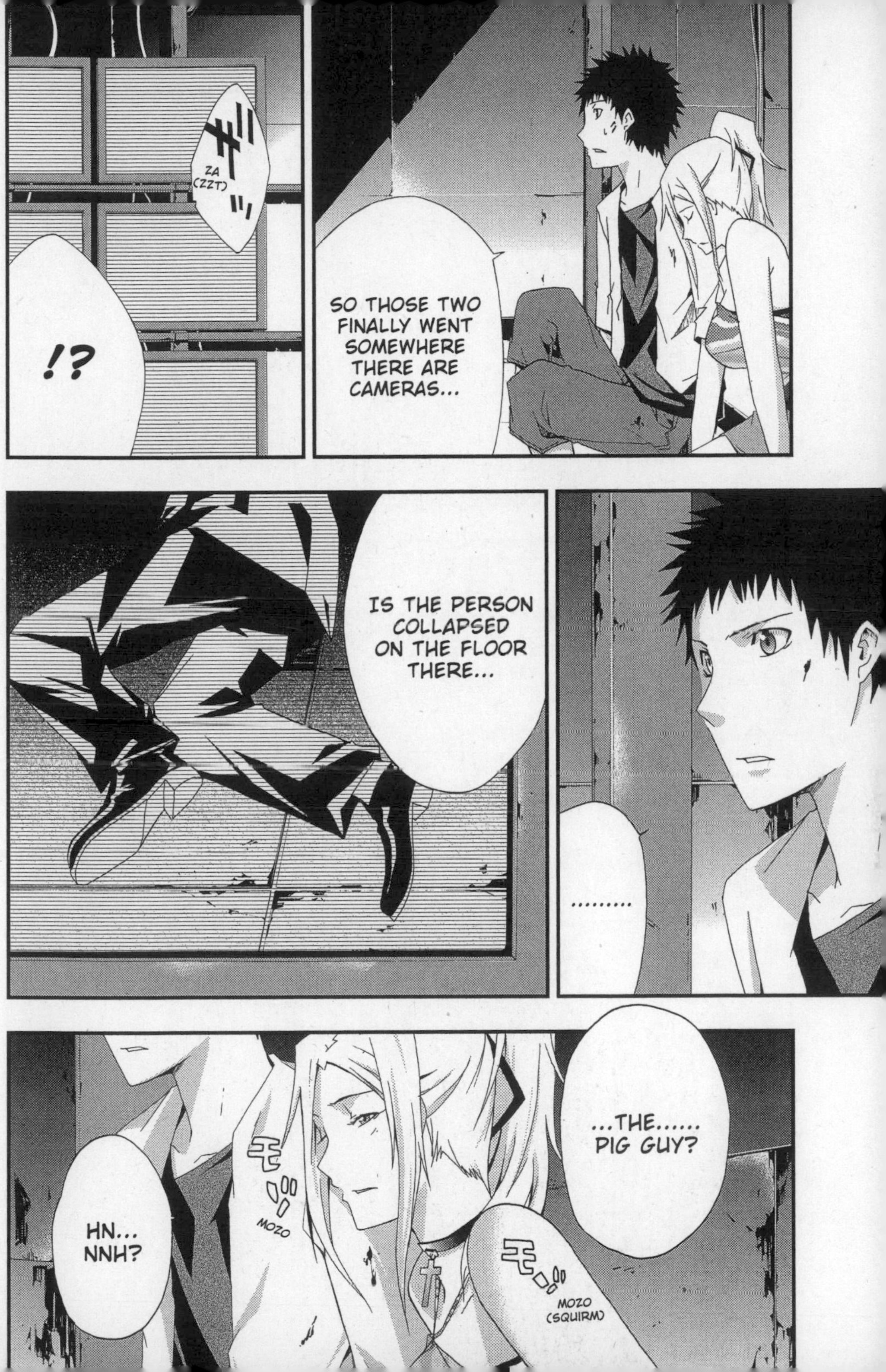
SO THOSE TWO FINALLY WENT SOMEWHERE THERE ARE CAMERAS...
ZA (ZZT)
!?
....
IS THE PERSON COLLAPSED ON THE FLOOR THERE...
...THE...... PIG GUY?
MOZO
MOZO (SQUIRM)
HN... NNH?

WHAT'S ALL THE FUSS?

MUKU
(RISE)

......HMM?

I FINALLY MANAGED TO NOD OFF...

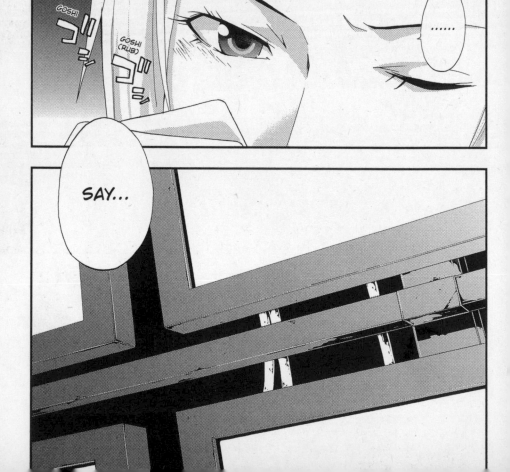

GOSHI

GOSHI
(RUB)

......

SAY...

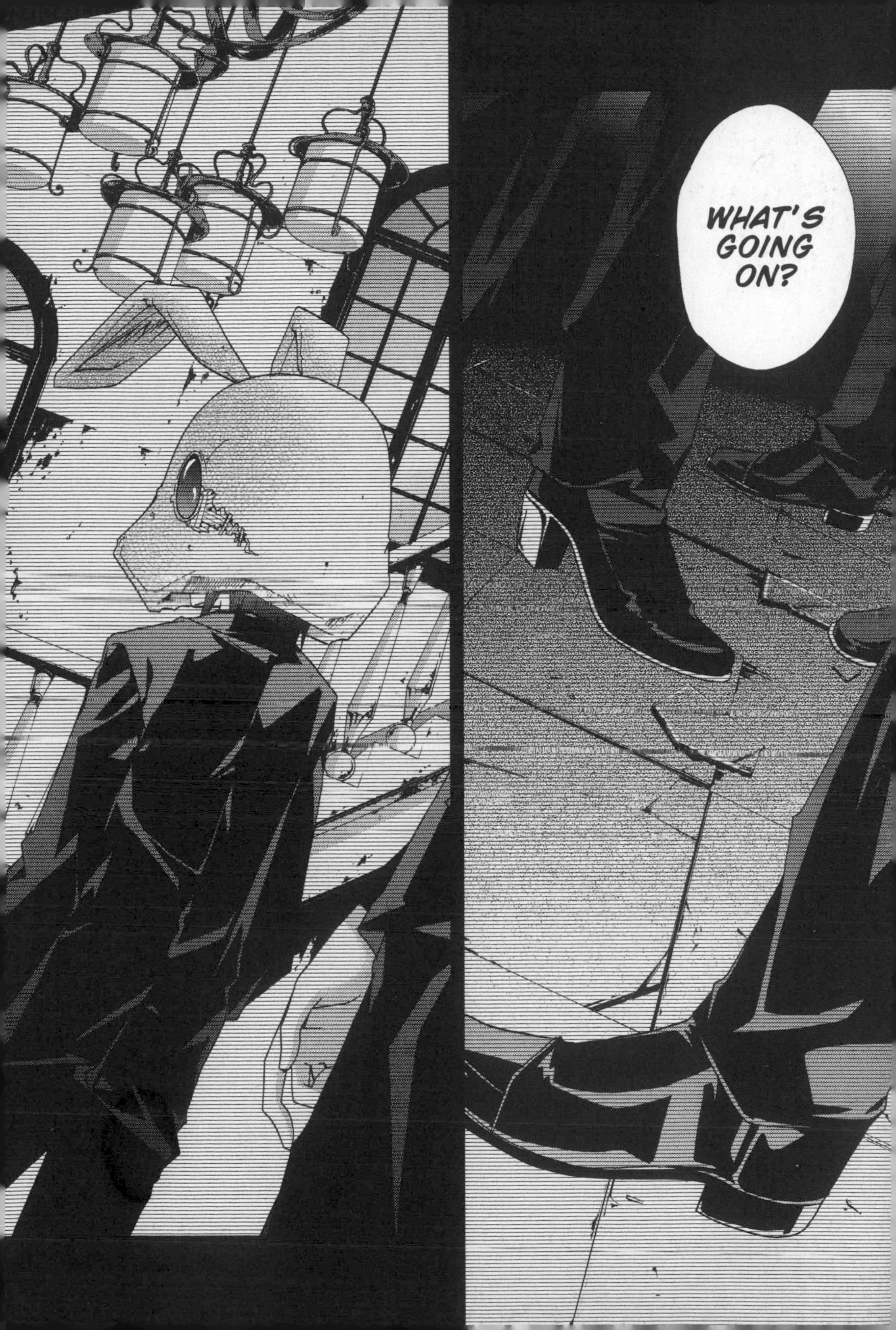
WHAT'S GOING ON?

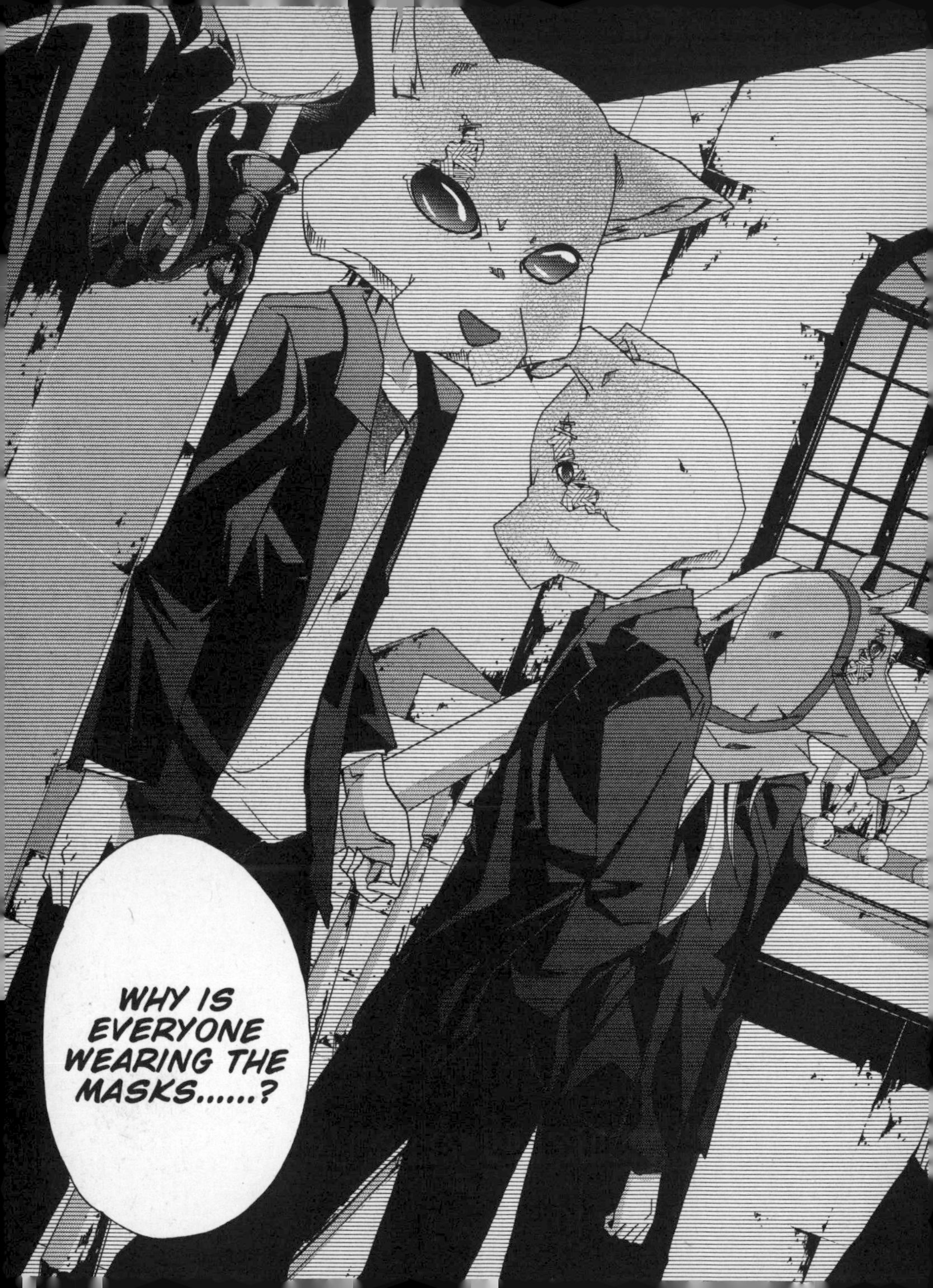
WHY IS EVERYONE WEARING THE MASKS......?

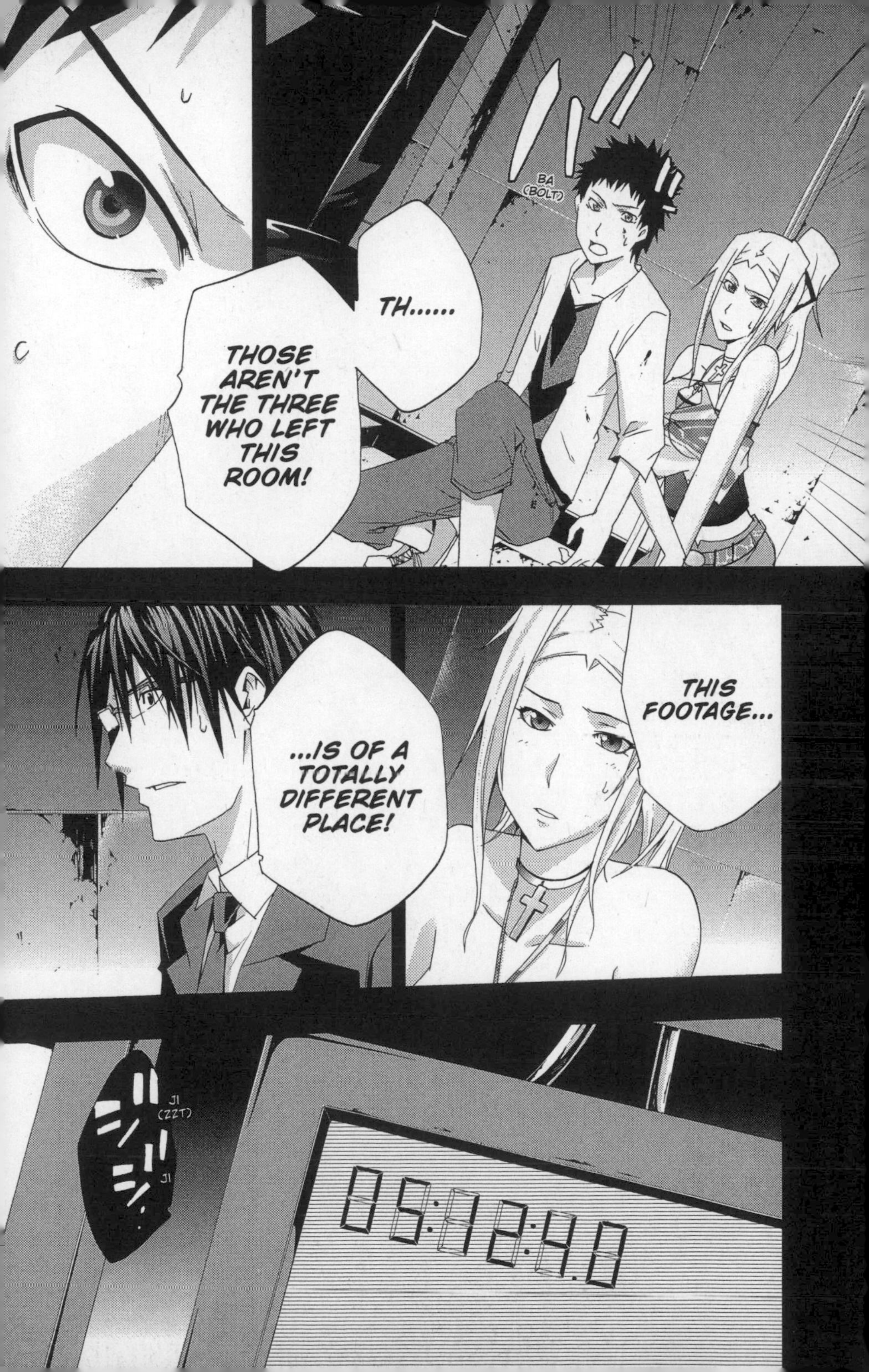
BA (BOLT)
TH......
THOSE AREN'T THE THREE WHO LEFT THIS ROOM!
THIS FOOTAGE...
...IS OF A TOTALLY DIFFERENT PLACE!
JI (ZZT)
JI

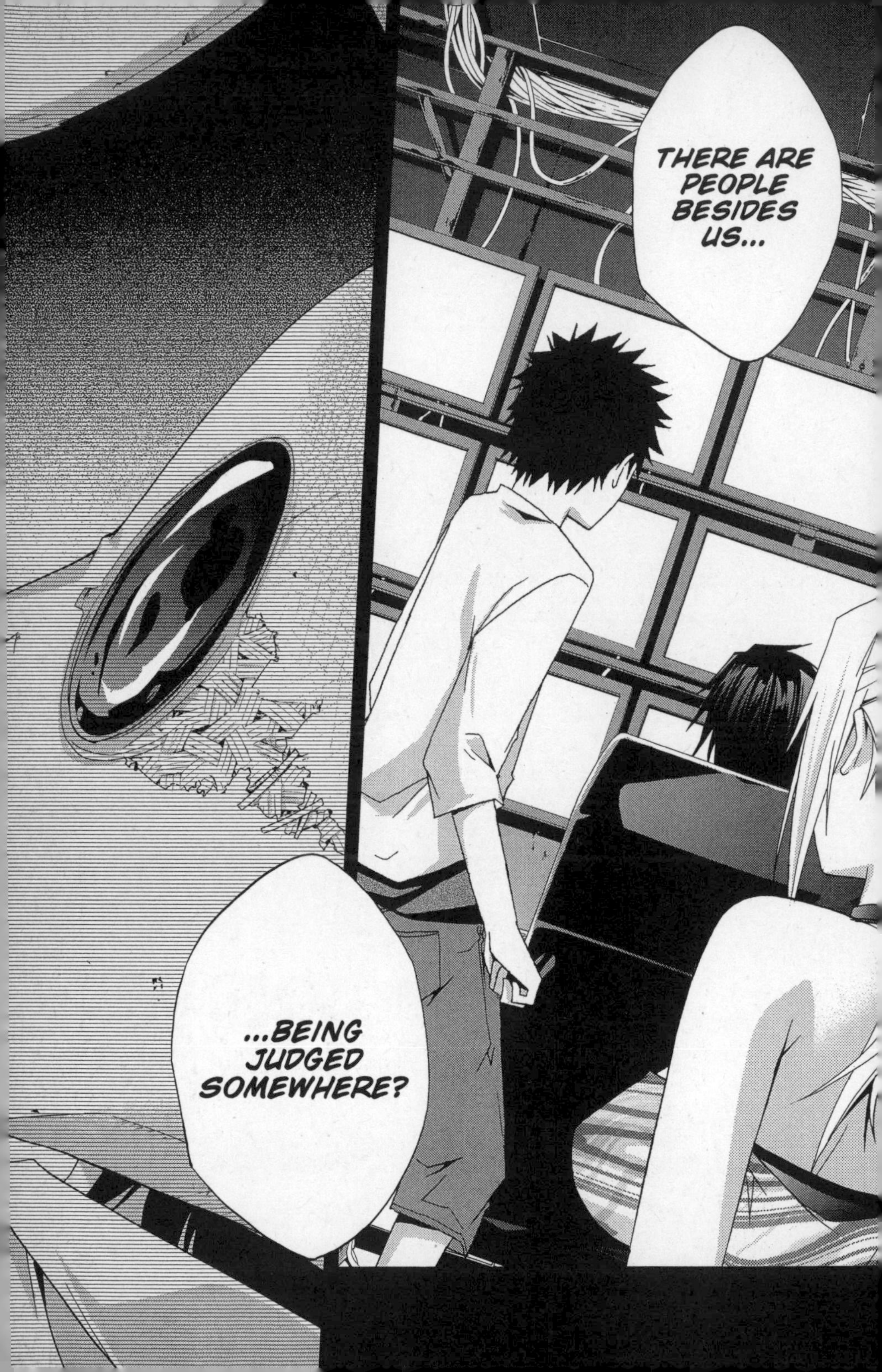
THERE ARE PEOPLE BESIDES US...
...BEING JUDGED SOMEWHERE?

JUDGE

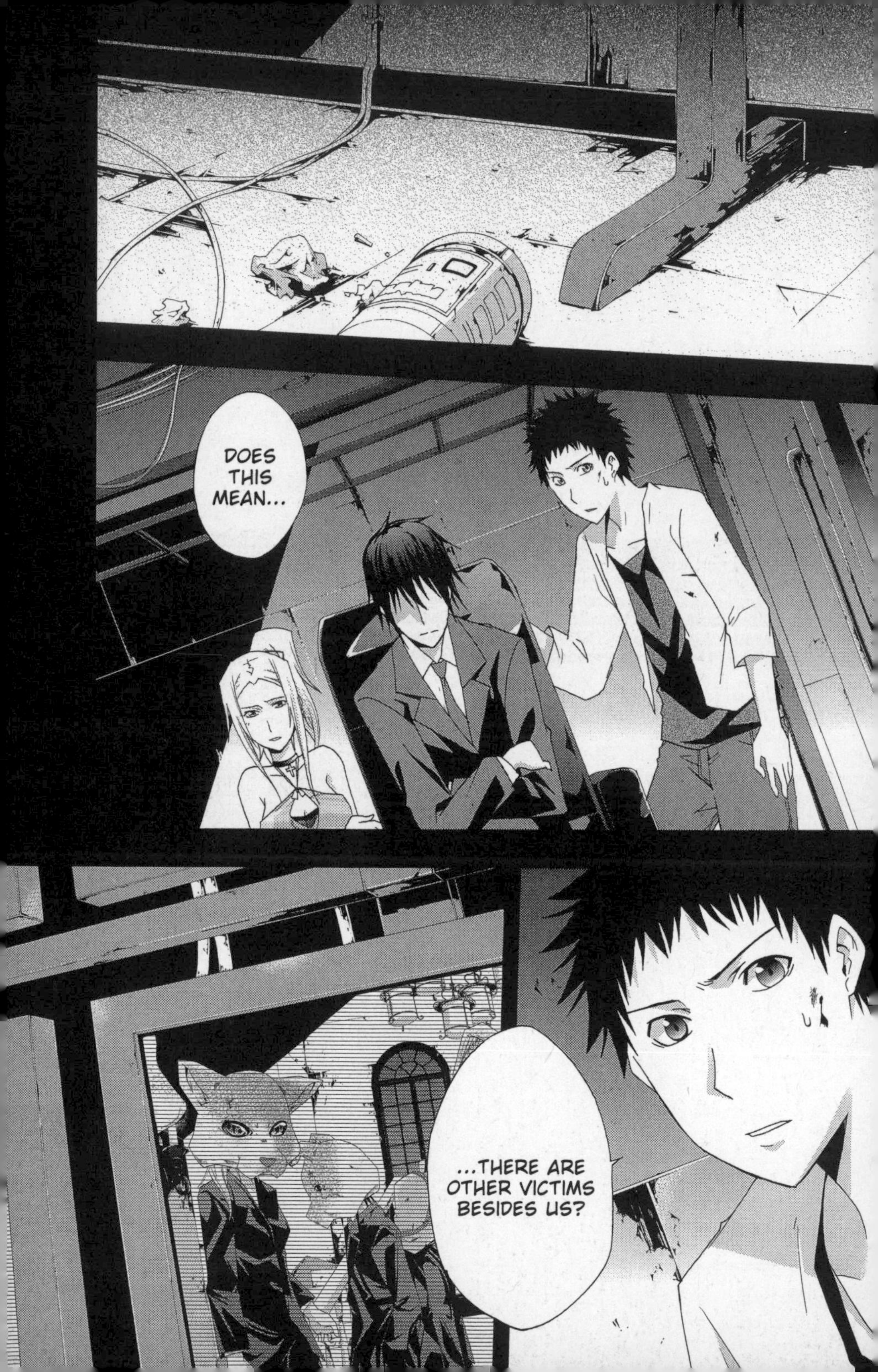
DOES THIS MEAN...
...THERE ARE OTHER VICTIMS BESIDES US?

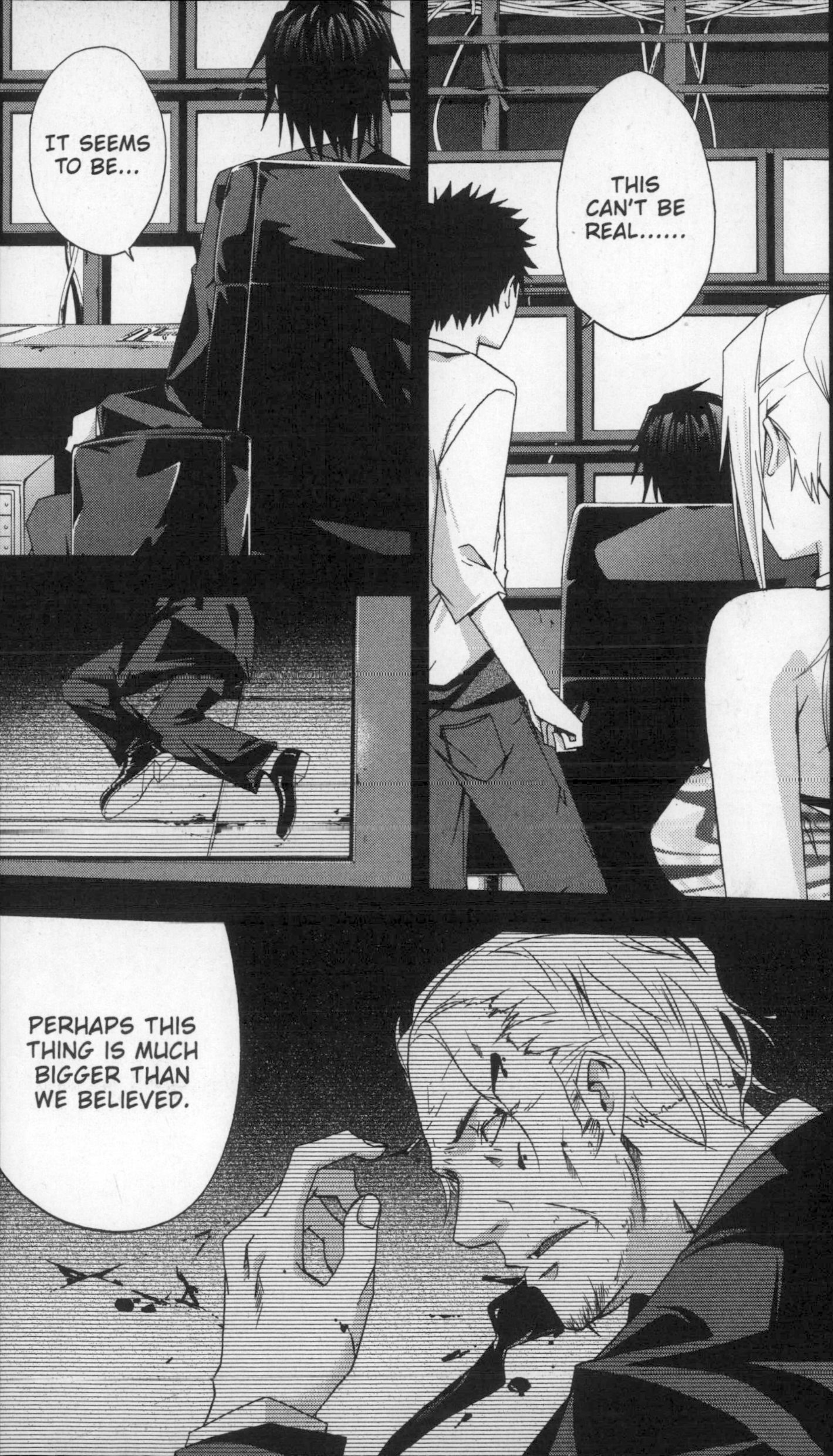
THIS CAN'T BE REAL......
IT SEEMS TO BE...
PERHAPS THIS THING IS MUCH BIGGER THAN WE BELIEVED.

CHAPTER 18 STAY OF EXECUTION

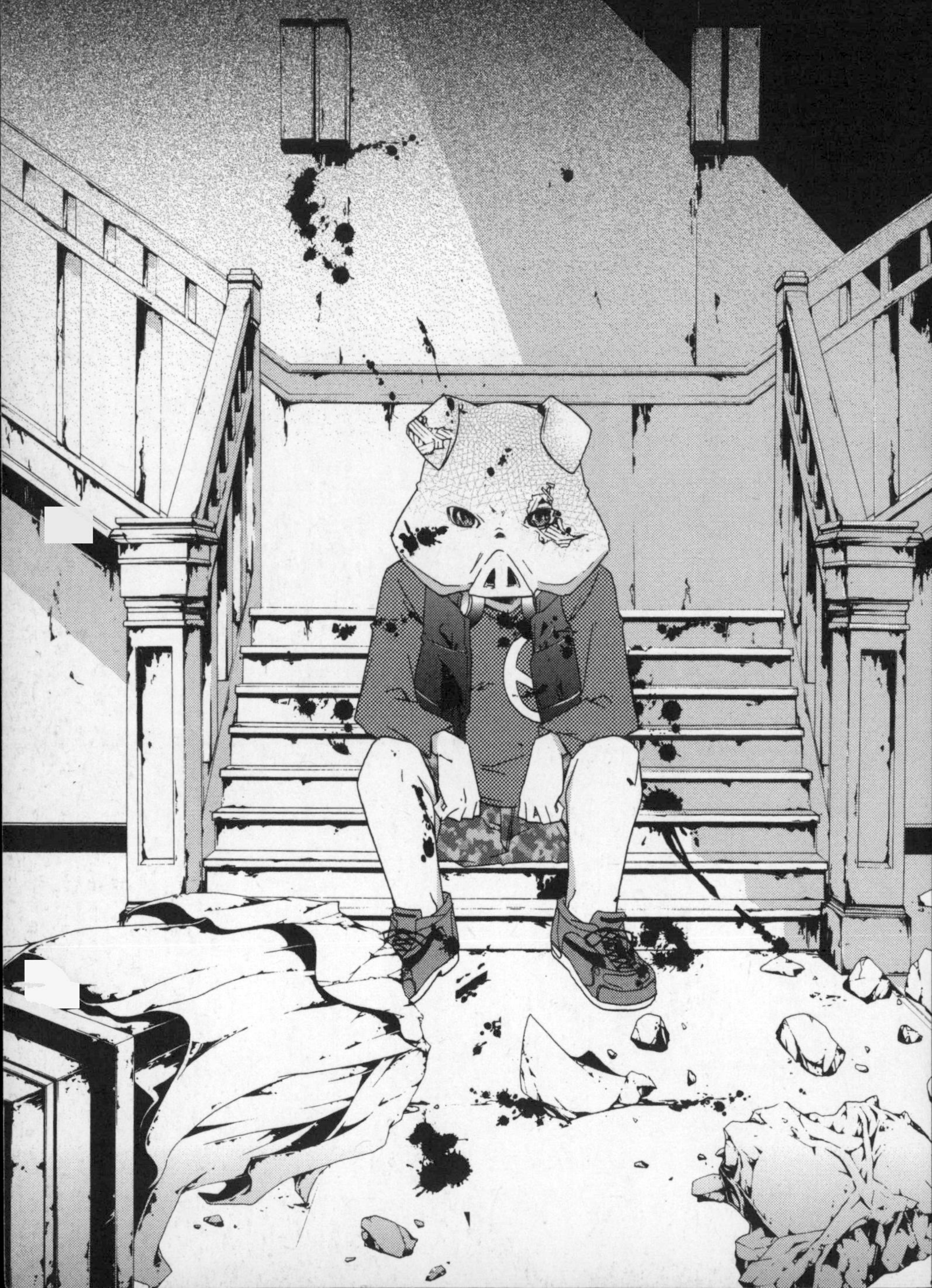

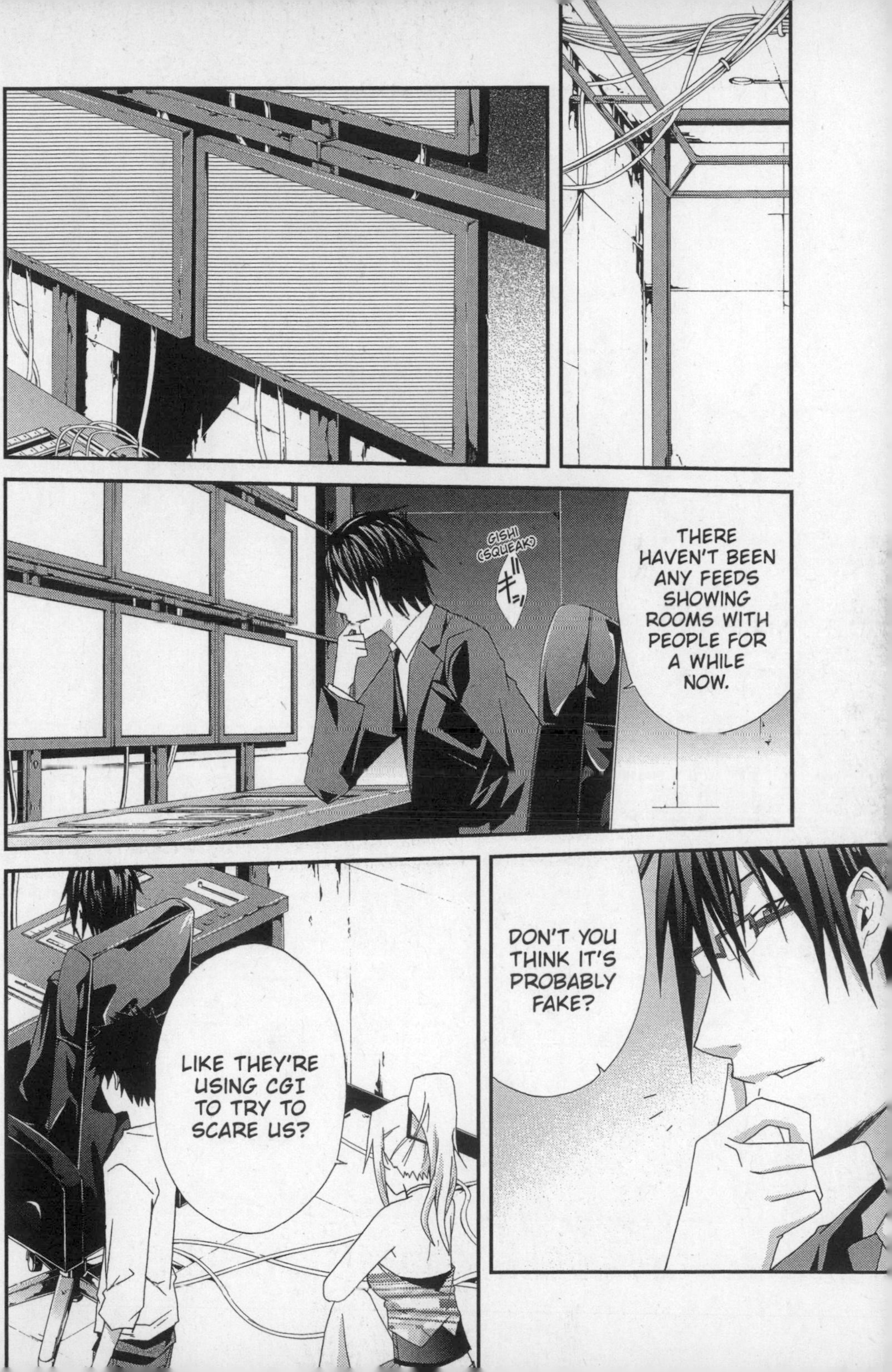
THERE HAVEN'T BEEN ANY FEEDS SHOWING ROOMS WITH PEOPLE FOR A WHILE NOW.
GISHI (SQUEAK)
DON'T YOU THINK IT'S PROBABLY FAKE?
LIKE THEY'RE USING CGI TO TRY TO SCARE US?

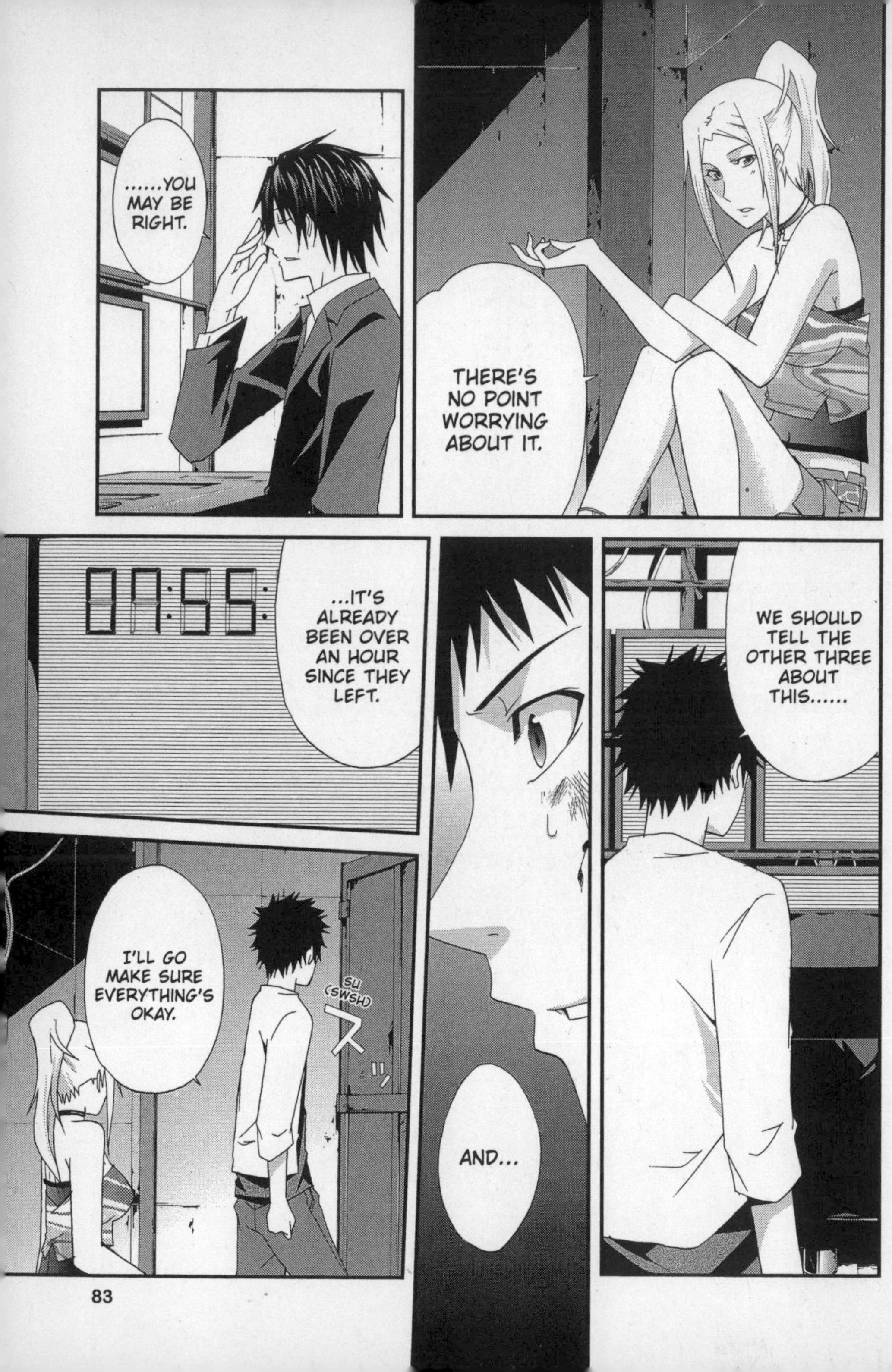
THERE'S NO POINT WORRYING ABOUT IT.
......YOU MAY BE RIGHT.
WE SHOULD TELL THE OTHER THREE ABOUT THIS......
AND...
...IT'S ALREADY BEEN OVER AN HOUR SINCE THEY LEFT.
01:55
I'LL GO MAKE SURE EVERYTHING'S OKAY.
SU (SWSH)

DO WHATEVER YOU WANT.

HAVE A SAFE TRIP!

HMMM.

......

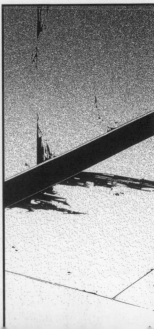

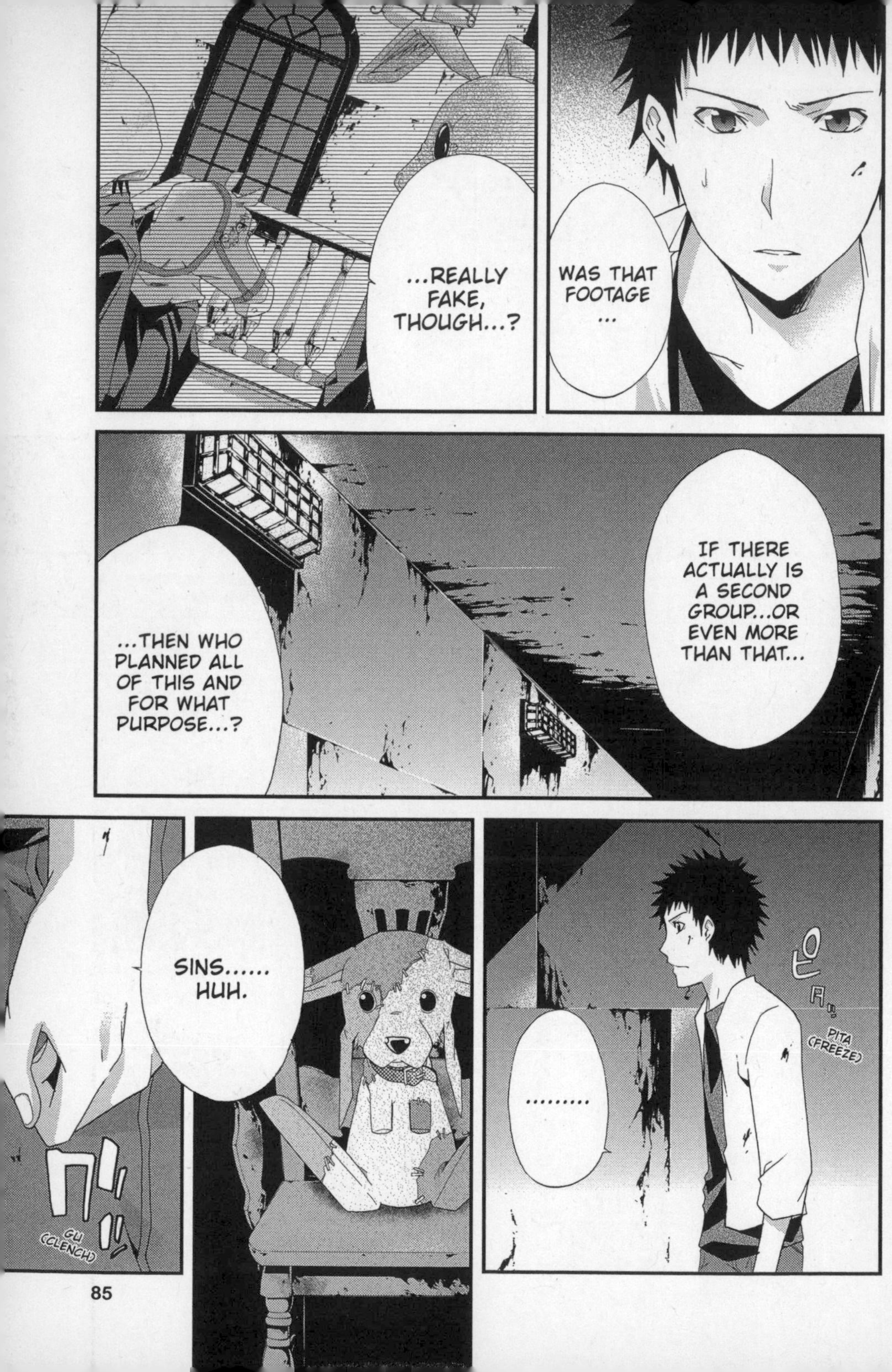
WAS THAT FOOTAGE ...
...REALLY FAKE, THOUGH...?
IF THERE ACTUALLY IS A SECOND GROUP...OR EVEN MORE THAN THAT...
...THEN WHO PLANNED ALL OF THIS AND FOR WHAT PURPOSE...?
PITA (FREEZE)
....
SINS...... HUH.
GU (CLENCH)

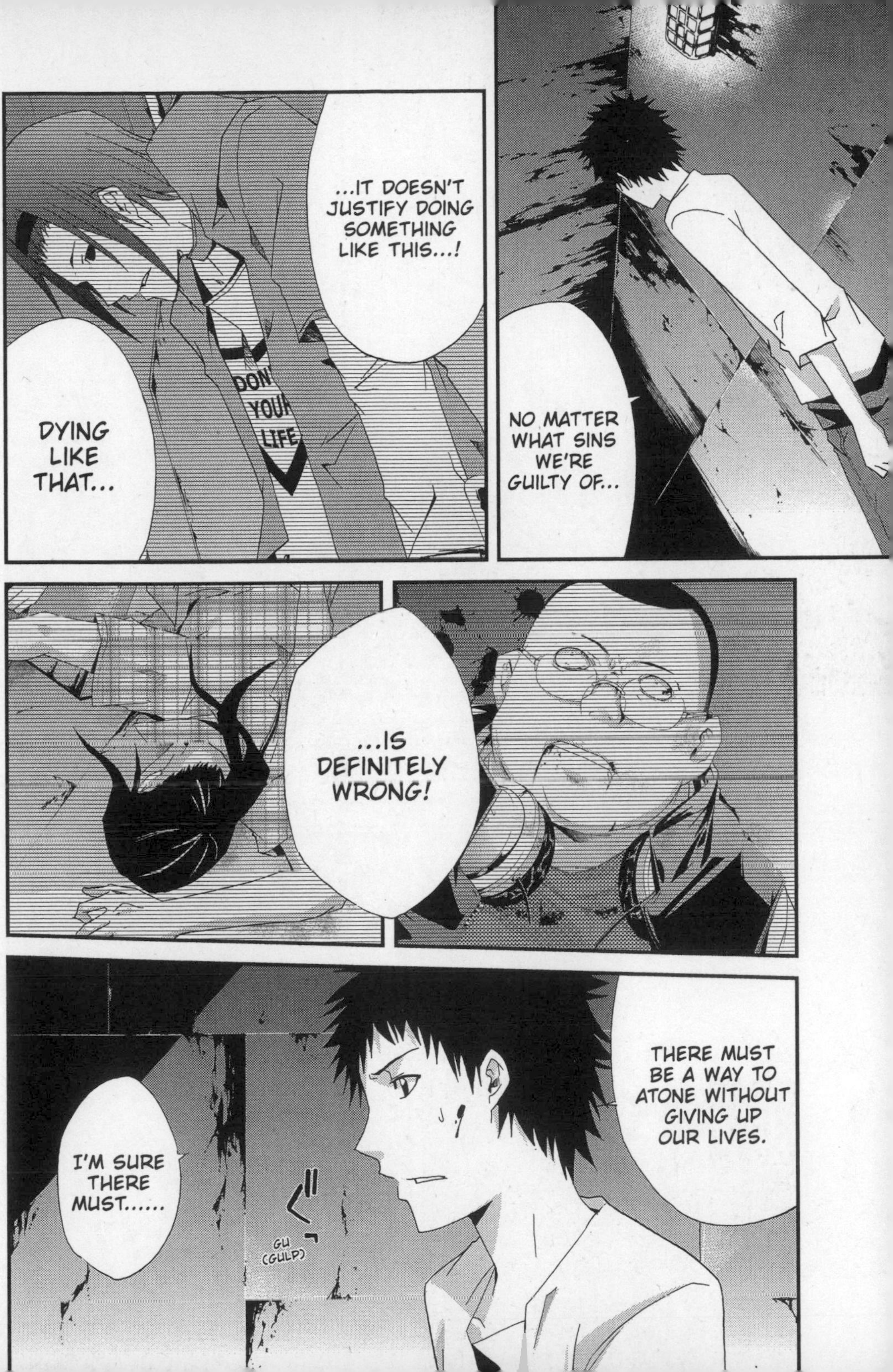
NO MATTER WHAT SINS WE'RE GUILTY OF...
...IT DOESN'T JUSTIFY DOING SOMETHING LIKE THIS...!
DYING LIKE THAT...
...IS DEFINITELY WRONG!
THERE MUST BE A WAY TO ATONE WITHOUT GIVING UP OUR LIVES.
GU (GULP)
I'M SURE THERE MUST......

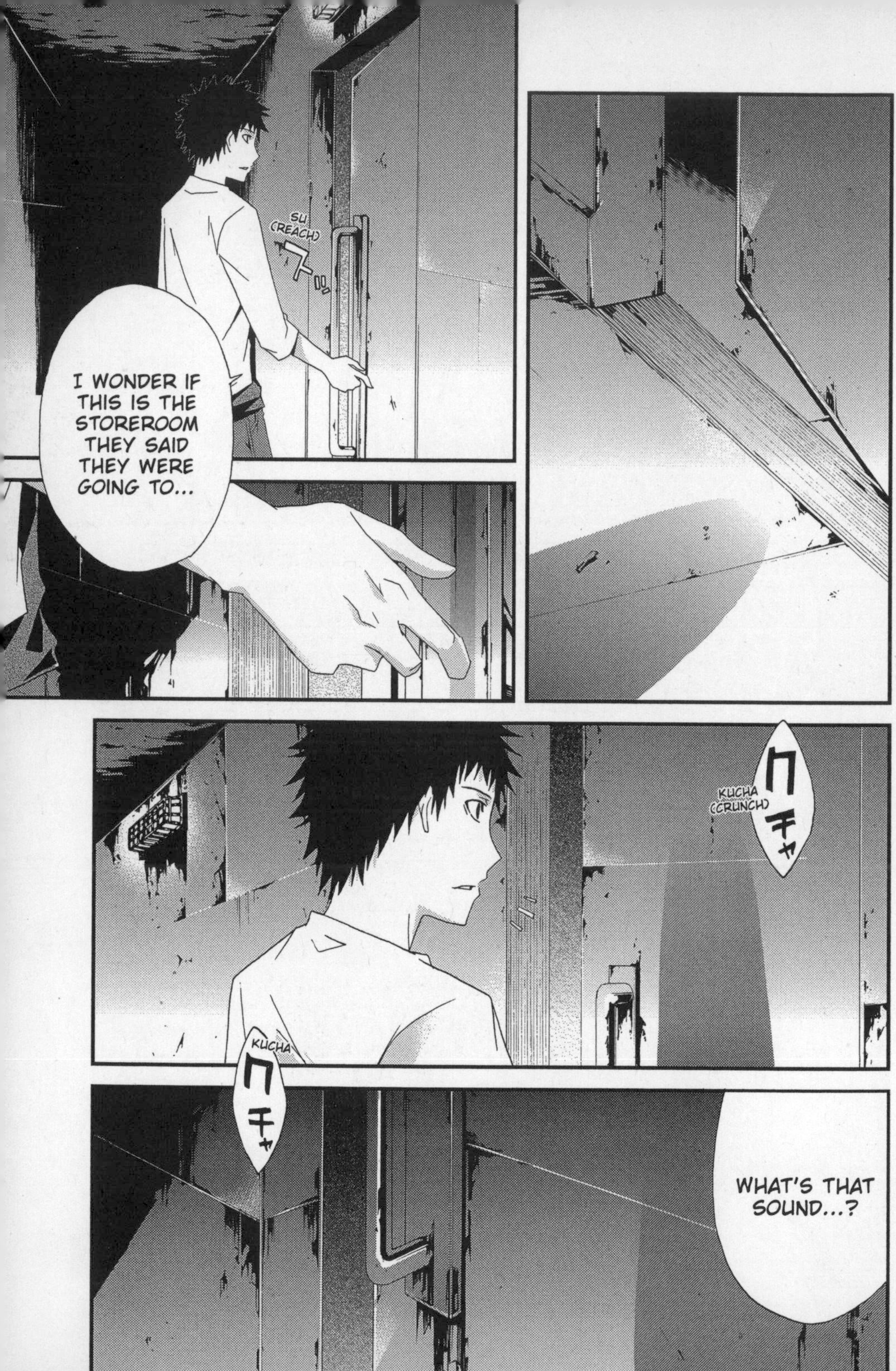
SU (REACH)
スッ
I WONDER IF THIS IS THE STOREROOM THEY SAID THEY WERE GOING TO...
KUCHA (CRUNCH)
クチャ
KUCHA
クチャ
WHAT'S THAT SOUND...?

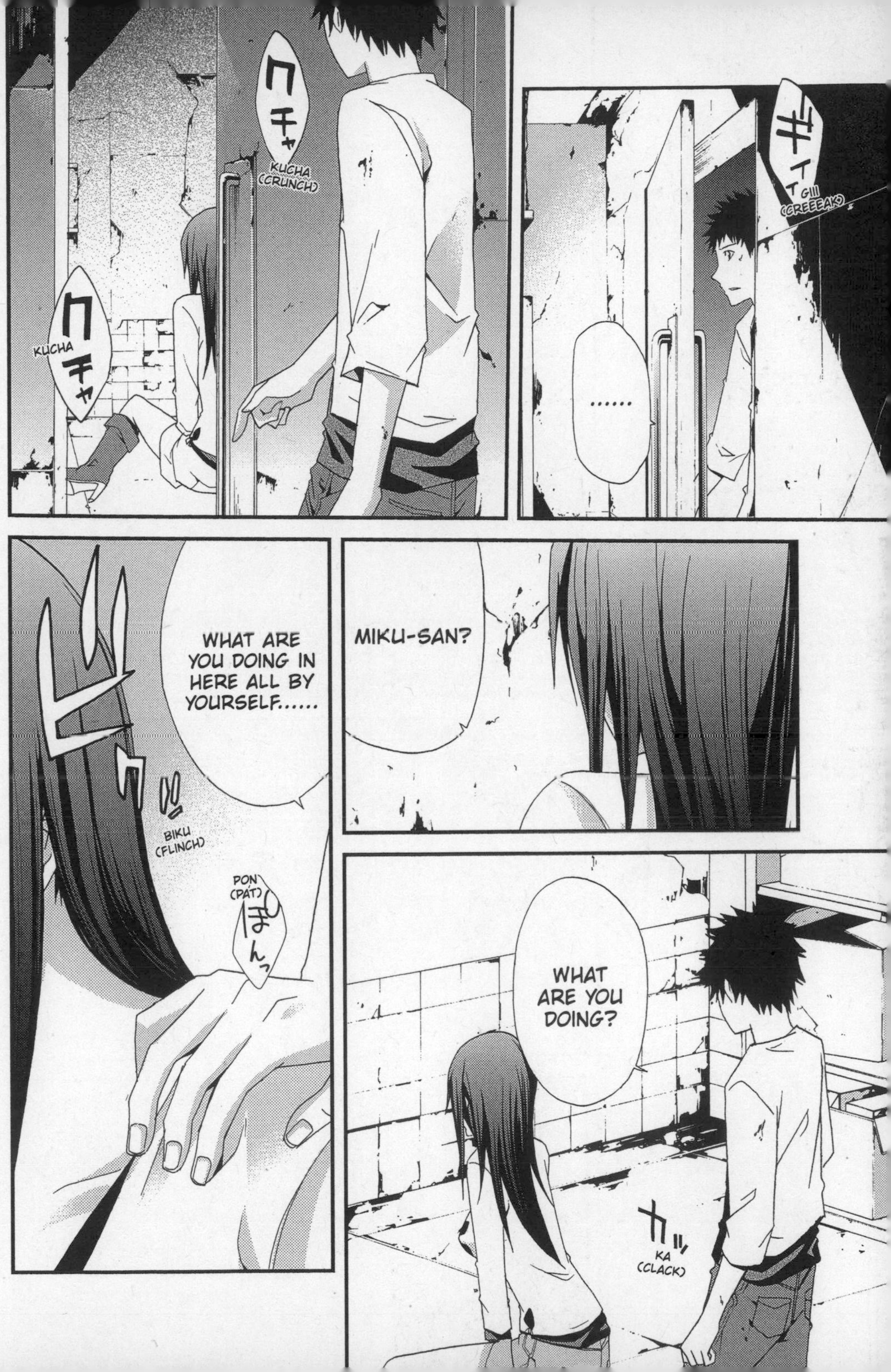
ギィィ
GIII (CREEEAK)
......
クチャ
KUCHA (CRUNCH)
クチャ
KUCHA
MIKU-SAN?
WHAT ARE YOU DOING?
カッ
KA (CLACK)
WHAT ARE YOU DOING IN HERE ALL BY YOURSELF......
ビクッ!!
BIKU (FLINCH)
PON (PAT)
ぽんっ

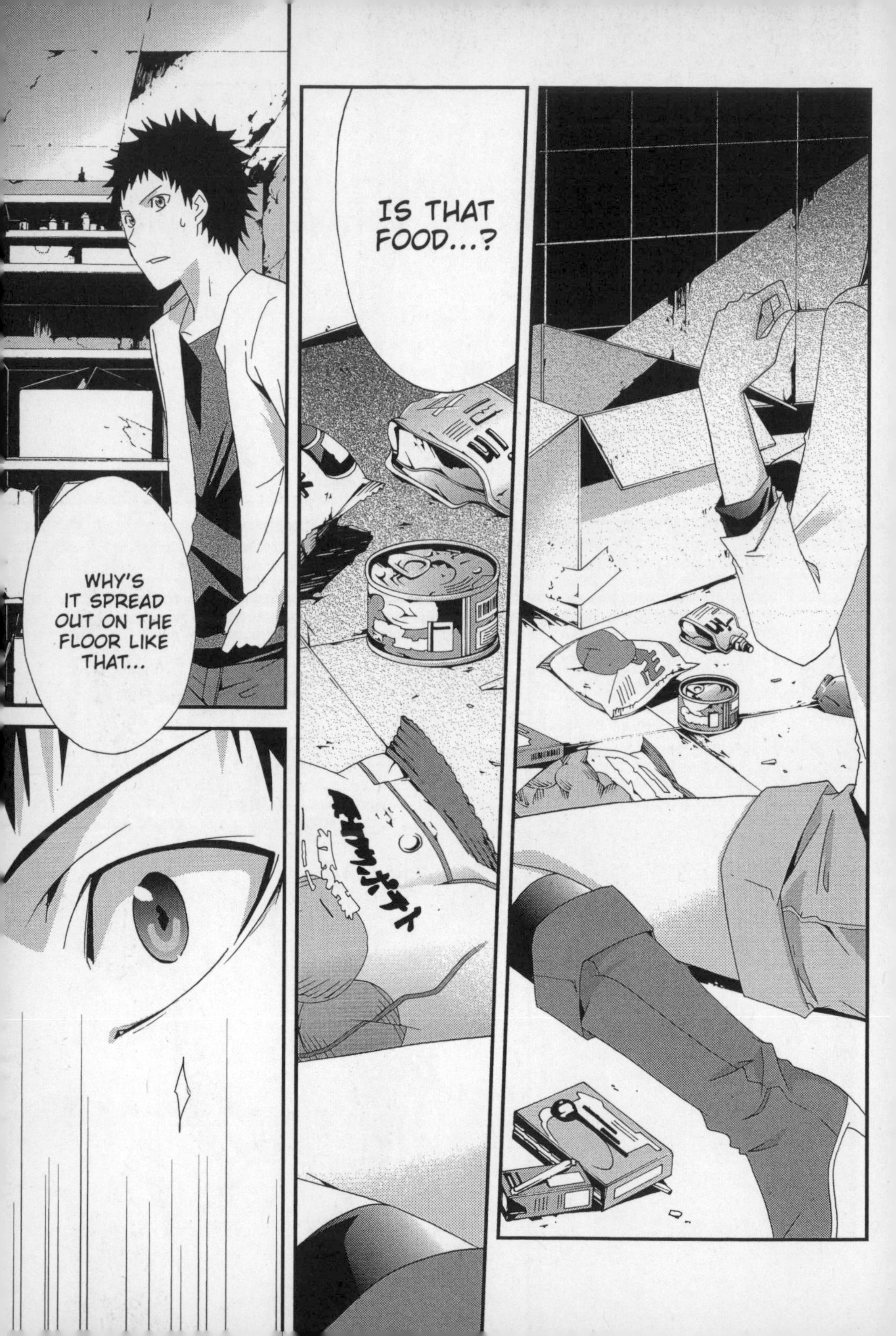
IS THAT FOOD...?
WHY'S IT SPREAD OUT ON THE FLOOR LIKE THAT...

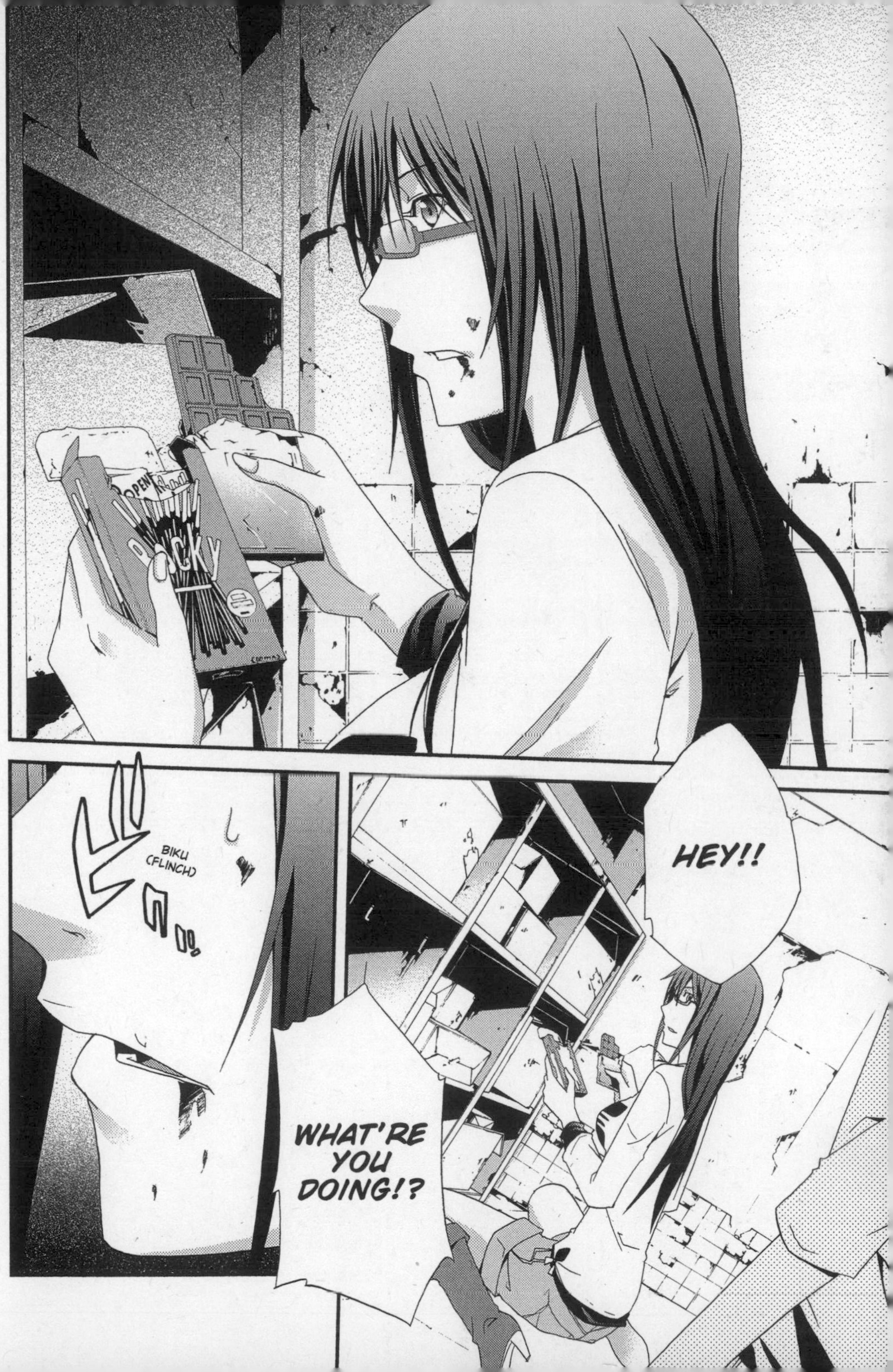
HEY!!
WHAT'RE YOU DOING!?
BIKU (FLINCH)

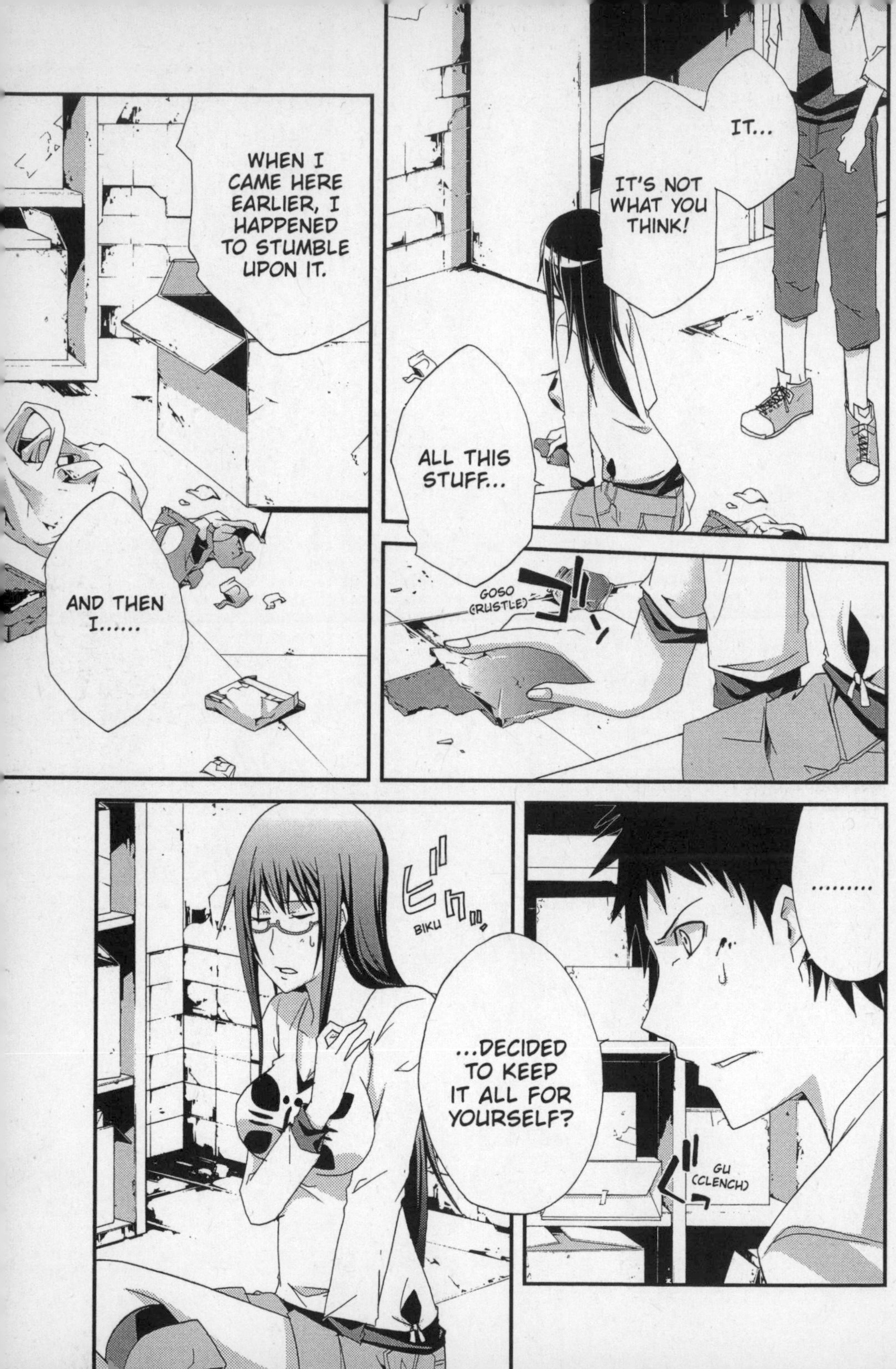
IT...
IT'S NOT WHAT YOU THINK!
ALL THIS STUFF...
GOSO (RUSTLE)
WHEN I CAME HERE EARLIER, I HAPPENED TO STUMBLE UPON IT.
AND THEN I......
....
GU (CLENCH)
...DECIDED TO KEEP IT ALL FOR YOURSELF?
BIKU

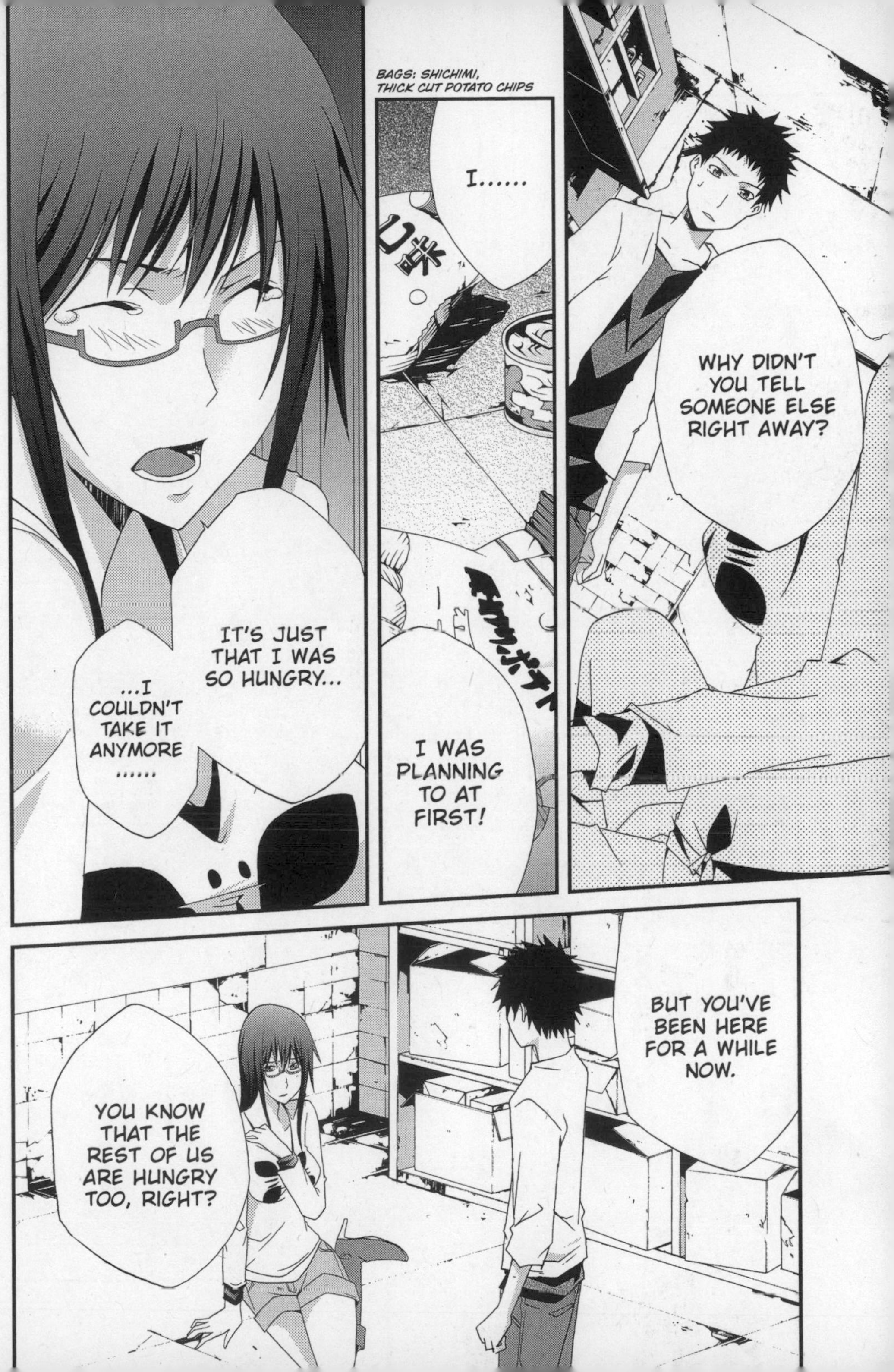
WHY DIDN'T YOU TELL SOMEONE ELSE RIGHT AWAY?
BAGS: SHICHIMI, THICK CUT POTATO CHIPS
I......
I WAS PLANNING TO AT FIRST!
IT'S JUST THAT I WAS SO HUNGRY...
...I COULDN'T TAKE IT ANYMORE ......
BUT YOU'VE BEEN HERE FOR A WHILE NOW.
YOU KNOW THAT THE REST OF US ARE HUNGRY TOO, RIGHT?

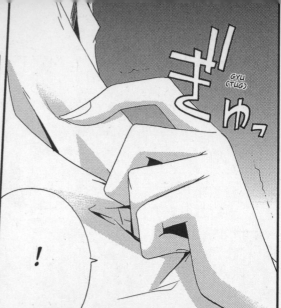

GYU
(TUG)

GU
(TENSE)

!

DON'T TELL
THEM...

PLEASE!

IF THEY FIND
OUT ABOUT
THIS...

...I'LL...
I'LL DEFINITELY
BE KILLED!

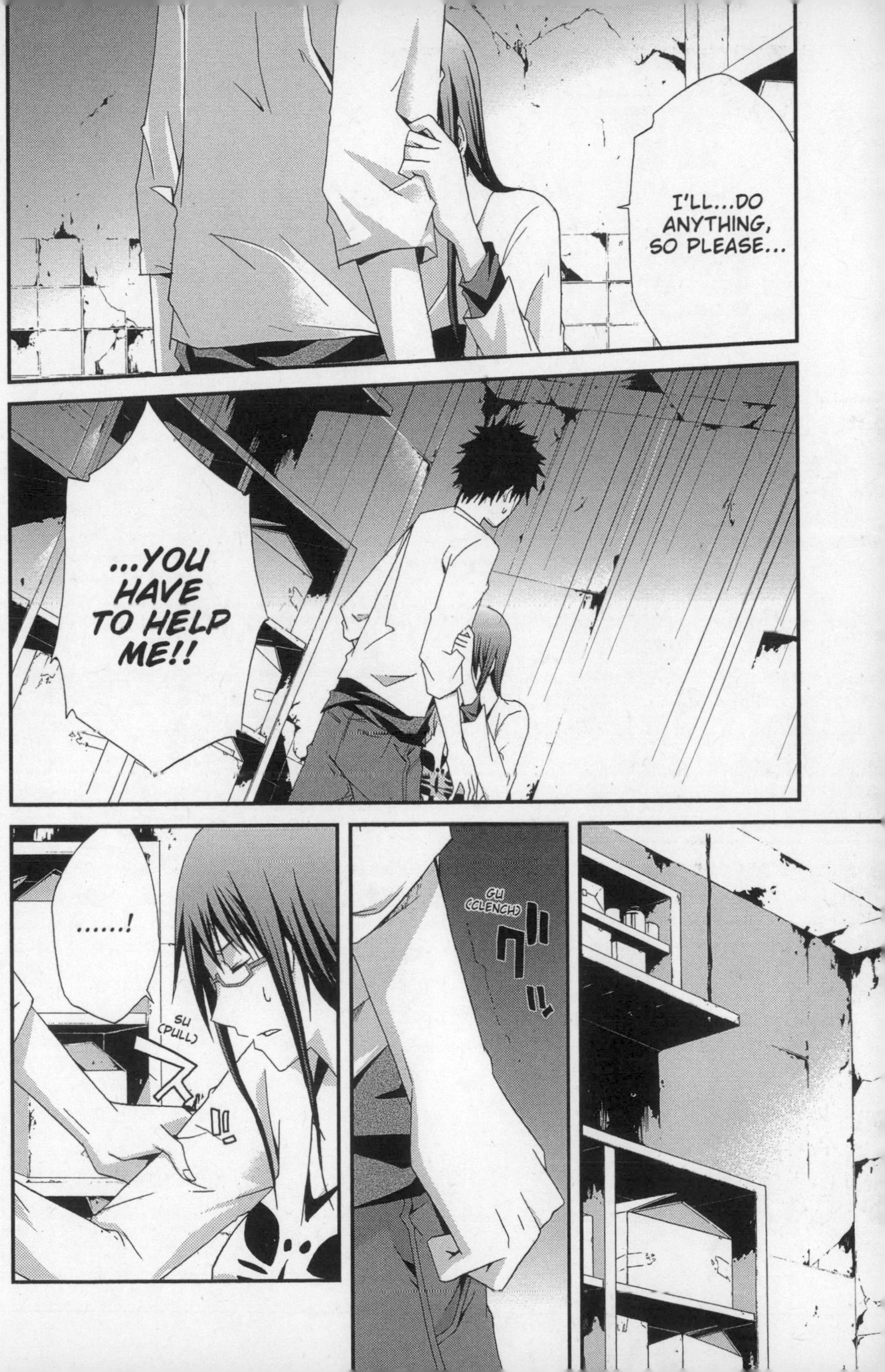
I'LL...DO ANYTHING, SO PLEASE...
...YOU HAVE TO HELP ME!!
GU (CLENCH)
......!
SU (PULL)

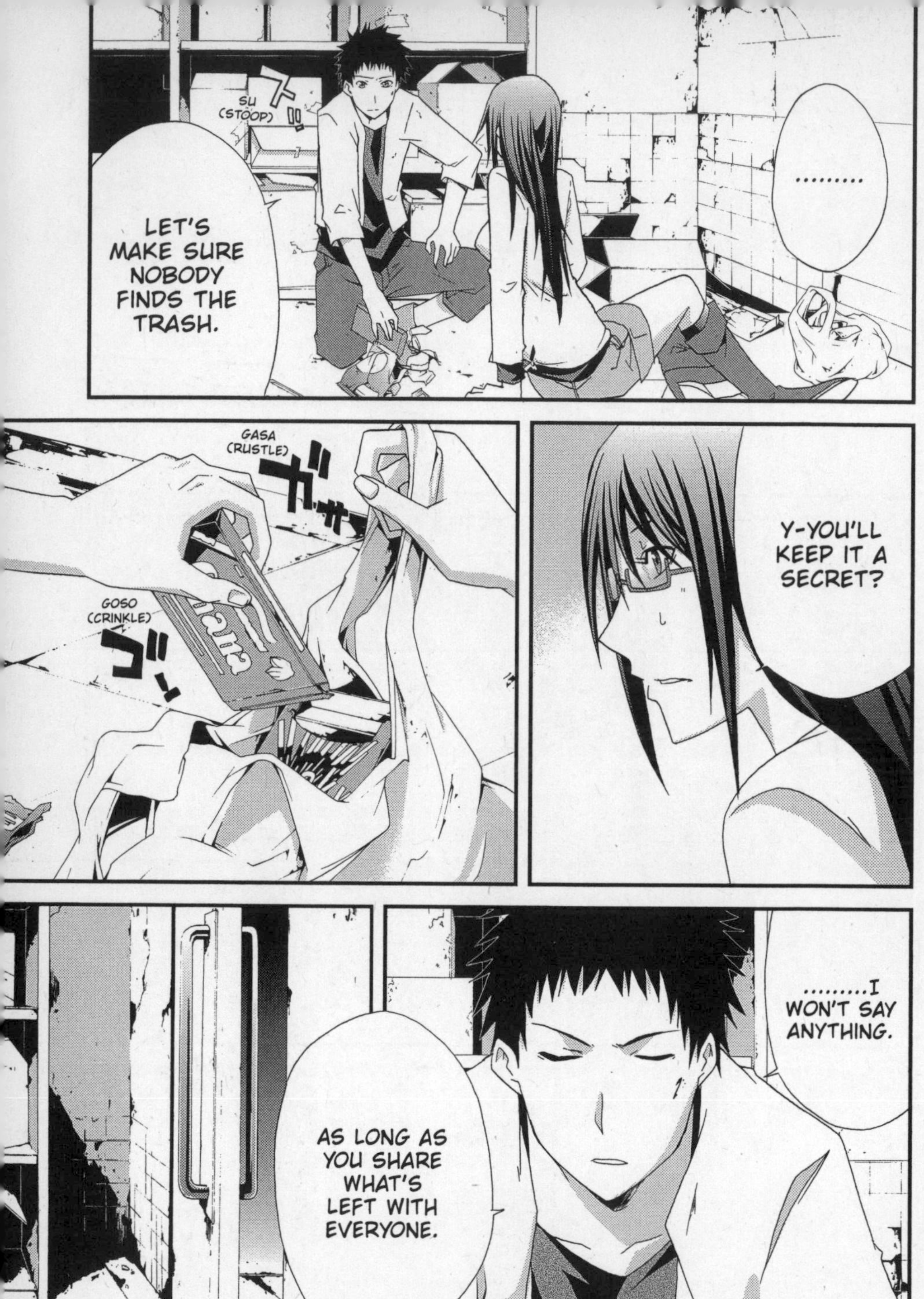
....
SU (STOOP)
LET'S MAKE SURE NOBODY FINDS THE TRASH.
Y-YOU'LL KEEP IT A SECRET?
GASA (RUSTLE)
GOSO (CRINKLE)
.........I WON'T SAY ANYTHING.
AS LONG AS YOU SHARE WHAT'S LEFT WITH EVERYONE.

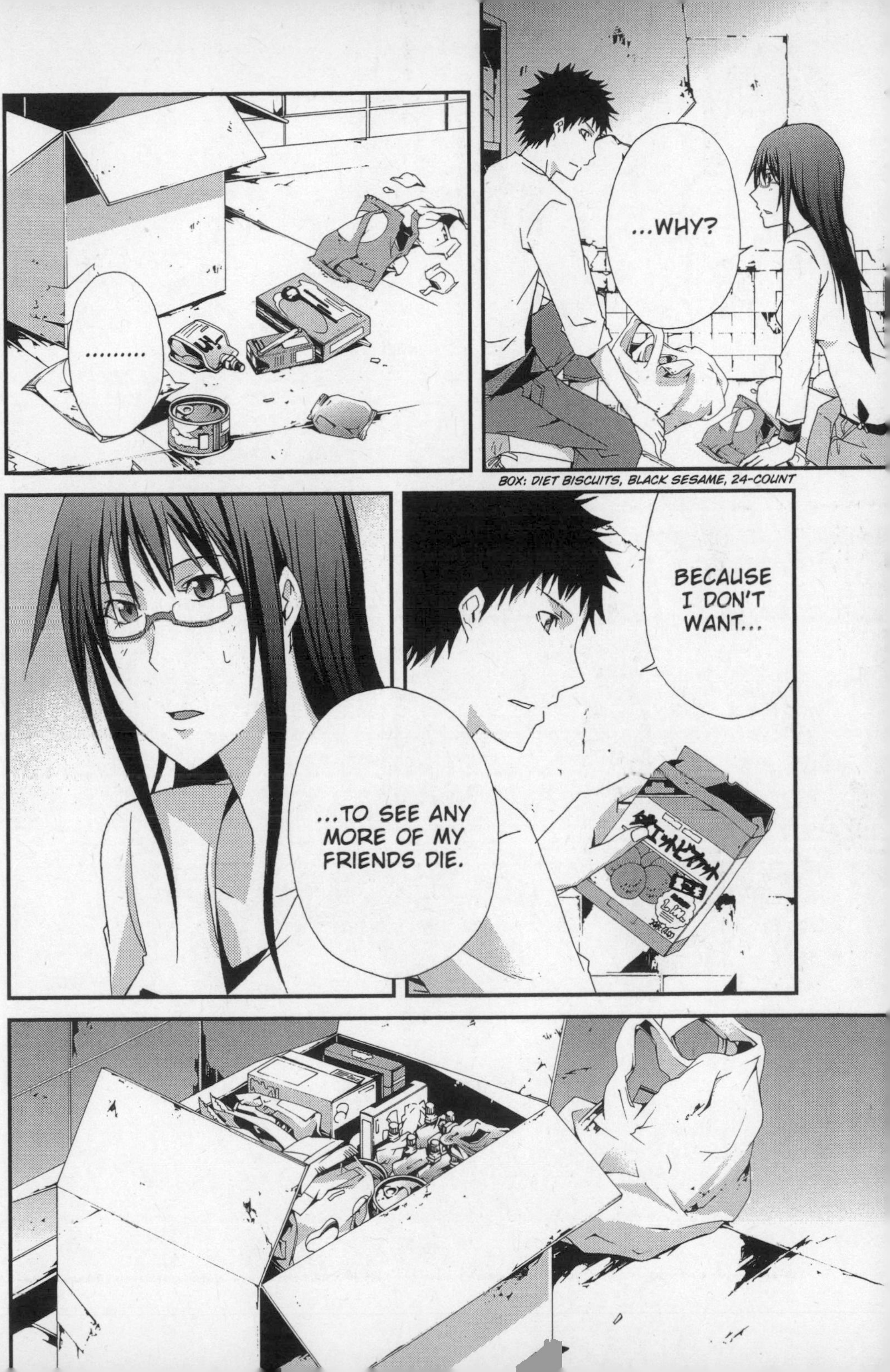
...WHY?
....
BECAUSE I DON'T WANT...
...TO SEE ANY MORE OF MY FRIENDS DIE.

BOX: DIET BISCUITS, BLACK SESAME, 24-COUNT

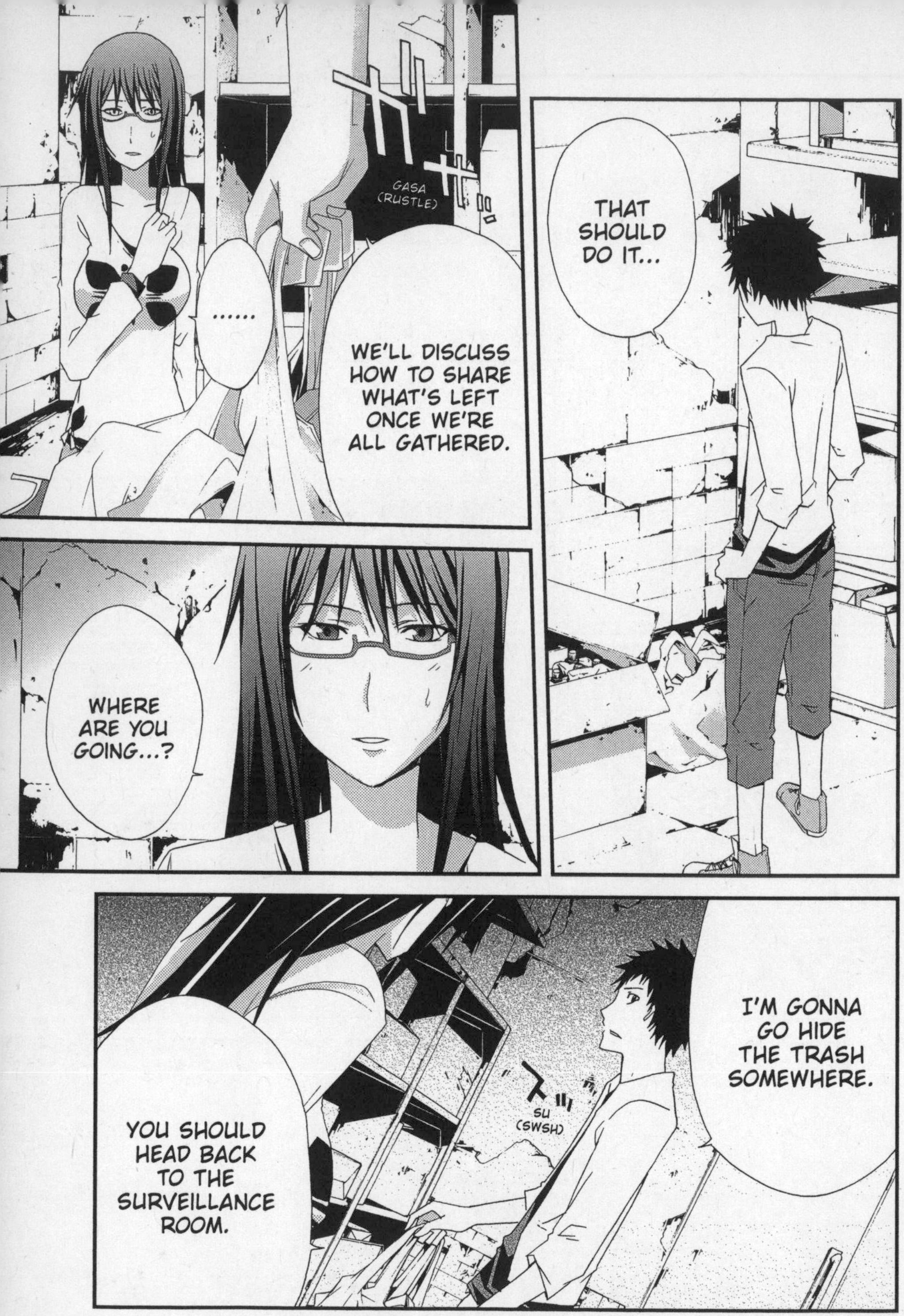
THAT SHOULD DO IT...
GASA (RUSTLE)
WE'LL DISCUSS HOW TO SHARE WHAT'S LEFT ONCE WE'RE ALL GATHERED.
......
WHERE ARE YOU GOING...?
I'M GONNA GO HIDE THE TRASH SOMEWHERE.
SU (SWSH)
YOU SHOULD HEAD BACK TO THE SURVEILLANCE ROOM.

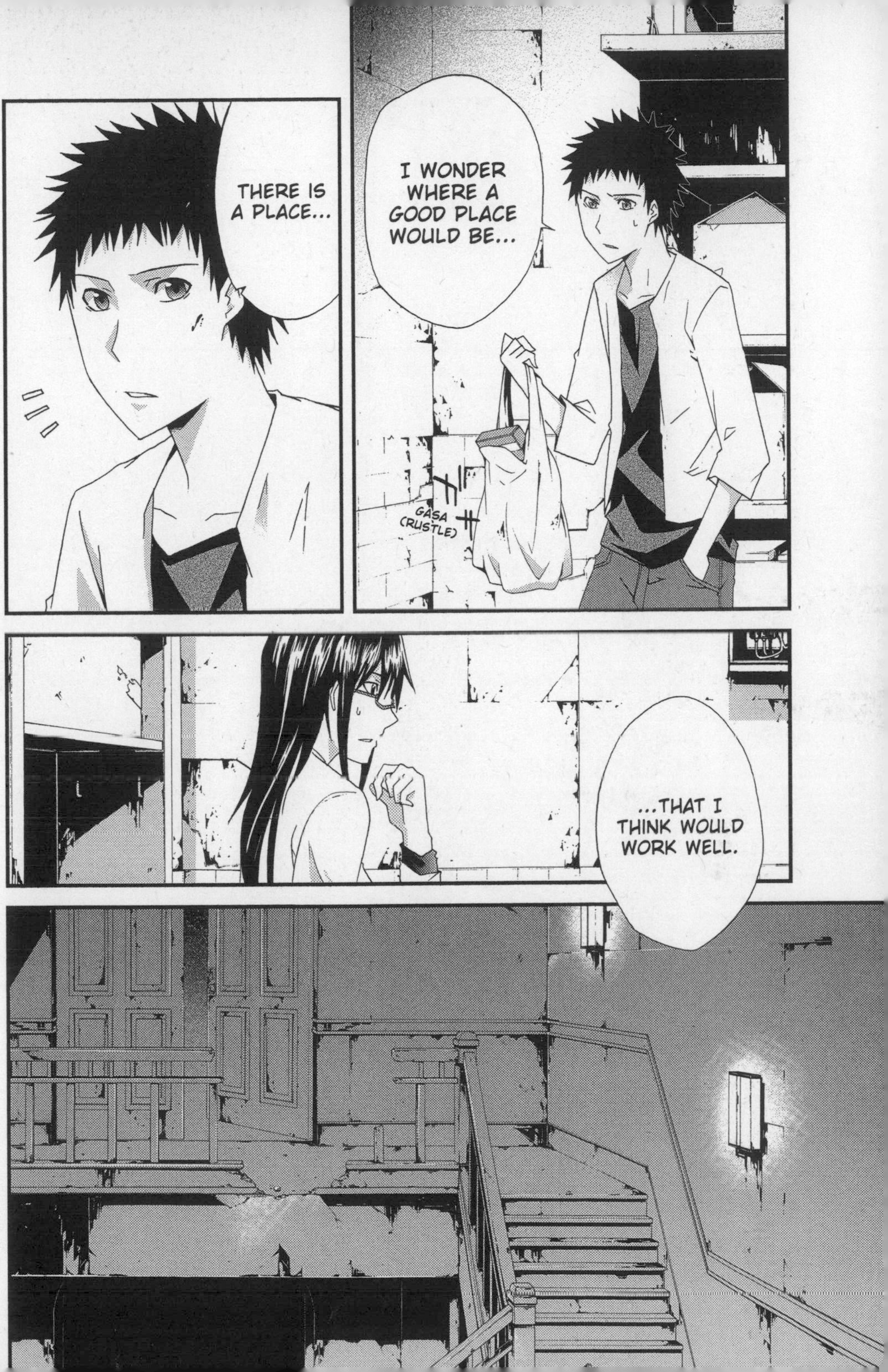
I WONDER WHERE A GOOD PLACE WOULD BE...
GASA (RUSTLE)
THERE IS A PLACE...
...THAT I THINK WOULD WORK WELL.

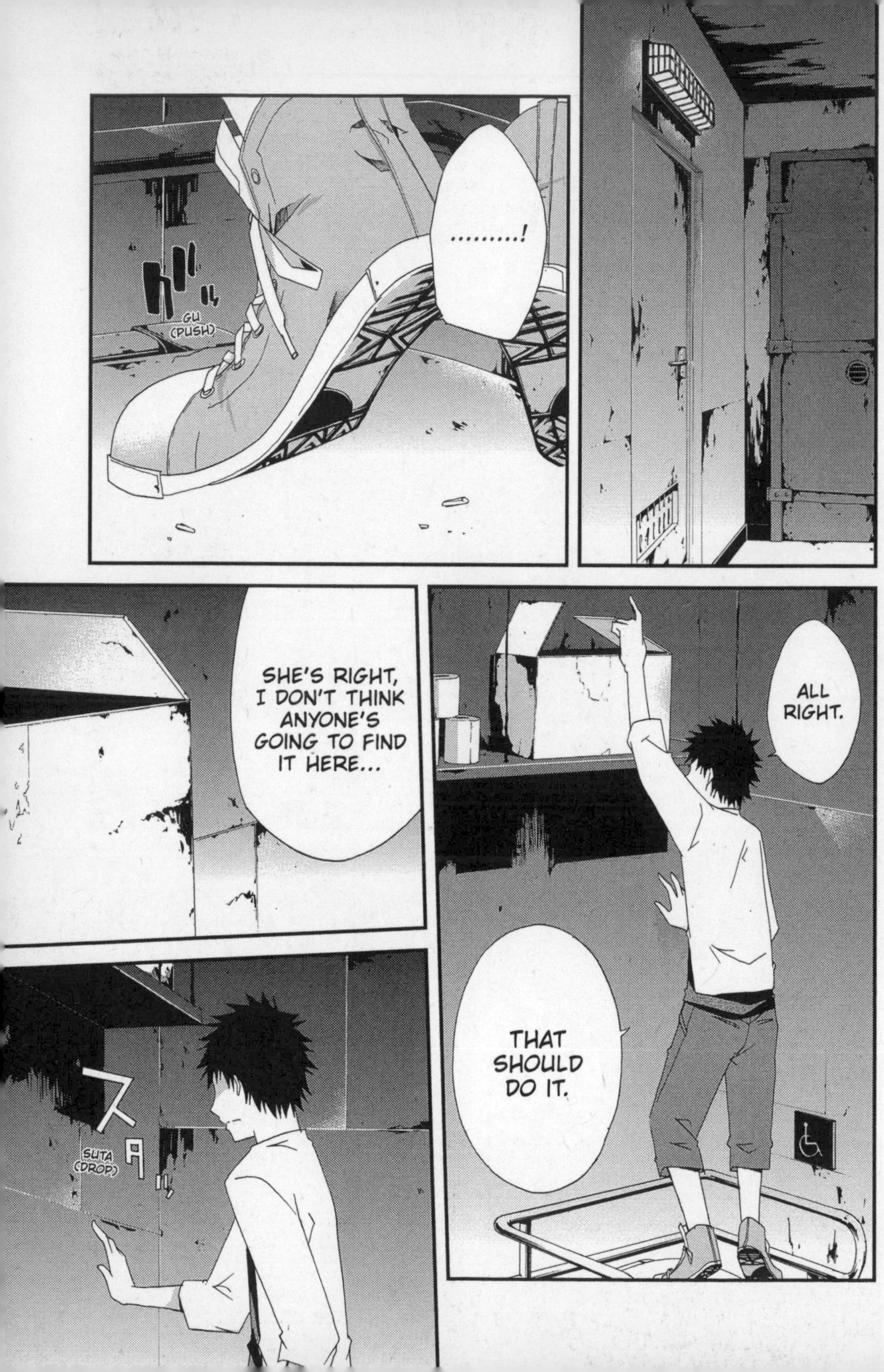
..........!
グッ
GU (PUSH)
ALL RIGHT.
THAT SHOULD DO IT.
SHE'S RIGHT, I DON'T THINK ANYONE'S GOING TO FIND IT HERE...
スタッ
SUTA (DROP)

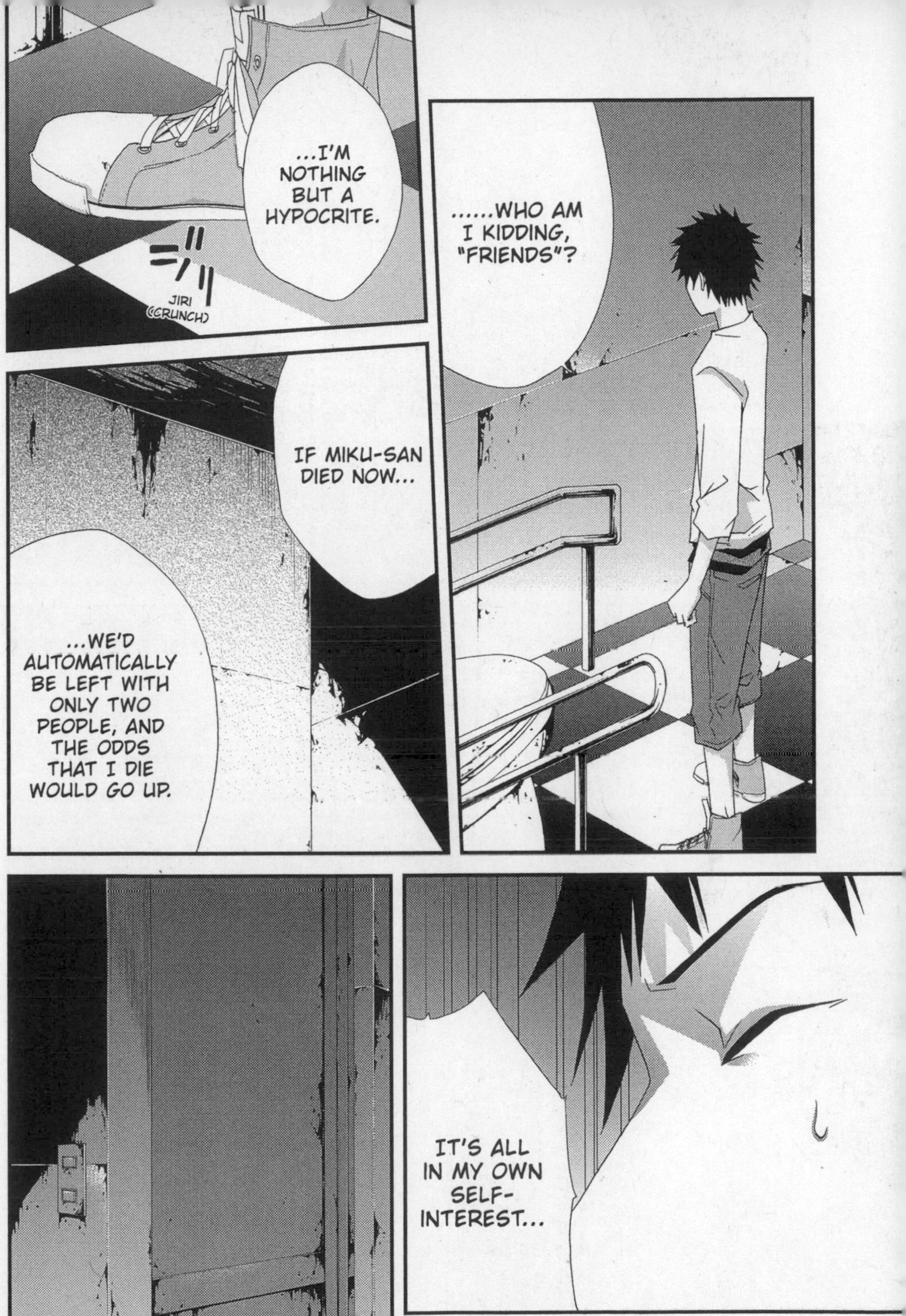
......WHO AM I KIDDING, "FRIENDS"?
...I'M NOTHING BUT A HYPOCRITE.
JIRI (CRUNCH)
IF MIKU-SAN DIED NOW...
...WE'D AUTOMATICALLY BE LEFT WITH ONLY TWO PEOPLE, AND THE ODDS THAT I DIE WOULD GO UP.
IT'S ALL IN MY OWN SELF-INTEREST...

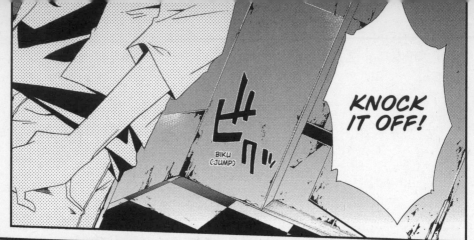

KNOCK
IT OFF!

BIKU
(JUMP)

......

LET GO
OF ME...

BIKU
(FLINCH)

SU
(REACH)

WHAT WAS
THAT...?

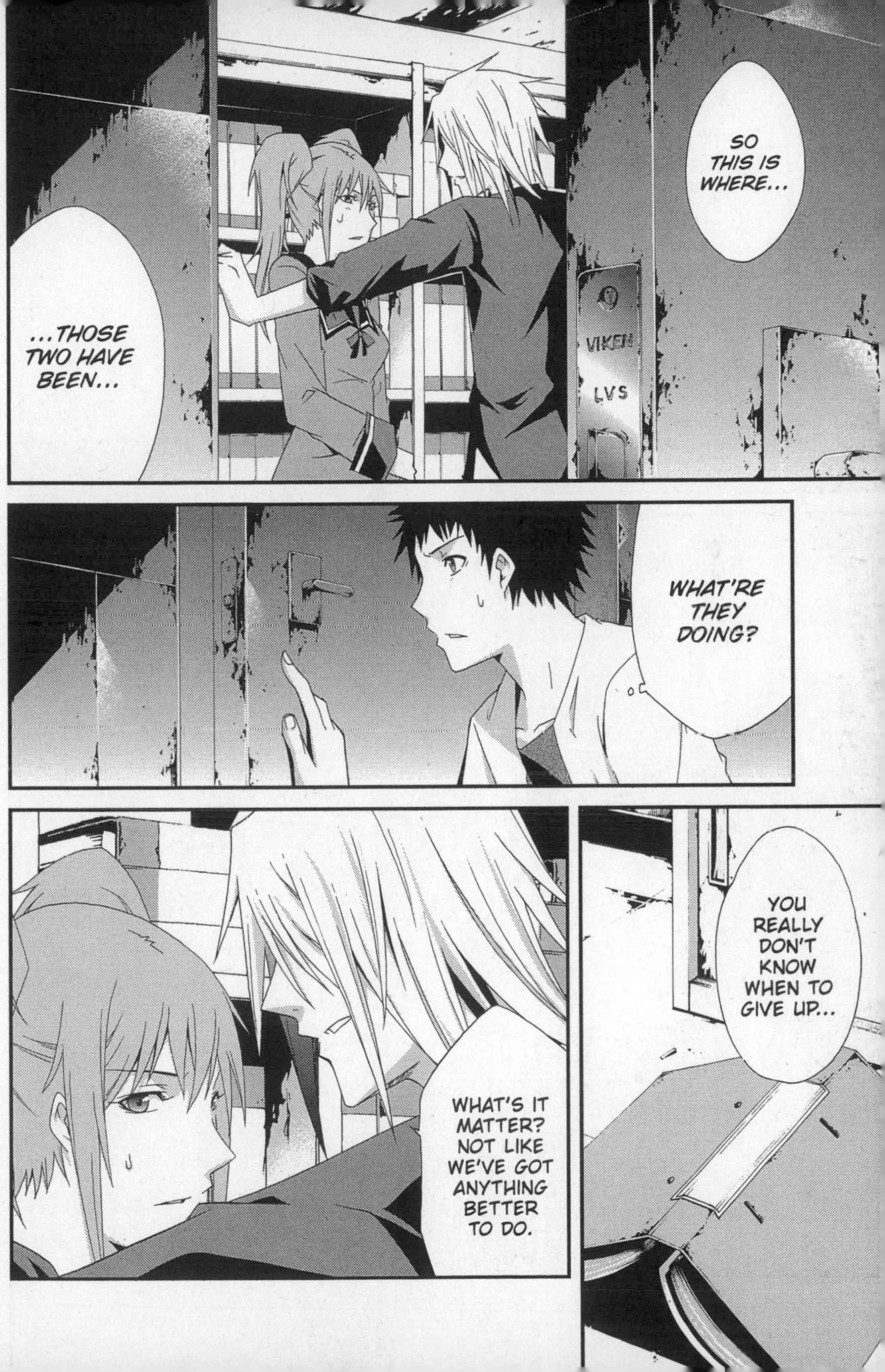
SO THIS IS WHERE...
VIKEN
LVS
...THOSE TWO HAVE BEEN...
WHAT'RE THEY DOING?
YOU REALLY DON'T KNOW WHEN TO GIVE UP...
WHAT'S IT MATTER? NOT LIKE WE'VE GOT ANYTHING BETTER TO DO.

C'MON.

STAYING IN THIS PLACE SO LONG, I CAN'T HELP BUT LOSE MY COOL.

...!

YOU KNOW I'VE GOT THIS GUN.

SAY...

...DON'T YOU WANNA LIVE TO MAKE IT OUTTA HERE?

CHAKI (CHAK)

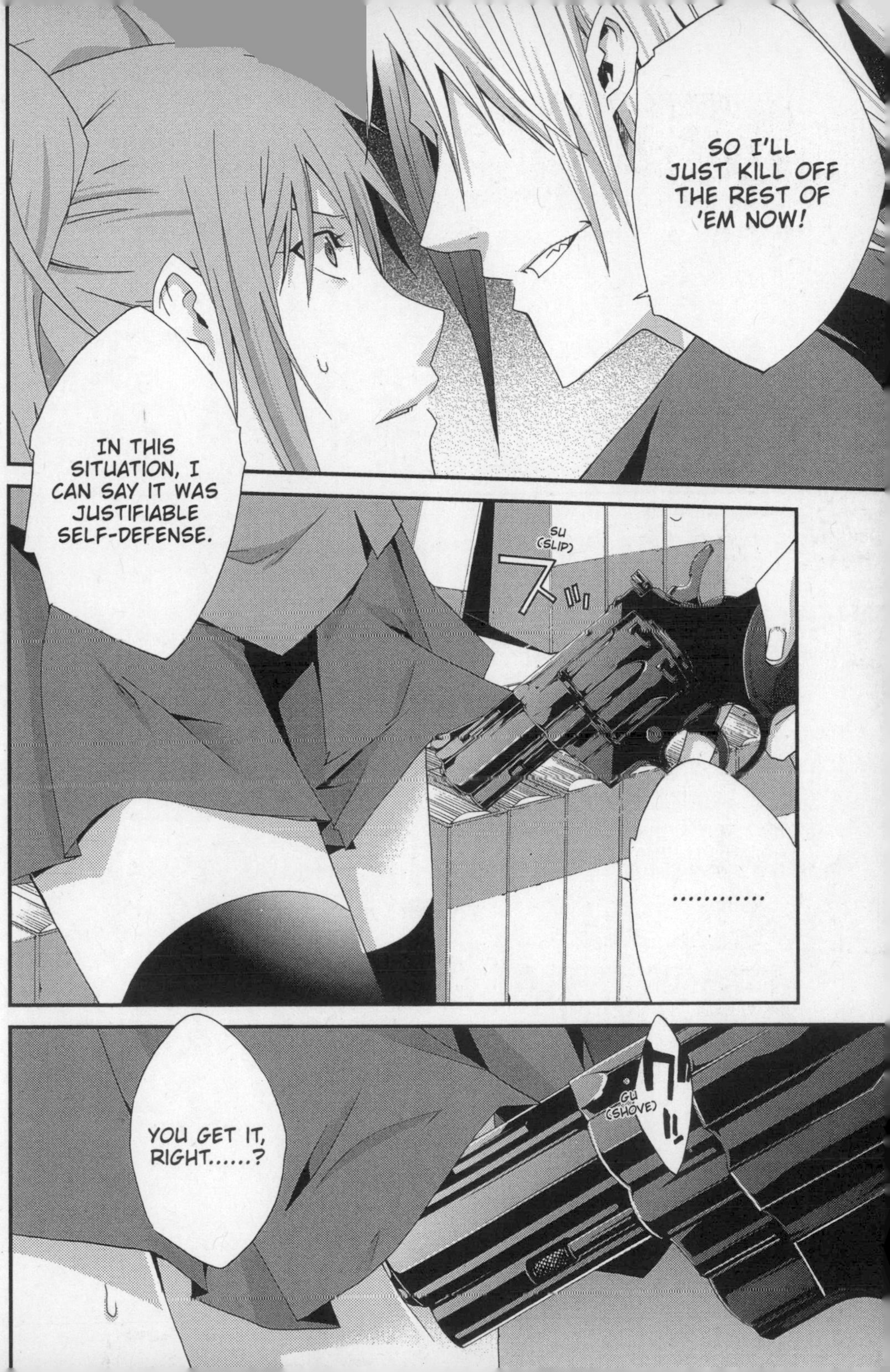
SO I'LL JUST KILL OFF THE REST OF 'EM NOW!
IN THIS SITUATION, I CAN SAY IT WAS JUSTIFIABLE SELF-DEFENSE.
....
SU (SLIP)
GU (SHOVE)
YOU GET IT, RIGHT......?

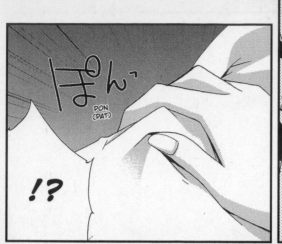

ぽん
PON
(PAT)

!?

THAT
BASTARD
...

ASAMI-
SAN...

SHH!

WHAT'S
GOING ON?
LOOKS LIKE
SOMETHING
EXCITING!

HEY...

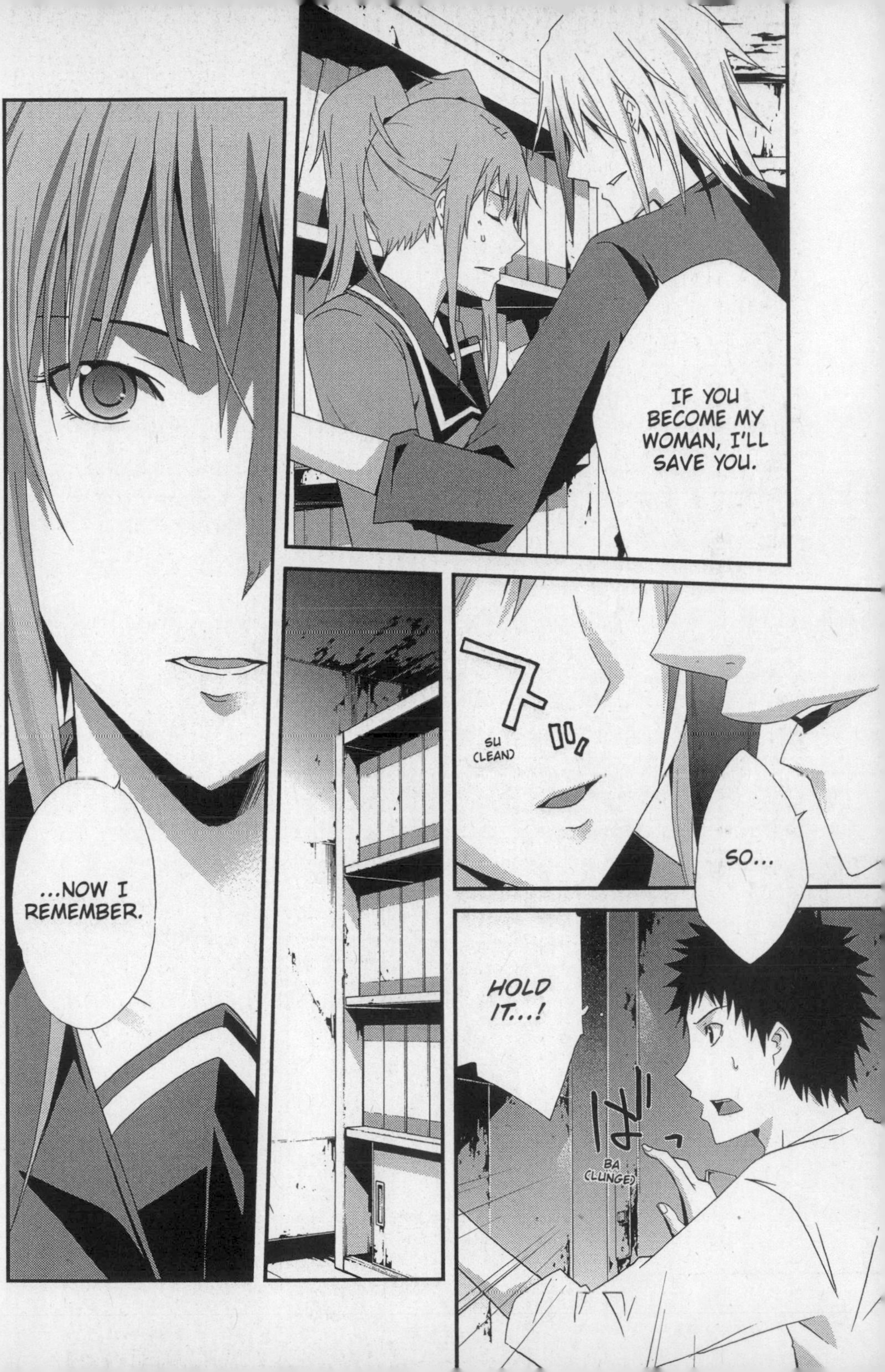
IF YOU BECOME MY WOMAN, I'LL SAVE YOU.
SU (LEAN)
SO...
HOLD IT...!
BA (LUNGE)
...NOW I REMEMBER.

YOU WERE THE VOCALIST FOR "GLORIOUS," WEREN'T YOU?

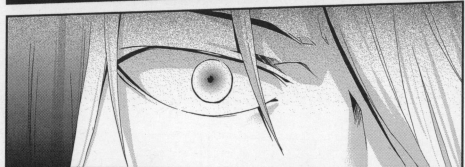

GLORIOUS?

I'M RIGHT, HUH?

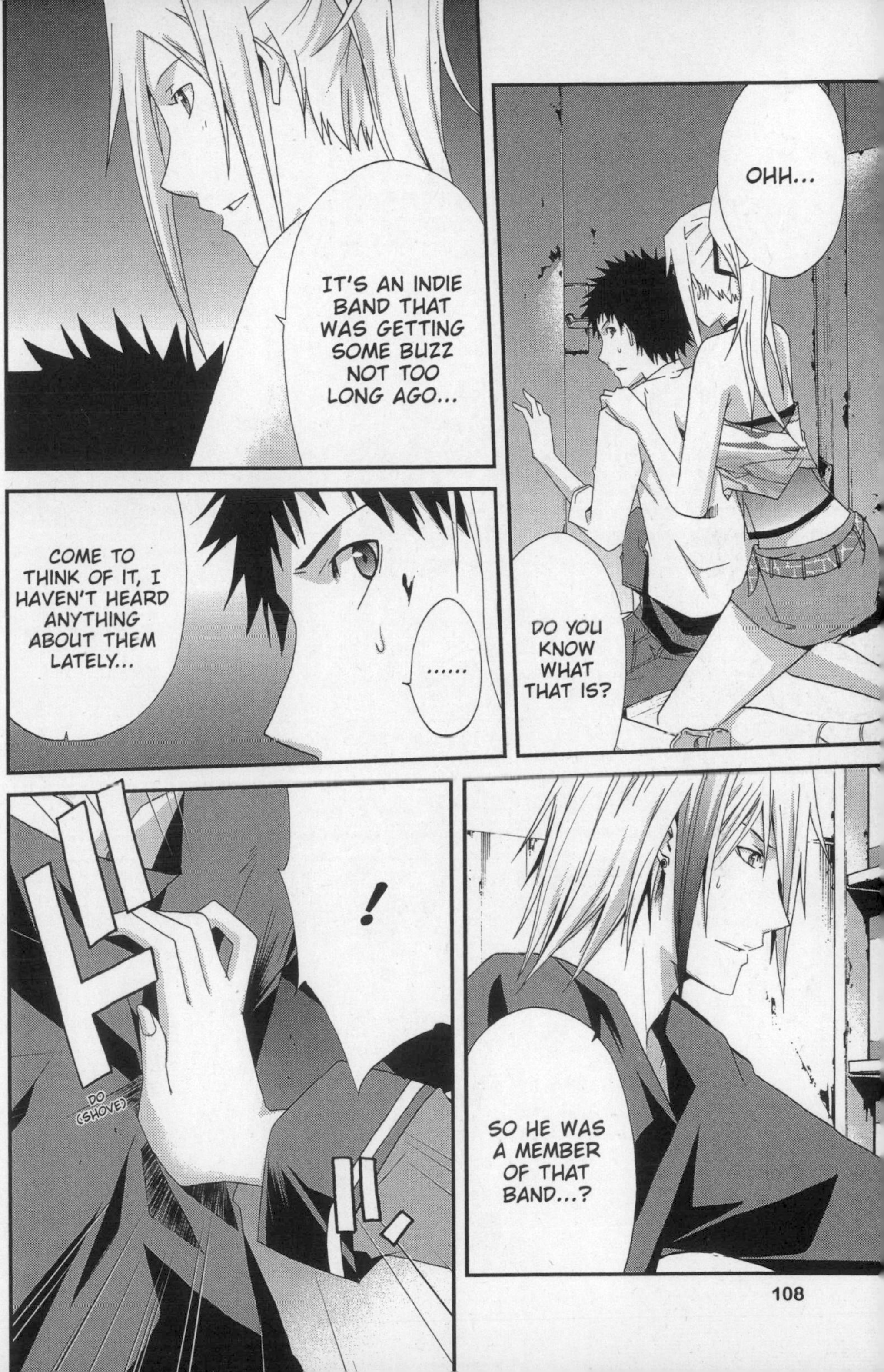
OHH...
DO YOU KNOW WHAT THAT IS?
IT'S AN INDIE BAND THAT WAS GETTING SOME BUZZ NOT TOO LONG AGO...
......
COME TO THINK OF IT, I HAVEN'T HEARD ANYTHING ABOUT THEM LATELY...
SO HE WAS A MEMBER OF THAT BAND...?
!
DO (SHOVE)

I SAW IT ON TV.

WHY, YOU...

GUESS THE RUMORS ABOUT YOU WERE TRUE.

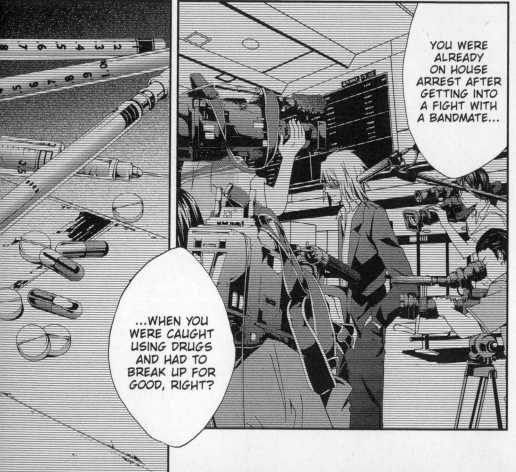

YOU WERE ALREADY ON HOUSE ARREST AFTER GETTING INTO A FIGHT WITH A BANDMATE...

...WHEN YOU WERE CAUGHT USING DRUGS AND HAD TO BREAK UP FOR GOOD, RIGHT?

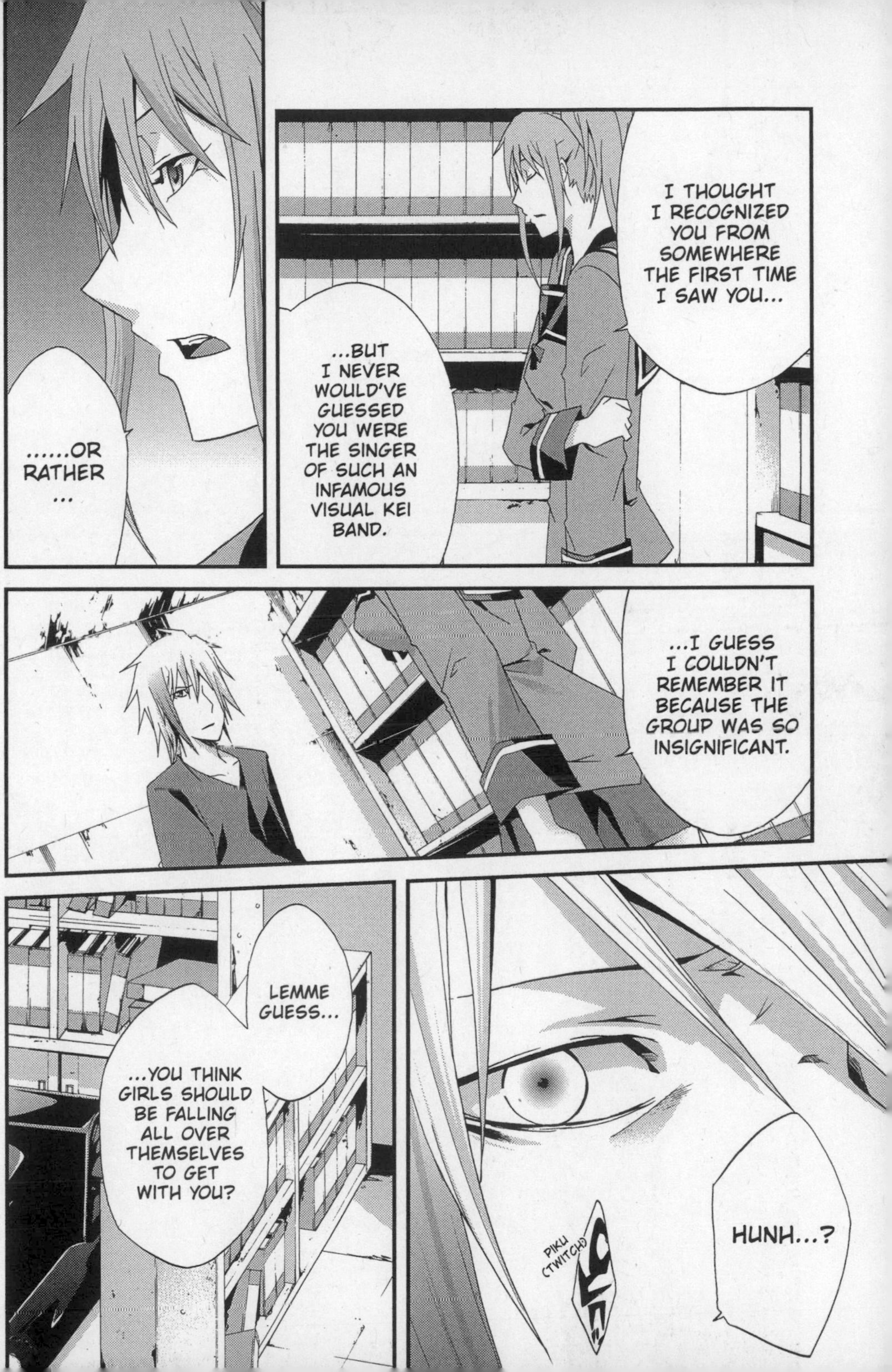
I THOUGHT I RECOGNIZED YOU FROM SOMEWHERE THE FIRST TIME I SAW YOU...
...BUT I NEVER WOULD'VE GUESSED YOU WERE THE SINGER OF SUCH AN INFAMOUS VISUAL KEI BAND.
......OR RATHER ...
...I GUESS I COULDN'T REMEMBER IT BECAUSE THE GROUP WAS SO INSIGNIFICANT.
PIKU (TWITCH)
HUNH...?
LEMME GUESS...
...YOU THINK GIRLS SHOULD BE FALLING ALL OVER THEMSELVES TO GET WITH YOU?

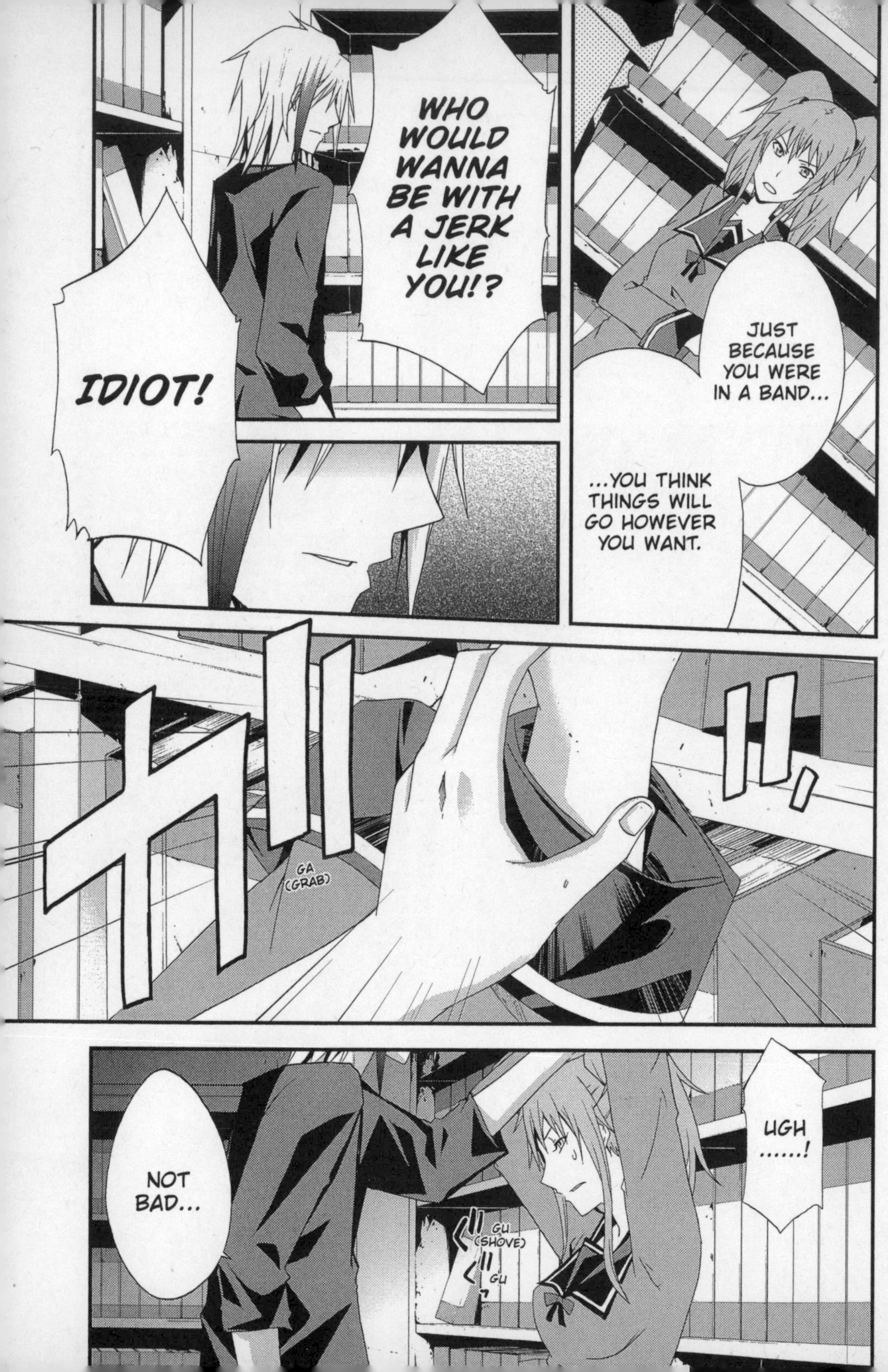
JUST BECAUSE YOU WERE IN A BAND...
...YOU THINK THINGS WILL GO HOWEVER YOU WANT.
WHO WOULD WANNA BE WITH A JERK LIKE YOU!?
IDIOT!
GA (GRAB)
UGH ......!
GU (SHOVE) GU
NOT BAD...

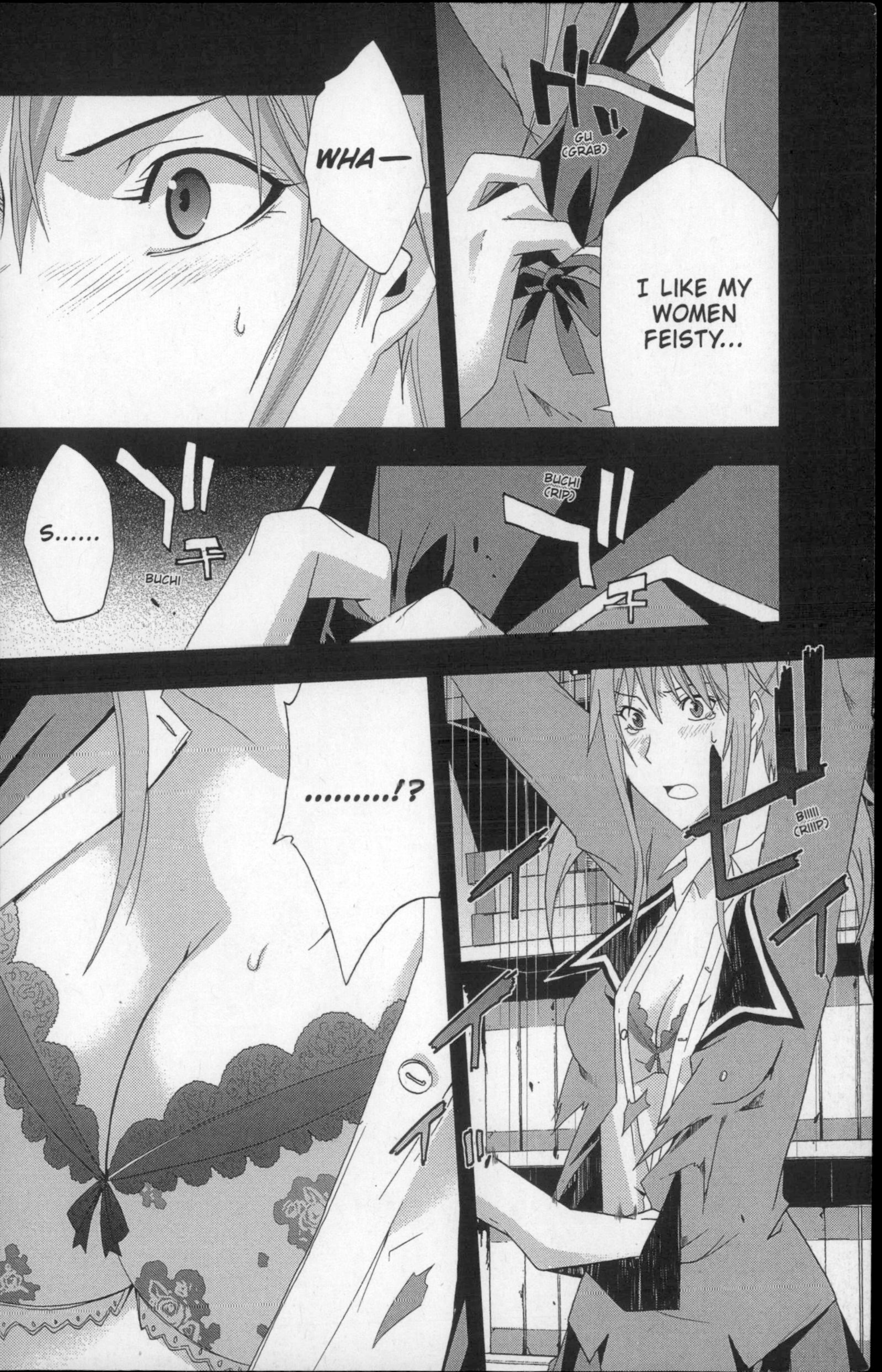
GU
(GRAB)
I LIKE MY WOMEN FEISTY...
WHA—
BUCHI
(RIP)
S......
BUCHI
BIIII
(RIIIP)
.........!?

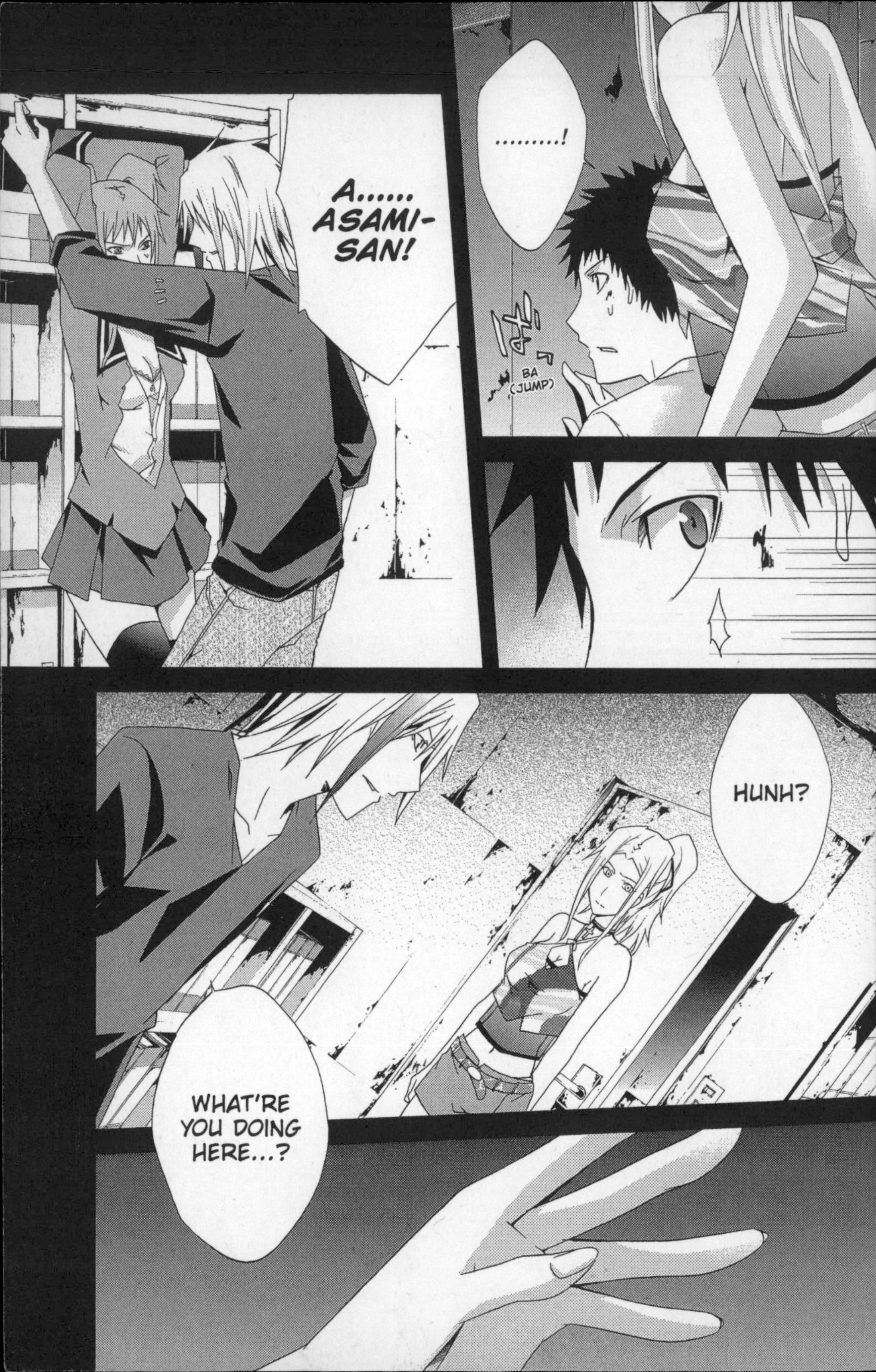
.........!
ばっ
BA (JUMP)
A...... ASAMI-SAN!
HUNH?
WHAT'RE YOU DOING HERE...?

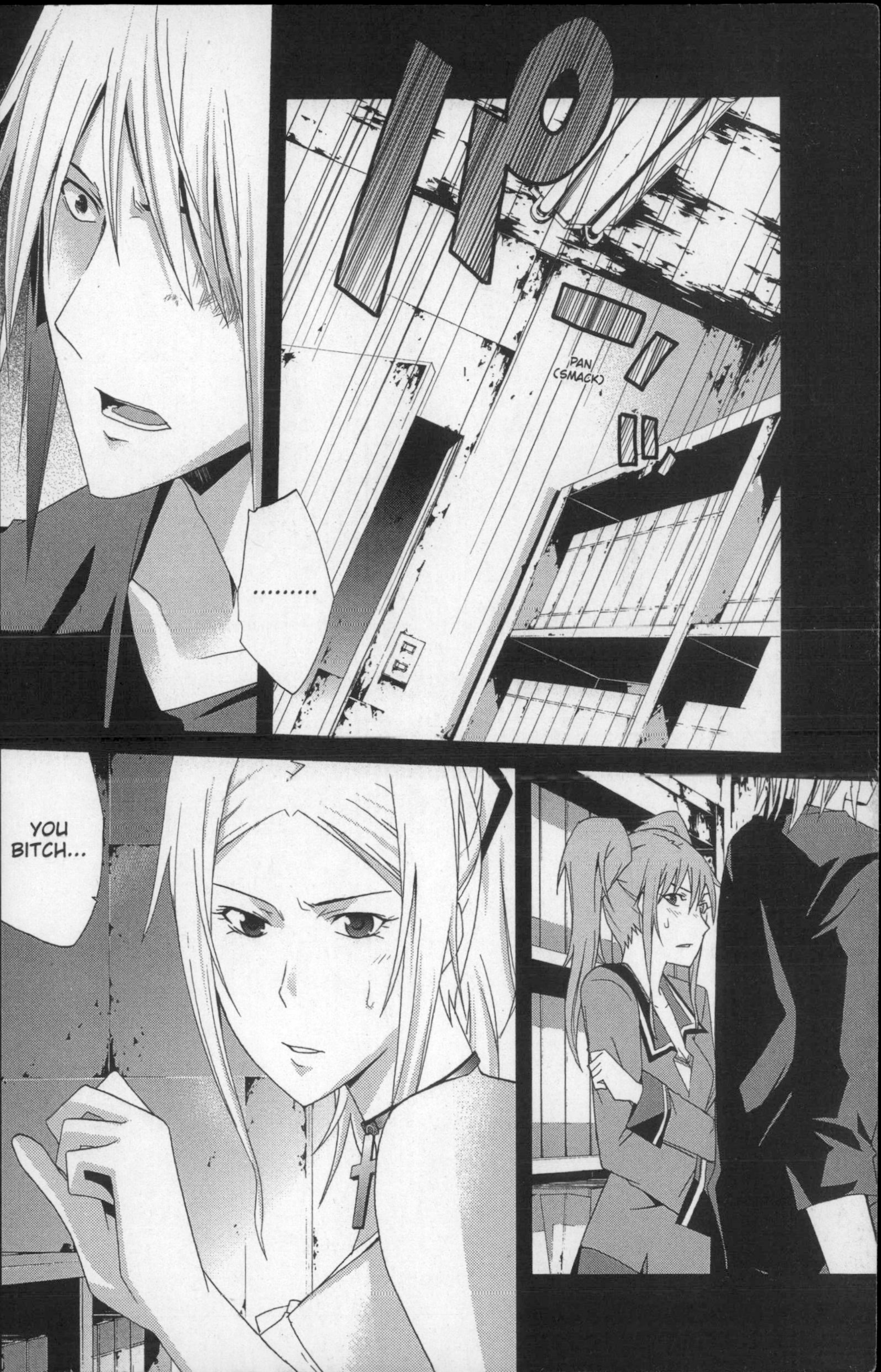
PAN (SMACK)
....
YOU BITCH...

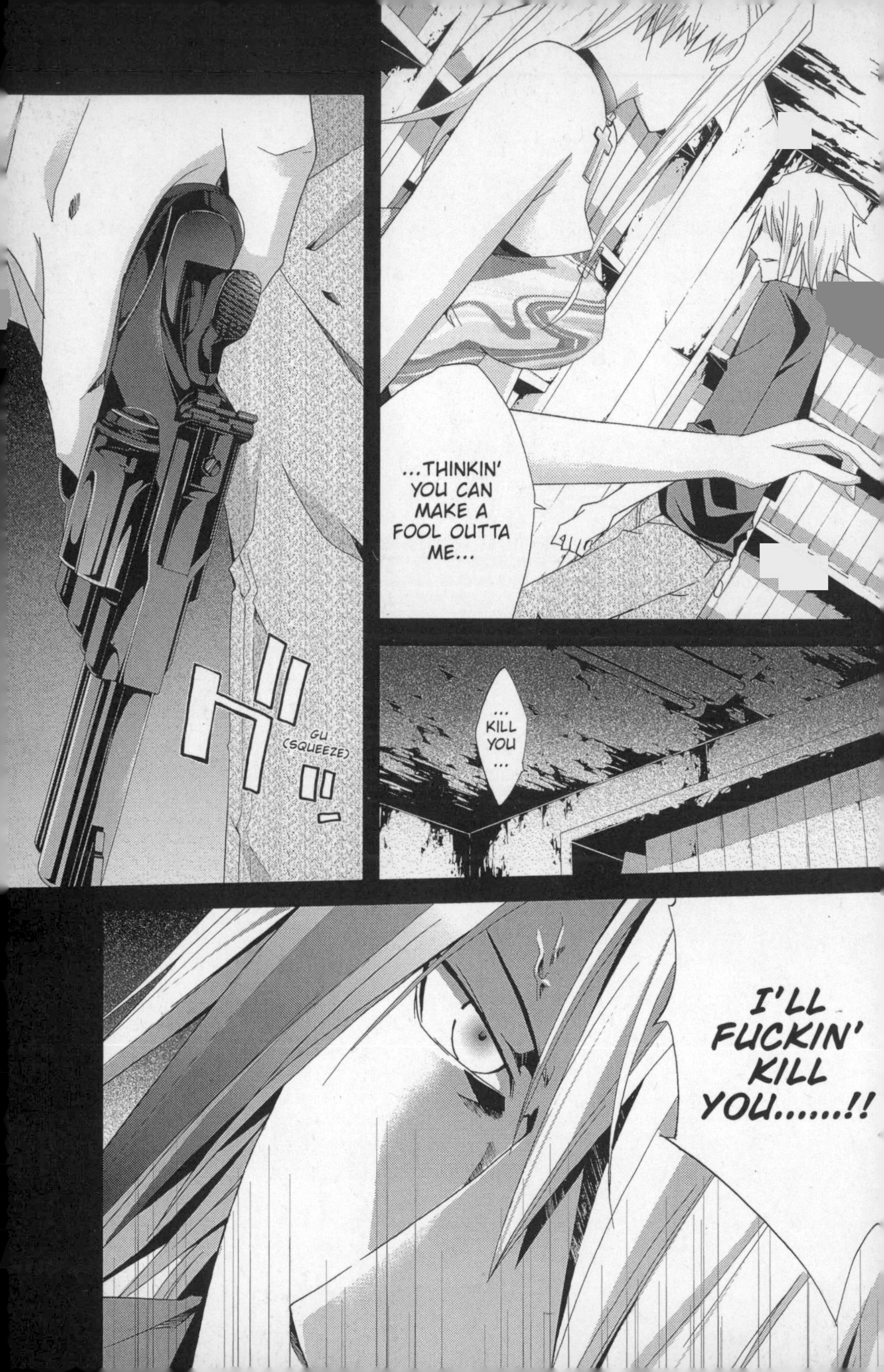
...THINKIN' YOU CAN MAKE A FOOL OUTTA ME...
... KILL YOU ...
GU (SQUEEZE)
I'LL FUCKIN' KILL YOU......!!

JUDGE

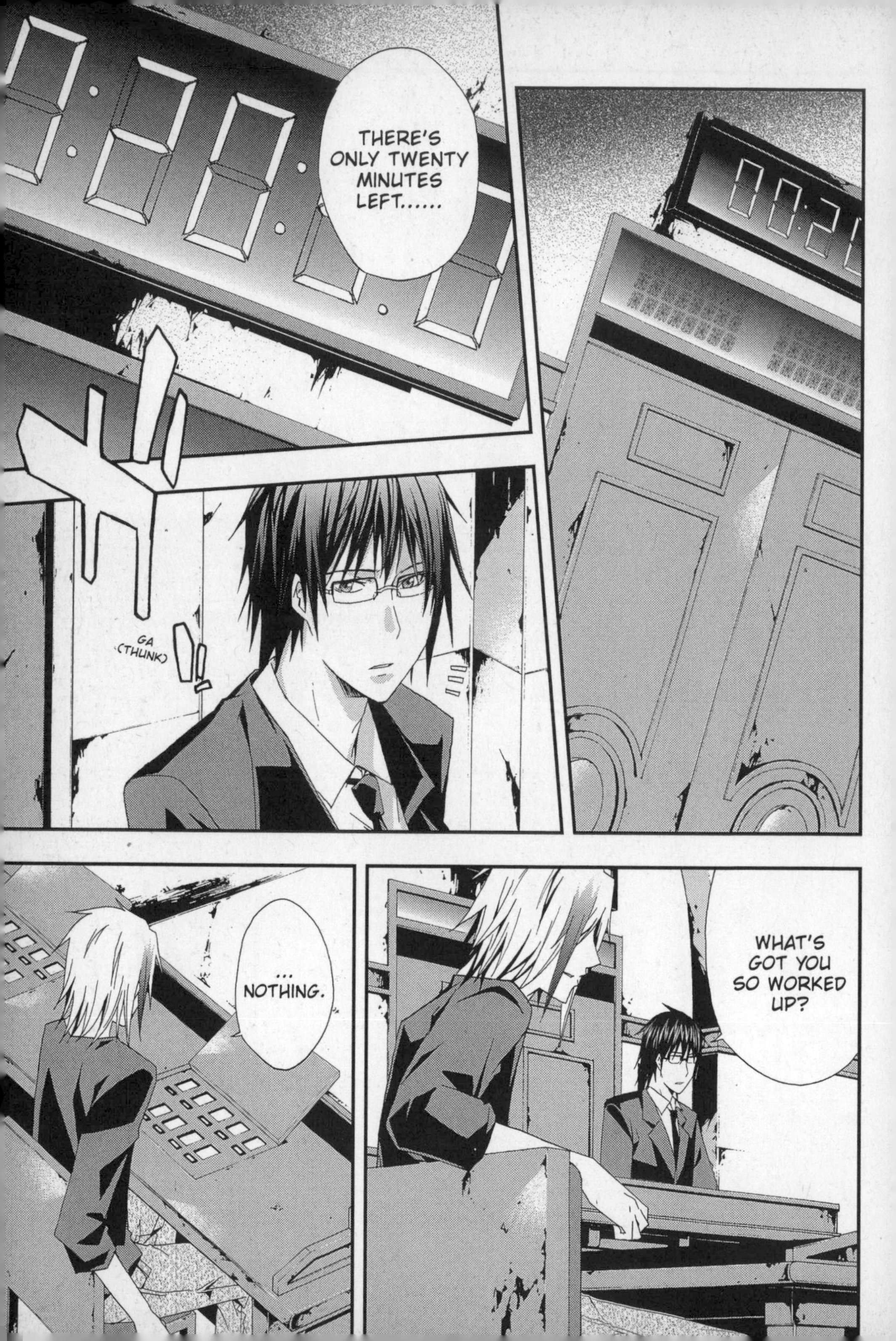
THERE'S ONLY TWENTY MINUTES LEFT......
GA (THUNK)
WHAT'S GOT YOU SO WORKED UP?
... NOTHING.

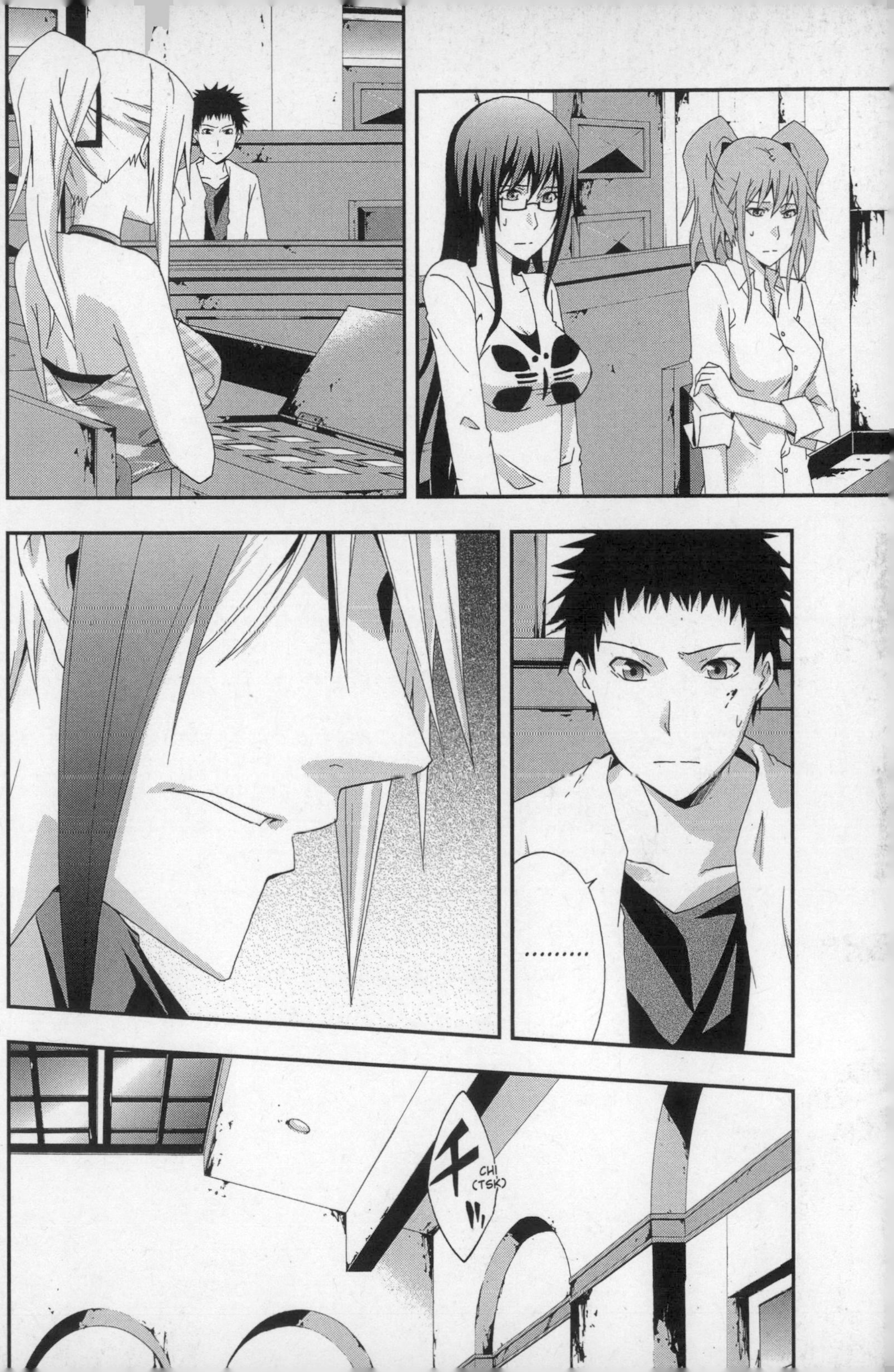
....
チッ
CHI (TSK)

CHAPTER 19 SPLIT

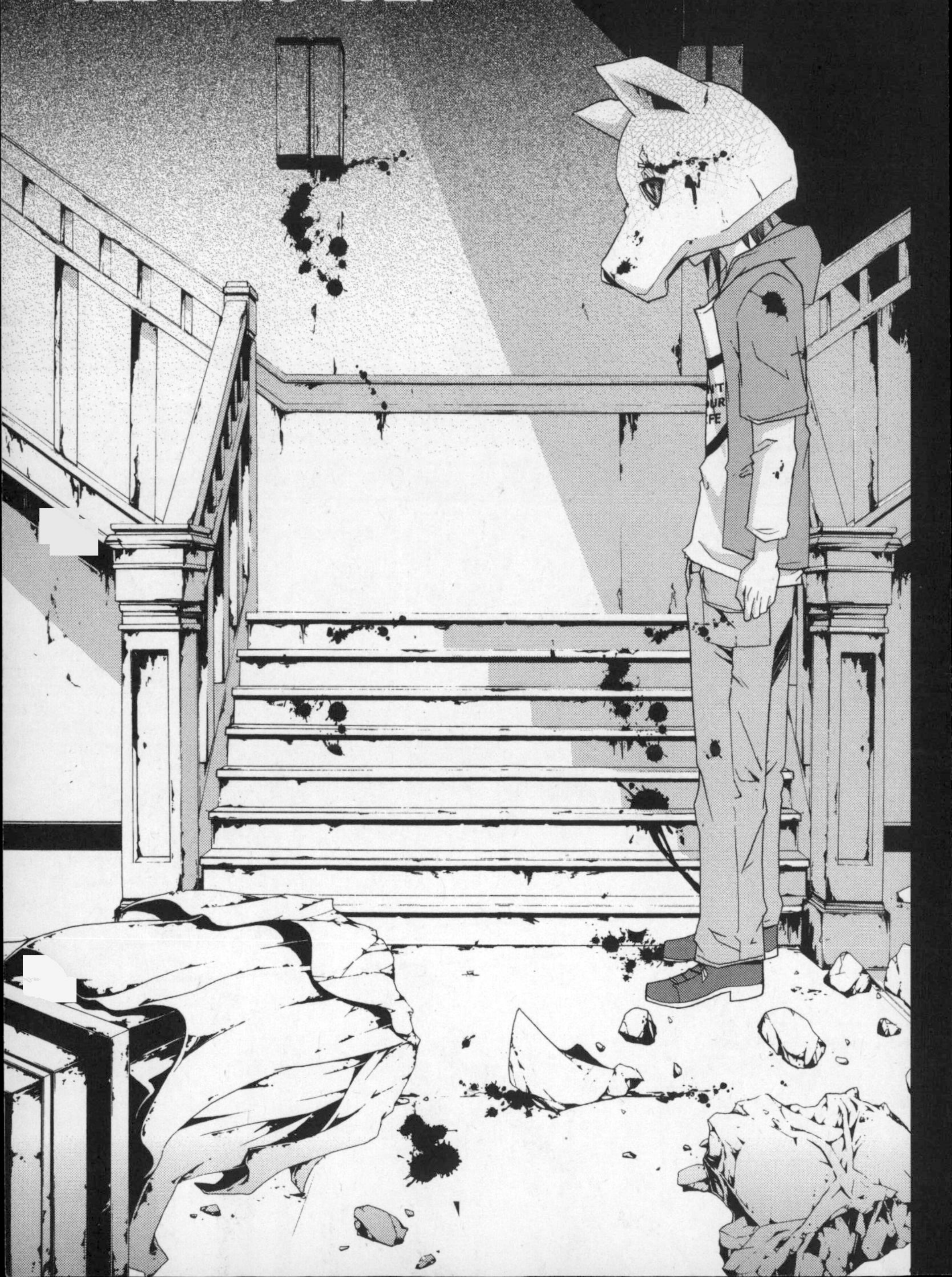

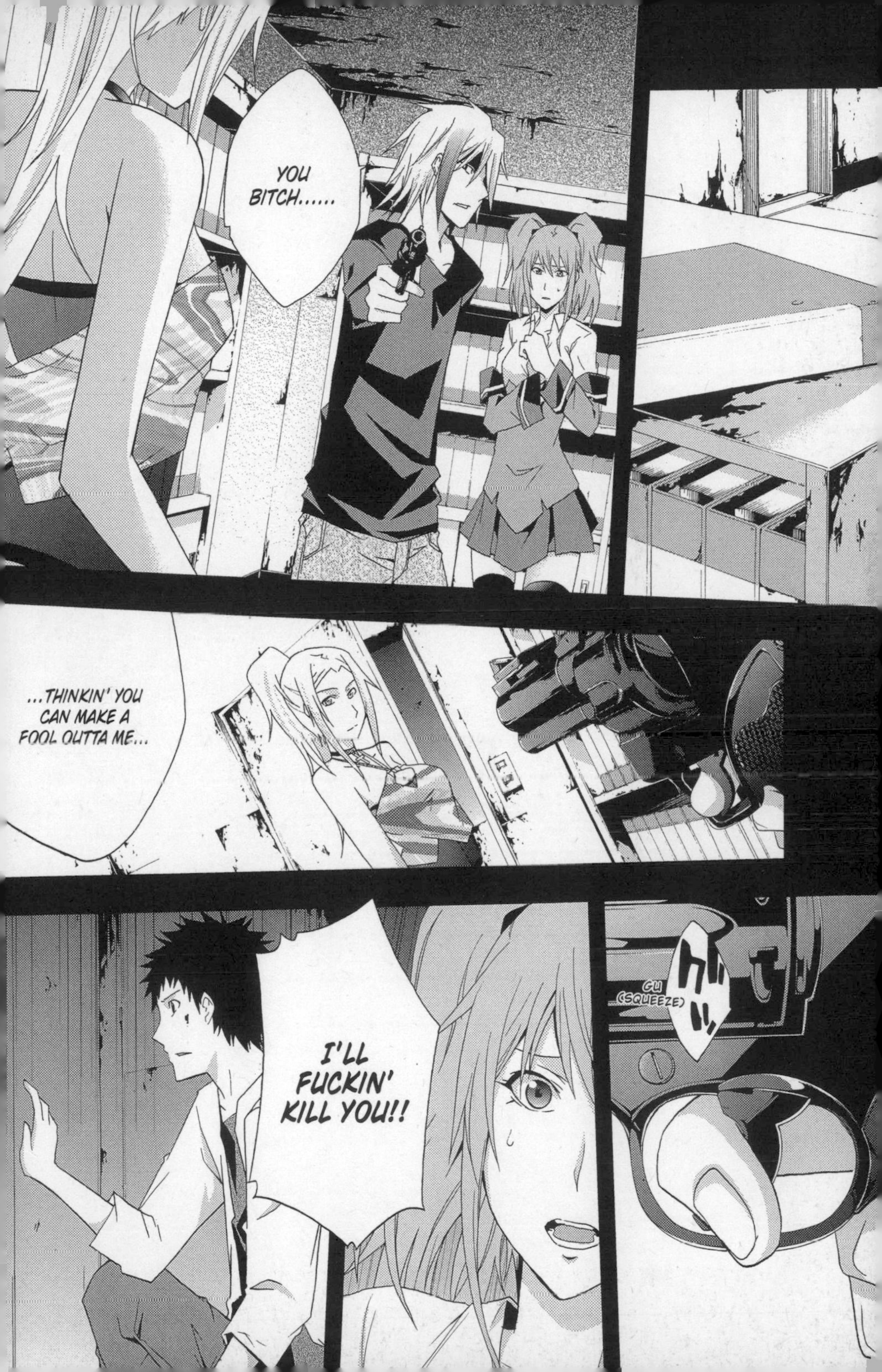
YOU BITCH......
...THINKIN' YOU CAN MAKE A FOOL OUTTA ME...
GU (SQUEEZE)
I'LL FUCKIN' KILL YOU!!

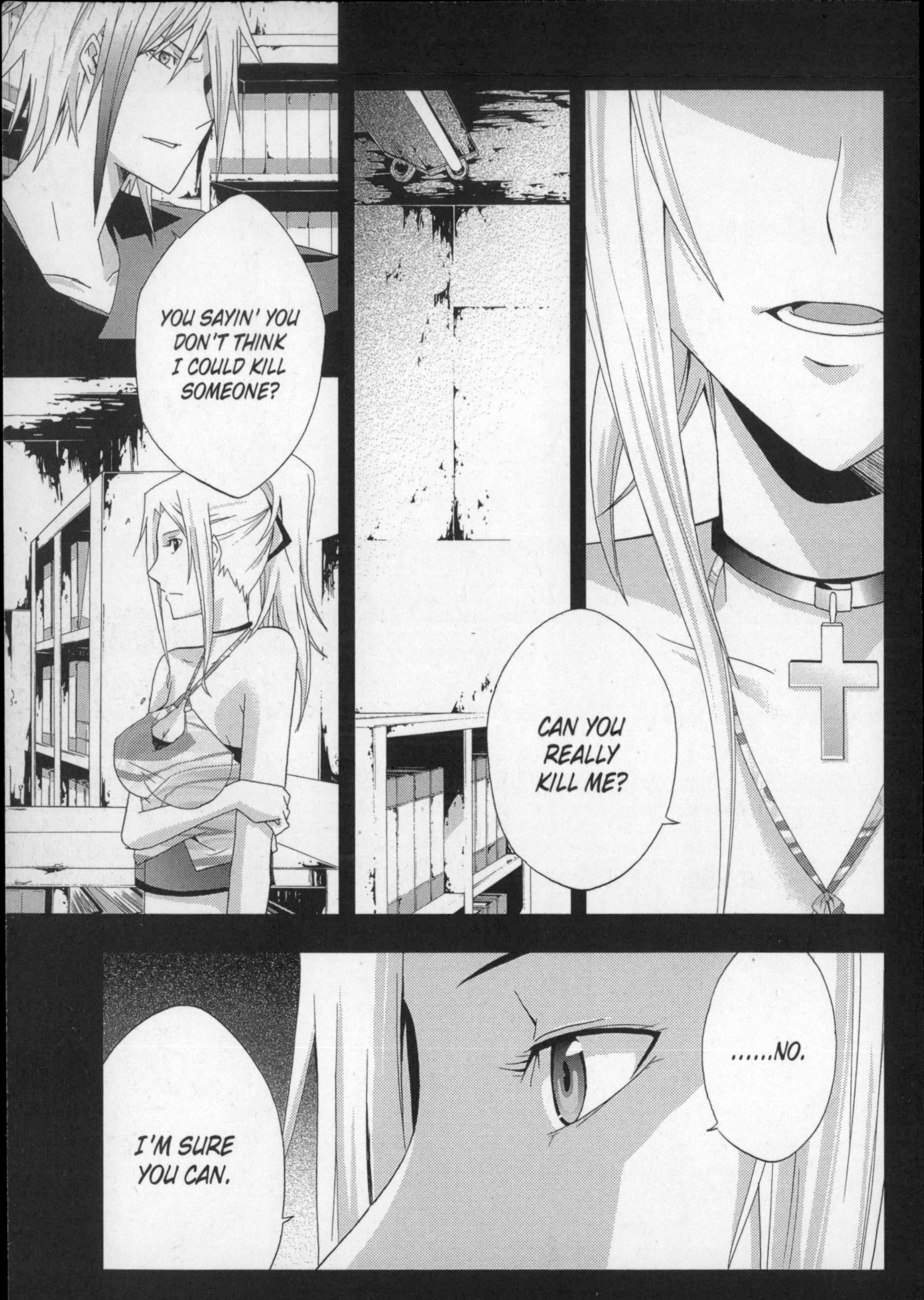
CAN YOU REALLY KILL ME?
YOU SAYIN' YOU DON'T THINK I COULD KILL SOMEONE?
......NO.
I'M SURE YOU CAN.

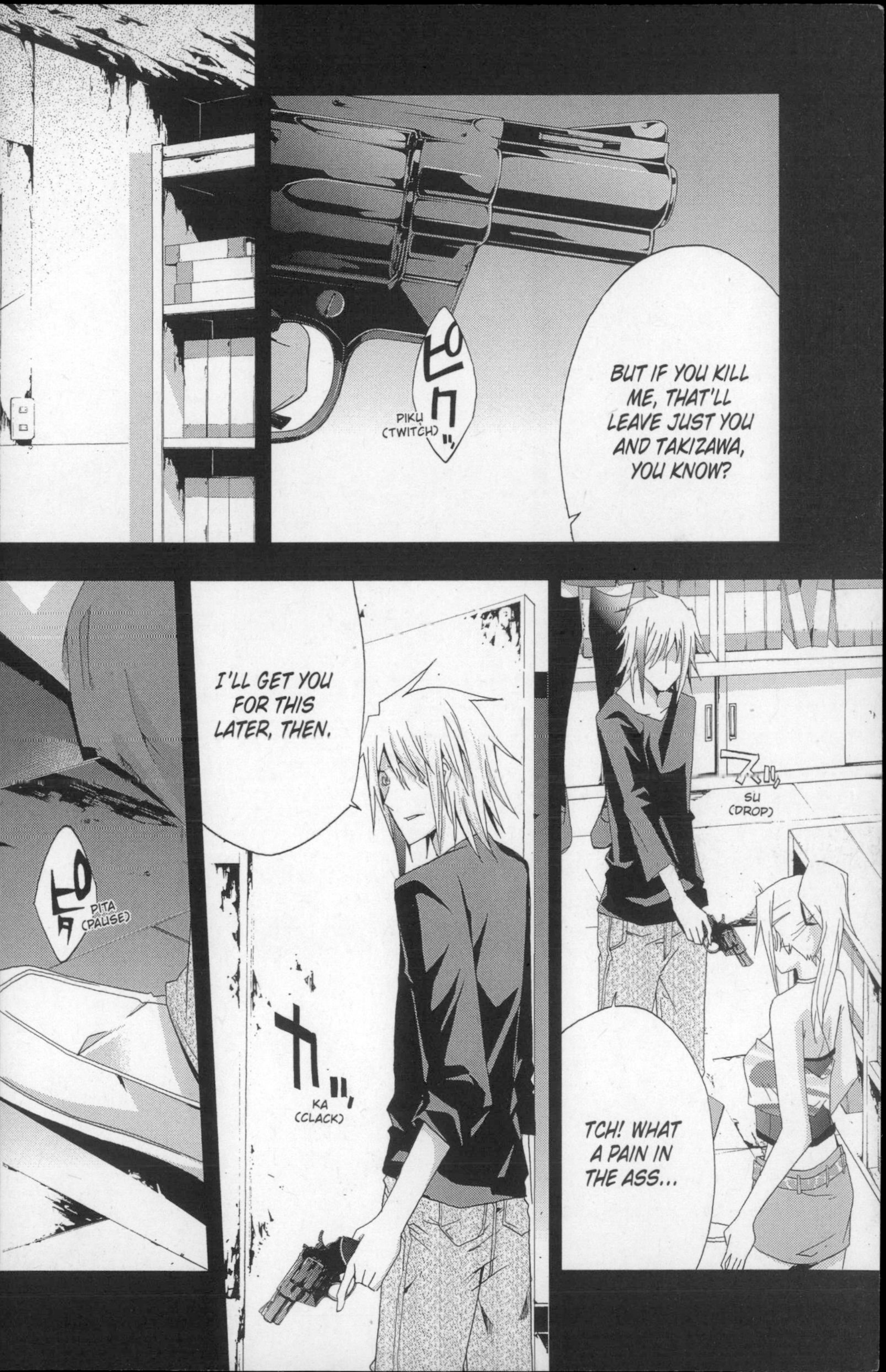
BUT IF YOU KILL ME, THAT'LL LEAVE JUST YOU AND TAKIZAWA, YOU KNOW?
PIKU (TWITCH)
SU (DROP)
TCH! WHAT A PAIN IN THE ASS...
I'LL GET YOU FOR THIS LATER, THEN.
KA (CLACK)
PITA (PAUSE)

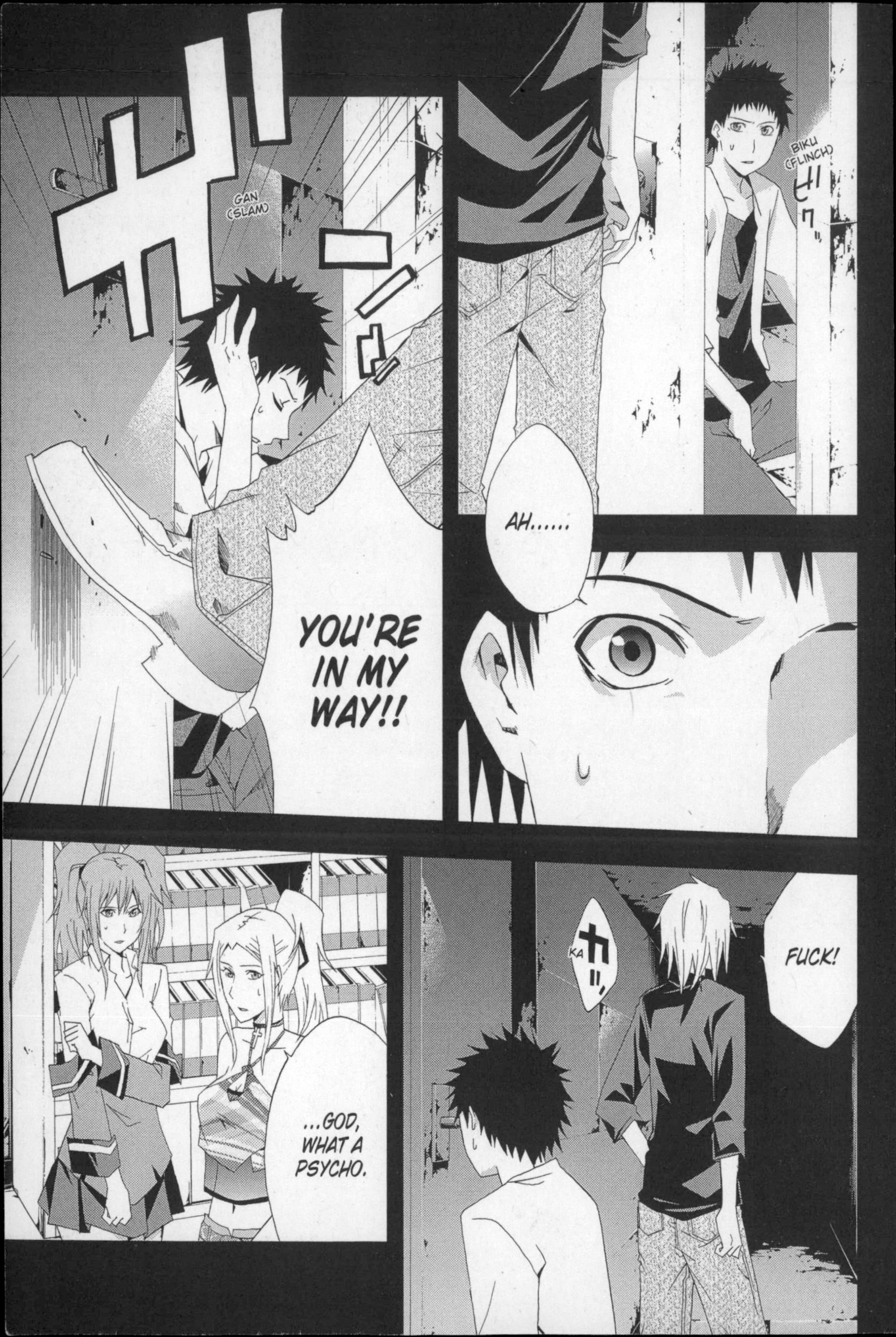

BIKU (FLINCH)
AH......
GAN (SLAM)
YOU'RE IN MY WAY!!
KA
FUCK!
...GOD, WHAT A PSYCHO.

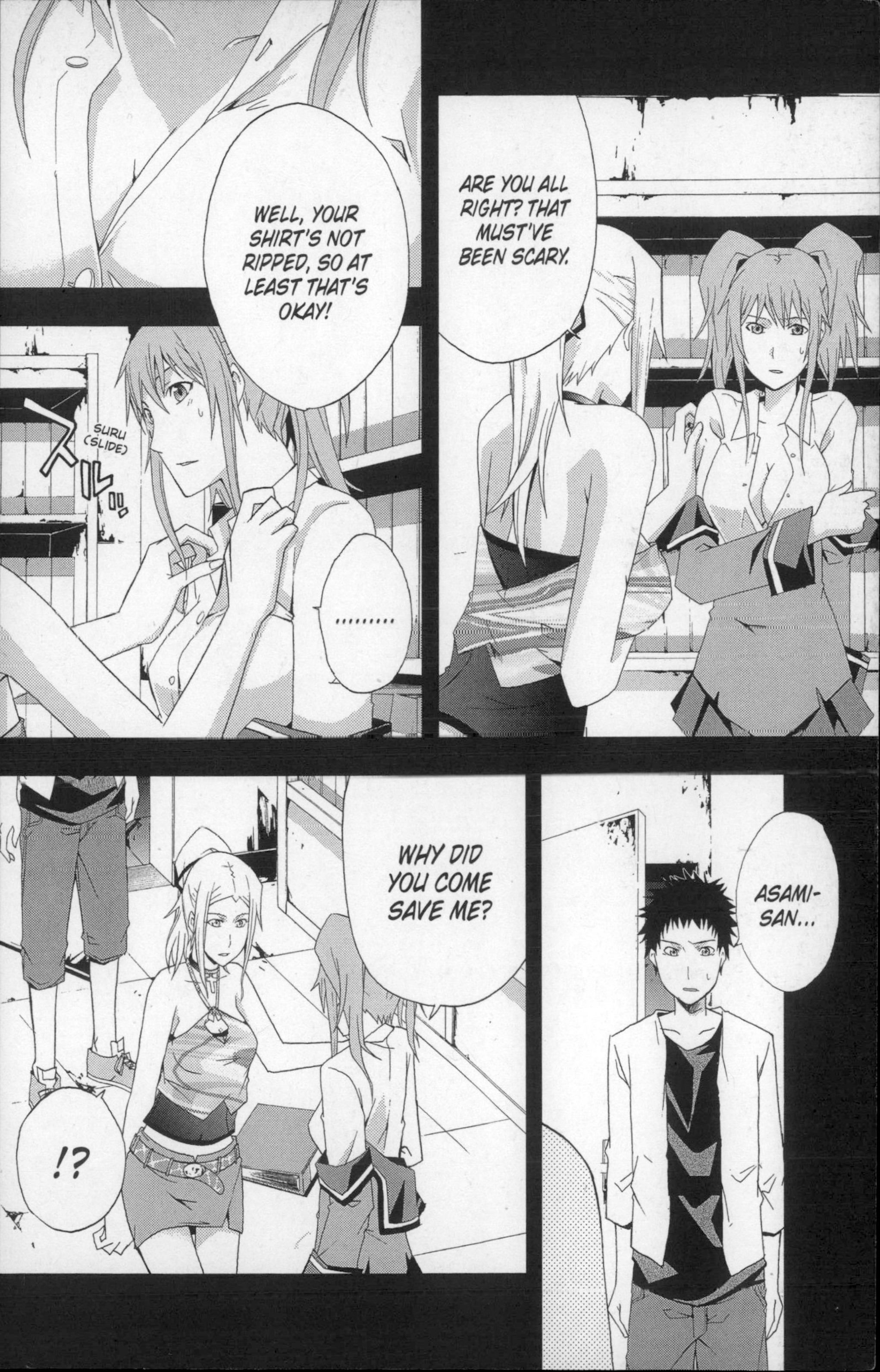
ARE YOU ALL RIGHT? THAT MUST'VE BEEN SCARY.
WELL, YOUR SHIRT'S NOT RIPPED, SO AT LEAST THAT'S OKAY!
SURU (SLIDE)
....
ASAMI-SAN...
WHY DID YOU COME SAVE ME?
!?

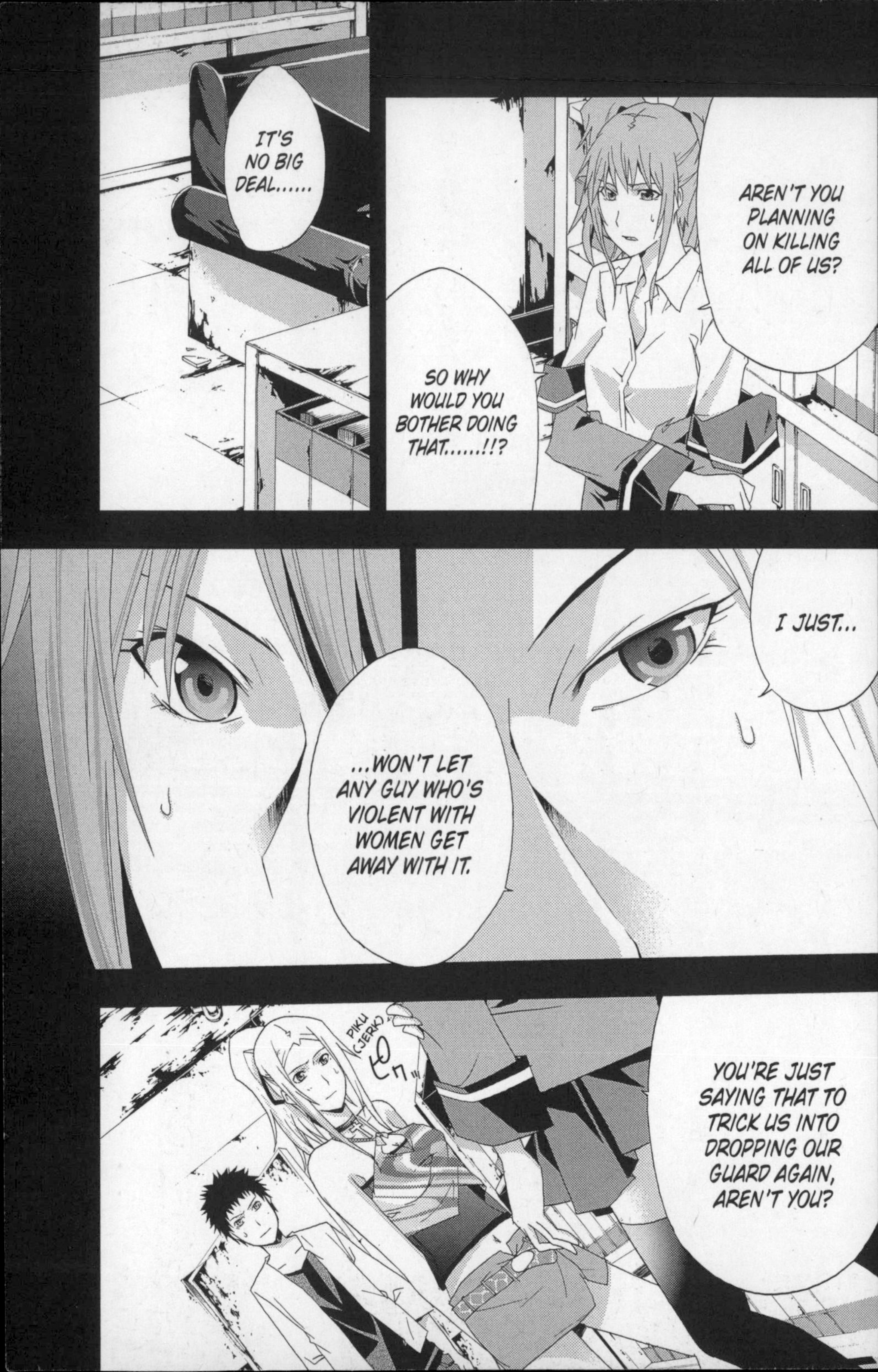
AREN'T YOU PLANNING ON KILLING ALL OF US?
SO WHY WOULD YOU BOTHER DOING THAT......!!?
IT'S NO BIG DEAL......
I JUST...
...WON'T LET ANY GUY WHO'S VIOLENT WITH WOMEN GET AWAY WITH IT.
YOU'RE JUST SAYING THAT TO TRICK US INTO DROPPING OUR GUARD AGAIN, AREN'T YOU?
PIKU (JERK)

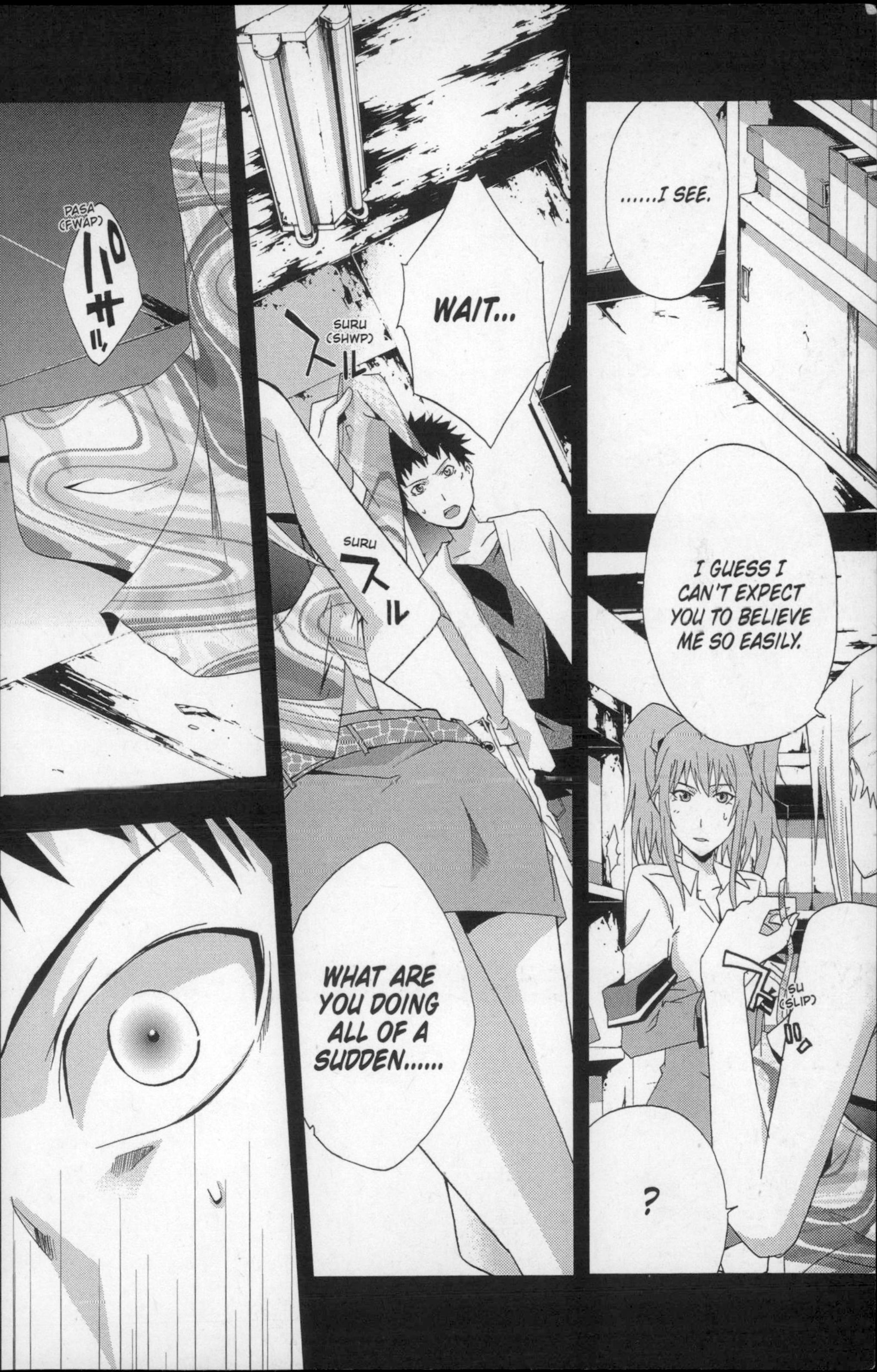
......I SEE.
I GUESS I CAN'T EXPECT YOU TO BELIEVE ME SO EASILY.
SU (SLIP)
スッ
?
WAIT...
SURU (SHWP)
スル
SURU
スル
WHAT ARE YOU DOING ALL OF A SUDDEN......
PASA (FWAP)
パサッ

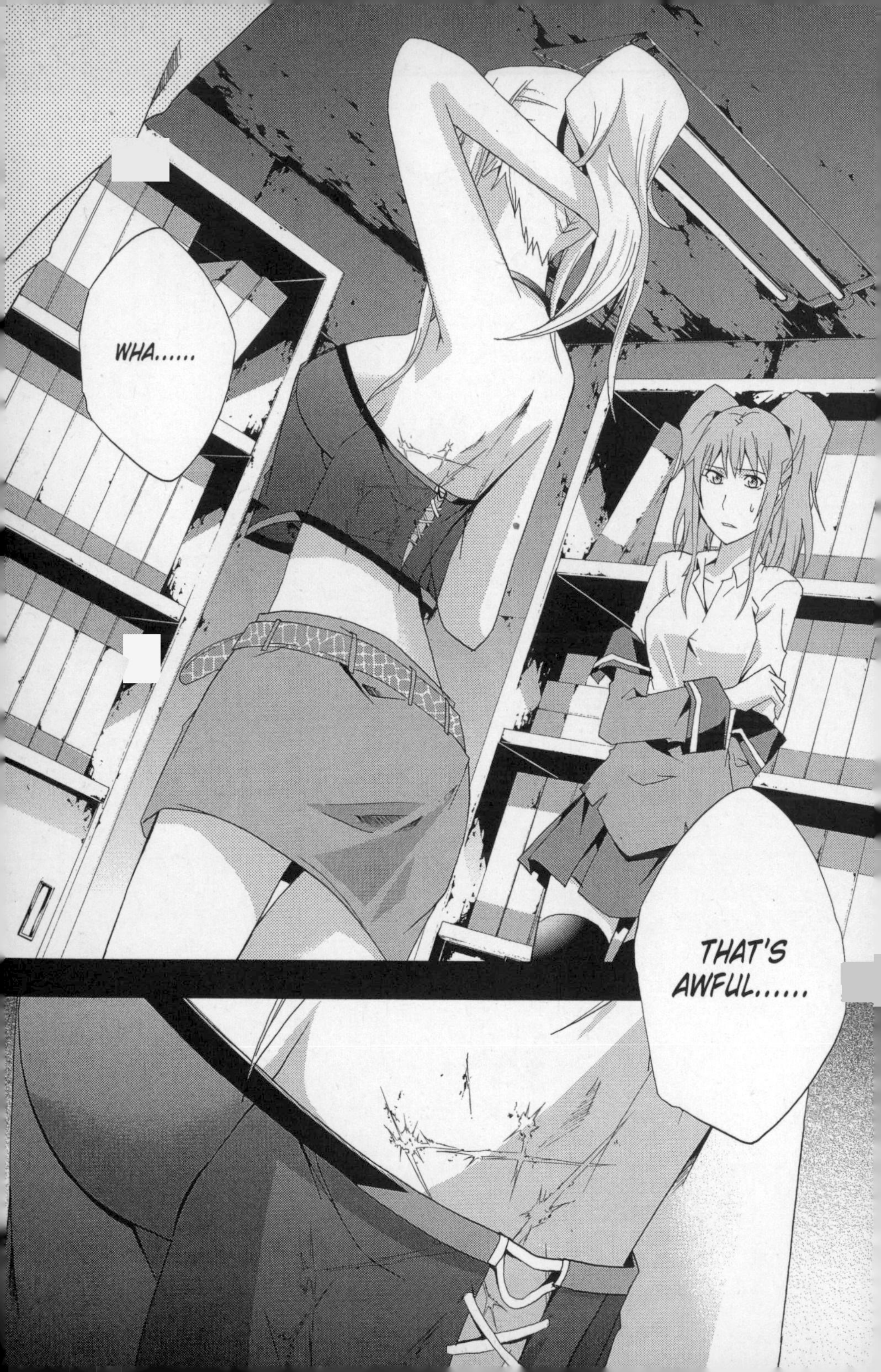
WHA......
THAT'S AWFUL......

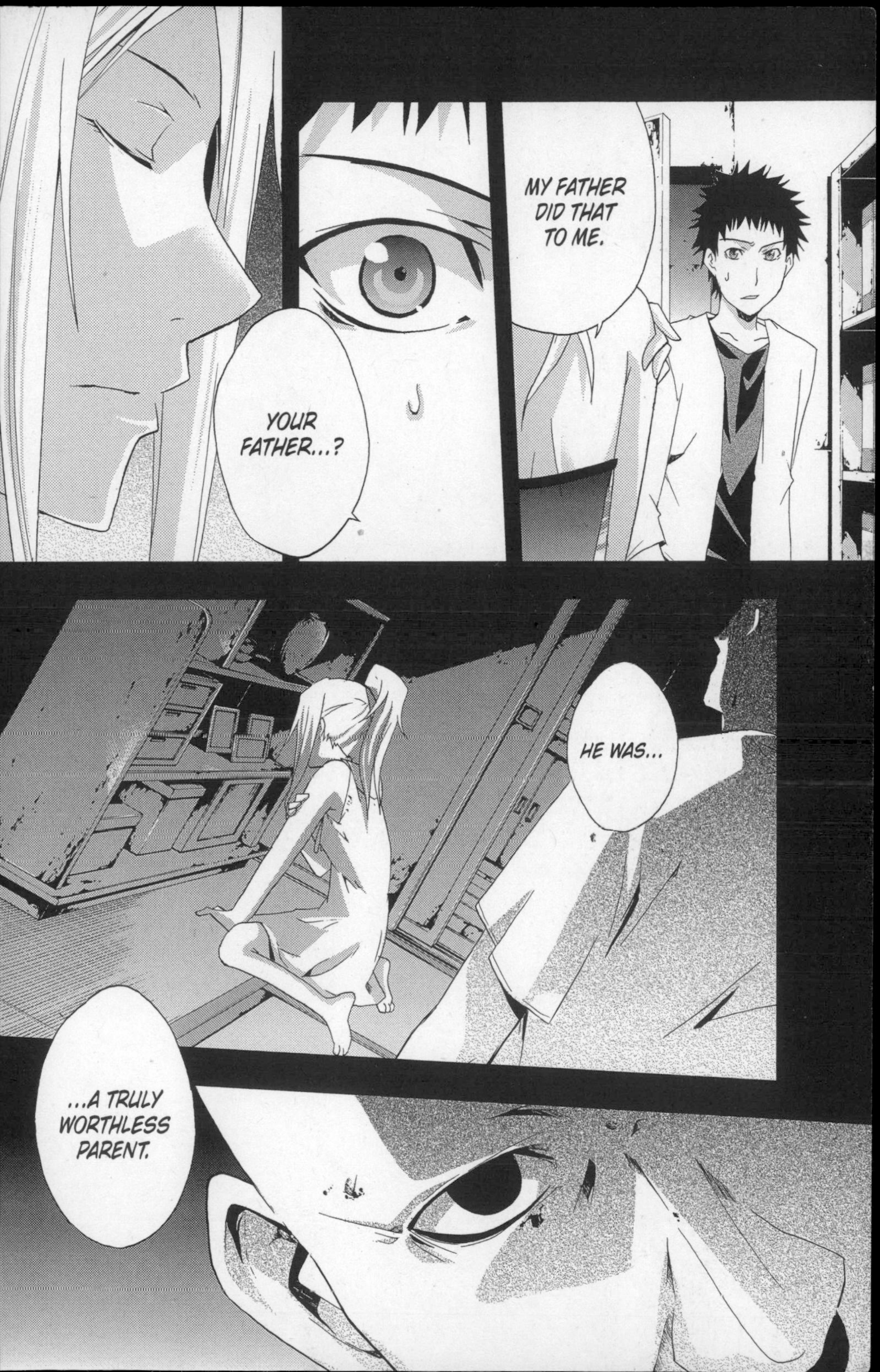
MY FATHER DID THAT TO ME.
YOUR FATHER...?
HE WAS...
...A TRULY WORTHLESS PARENT.

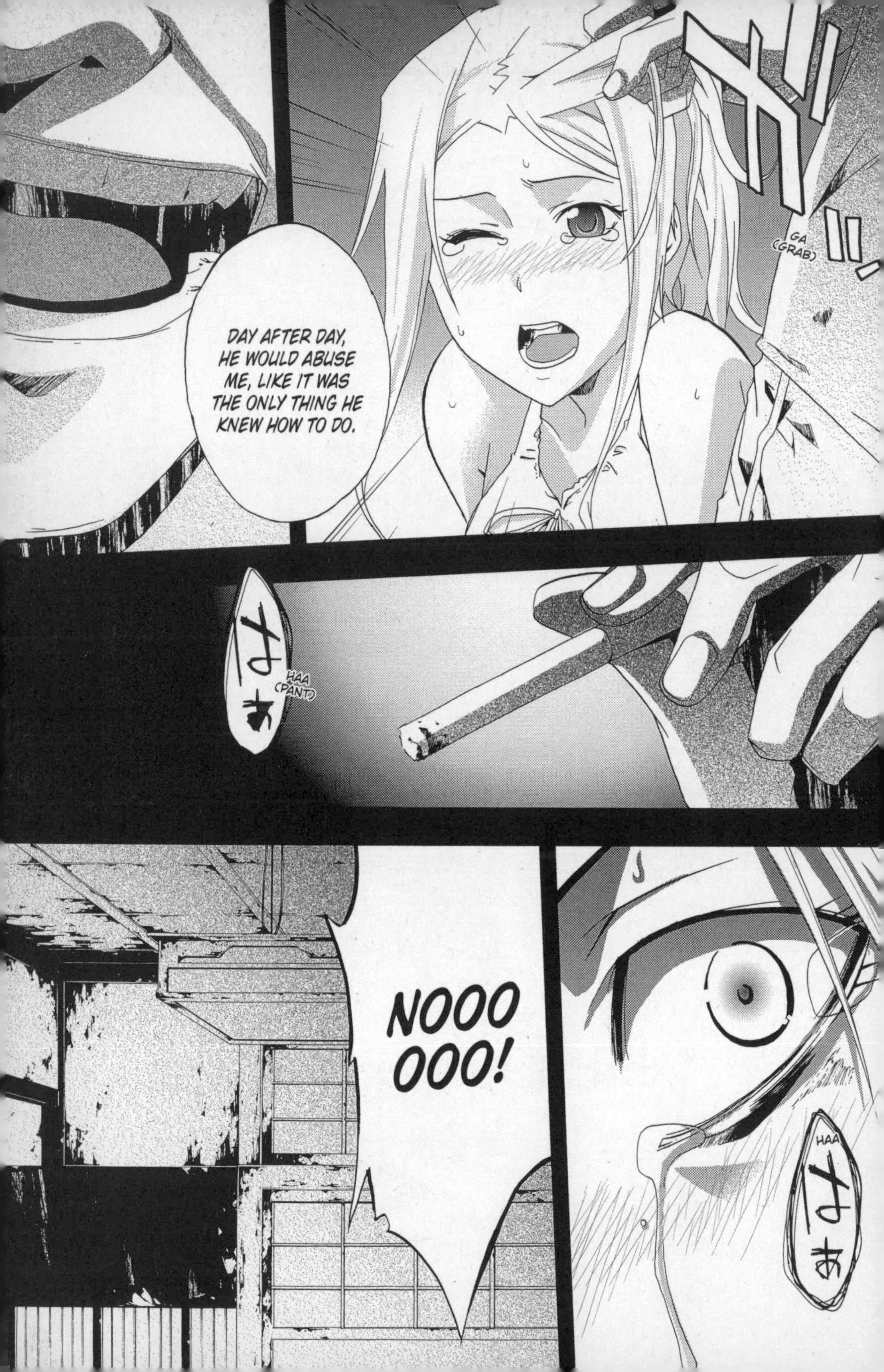
GA (GRAB)
DAY AFTER DAY, HE WOULD ABUSE ME, LIKE IT WAS THE ONLY THING HE KNEW HOW TO DO.
はあ
HAA (PANT)
はあ
HAA
NOOOOOO!

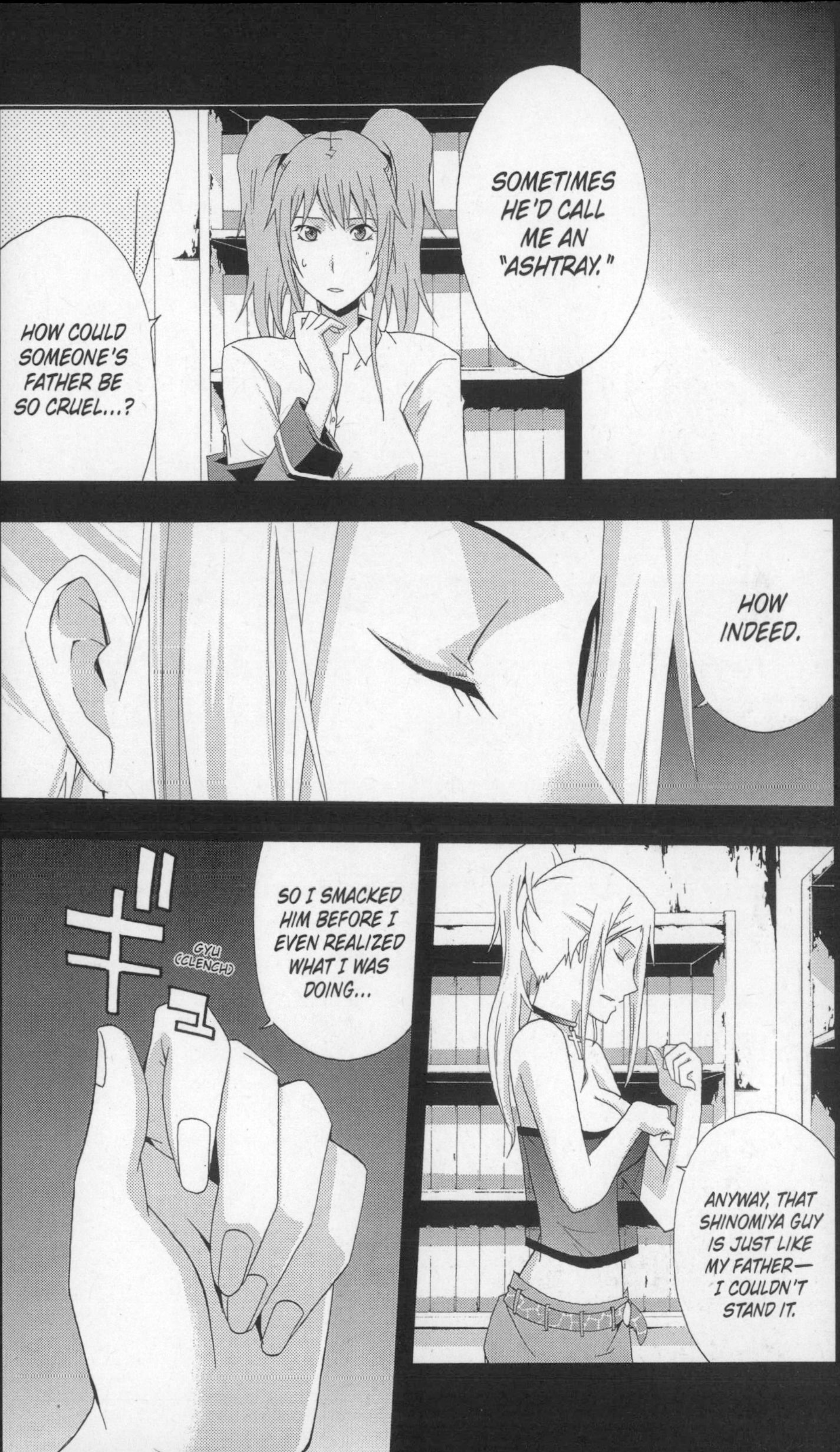
SOMETIMES HE'D CALL ME AN "ASHTRAY."
HOW COULD SOMEONE'S FATHER BE SO CRUEL...?
HOW INDEED.
ANYWAY, THAT SHINOMIYA GUY IS JUST LIKE MY FATHER— I COULDN'T STAND IT.
SO I SMACKED HIM BEFORE I EVEN REALIZED WHAT I WAS DOING...
GYU (CLENCH)

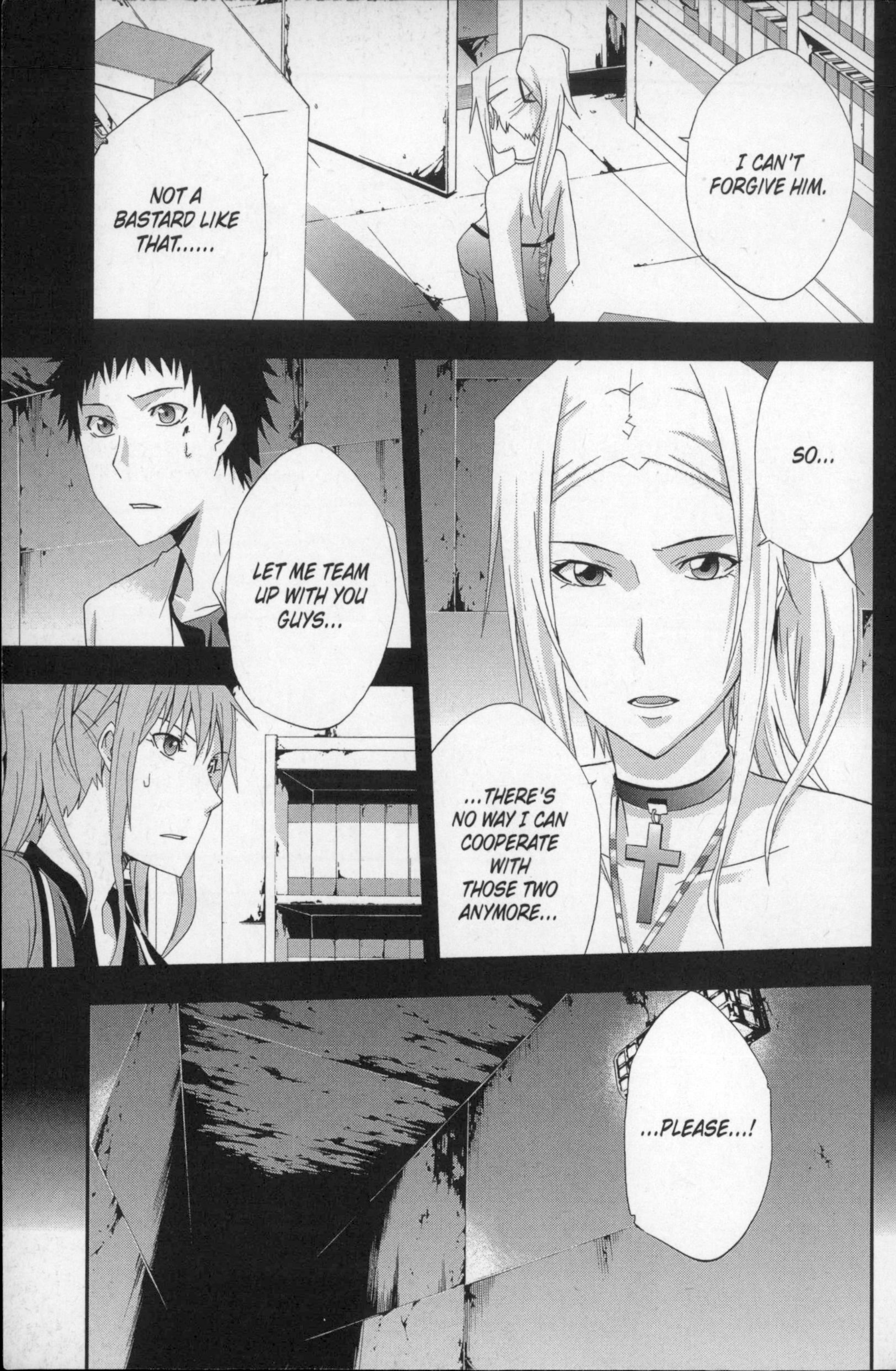
I CAN'T FORGIVE HIM.
NOT A BASTARD LIKE THAT......
SO...
...THERE'S NO WAY I CAN COOPERATE WITH THOSE TWO ANYMORE...
LET ME TEAM UP WITH YOU GUYS...
...PLEASE...!

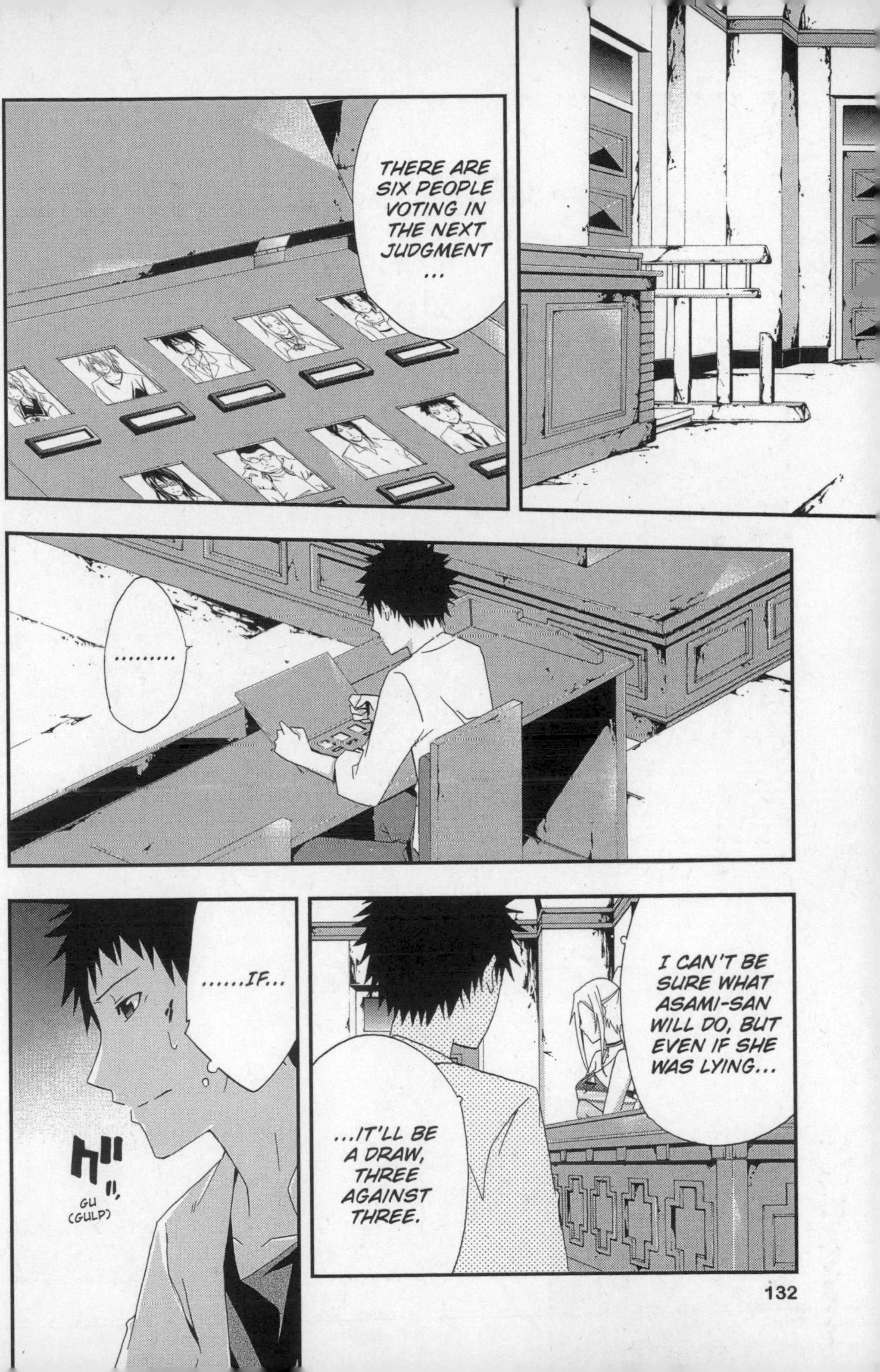
THERE ARE SIX PEOPLE VOTING IN THE NEXT JUDGMENT ...
....
I CAN'T BE SURE WHAT ASAMI-SAN WILL DO, BUT EVEN IF SHE WAS LYING...
...IT'LL BE A DRAW, THREE AGAINST THREE.
......IF...
GU (GULP)

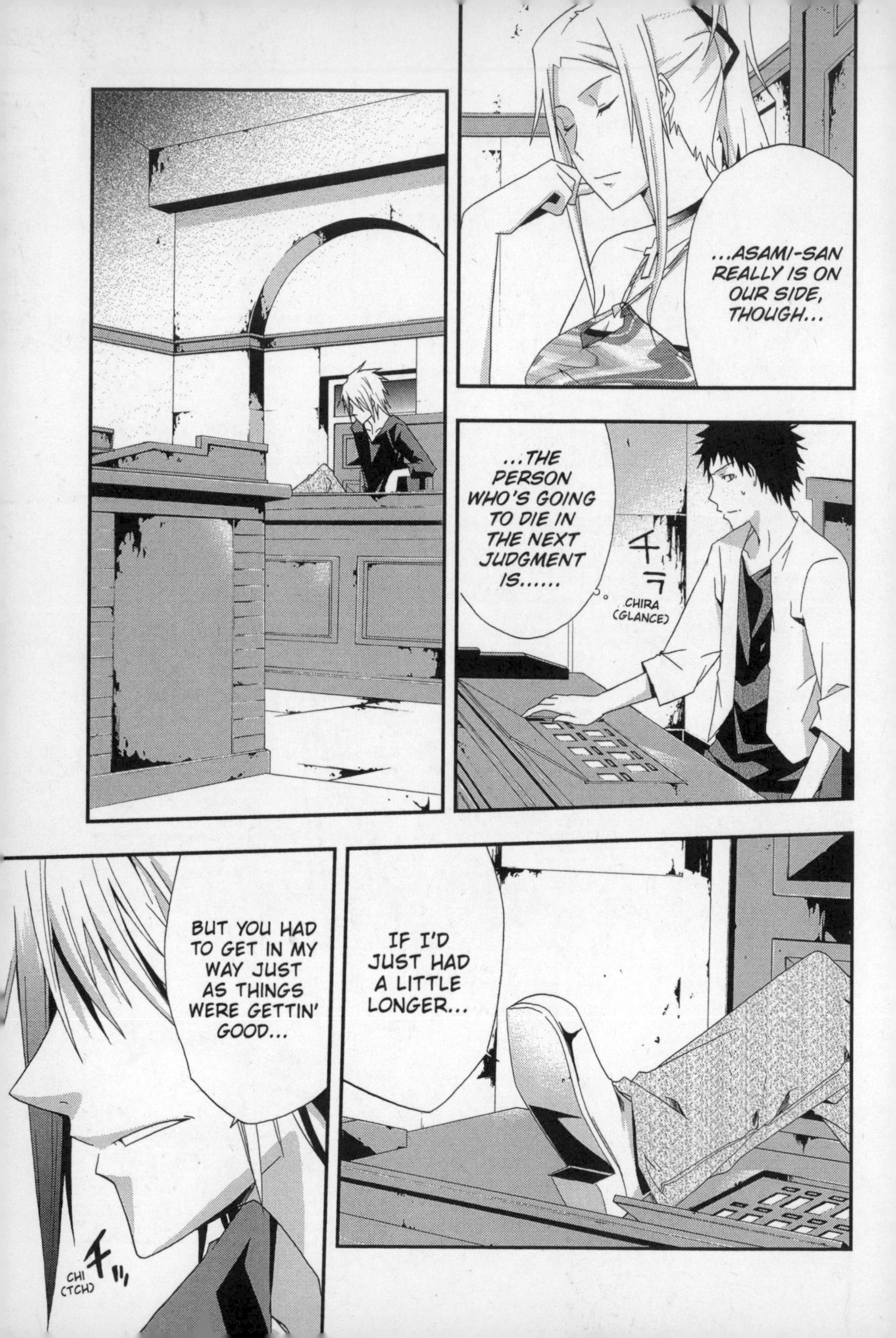
...ASAMI-SAN REALLY IS ON OUR SIDE, THOUGH...
...THE PERSON WHO'S GOING TO DIE IN THE NEXT JUDGMENT IS......
CHIRA (GLANCE)
IF I'D JUST HAD A LITTLE LONGER...
BUT YOU HAD TO GET IN MY WAY JUST AS THINGS WERE GETTIN' GOOD...
CHI (TCH)

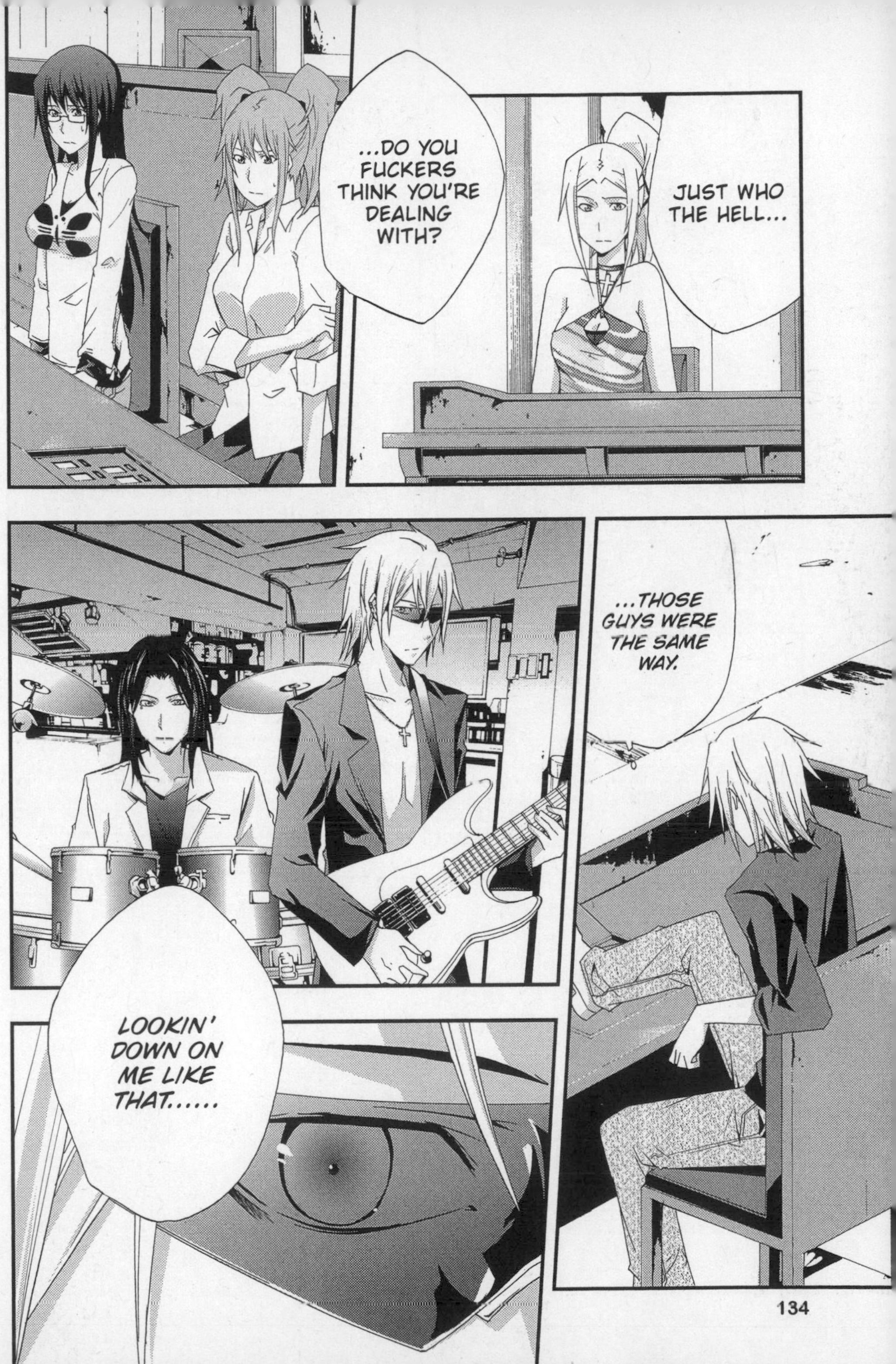
JUST WHO THE HELL...
...DO YOU FUCKERS THINK YOU'RE DEALING WITH?
...THOSE GUYS WERE THE SAME WAY.
LOOKIN' DOWN ON ME LIKE THAT......

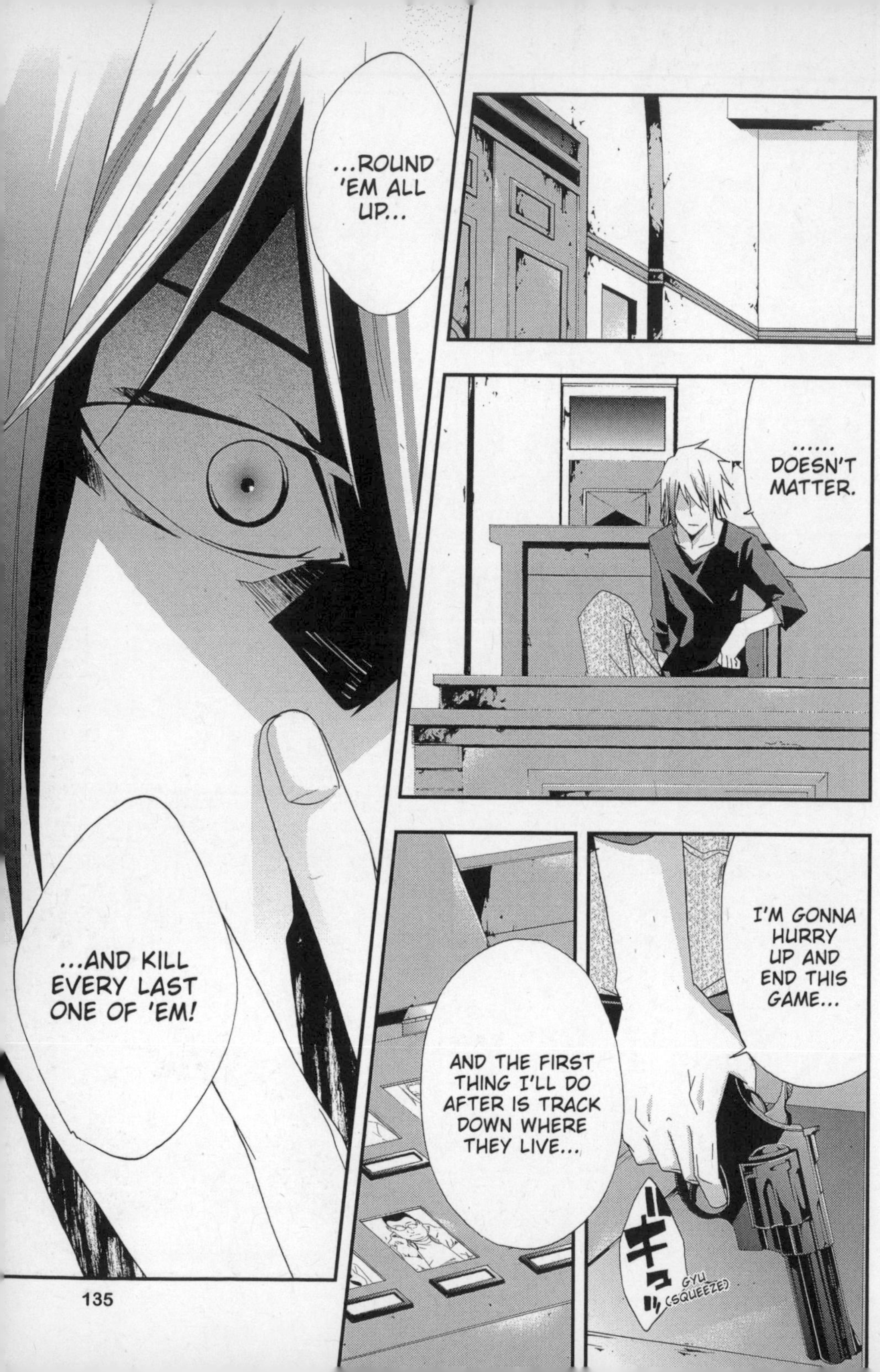
...... DOESN'T MATTER.
I'M GONNA HURRY UP AND END THIS GAME...
AND THE FIRST THING I'LL DO AFTER IS TRACK DOWN WHERE THEY LIVE...
GYU (SQUEEZE)
...ROUND 'EM ALL UP...
...AND KILL EVERY LAST ONE OF 'EM!

=BEEEP=

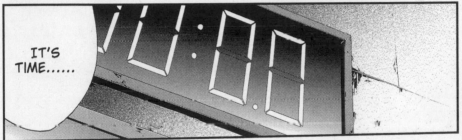

IT'S
TIME......

I GUESS
THIS TIME
THERE WON'T
BE ANY
TRICKS...

...AND IT
WILL JUST BE
A STRAIGHT-
FORWARD
JUDGMENT.

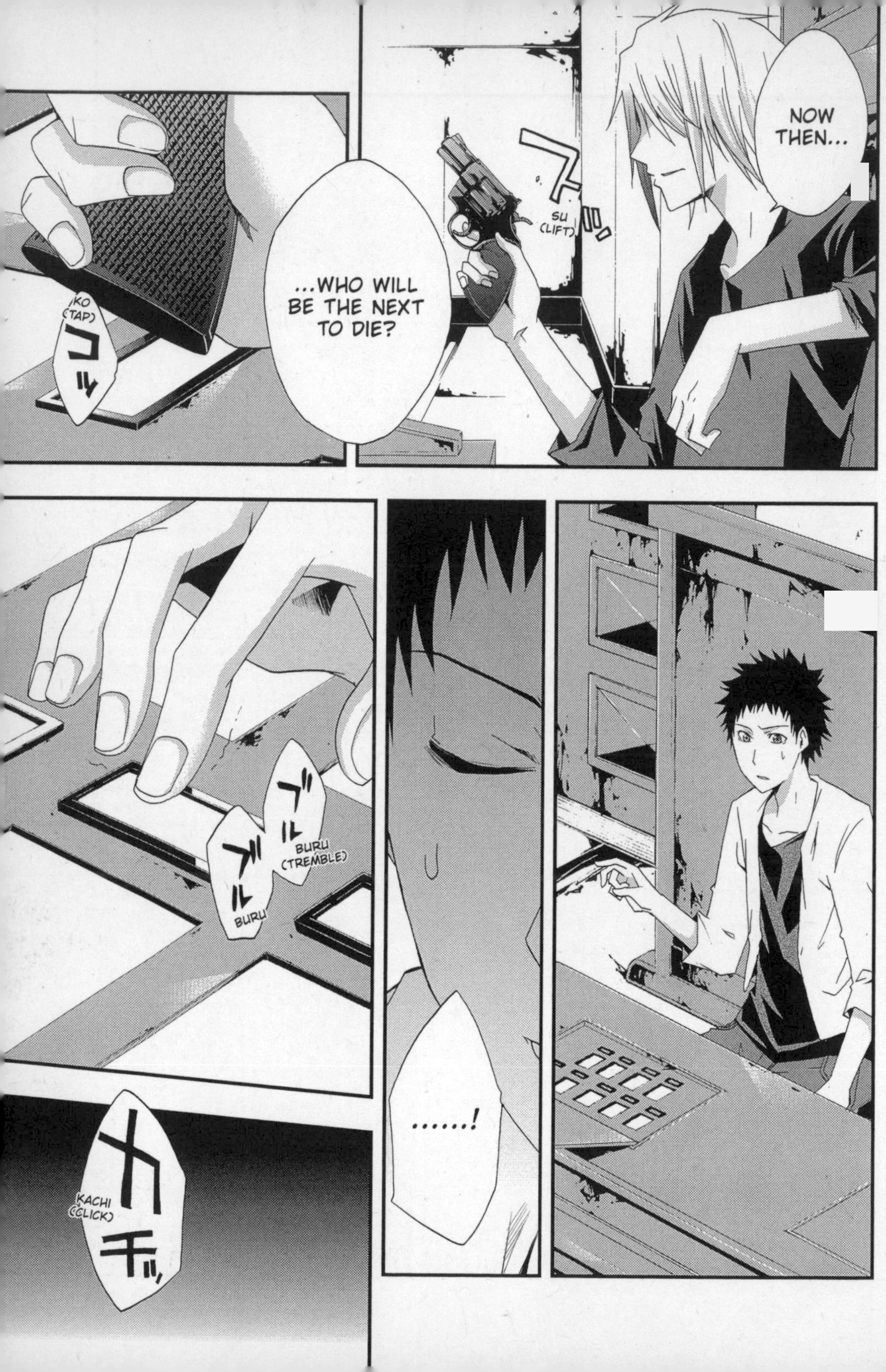
NOW THEN...
SU (LIFT)
...WHO WILL BE THE NEXT TO DIE?
KO (TAP)
......!
BURU (TREMBLE)
BURU
KACHI (CLICK)

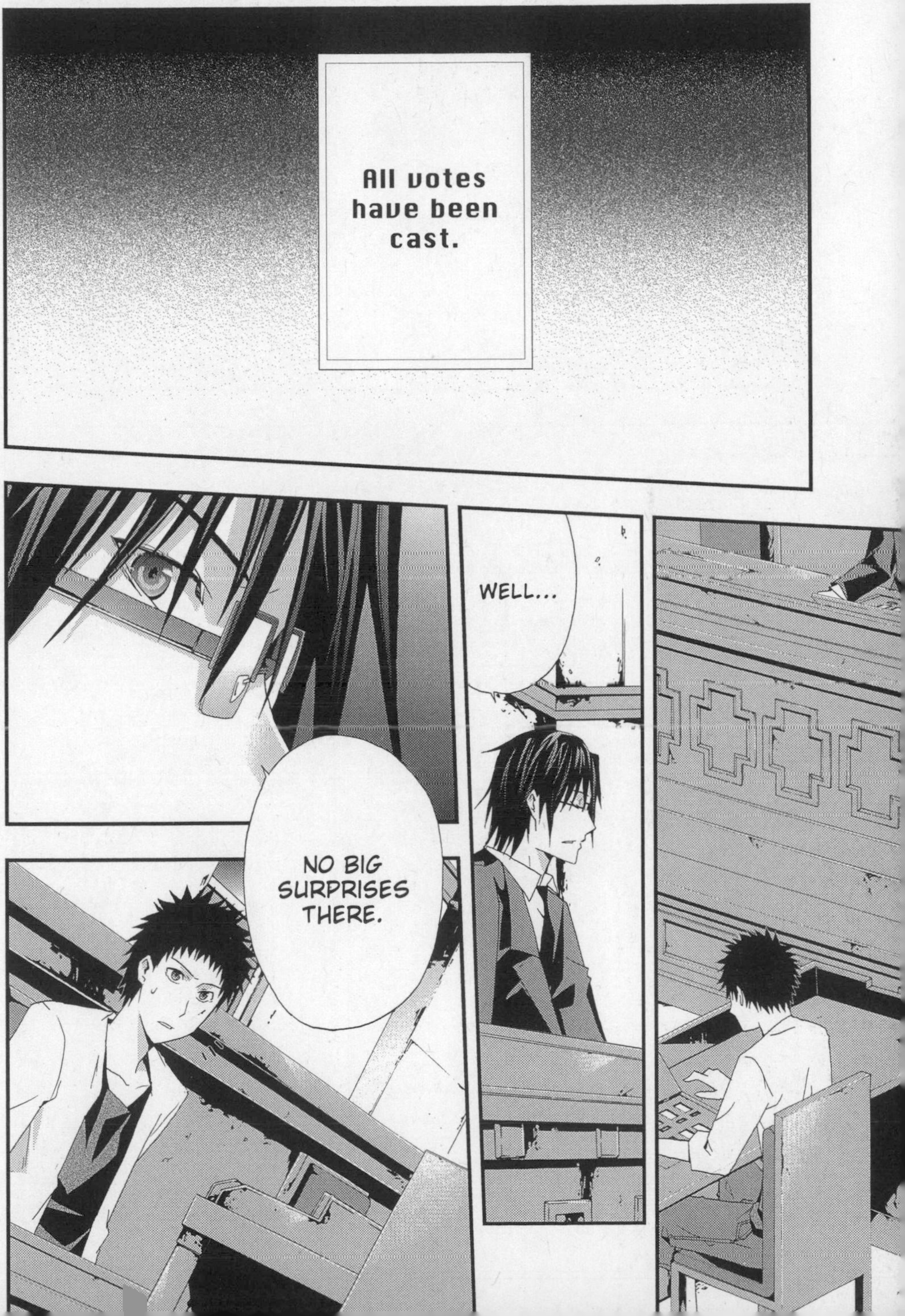
All votes have been cast.
WELL...
NO BIG SURPRISES THERE.

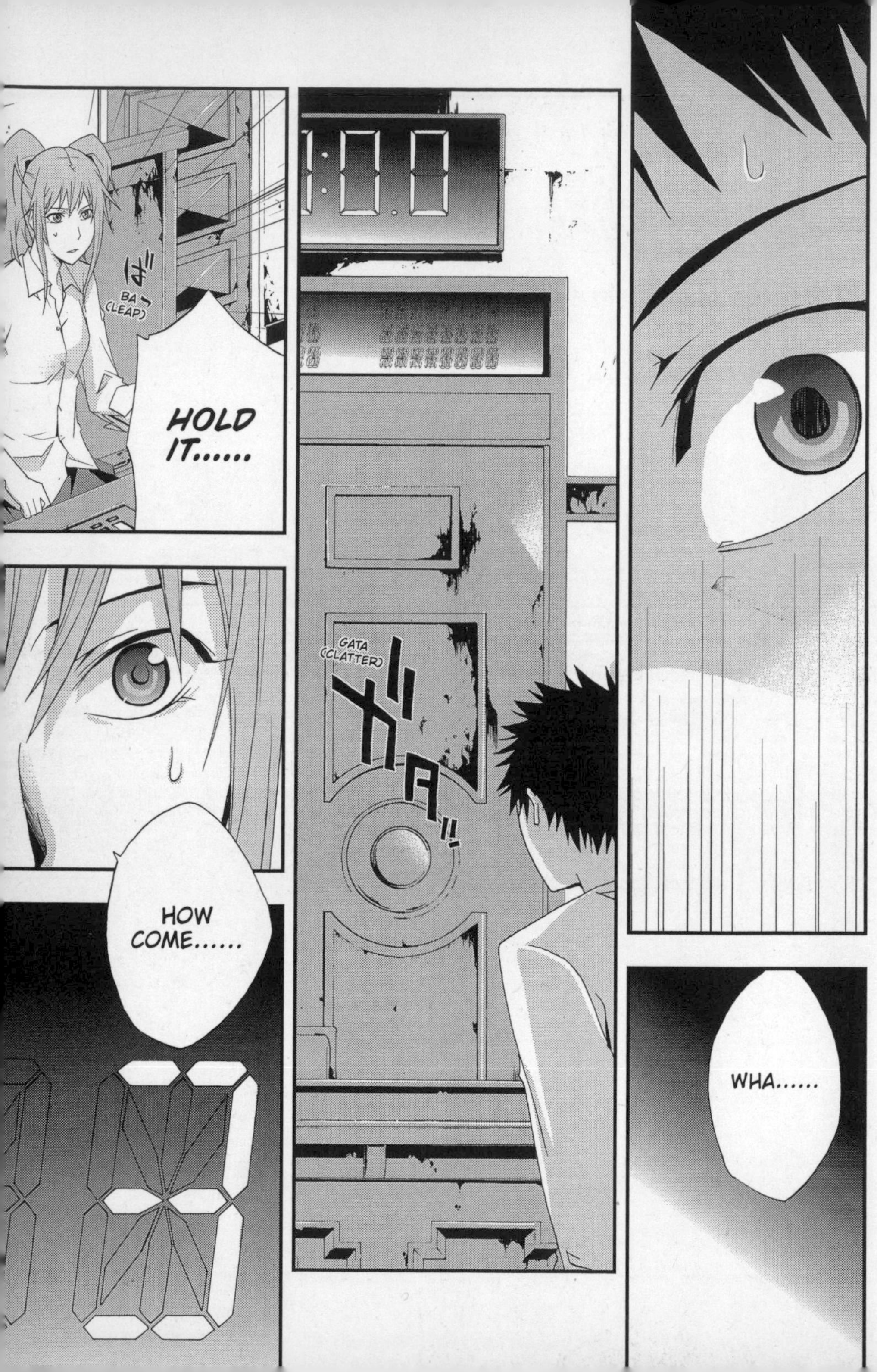
WHA......
ガタッ!!
GATA (CLATTER)
ばっ
BA (LEAP)
HOLD IT......
HOW COME......

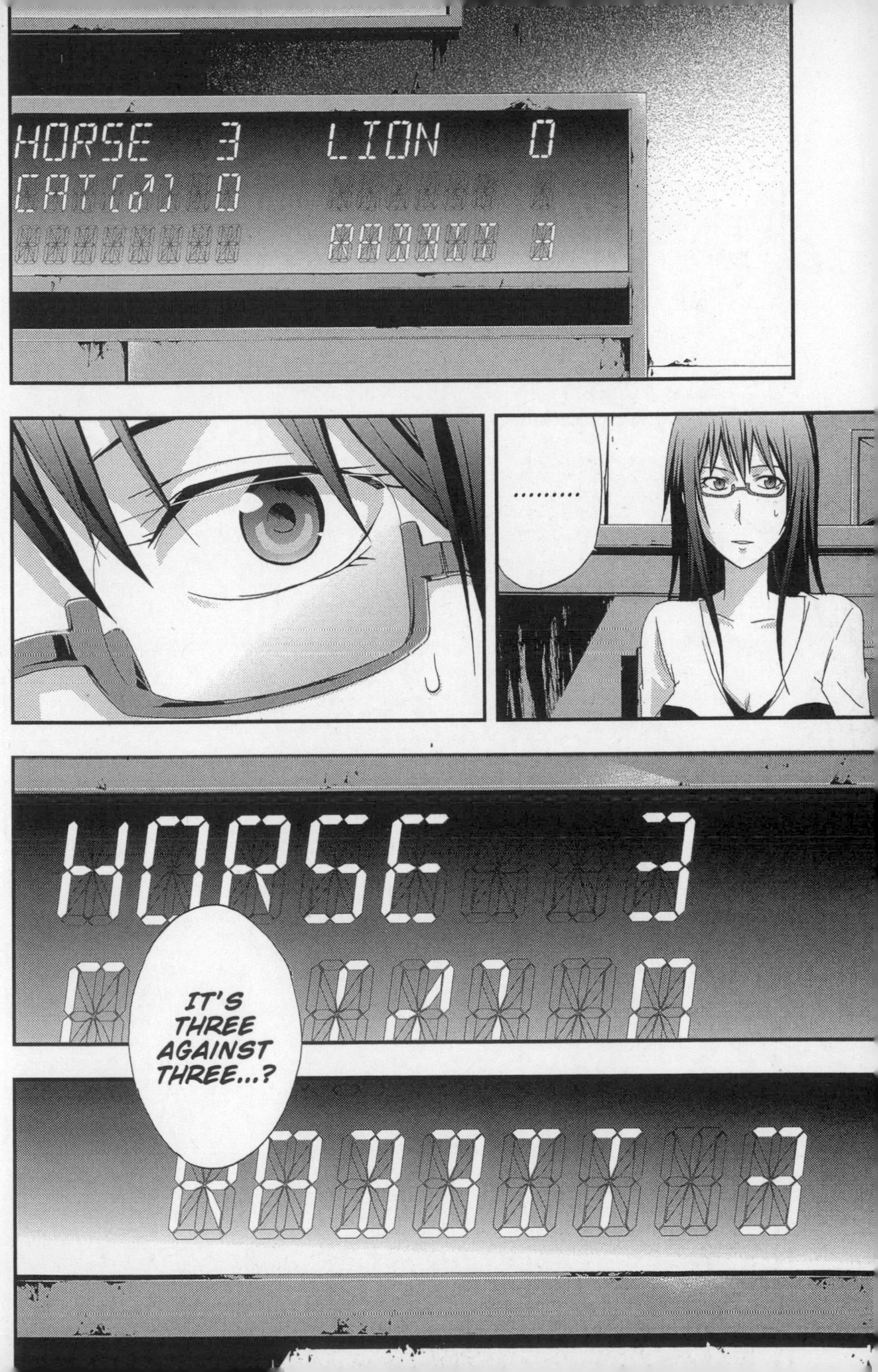
HORSE 3
LION 0
CAT[♂] 0
....
HORSE 3
IT'S THREE AGAINST THREE...?

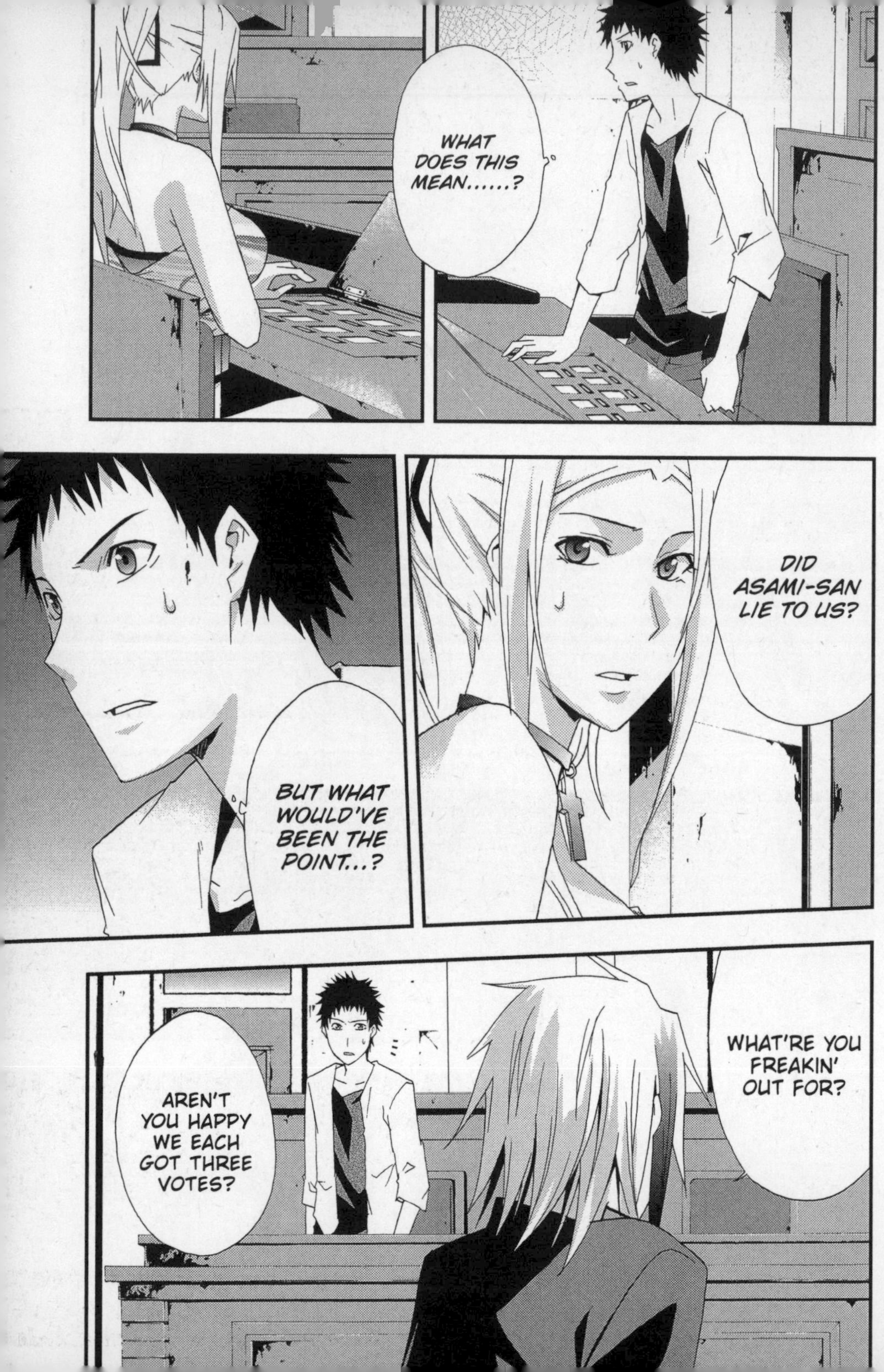
WHAT DOES THIS MEAN......?
DID ASAMI-SAN LIE TO US?
BUT WHAT WOULD'VE BEEN THE POINT...?
WHAT'RE YOU FREAKIN' OUT FOR?
AREN'T YOU HAPPY WE EACH GOT THREE VOTES?

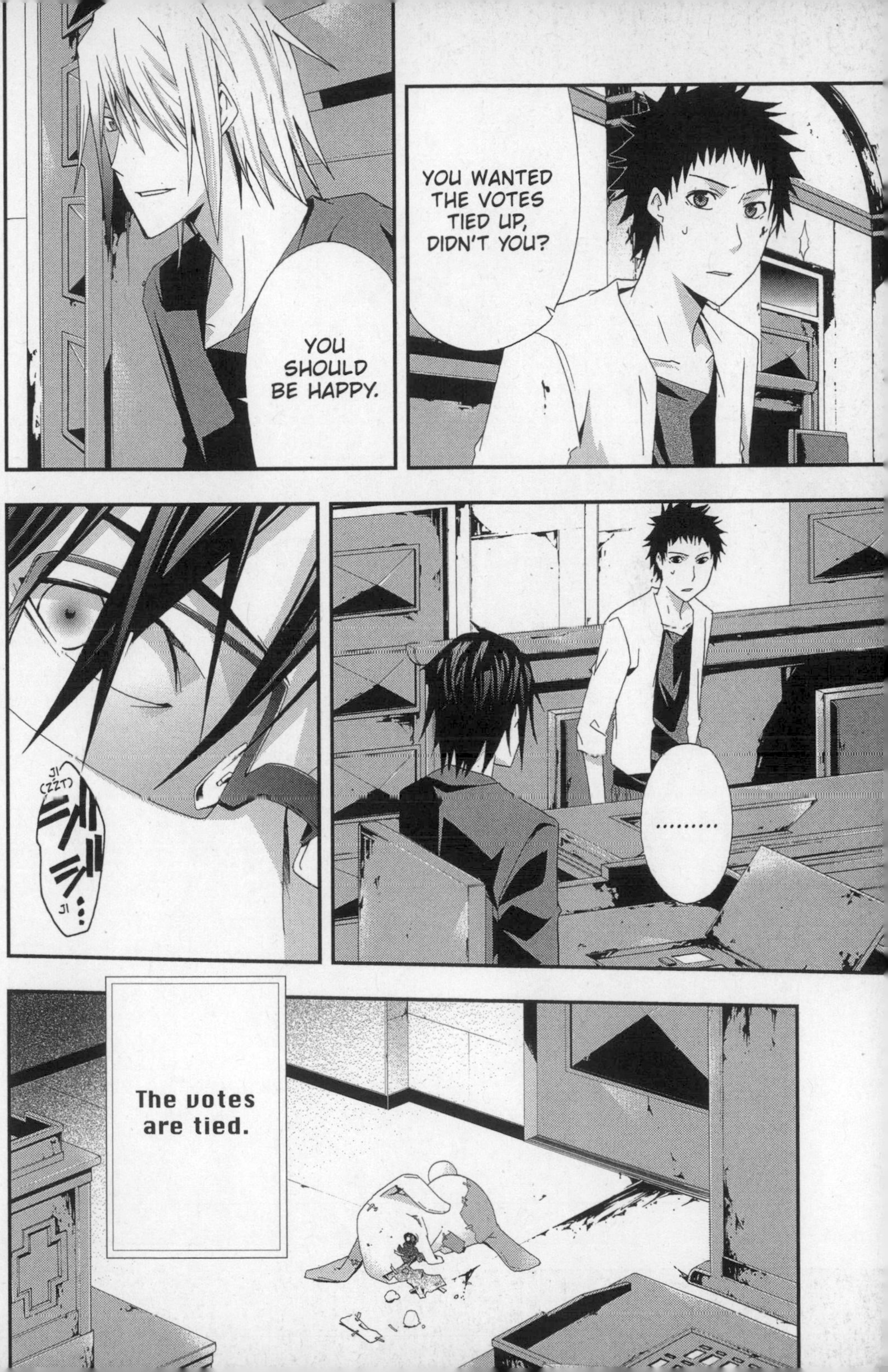
YOU WANTED THE VOTES TIED UP, DIDN'T YOU?
YOU SHOULD BE HAPPY.
....
JI (ZZZT) JI
The votes are tied.

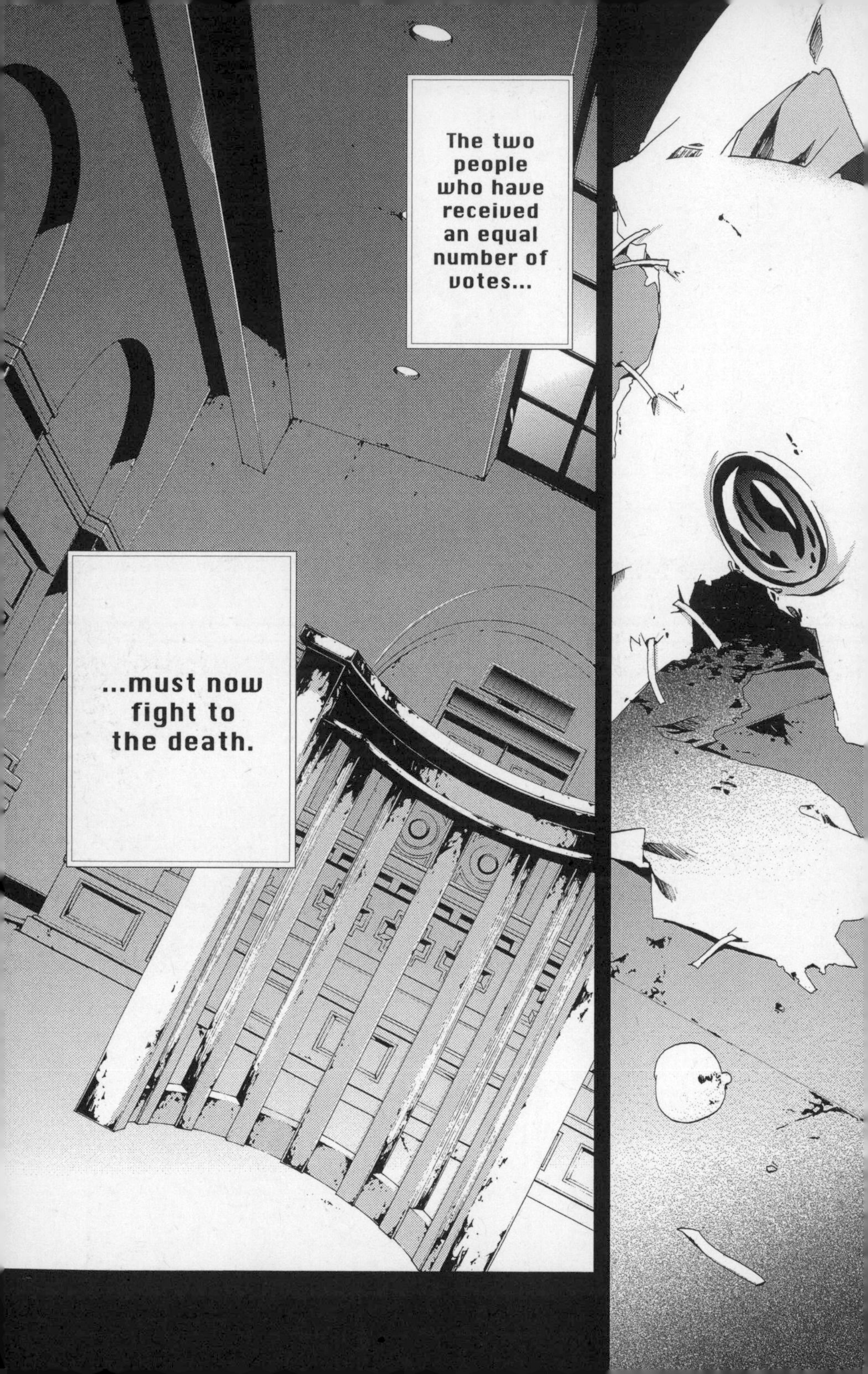
The two people who have received an equal number of votes...
...must now fight to the death.

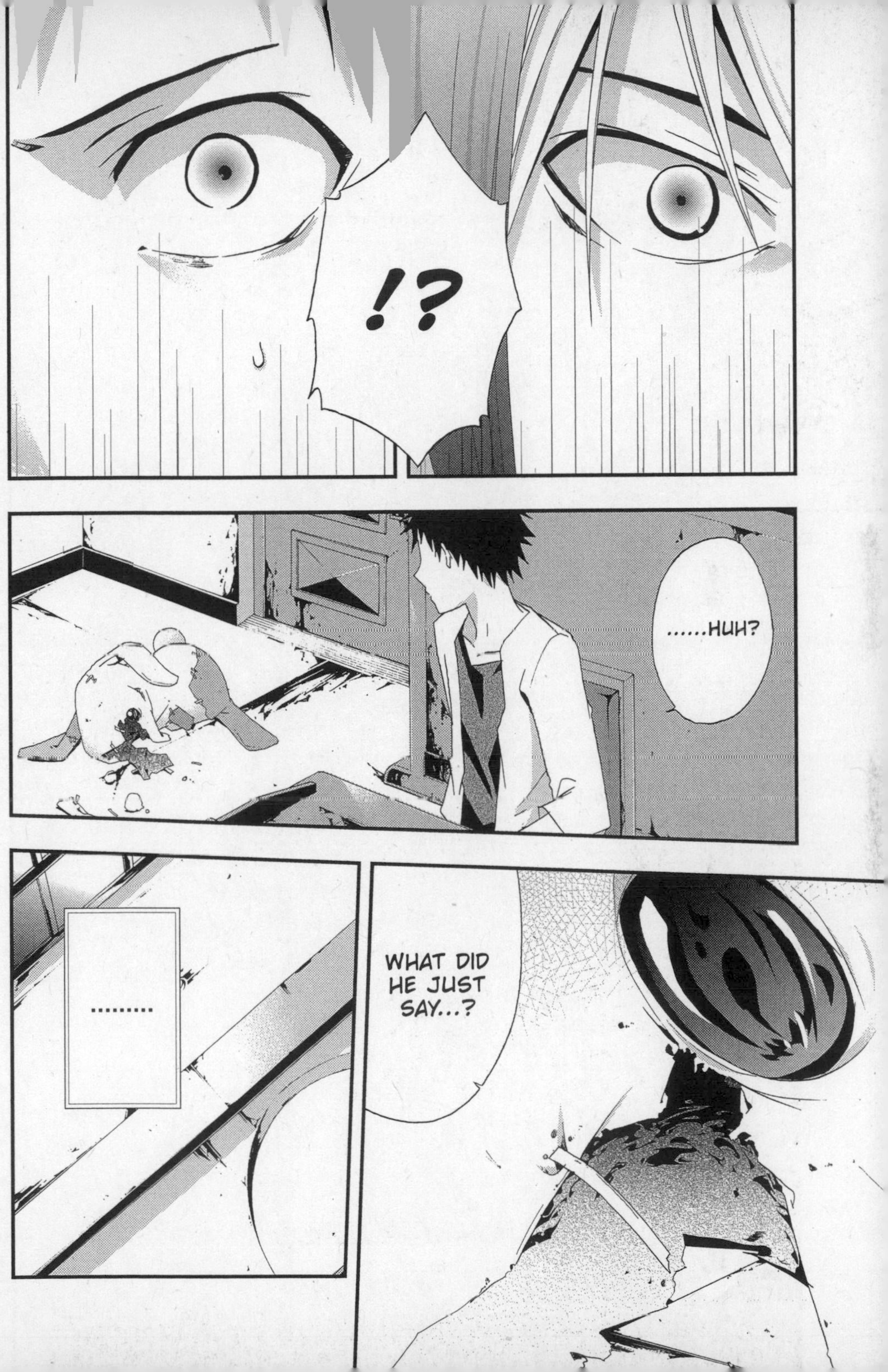
!?
......HUH?
WHAT DID HE JUST SAY...?
....

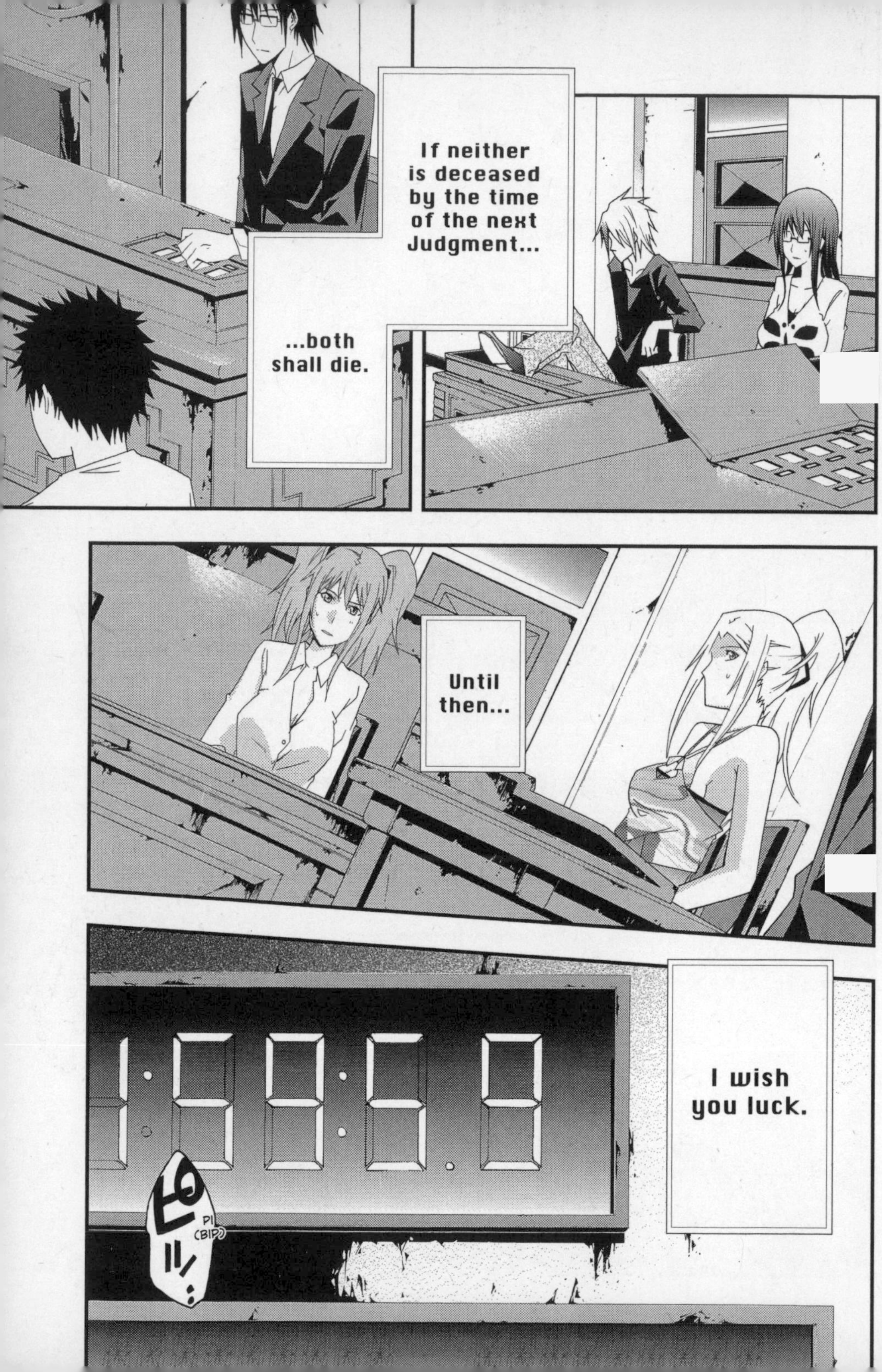
If neither is deceased by the time of the next Judgment...
...both shall die.
Until then...
I wish you luck.
PI (BIP)

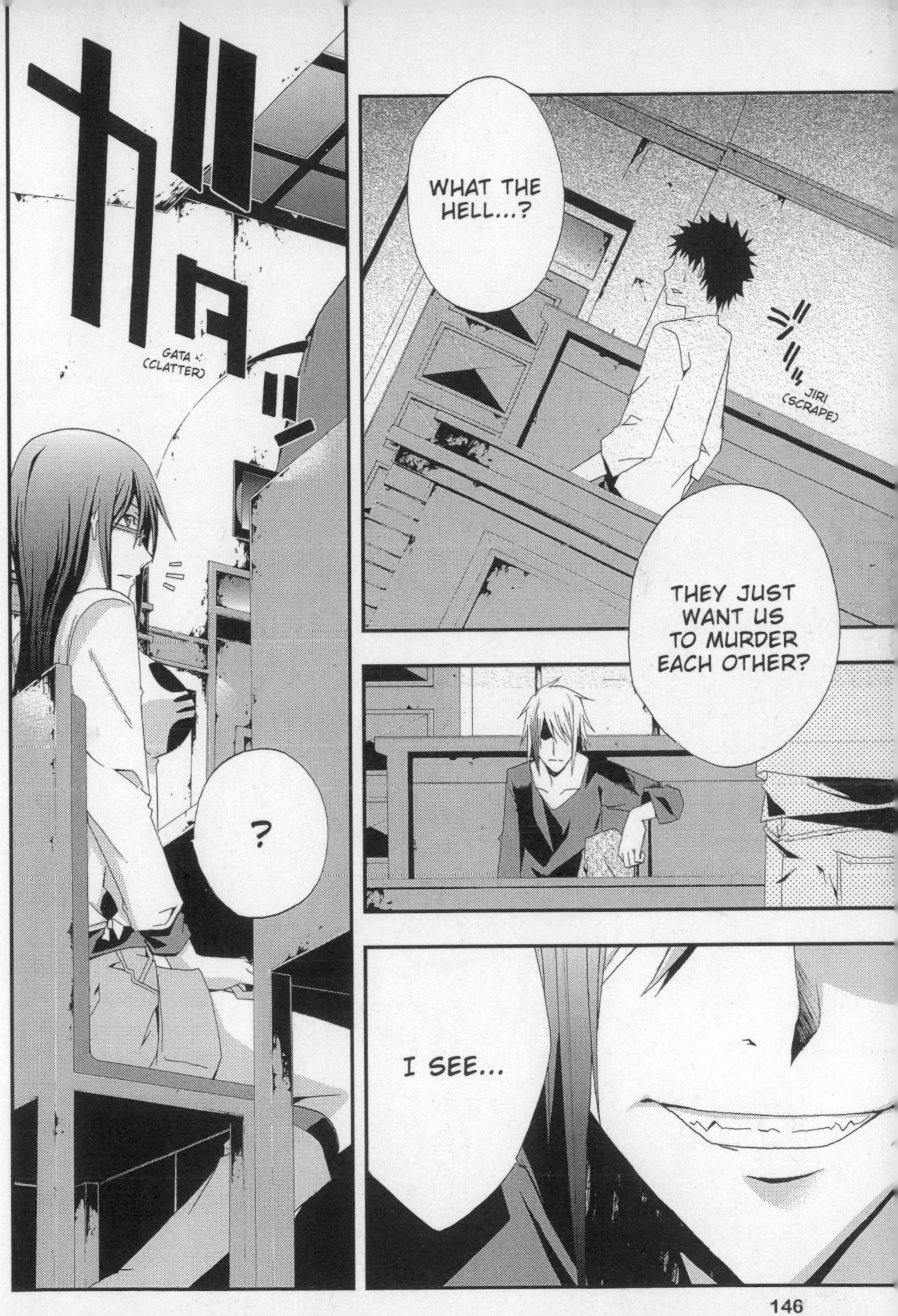
WHAT THE HELL...?
ジリ
JIRI (SCRAPE)
THEY JUST WANT US TO MURDER EACH OTHER?
I SEE...
ガタッ
GATA (CLATTER)
?

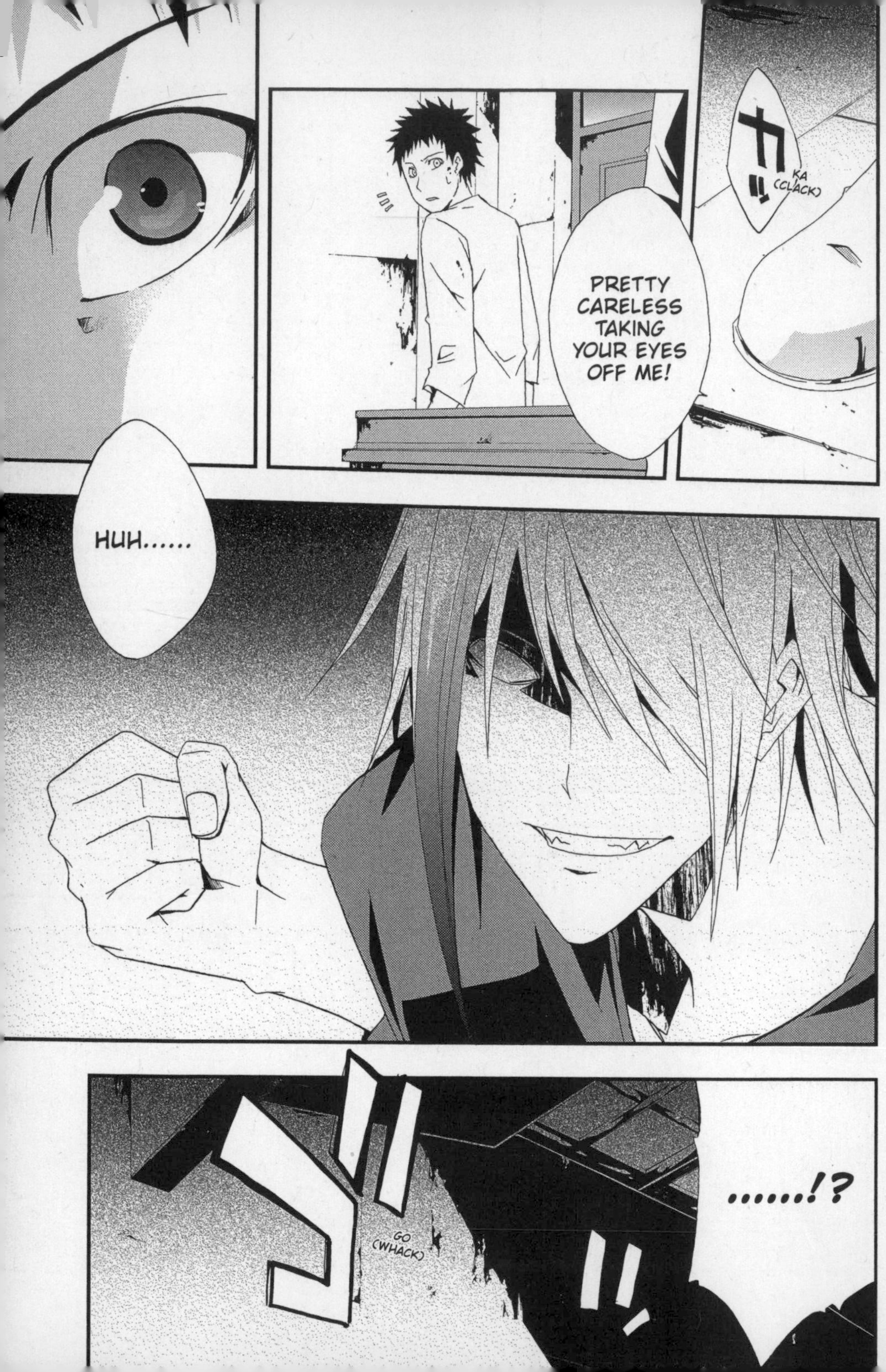
KA (CLACK)
PRETTY CARELESS TAKING YOUR EYES OFF ME!
HUH......
......!?
GO (WHACK)

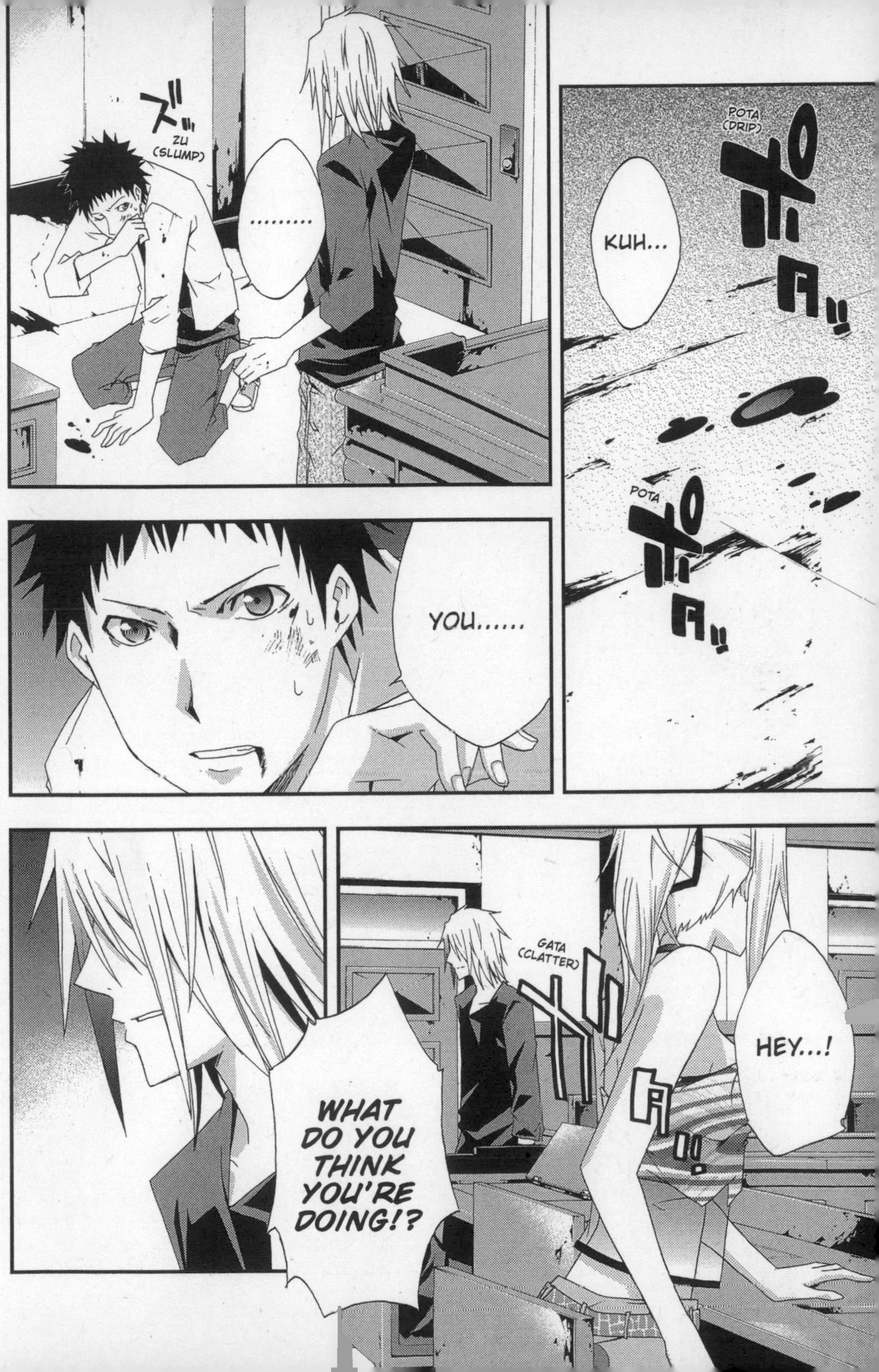
POTA (DRIP)
KUH...
POTA
ZU (SLUMP)
....
YOU......
GATA (CLATTER)
HEY...!
WHAT DO YOU THINK YOU'RE DOING!?

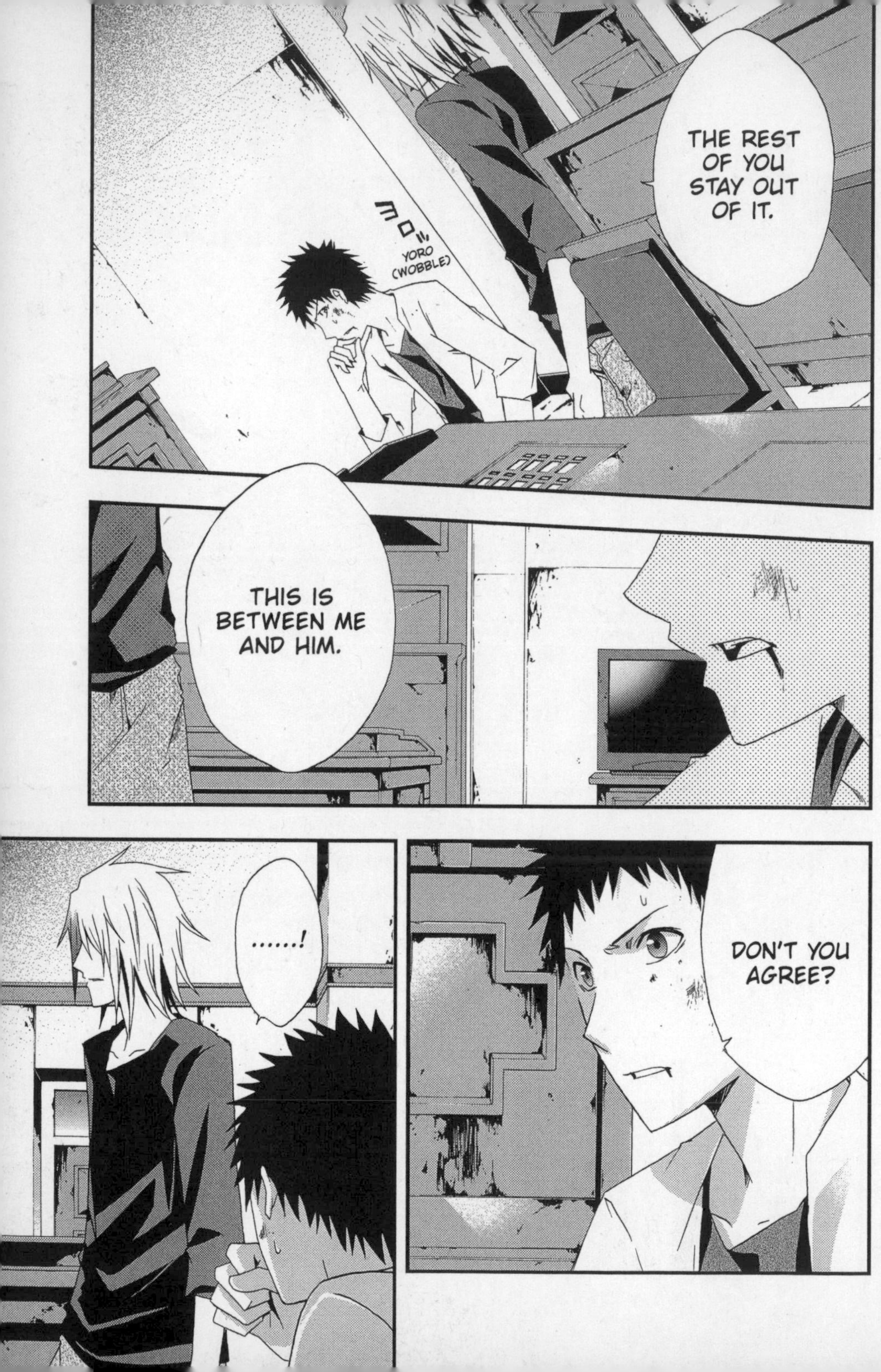
THE REST OF YOU STAY OUT OF IT.
ヨロ
YORO (WOBBLE)
THIS IS BETWEEN ME AND HIM.
DON'T YOU AGREE?
......!

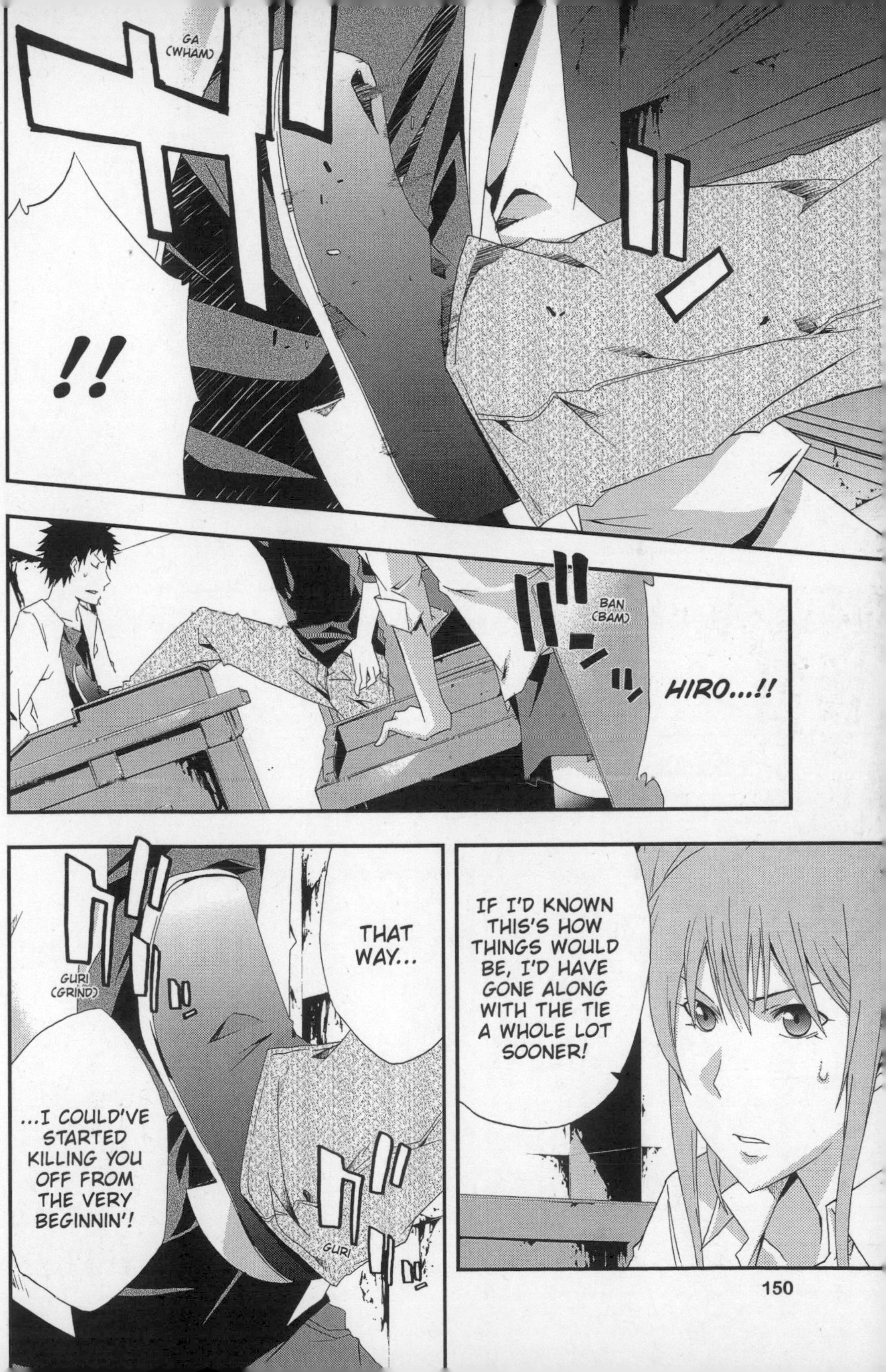
GA (WHAM)
!!
BAN (BAM)
HIRO...!!
IF I'D KNOWN THIS'S HOW THINGS WOULD BE, I'D HAVE GONE ALONG WITH THE TIE A WHOLE LOT SOONER!
THAT WAY...
GURI (GRIND)
...I COULD'VE STARTED KILLING YOU OFF FROM THE VERY BEGINNIN'!
GURI

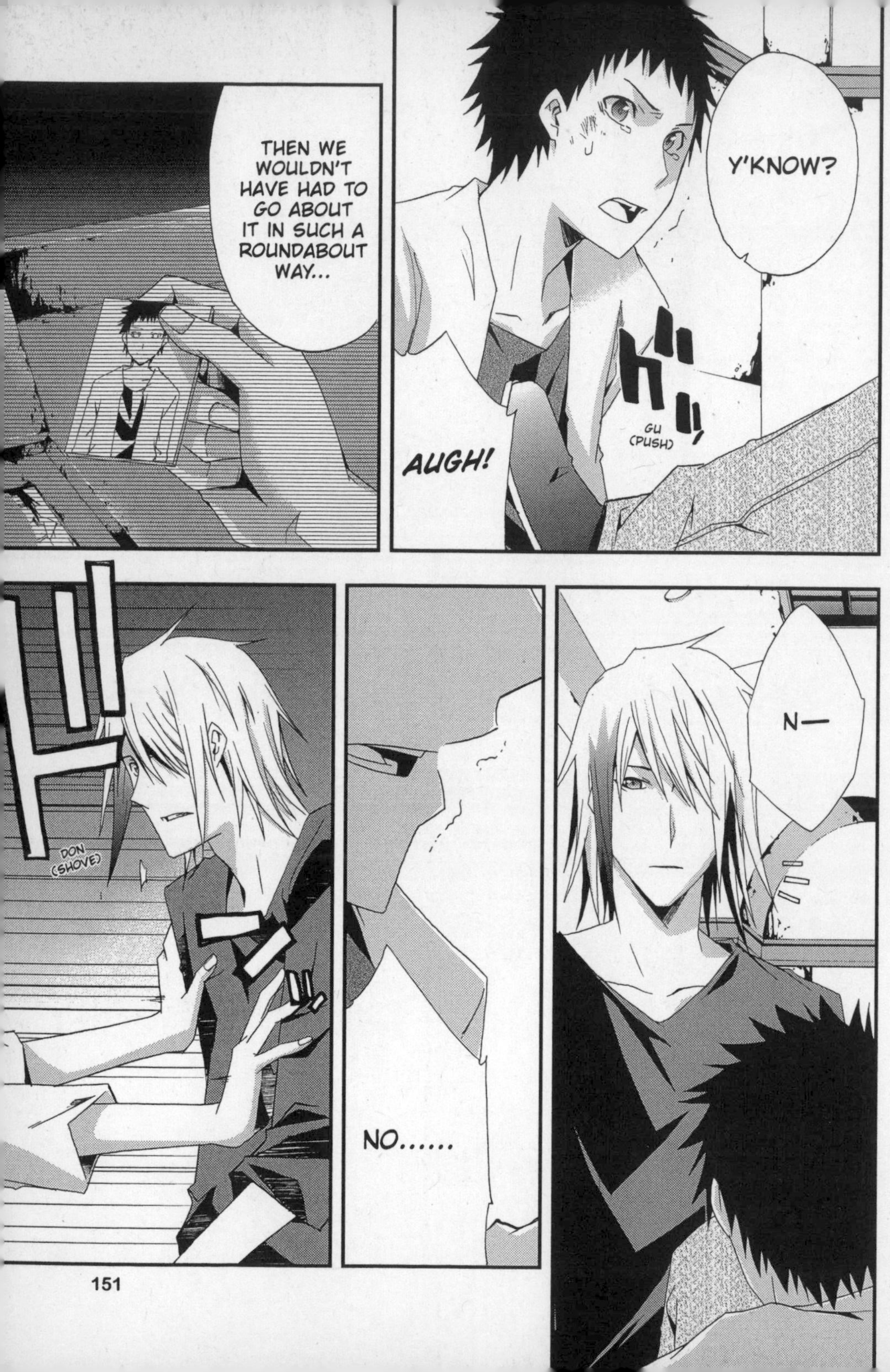
Y'KNOW?
GU (PUSH)
AUGH!
THEN WE WOULDN'T HAVE HAD TO GO ABOUT IT IN SUCH A ROUNDABOUT WAY...
N—
NO......
DON (SHOVE)

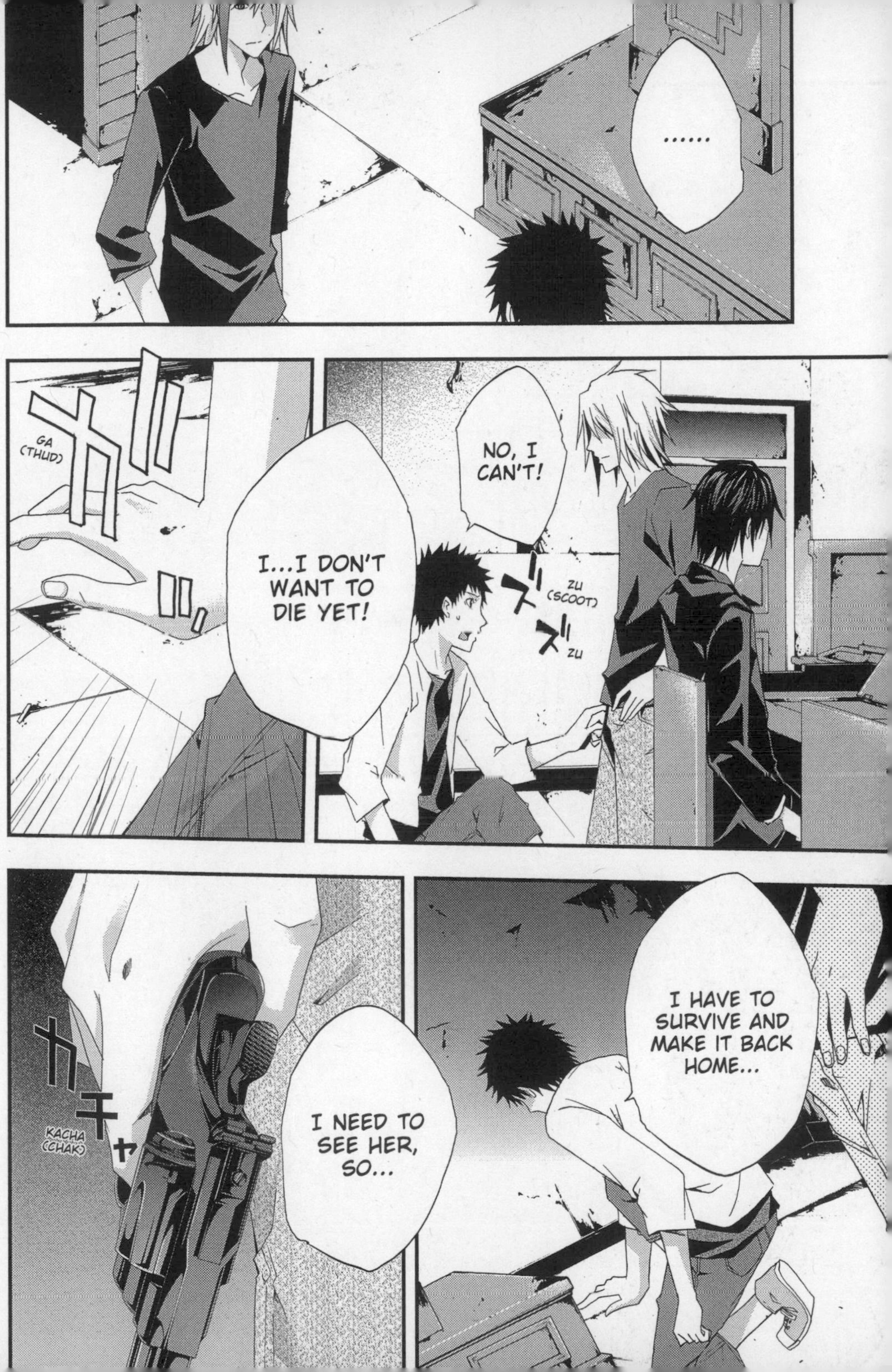
……
NO, I CAN'T!
I...I DON'T WANT TO DIE YET!
ズッ
ZU (SCOOT)
ズッ
ZU
ガッ
GA (THUD)
I HAVE TO SURVIVE AND MAKE IT BACK HOME...
I NEED TO SEE HER, SO...
カチャ
KACHA (CHAK)

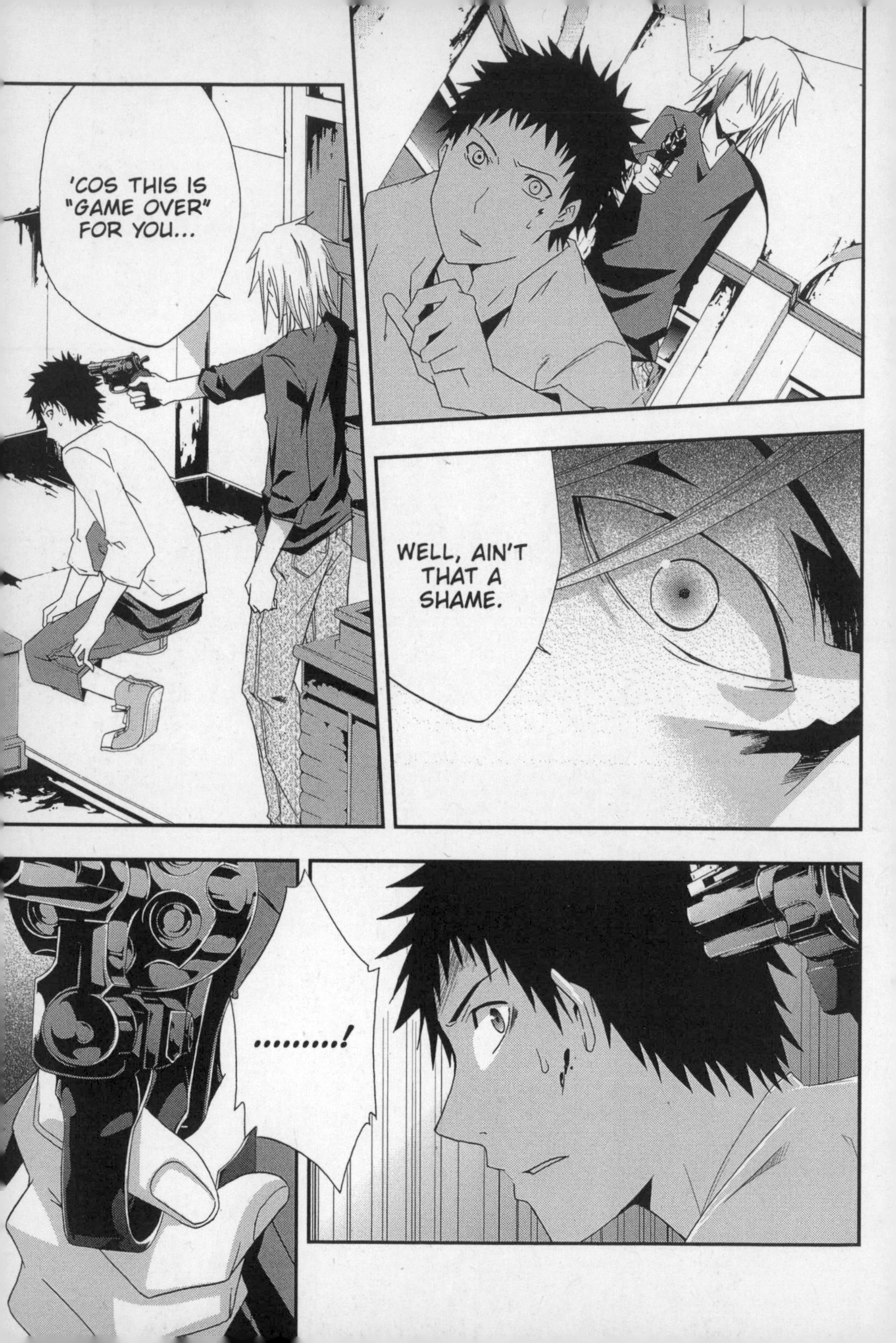
WELL, AIN'T THAT A SHAME.
'COS THIS IS "GAME OVER" FOR YOU...
.........!

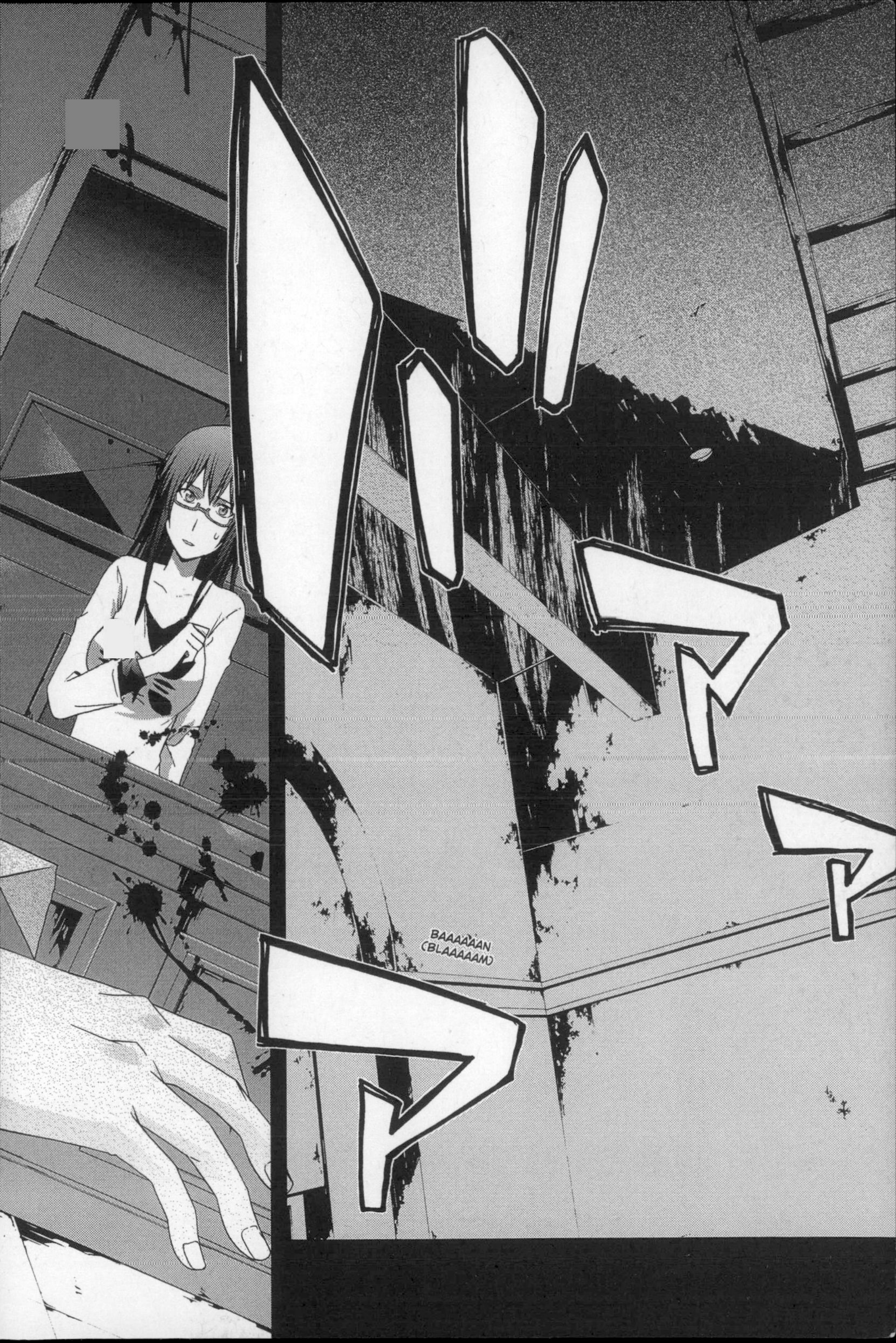
BAAAAAAN
(BLAAAAAM)

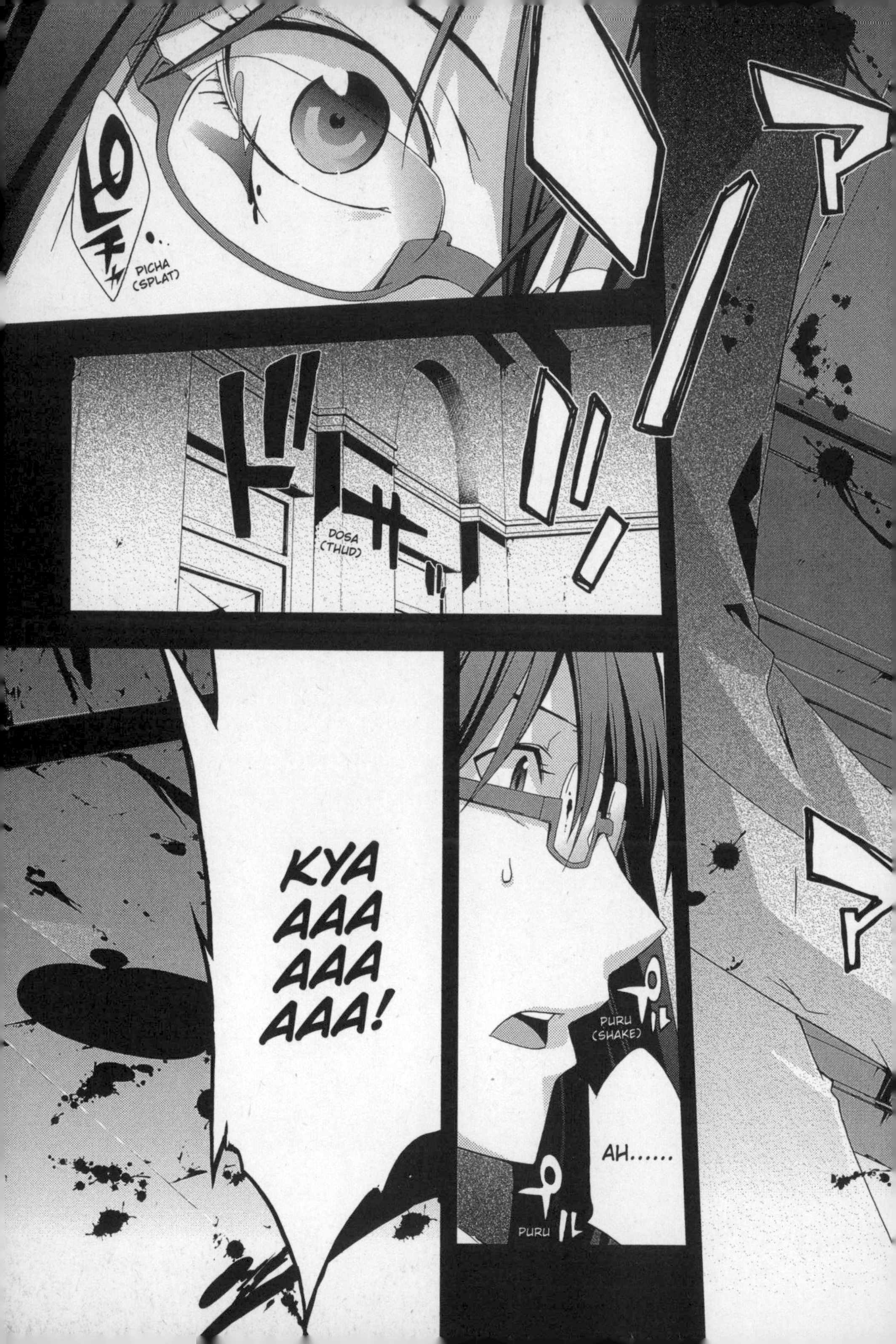
PICHA (SPLAT)
DOSA (THUD)
PURU (SHAKE)
AH......
PURU
KYA AAA AAA AAA!

JUDGE

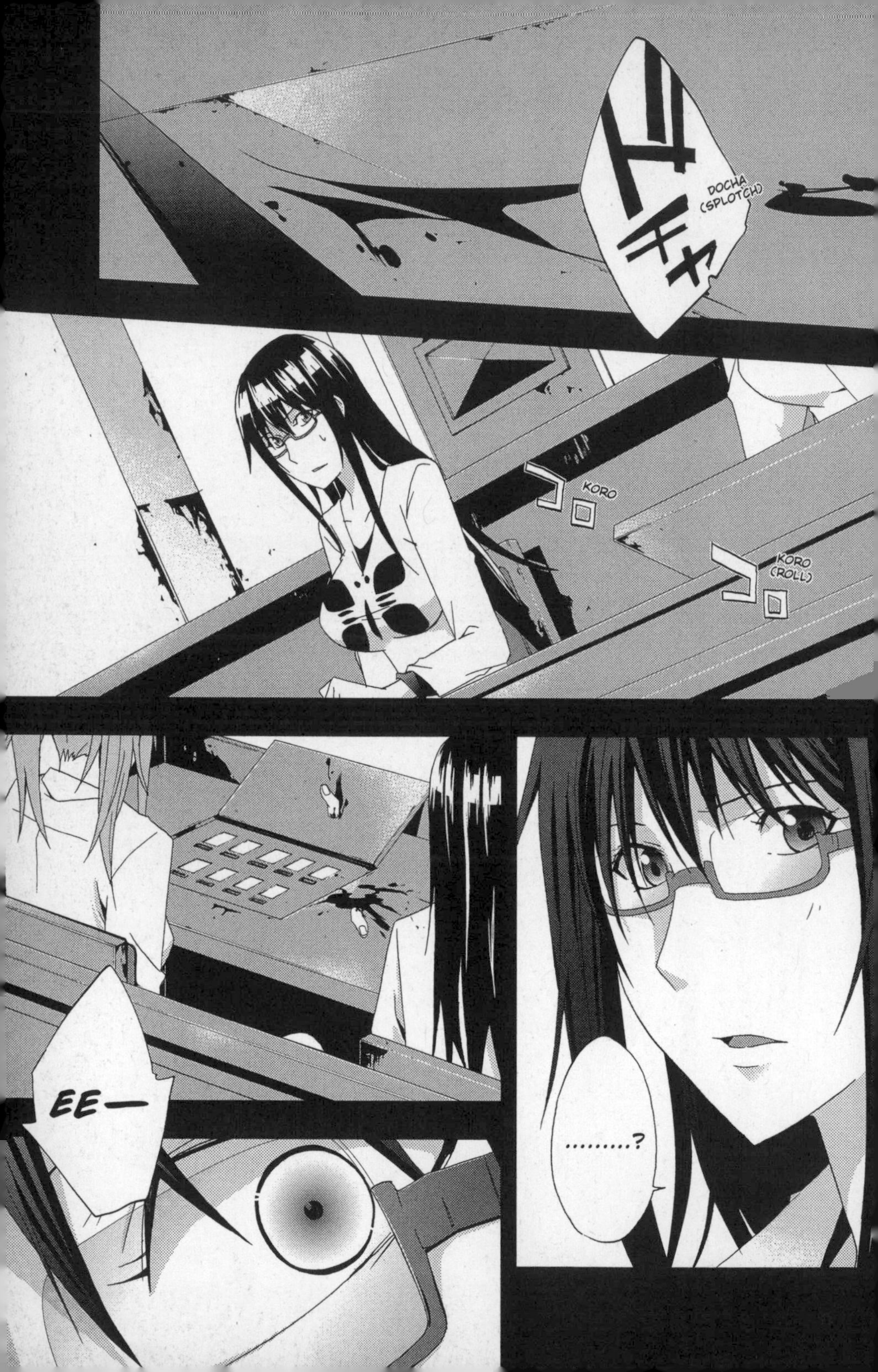
ドチャ
DOCHA (SPLOTCH)
コロ
KORO
コロ
KORO (ROLL)
..........?
EE—

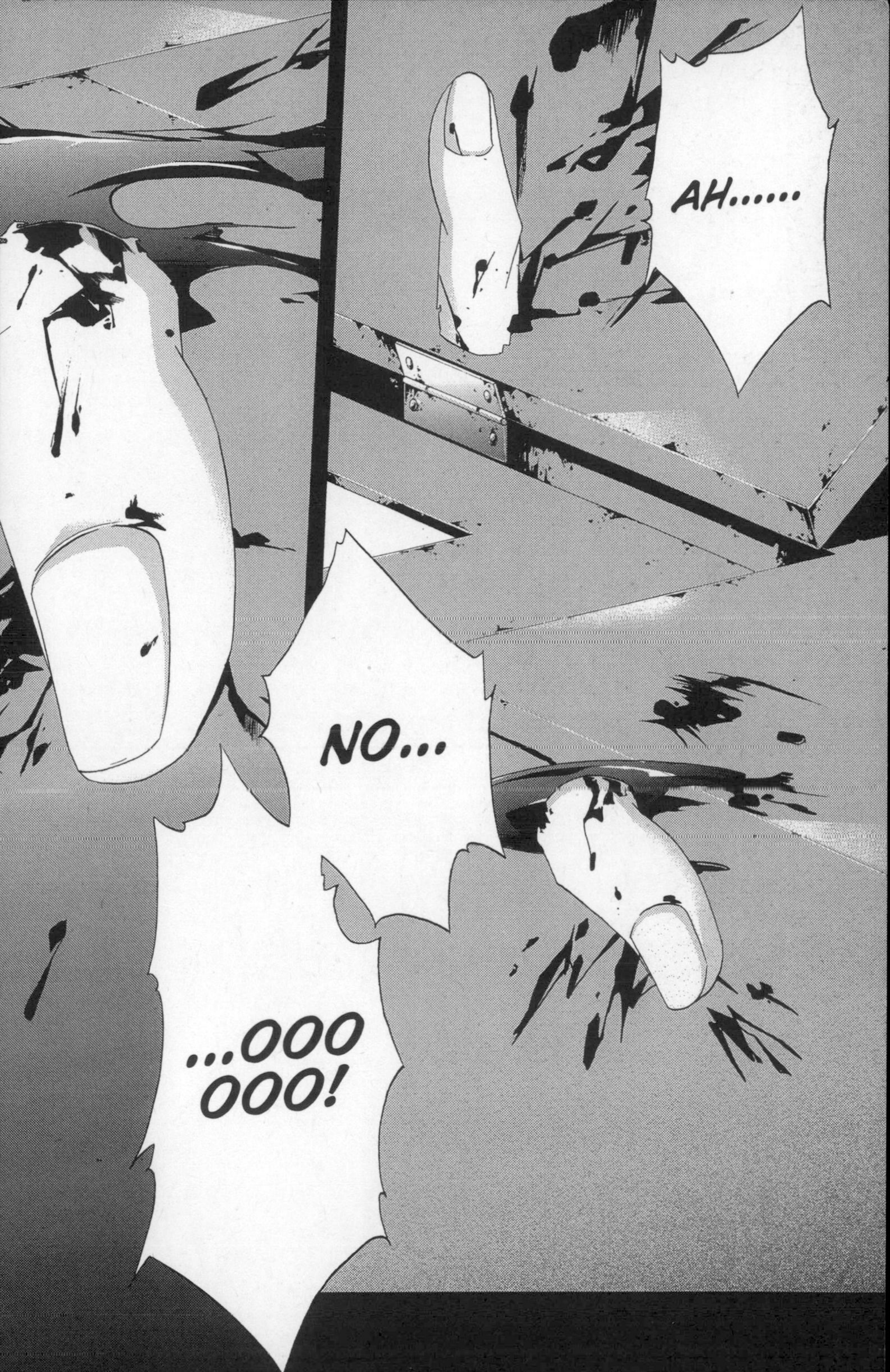
AH......
NO...
...OOO OOO!

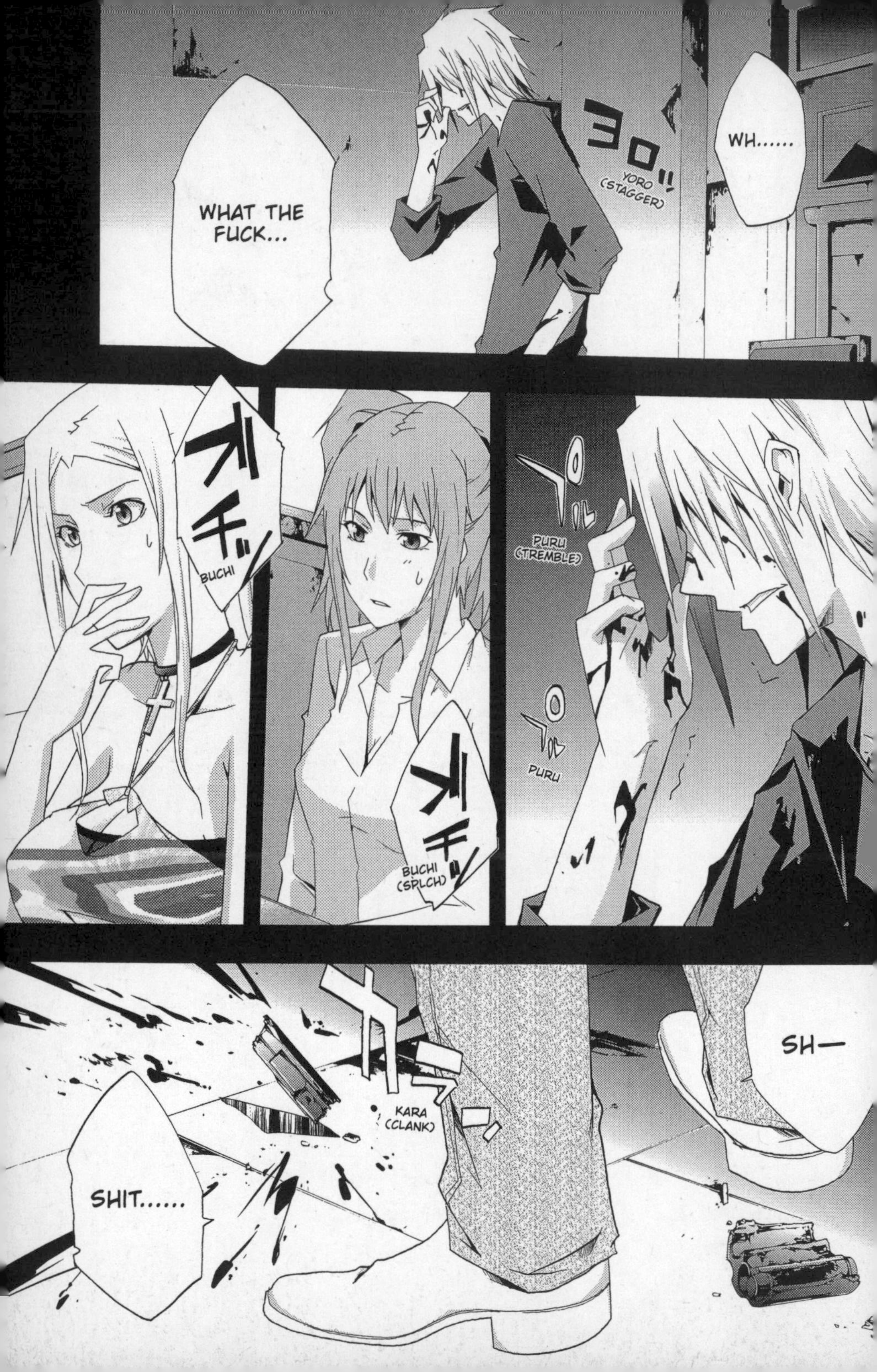

WH......
YORO (STAGGER)
WHAT THE FUCK...
PURU (TREMBLE)
PURU
BUCHI (SPLCH)
BUCHI
SH—
KARA (CLANK)
SHIT......

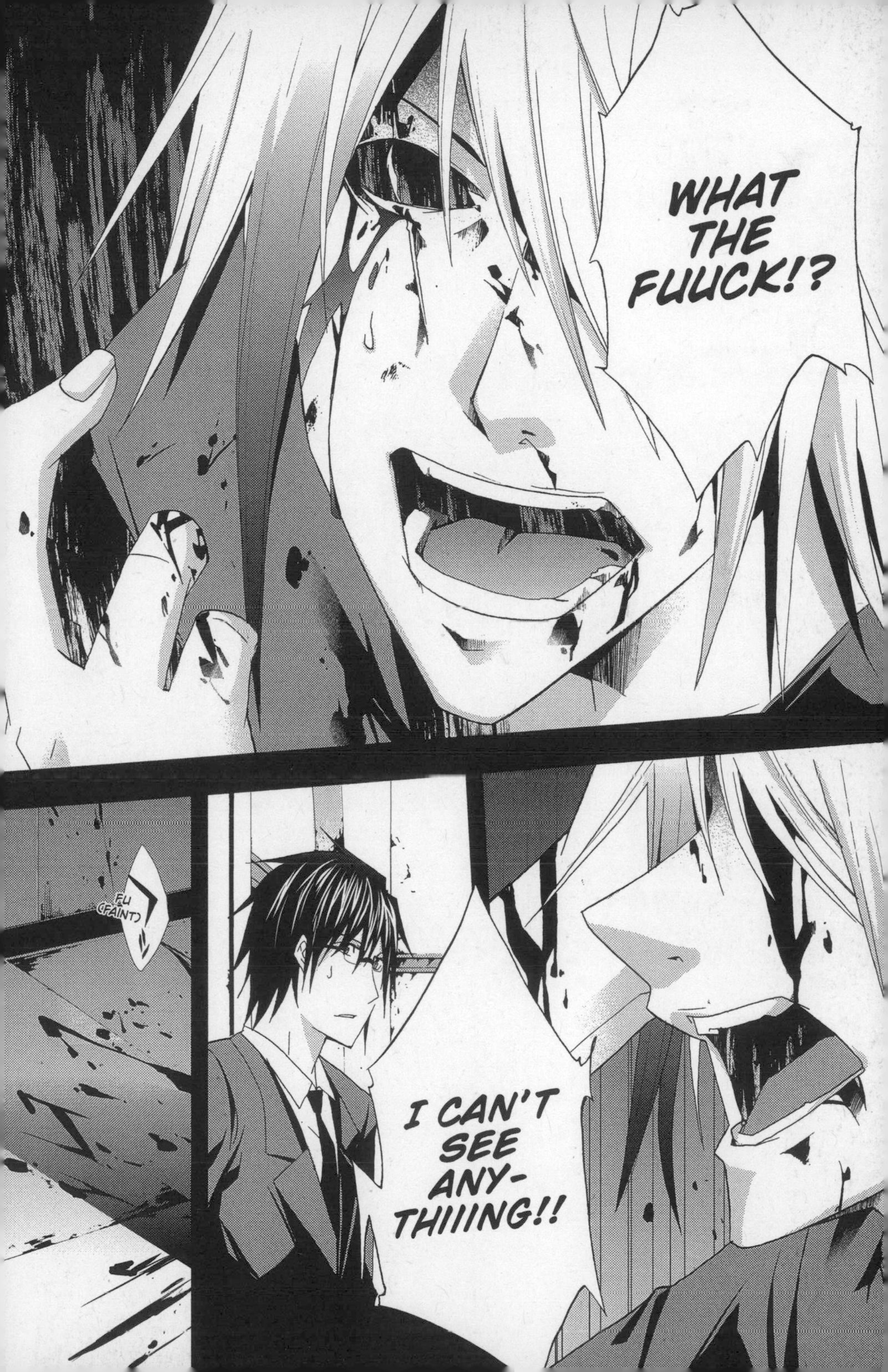
WHAT THE FUUCK!?
I CAN'T SEE ANY-THIIING!!
FU (FAINT)

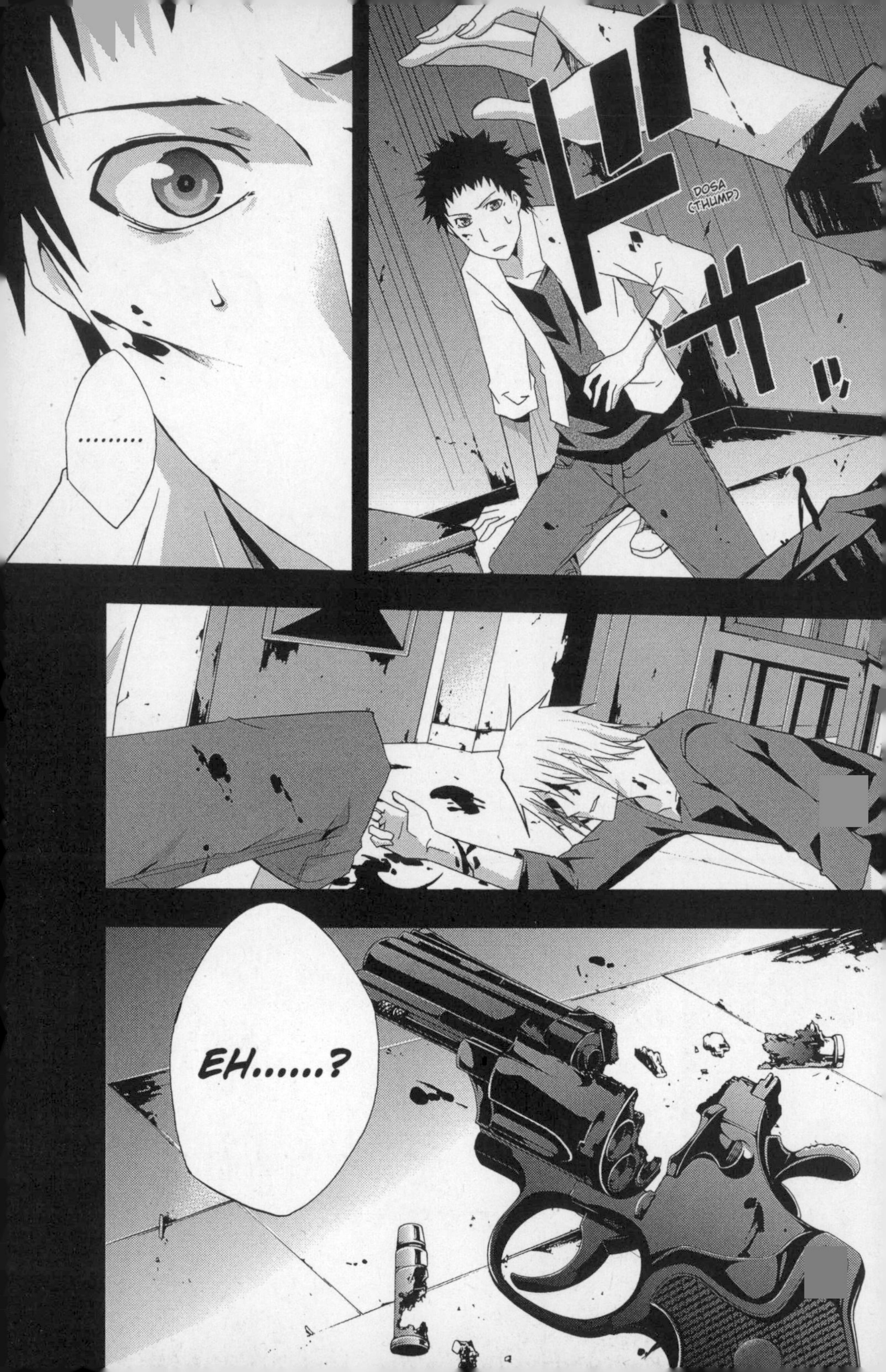
ドサッ
DOSA
(THUMP)
....
EH......?

CHAPTER 20 MATERIAL EVIDENCE

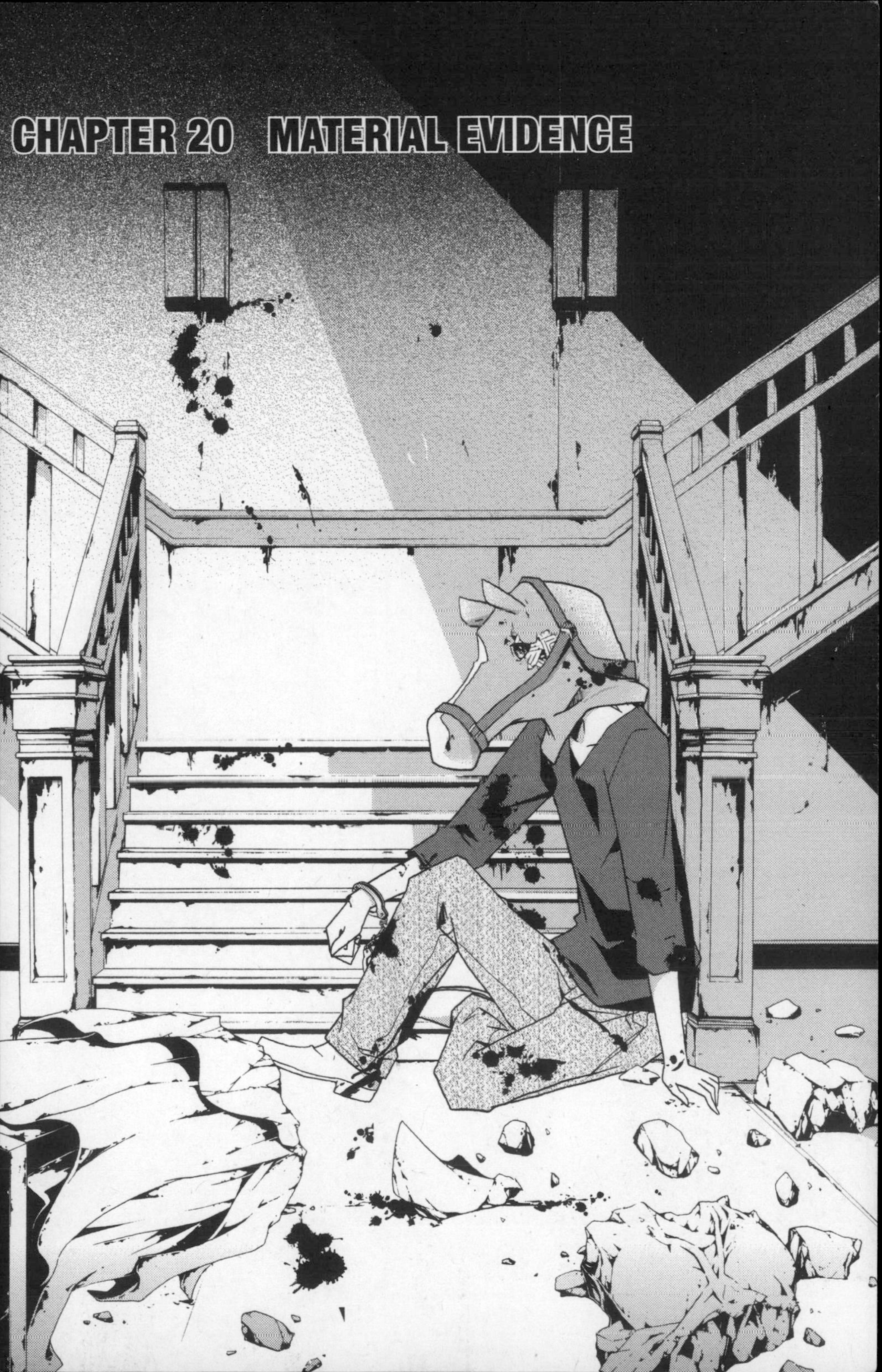

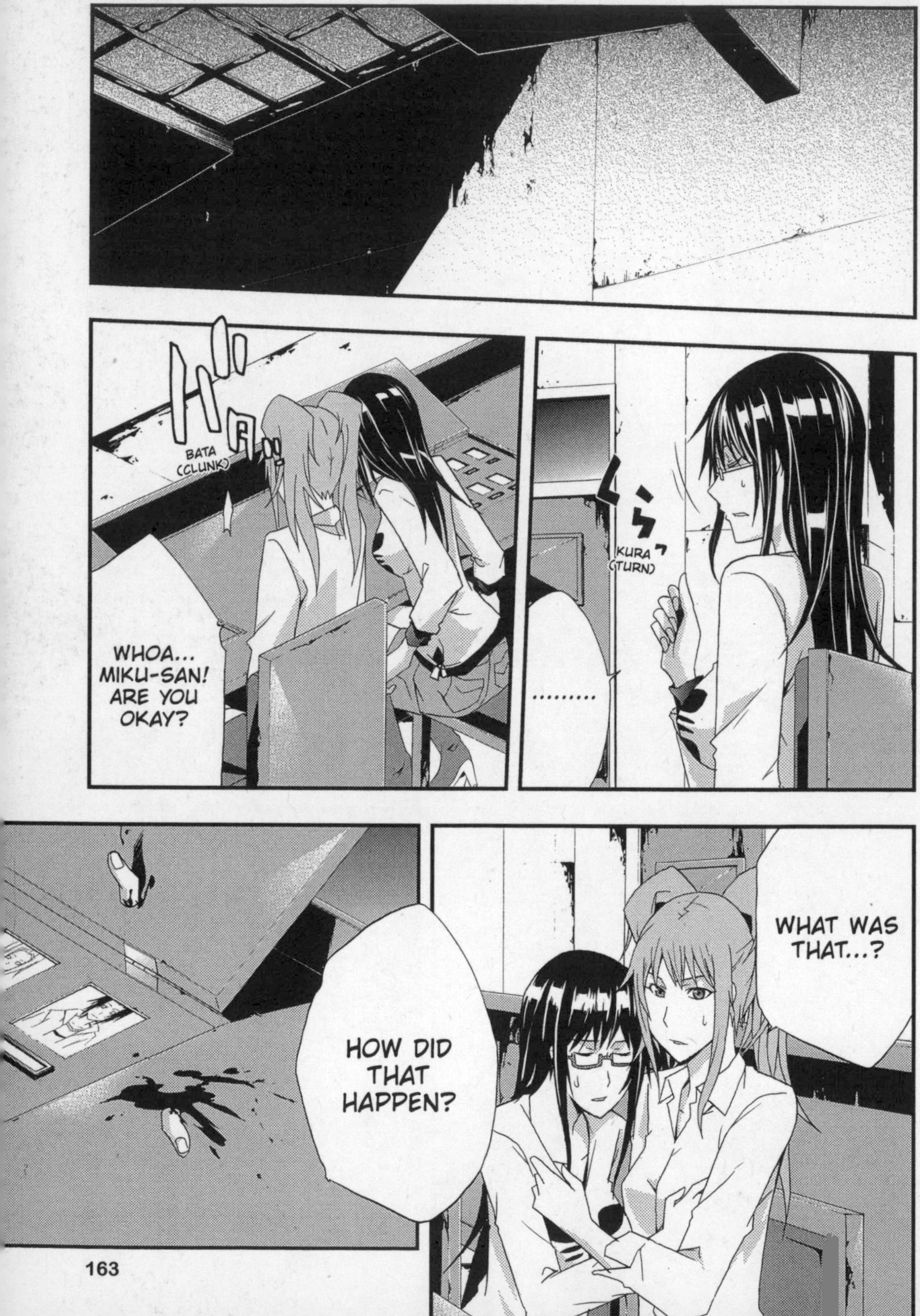

KURA
(TURN)
....
BATA
(CLUNK)
WHOA... MIKU-SAN! ARE YOU OKAY?
WHAT WAS THAT...?
HOW DID THAT HAPPEN?

GU
(CLENCH)

UH......!

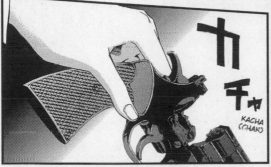

カチャ

KACHA
(CHAK)

カッ

KA
(CLACK)

THE GUN
MISFIRED
......

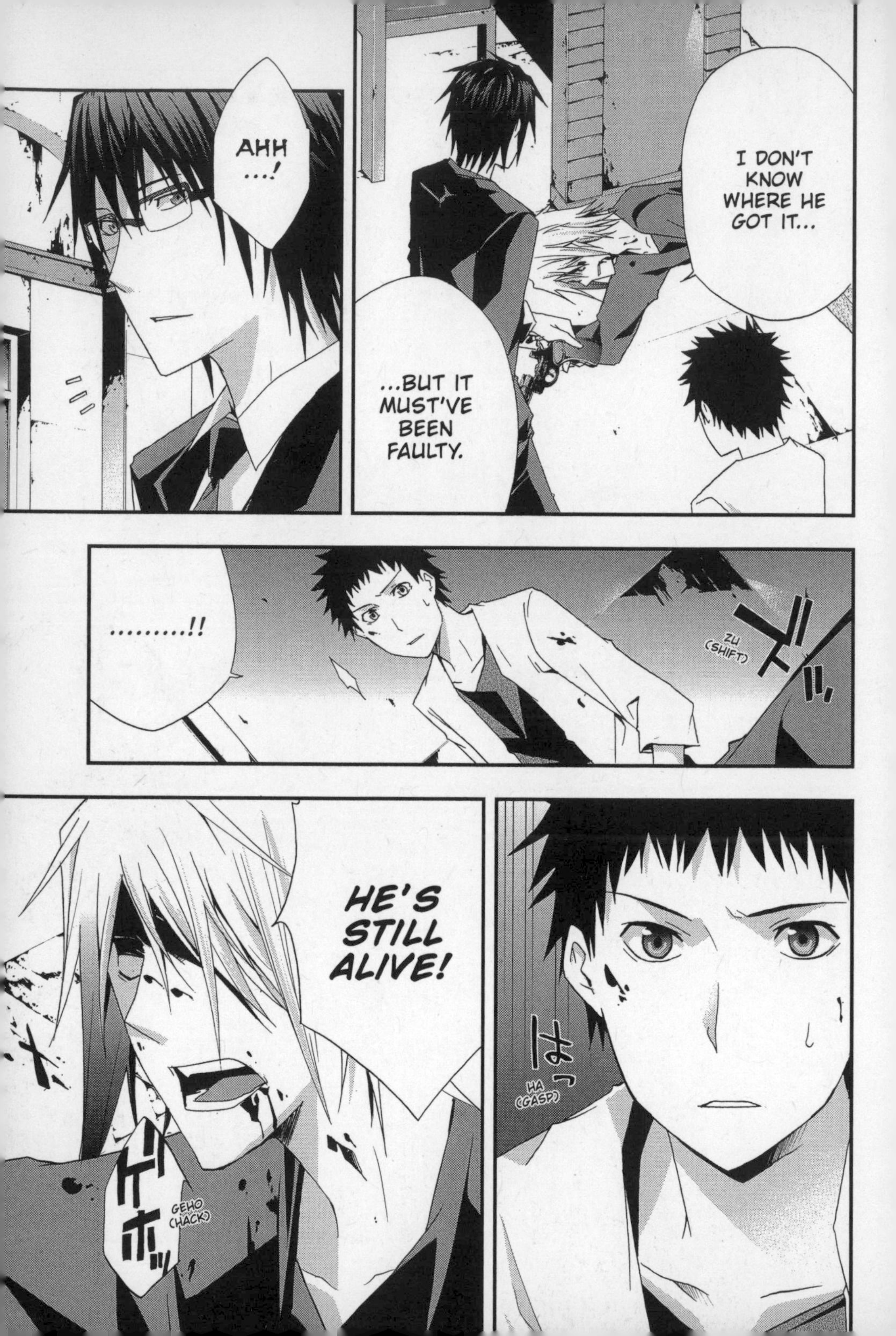
I DON'T KNOW WHERE HE GOT IT...
...BUT IT MUST'VE BEEN FAULTY.
AHH ...!
..........!!
ZU (SHIFT)
HA (GASP)
HE'S STILL ALIVE!
GEHO (HACK)

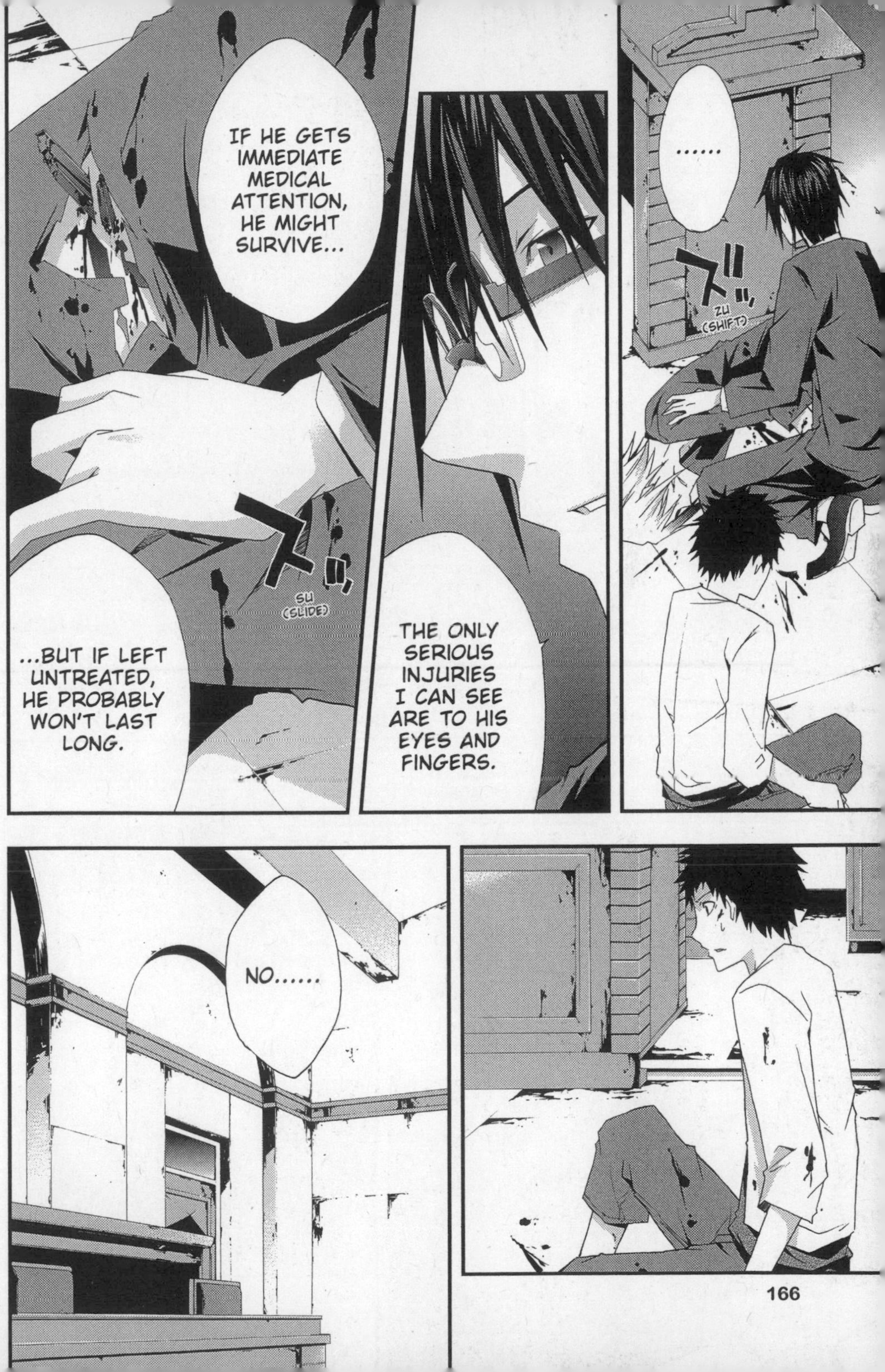
......
ZU (SHIFT)
THE ONLY SERIOUS INJURIES I CAN SEE ARE TO HIS EYES AND FINGERS.
IF HE GETS IMMEDIATE MEDICAL ATTENTION, HE MIGHT SURVIVE...
SU (SLIDE)
...BUT IF LEFT UNTREATED, HE PROBABLY WON'T LAST LONG.
NO......

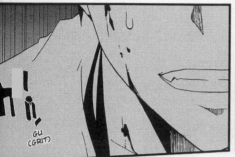

GU
(GRIT)

WHAT DO
YOU THINK
YOU'RE
DOING?

BA
(LUNGE)

......!

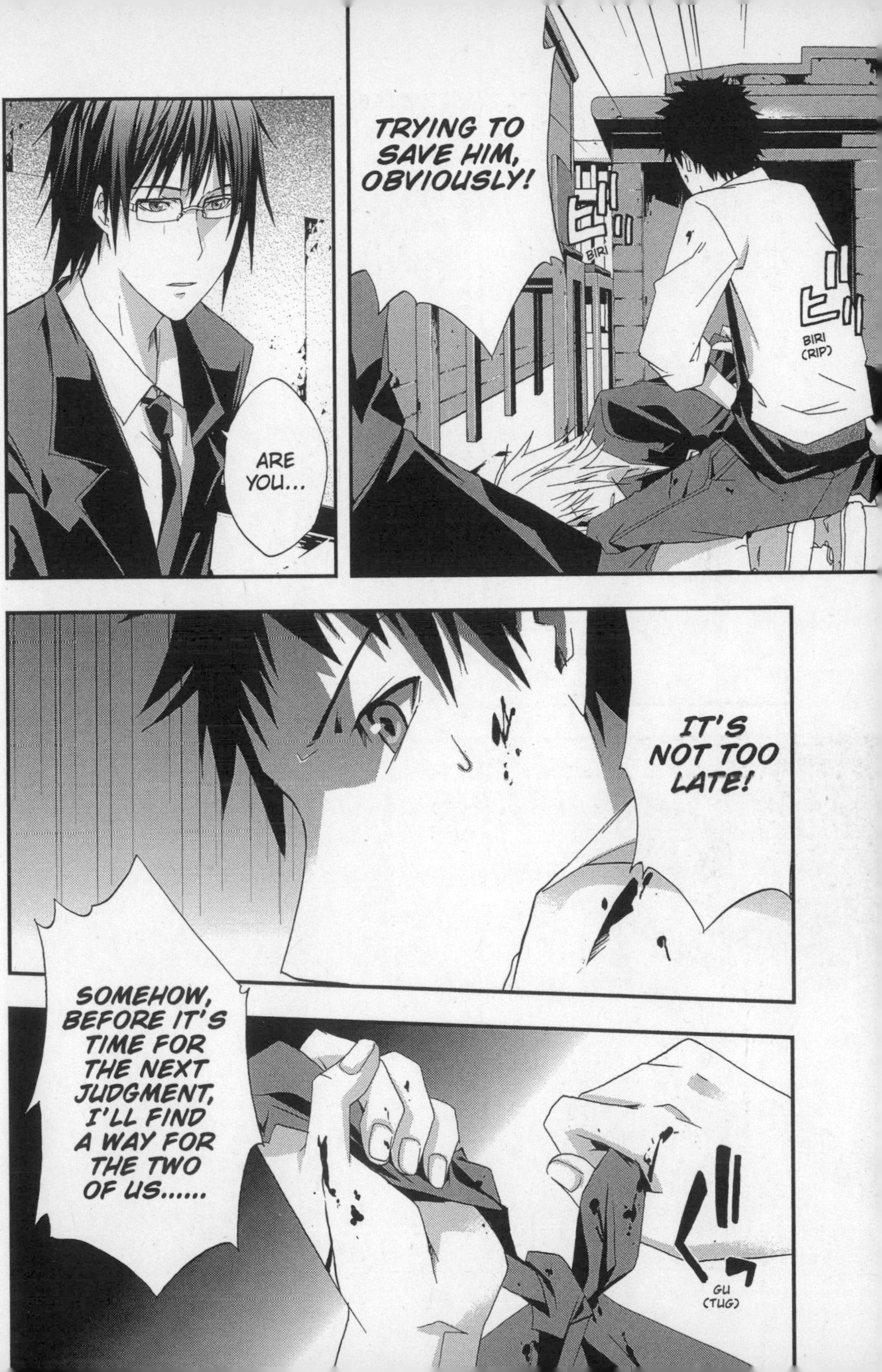
TRYING TO SAVE HIM, OBVIOUSLY!
BIRI
BIRI (RIP)
ARE YOU...
IT'S NOT TOO LATE!
SOMEHOW, BEFORE IT'S TIME FOR THE NEXT JUDGMENT, I'LL FIND A WAY FOR THE TWO OF US......
GU (TUG)

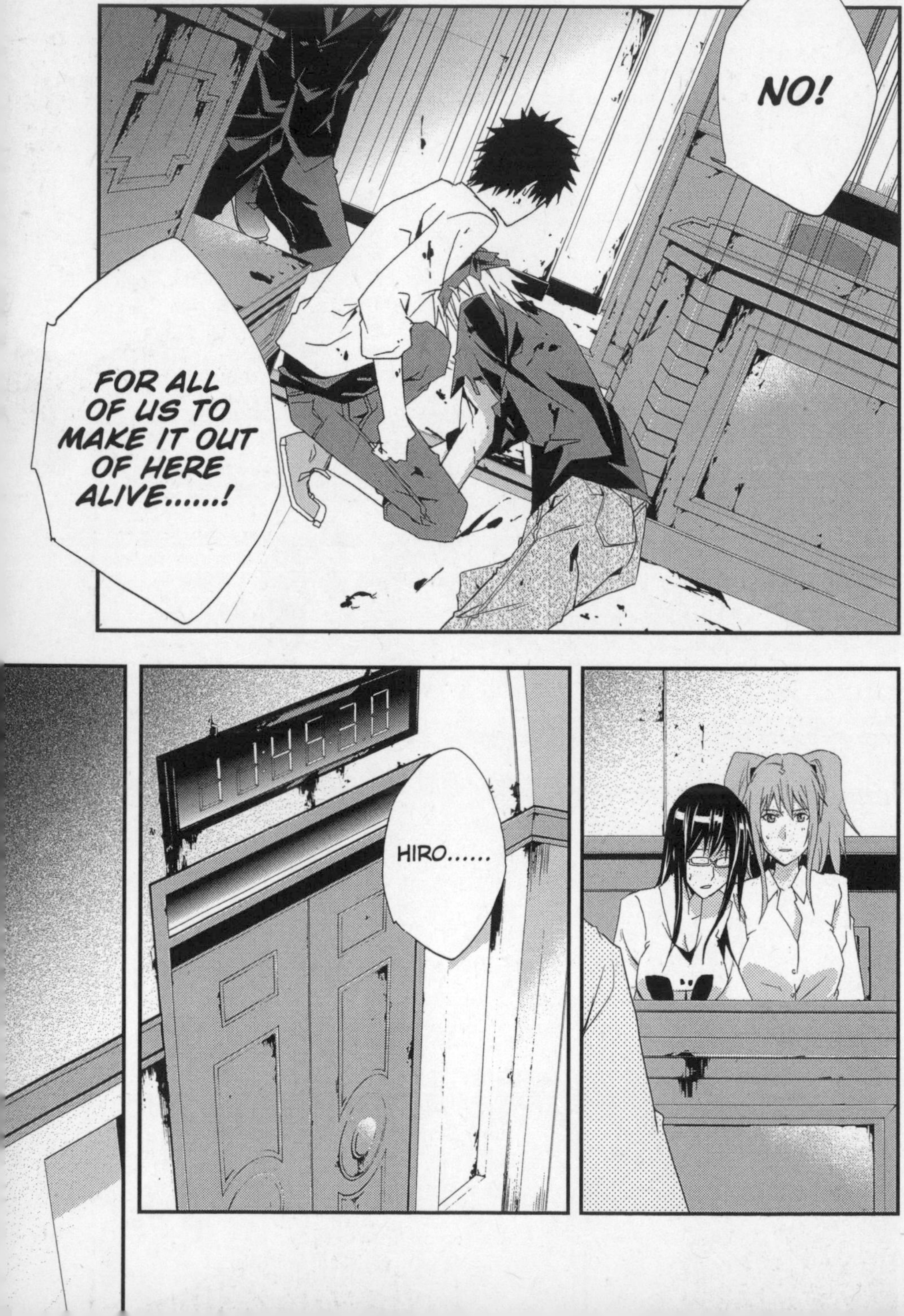
NO!
FOR ALL OF US TO MAKE IT OUT OF HERE ALIVE......!
HIRO......

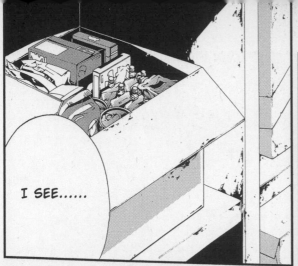

KACHA
(CLACK)

I SEE......

SU
(SHF)

PACKAGE: CAN'T STOP EATING, 2 MINS MICROWAVE

SO WHAT HE SAID WAS TRUE...

...ABOUT THERE BEING PLENTY OF FOOD IN HERE.

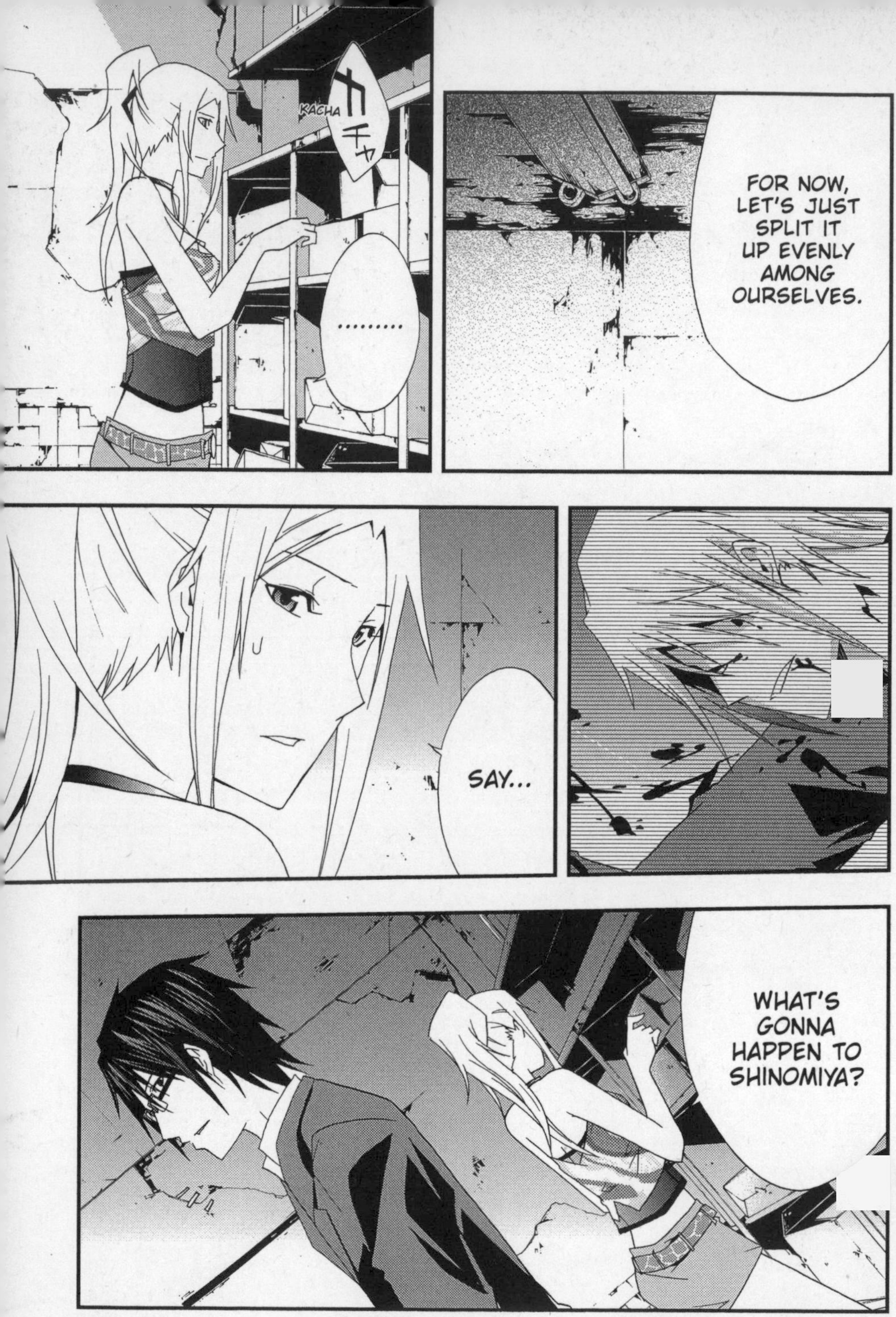
FOR NOW, LET'S JUST SPLIT IT UP EVENLY AMONG OURSELVES.
カチャ
KACHA
....
SAY...
WHAT'S GONNA HAPPEN TO SHINOMIYA?

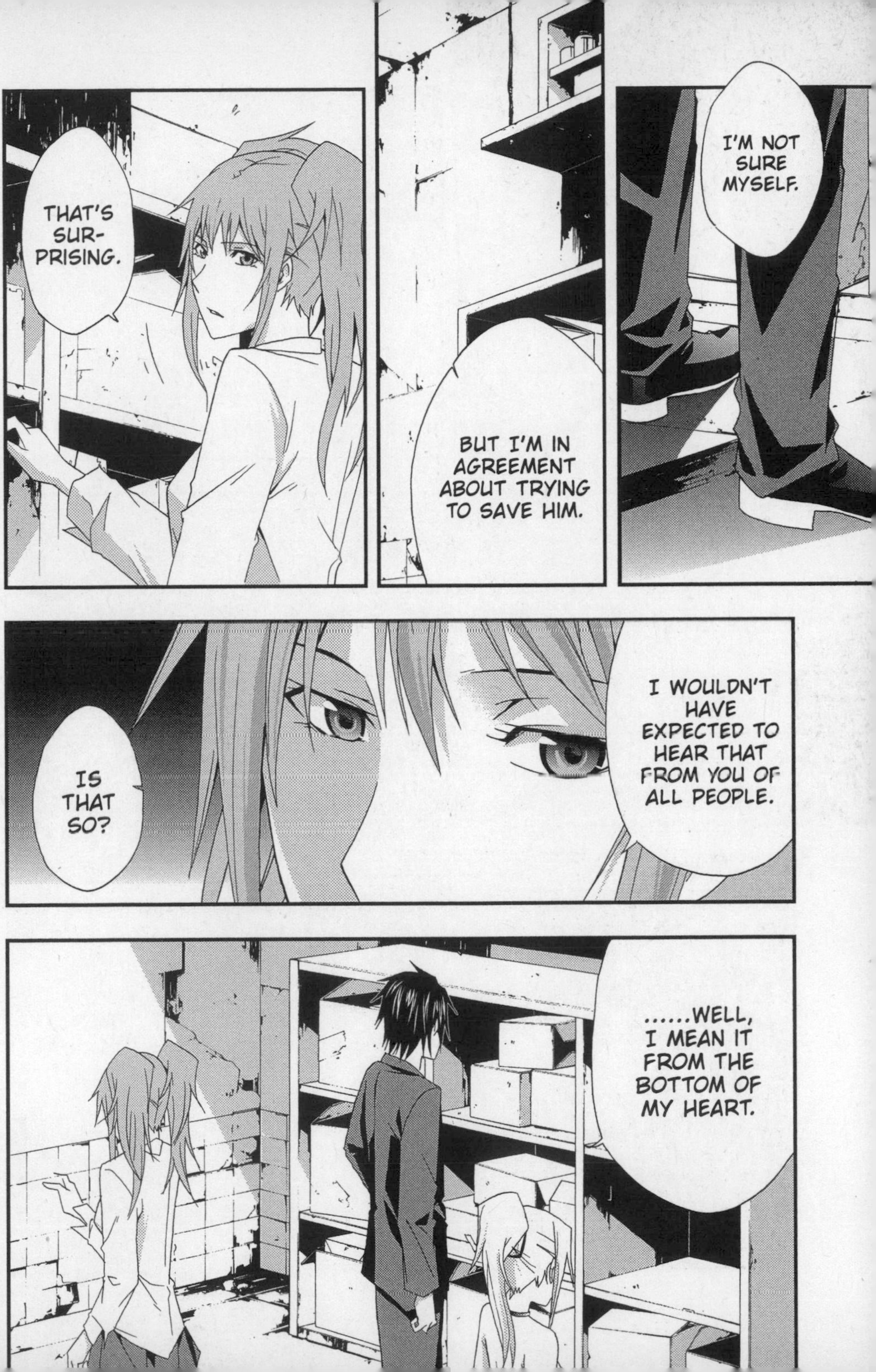
I'M NOT SURE MYSELF.
BUT I'M IN AGREEMENT ABOUT TRYING TO SAVE HIM.
THAT'S SUR-PRISING.
I WOULDN'T HAVE EXPECTED TO HEAR THAT FROM YOU OF ALL PEOPLE.
IS THAT SO?
......WELL, I MEAN IT FROM THE BOTTOM OF MY HEART.

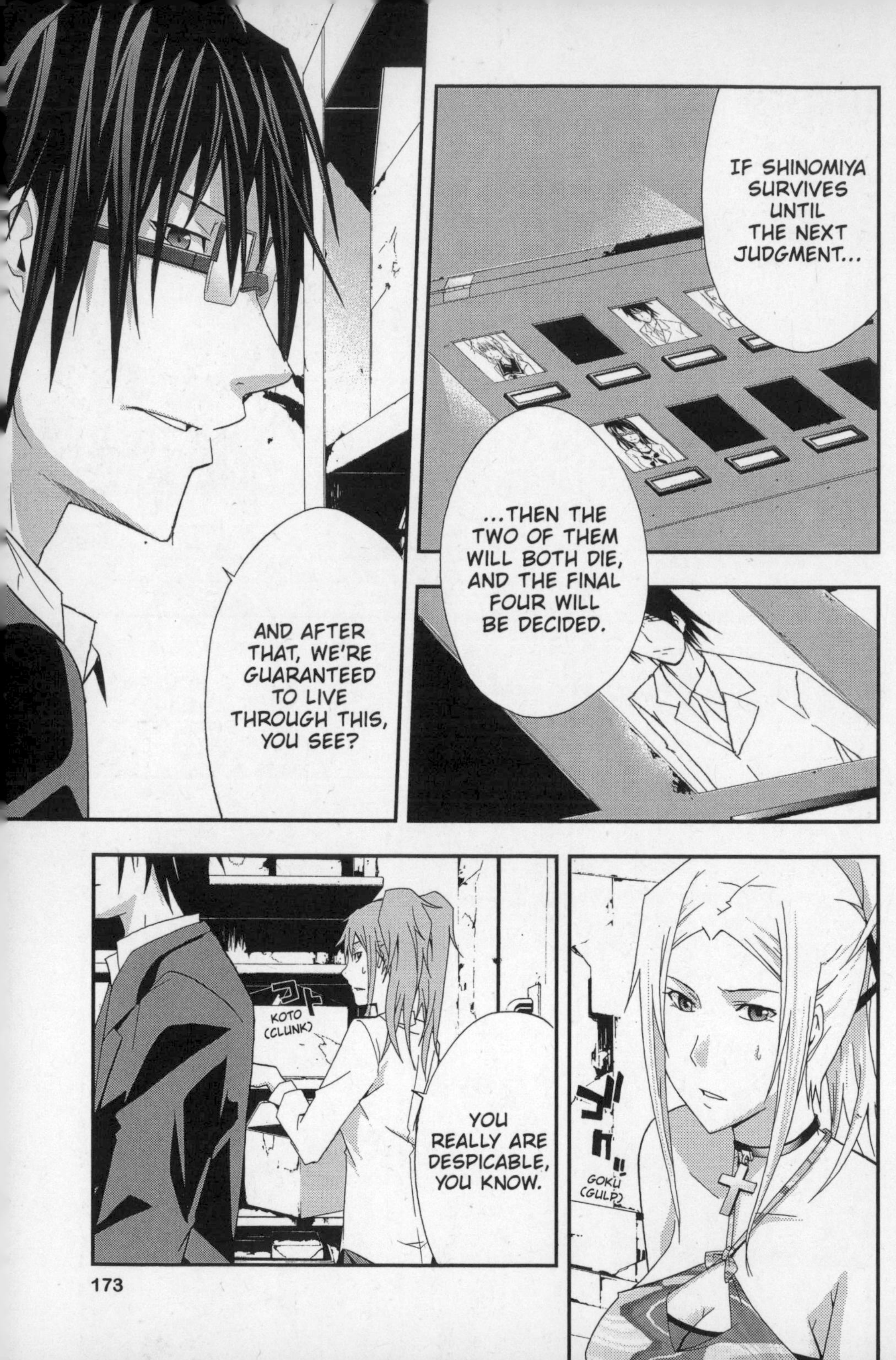
IF SHINOMIYA SURVIVES UNTIL THE NEXT JUDGMENT...
...THEN THE TWO OF THEM WILL BOTH DIE, AND THE FINAL FOUR WILL BE DECIDED.
AND AFTER THAT, WE'RE GUARANTEED TO LIVE THROUGH THIS, YOU SEE?
GOKU (GULP)
KOTO (CLUNK)
YOU REALLY ARE DESPICABLE, YOU KNOW.

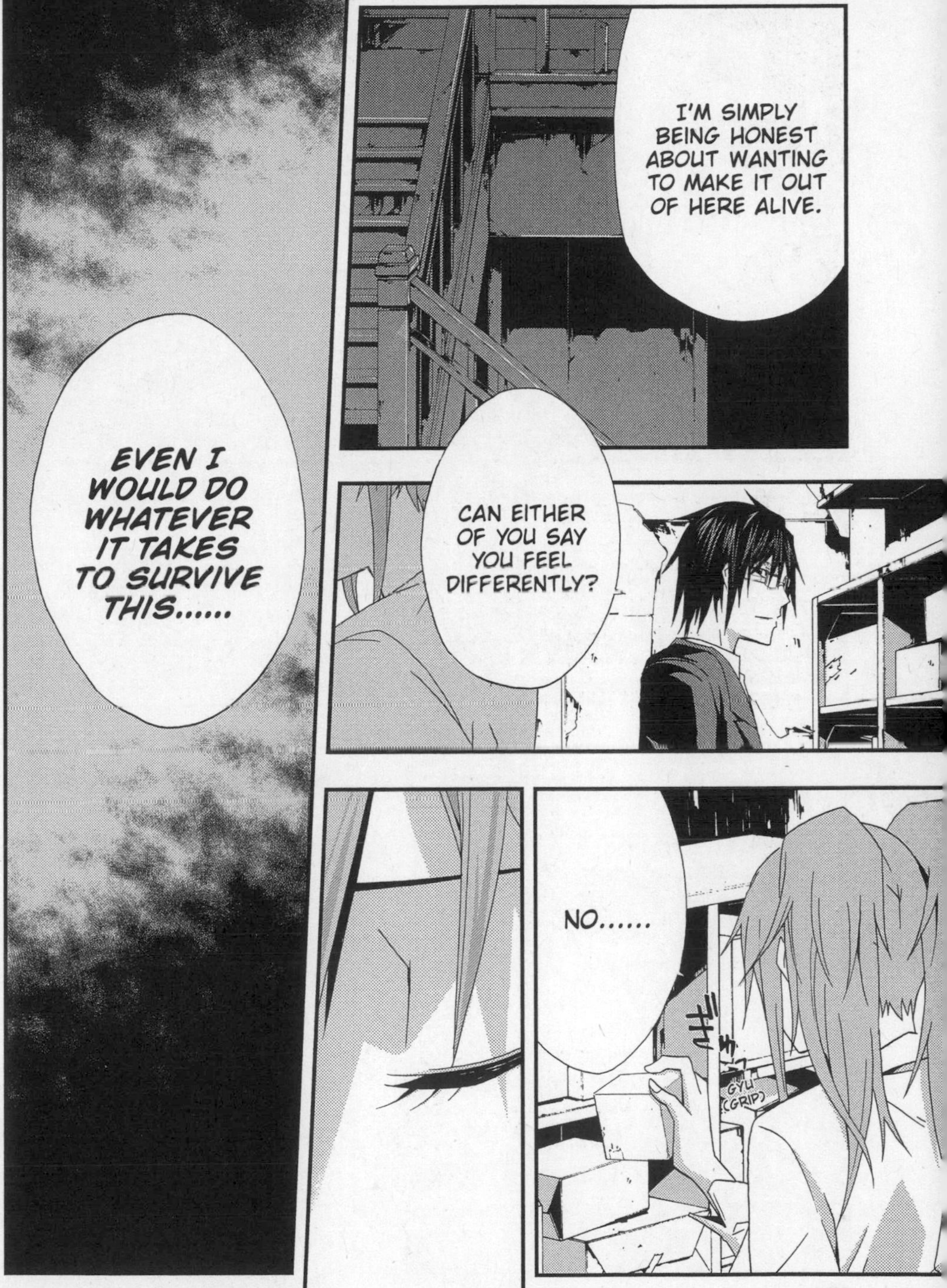
I'M SIMPLY BEING HONEST ABOUT WANTING TO MAKE IT OUT OF HERE ALIVE.
CAN EITHER OF YOU SAY YOU FEEL DIFFERENTLY?
NO......
GYU (GRIP)
EVEN I WOULD DO WHATEVER IT TAKES TO SURVIVE THIS......

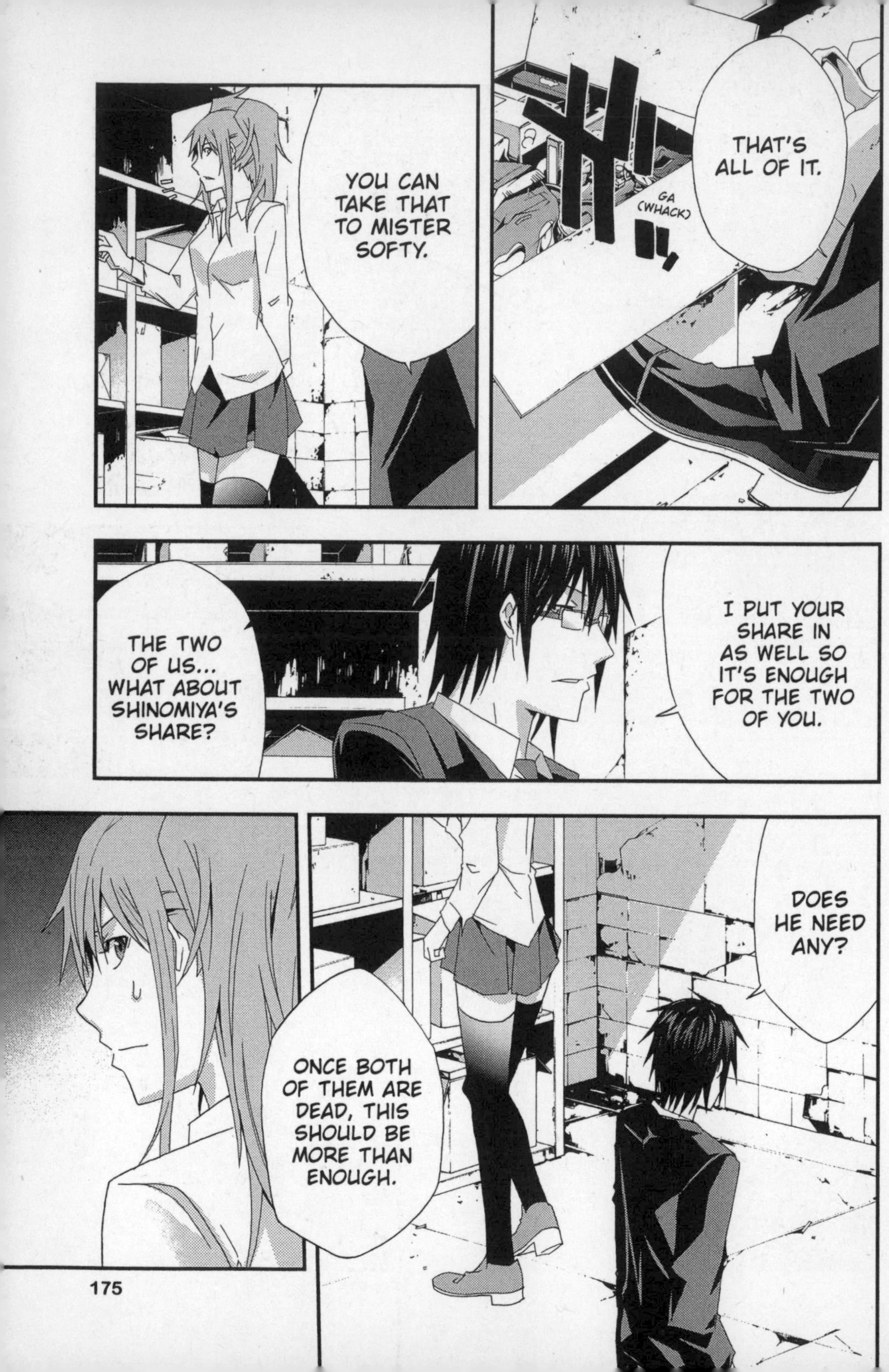
THAT'S ALL OF IT.
GA (WHACK)
YOU CAN TAKE THAT TO MISTER SOFTY.
I PUT YOUR SHARE IN AS WELL SO IT'S ENOUGH FOR THE TWO OF YOU.
THE TWO OF US... WHAT ABOUT SHINOMIYA'S SHARE?
DOES HE NEED ANY?
ONCE BOTH OF THEM ARE DEAD, THIS SHOULD BE MORE THAN ENOUGH.

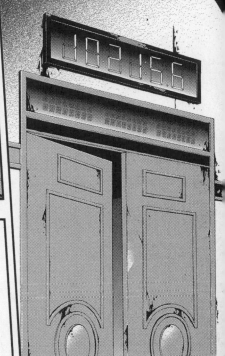

HOW'S HE DOING?

GYU
(SQUEEZE)

I MANAGED TO STOP THE BLEEDING.

DOSA
(THUD)

....

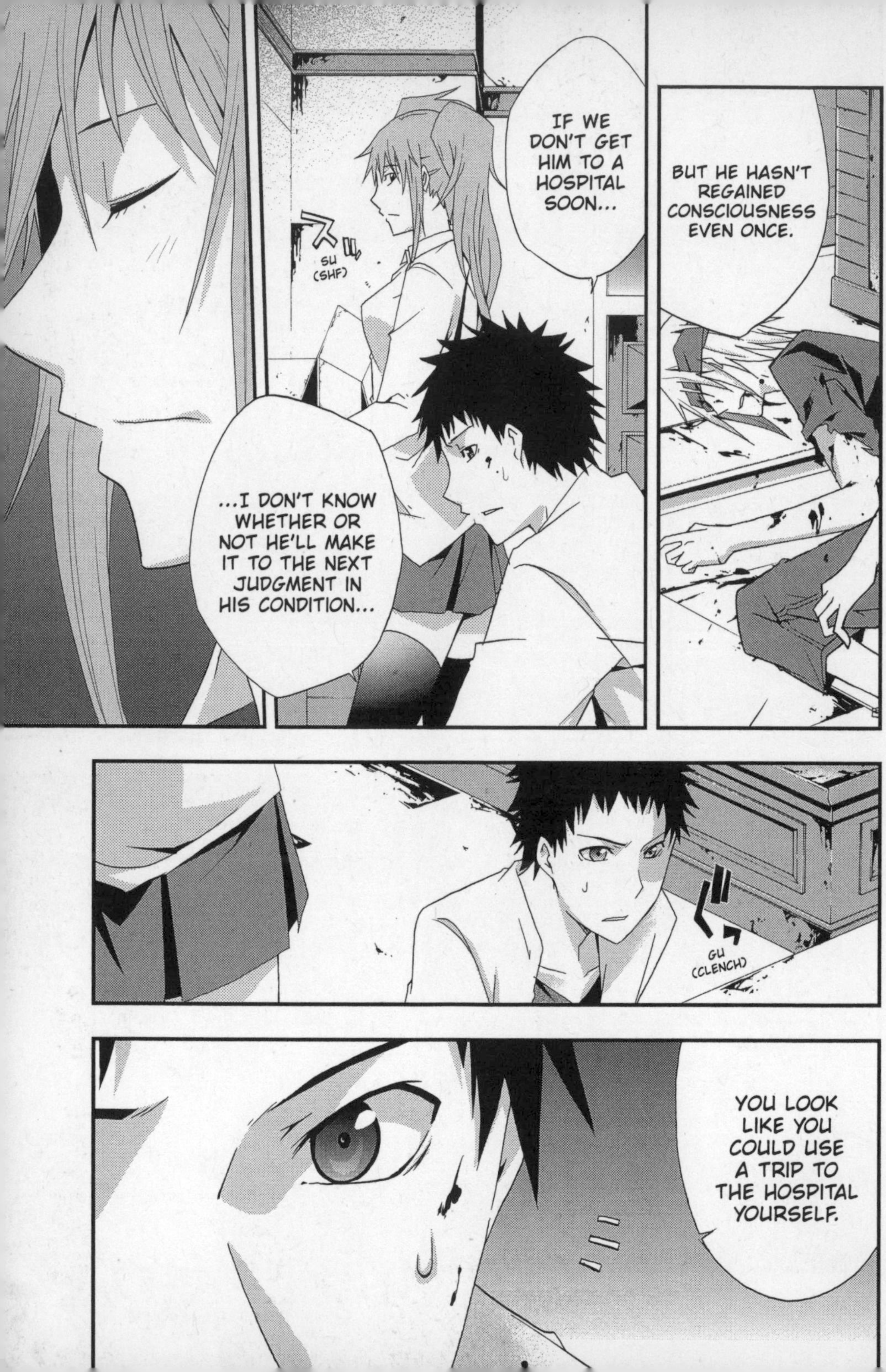
BUT HE HASN'T REGAINED CONSCIOUSNESS EVEN ONCE.
IF WE DON'T GET HIM TO A HOSPITAL SOON...
SU (SHF)
...I DON'T KNOW WHETHER OR NOT HE'LL MAKE IT TO THE NEXT JUDGMENT IN HIS CONDITION...
GU (CLENCH)
YOU LOOK LIKE YOU COULD USE A TRIP TO THE HOSPITAL YOURSELF.

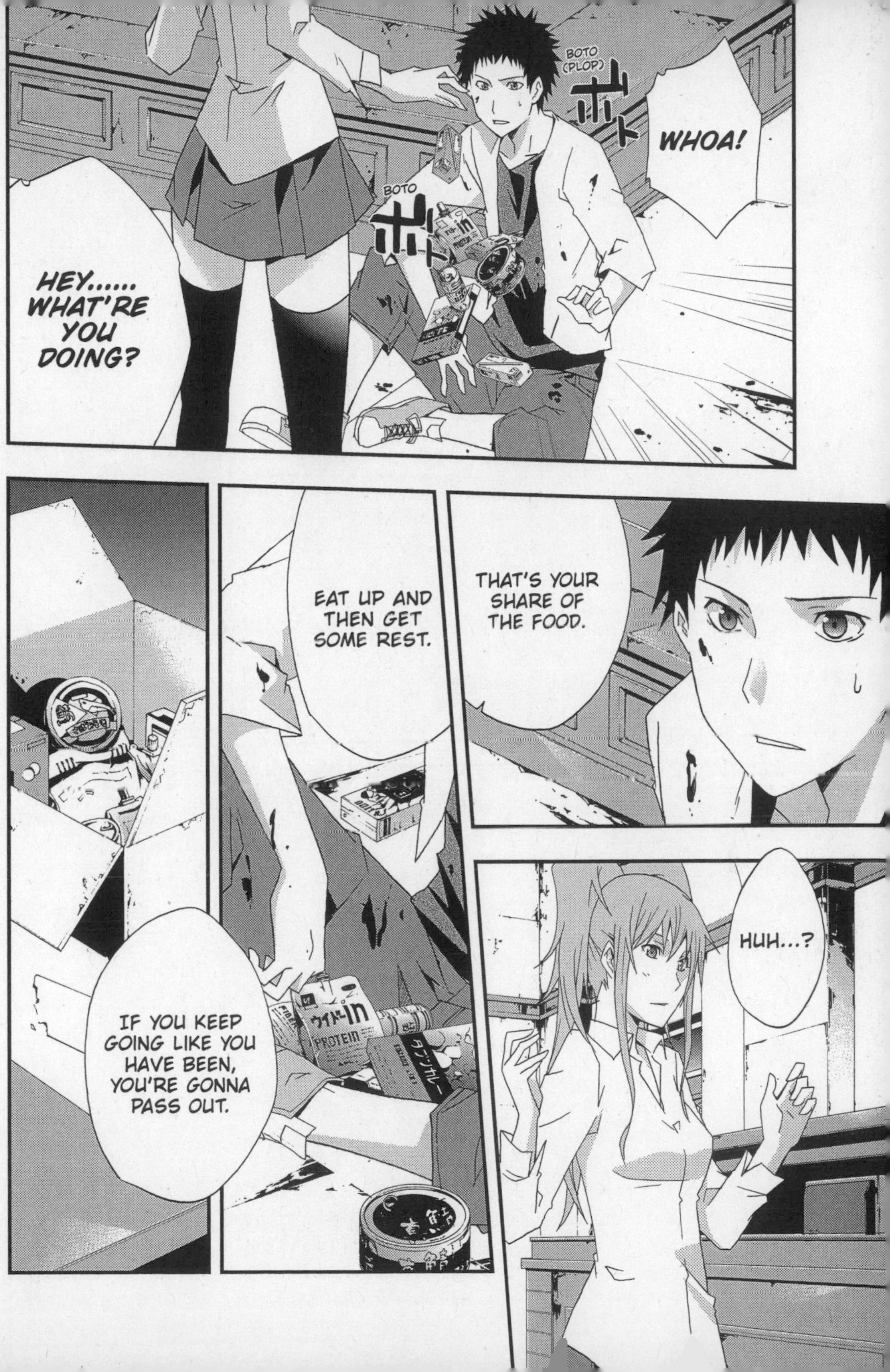
WHOA!
BOTO (PLOP) ボト
BOTO ボト
HEY...... WHAT'RE YOU DOING?
THAT'S YOUR SHARE OF THE FOOD.
HUH...?
EAT UP AND THEN GET SOME REST.
IF YOU KEEP GOING LIKE YOU HAVE BEEN, YOU'RE GONNA PASS OUT.

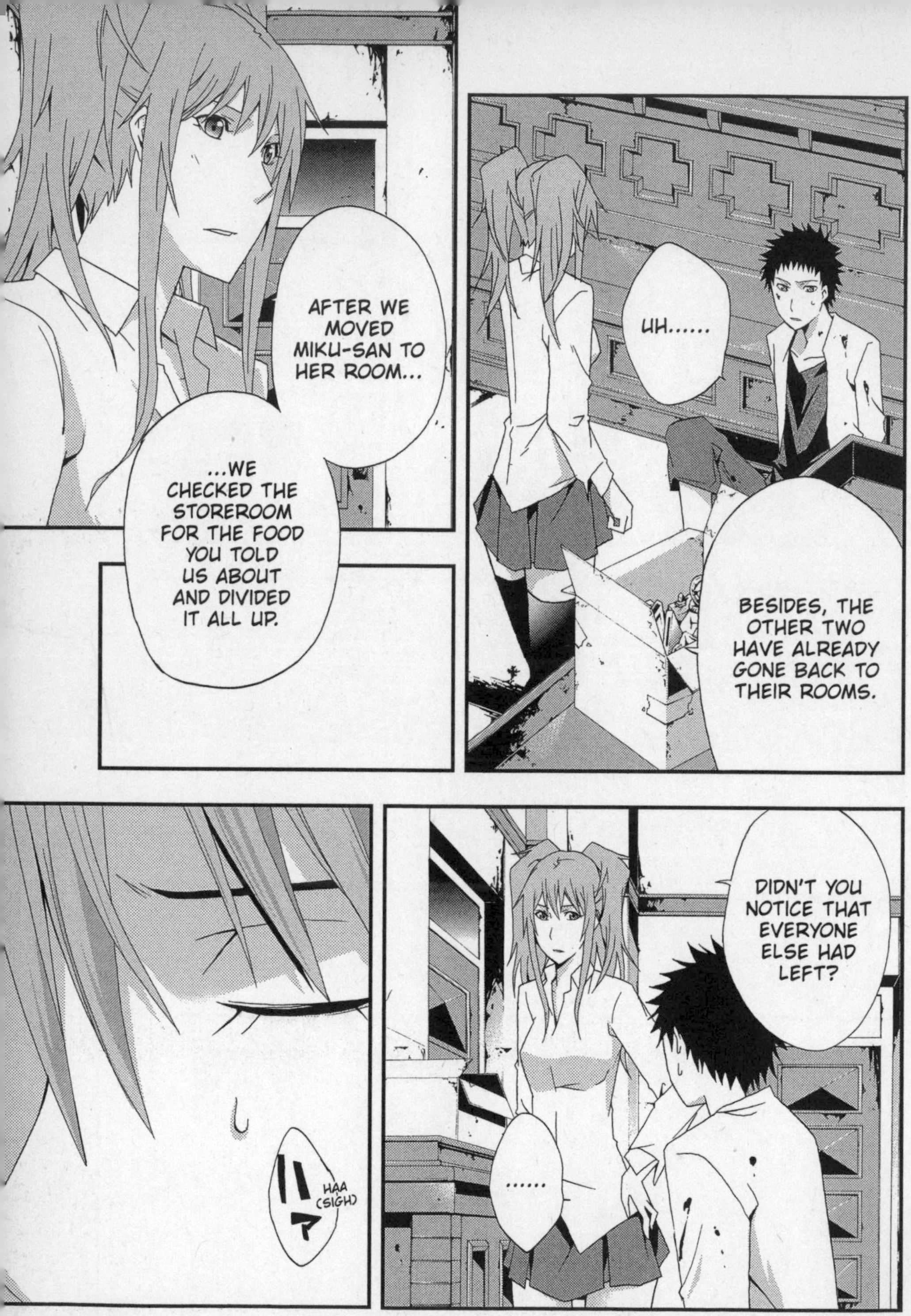
UH......
BESIDES, THE OTHER TWO HAVE ALREADY GONE BACK TO THEIR ROOMS.
AFTER WE MOVED MIKU-SAN TO HER ROOM...
...WE CHECKED THE STOREROOM FOR THE FOOD YOU TOLD US ABOUT AND DIVIDED IT ALL UP.
DIDN'T YOU NOTICE THAT EVERYONE ELSE HAD LEFT?
......
ハァ
HAA (SIGH)

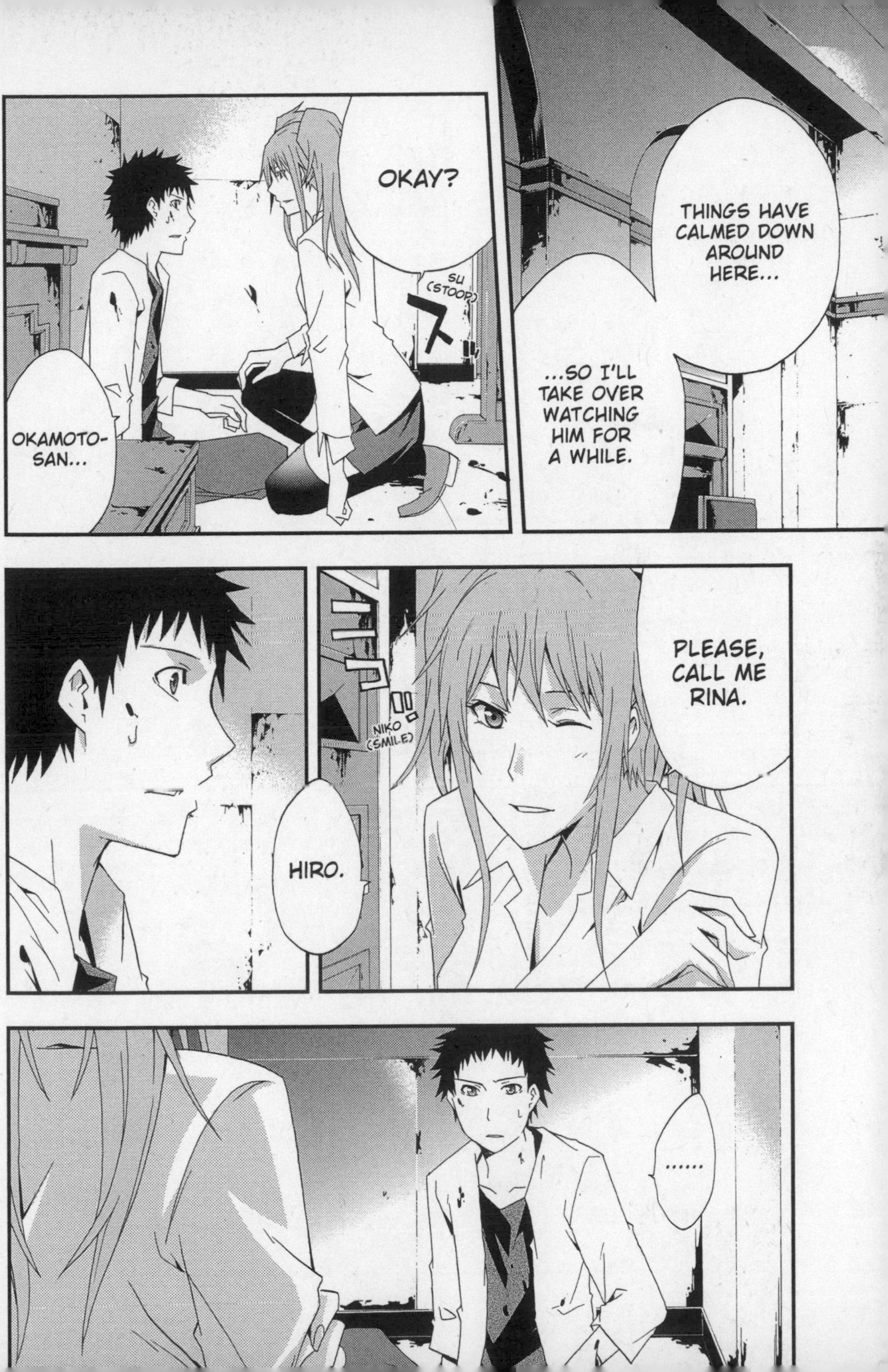
THINGS HAVE CALMED DOWN AROUND HERE...
...SO I'LL TAKE OVER WATCHING HIM FOR A WHILE.
OKAY?
SU (STOOP)
OKAMOTO-SAN...
PLEASE, CALL ME RINA.
NIKO (SMILE)
HIRO.
......

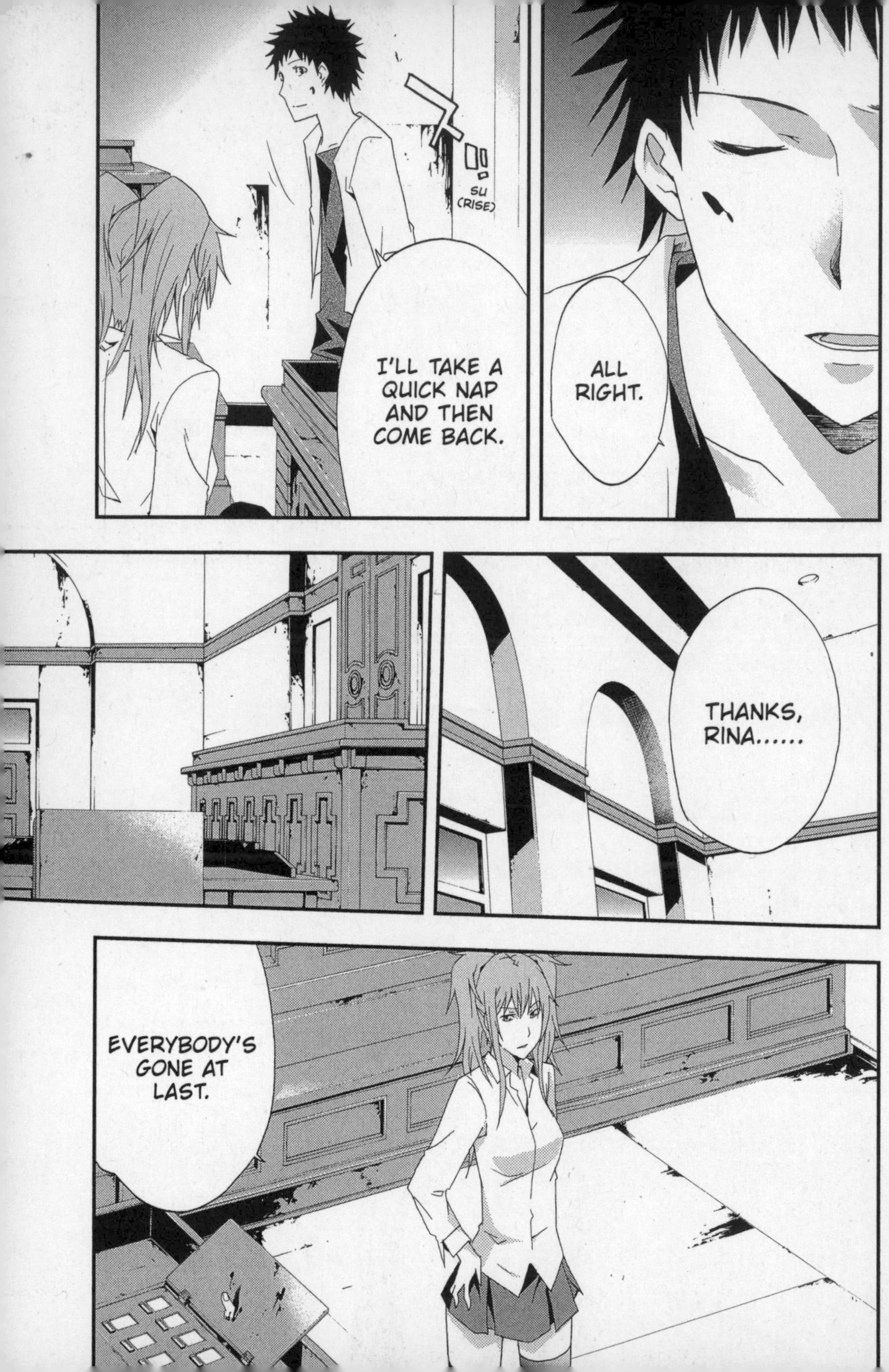
ALL RIGHT.
SU (RISE)
I'LL TAKE A QUICK NAP AND THEN COME BACK.
THANKS, RINA......
EVERYBODY'S GONE AT LAST.

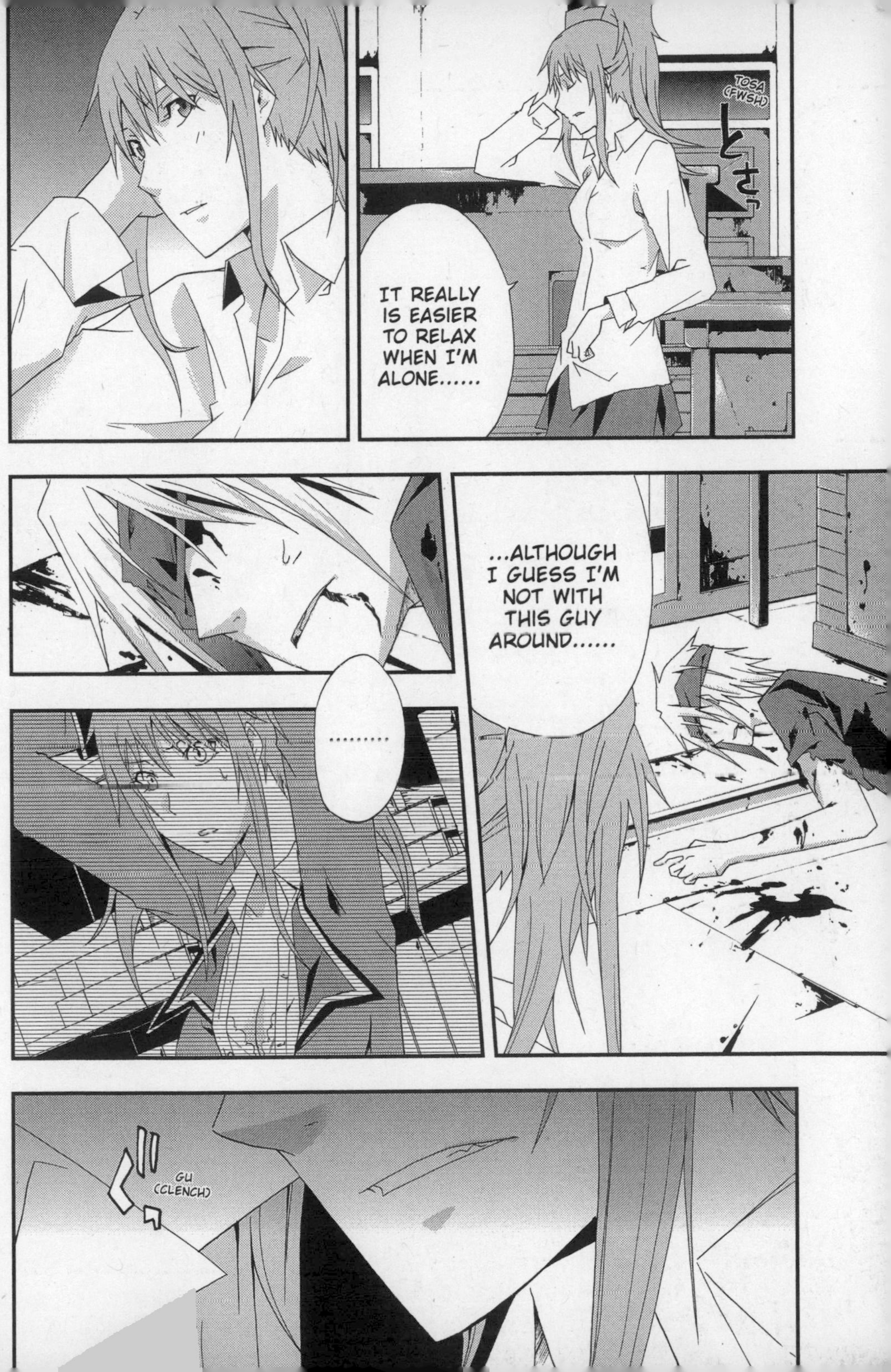
とさっ
TOSA (FWSH)
IT REALLY IS EASIER TO RELAX WHEN I'M ALONE......
...ALTHOUGH I GUESS I'M NOT WITH THIS GUY AROUND......
....
ぐっ
GU (CLENCH)

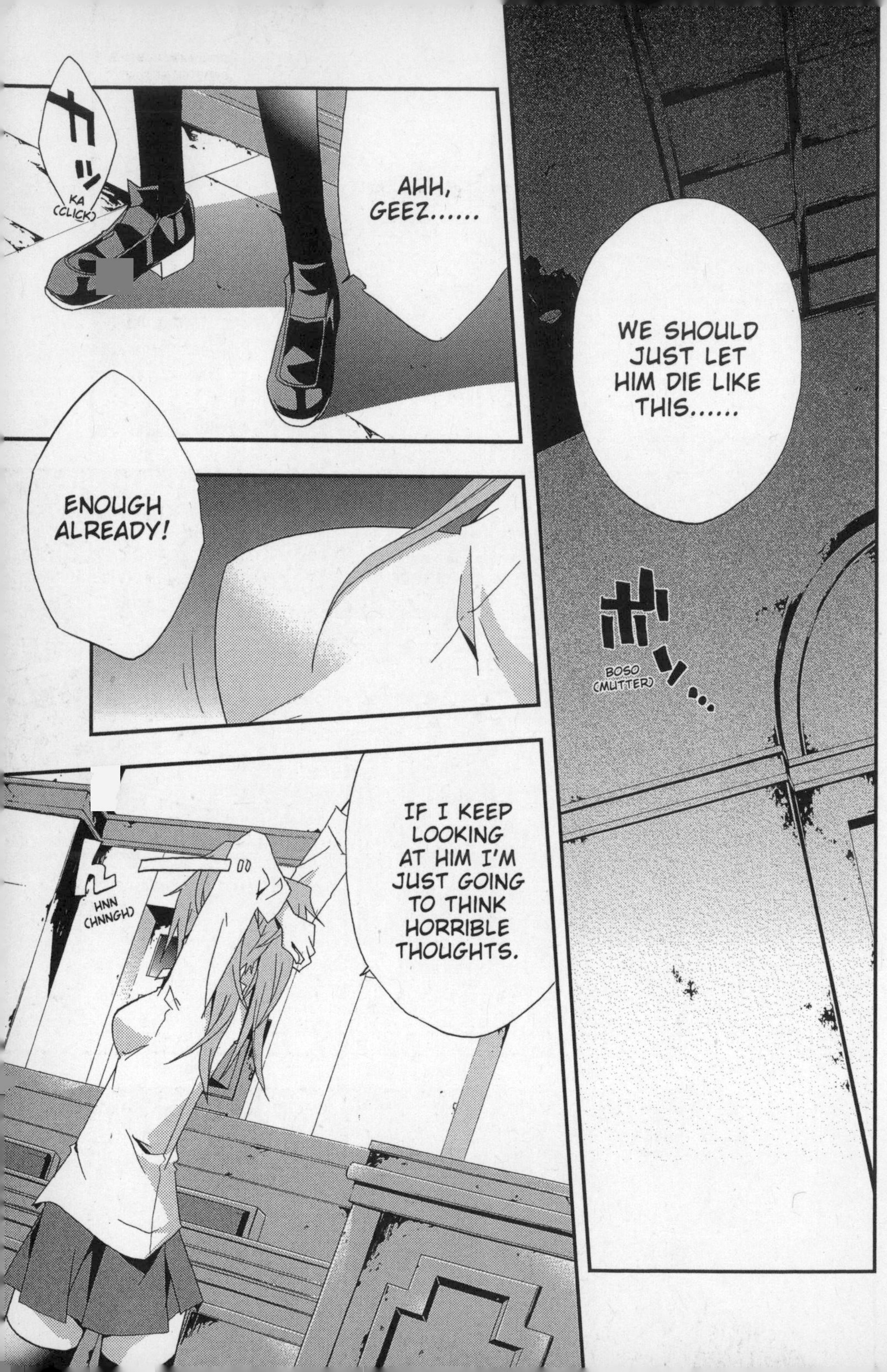
WE SHOULD JUST LET HIM DIE LIKE THIS......
BOSO (MUTTER)
AHH, GEEZ......
KA (CLICK)
ENOUGH ALREADY!
IF I KEEP LOOKING AT HIM I'M JUST GOING TO THINK HORRIBLE THOUGHTS.
HNN (HNNGH)

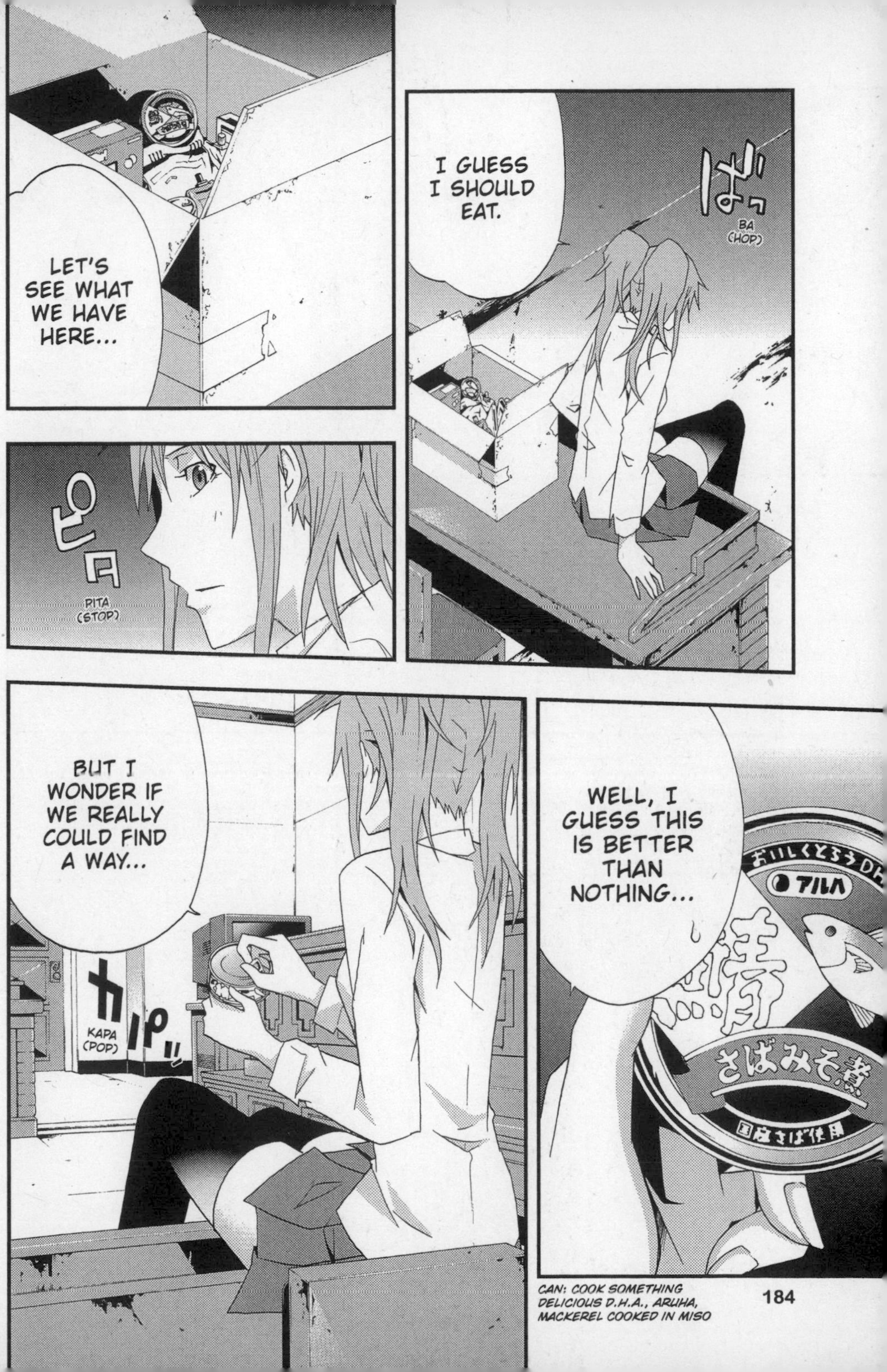
I GUESS I SHOULD EAT.
ぱっ
BA (HOP)
LET'S SEE WHAT WE HAVE HERE...
ピタ
PITA (STOP)
WELL, I GUESS THIS IS BETTER THAN NOTHING...
アルハ
さばみそ煮
BUT I WONDER IF WE REALLY COULD FIND A WAY...
カパッ
KAPA (POP)

CAN: COOK SOMETHING DELICIOUS D.H.A., ARUHA, MACKEREL COOKED IN MISO

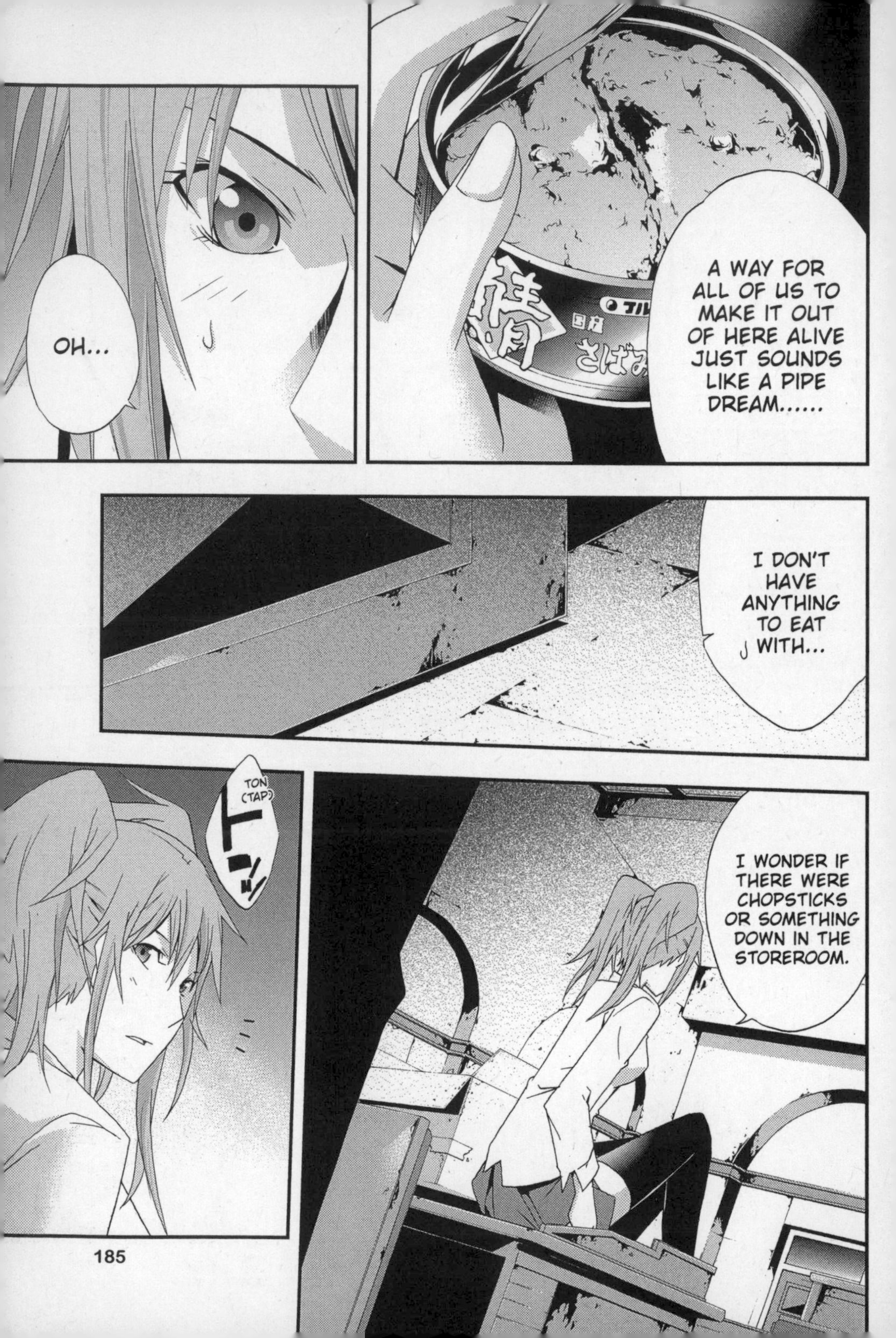
A WAY FOR ALL OF US TO MAKE IT OUT OF HERE ALIVE JUST SOUNDS LIKE A PIPE DREAM......
OH...
I DON'T HAVE ANYTHING TO EAT WITH...
I WONDER IF THERE WERE CHOPSTICKS OR SOMETHING DOWN IN THE STOREROOM.
TON (TAP)

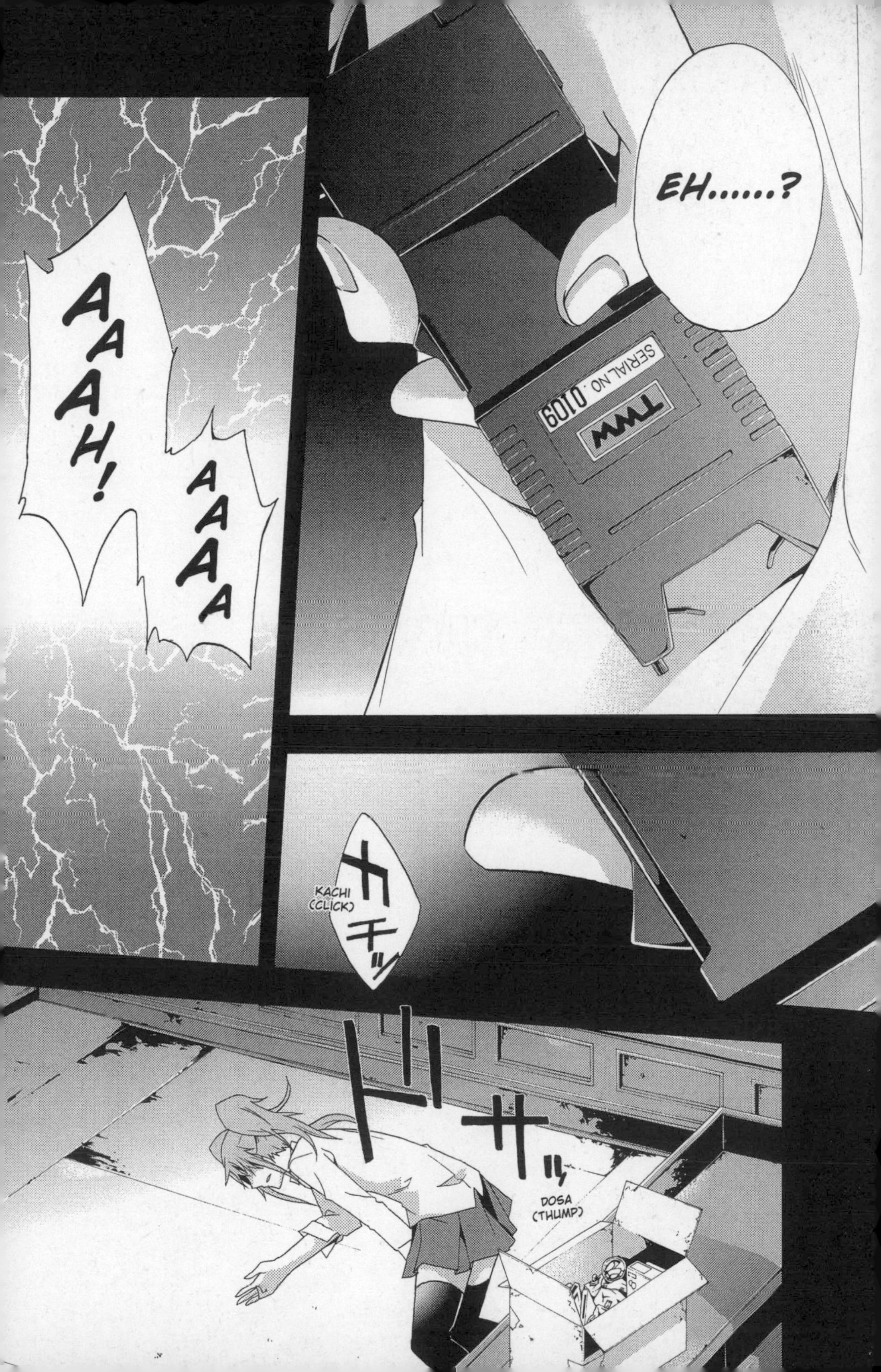
EH......?
KACHI (CLICK)
AAAAH!
AAAAA
DOSA (THUMP)

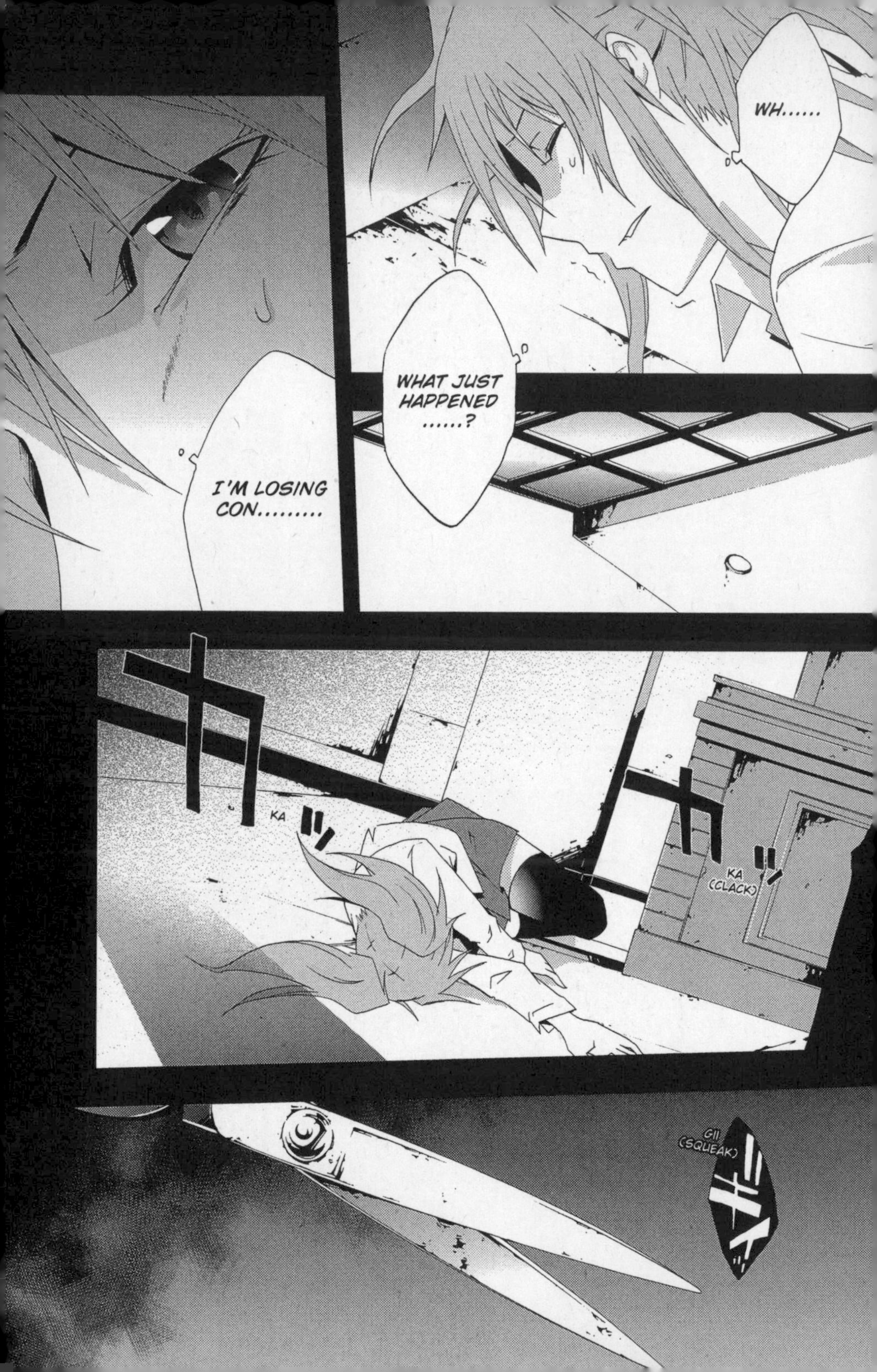
WH......
WHAT JUST HAPPENED ......?
I'M LOSING CON.........
KA (CLACK)
KA
GII (SQUEAK)

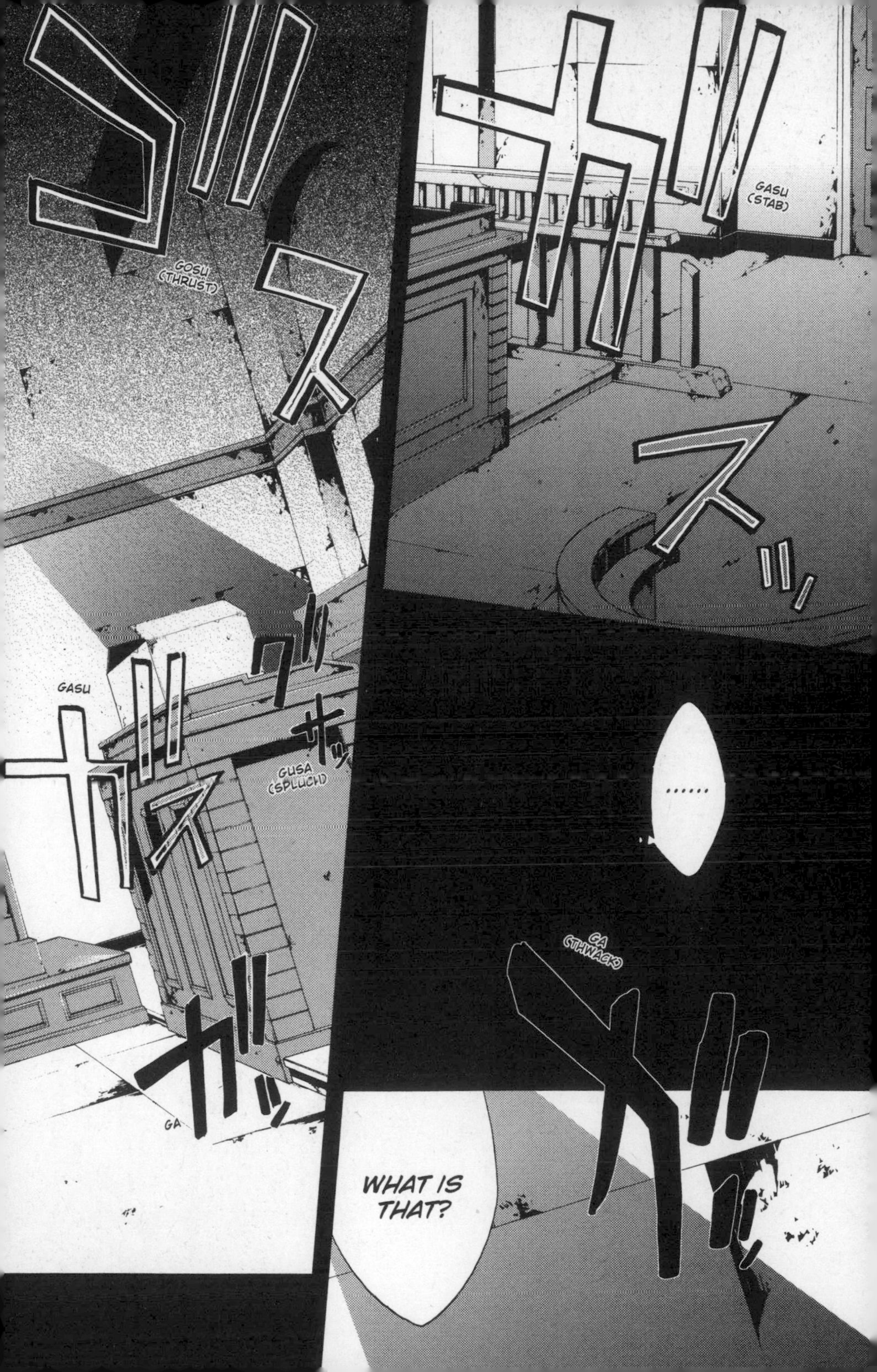
GASU (STAB)
......
GA (THWACK)
WHAT IS THAT?
GOSU (THRUST)
GASU
GUSA (SPLUCH)
GA

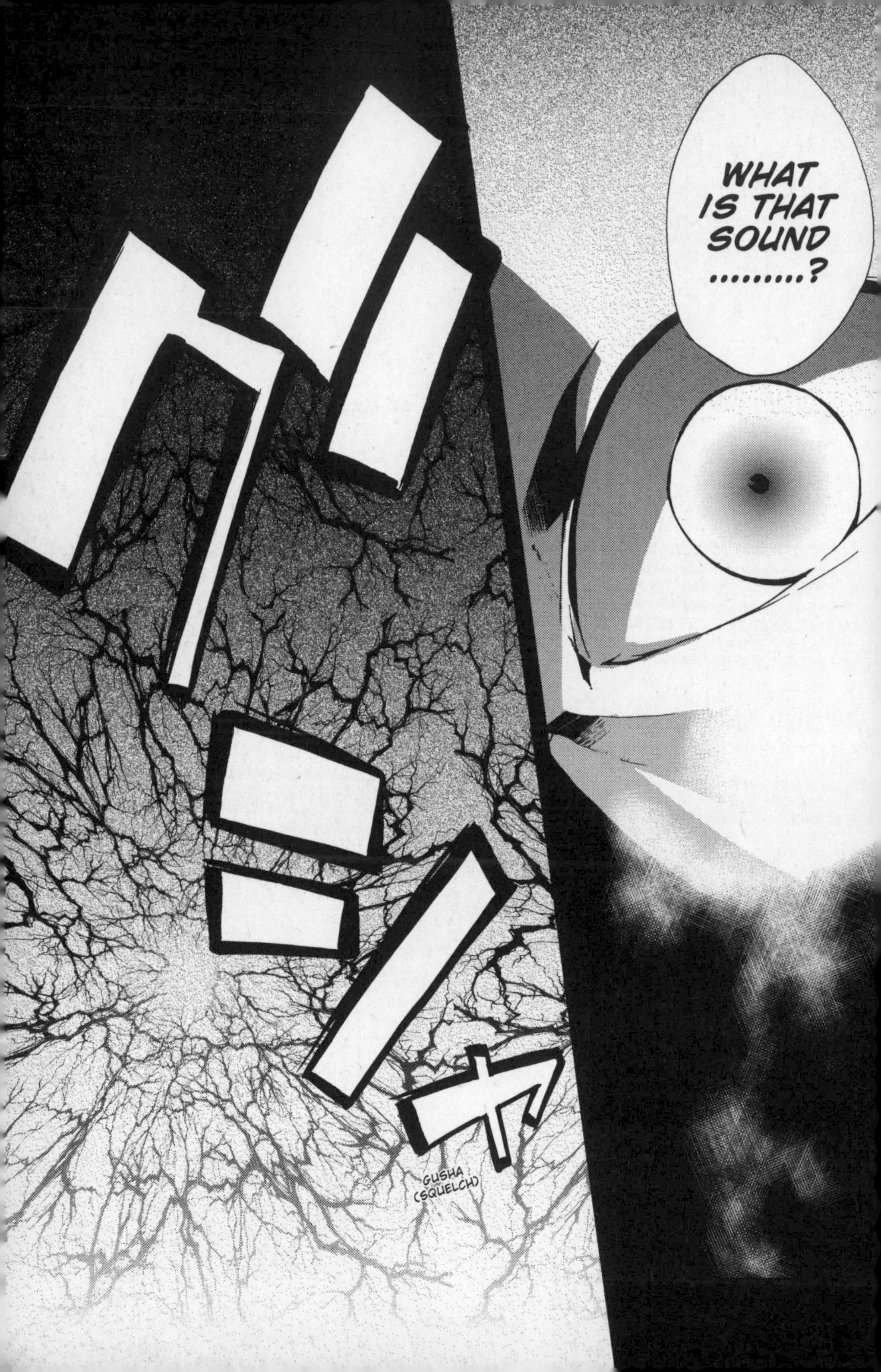
WHAT IS THAT SOUND ....?
GUSHA (SQUELCH)

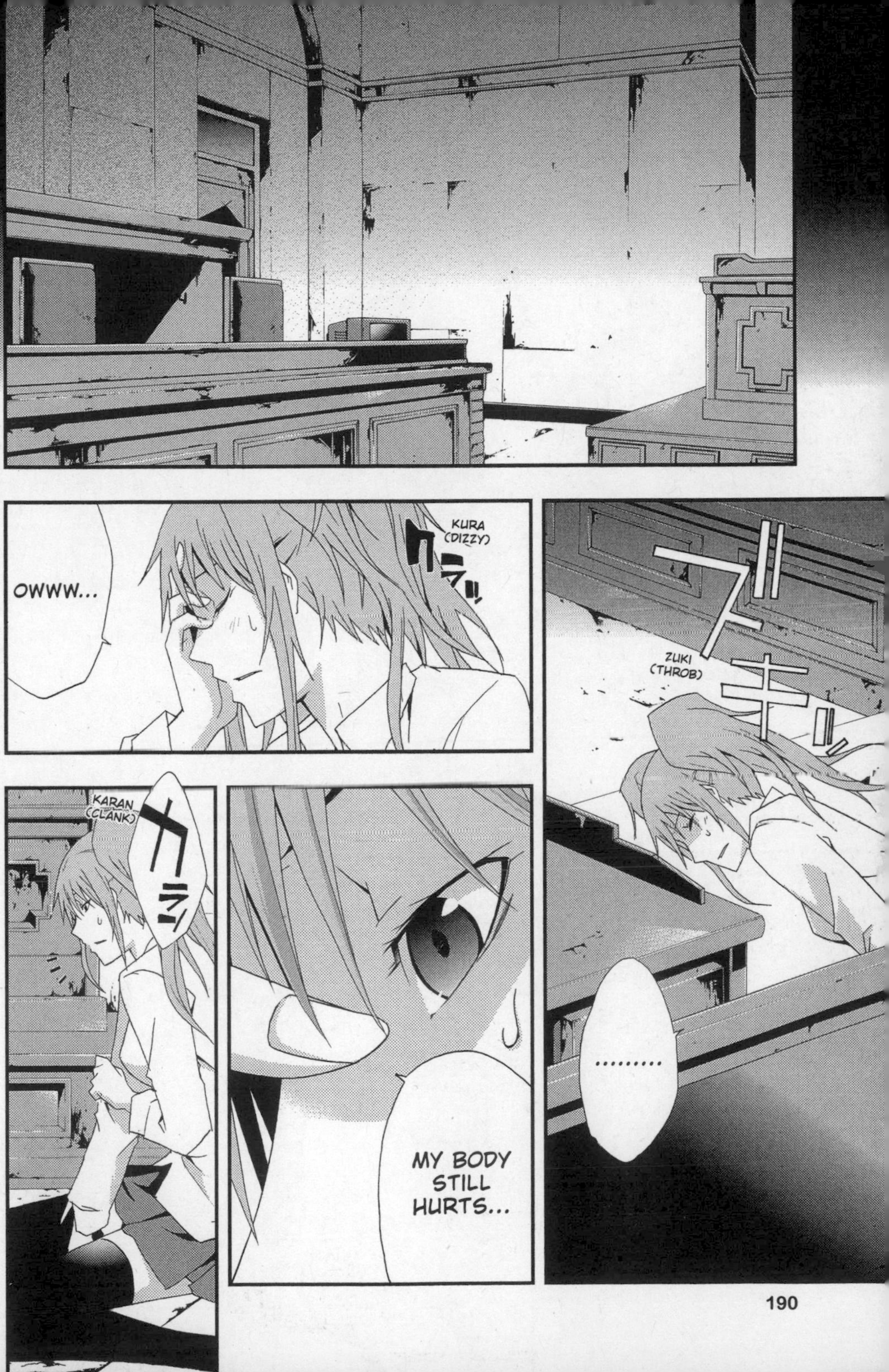
ZUKI (THROB)
....
KURA (DIZZY)
OWWW...
MY BODY STILL HURTS...
KARAN (CLANK)

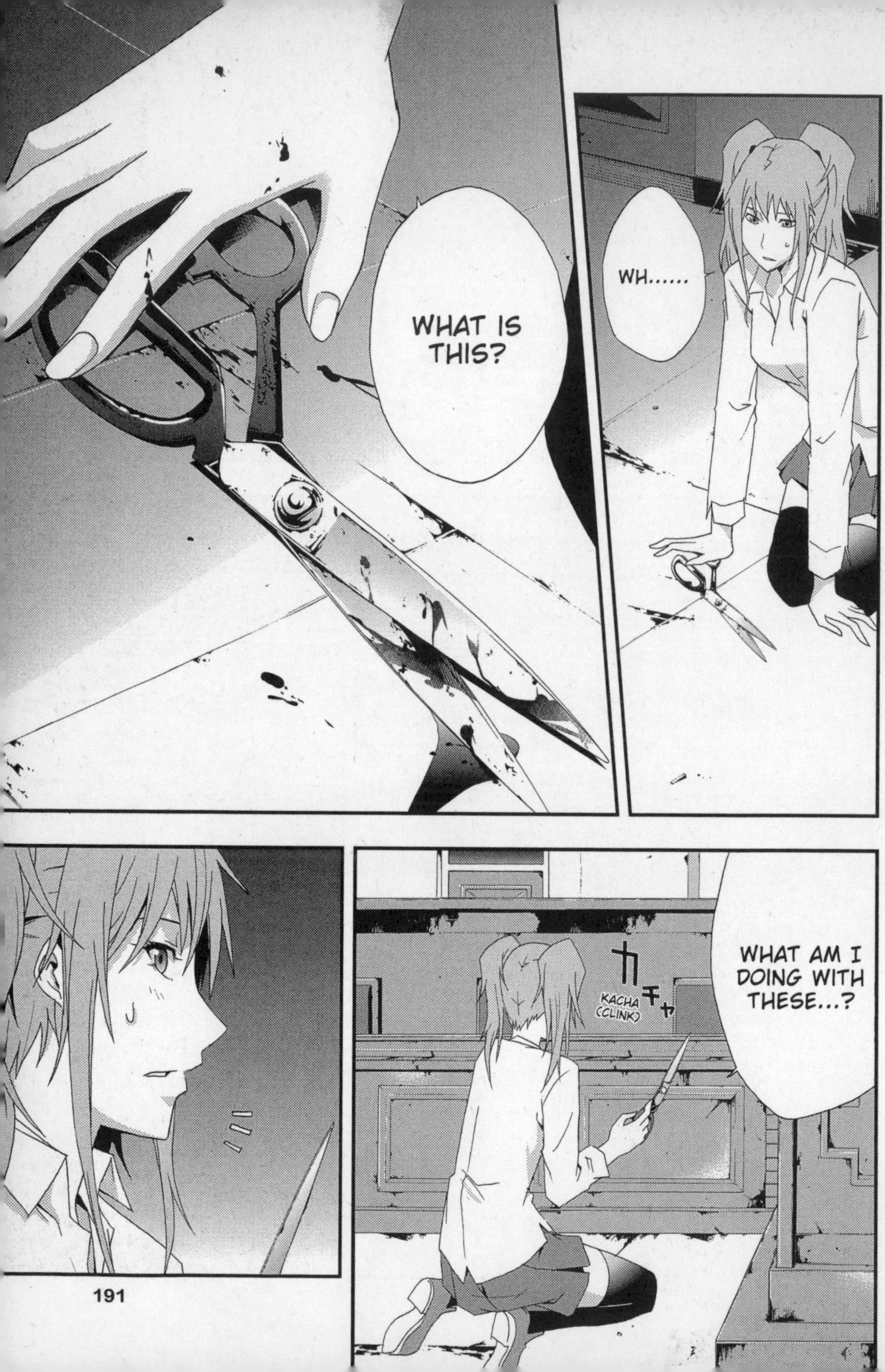
WH......
WHAT IS THIS?
WHAT AM I DOING WITH THESE...?
カチャ
KACHA (CLINK)

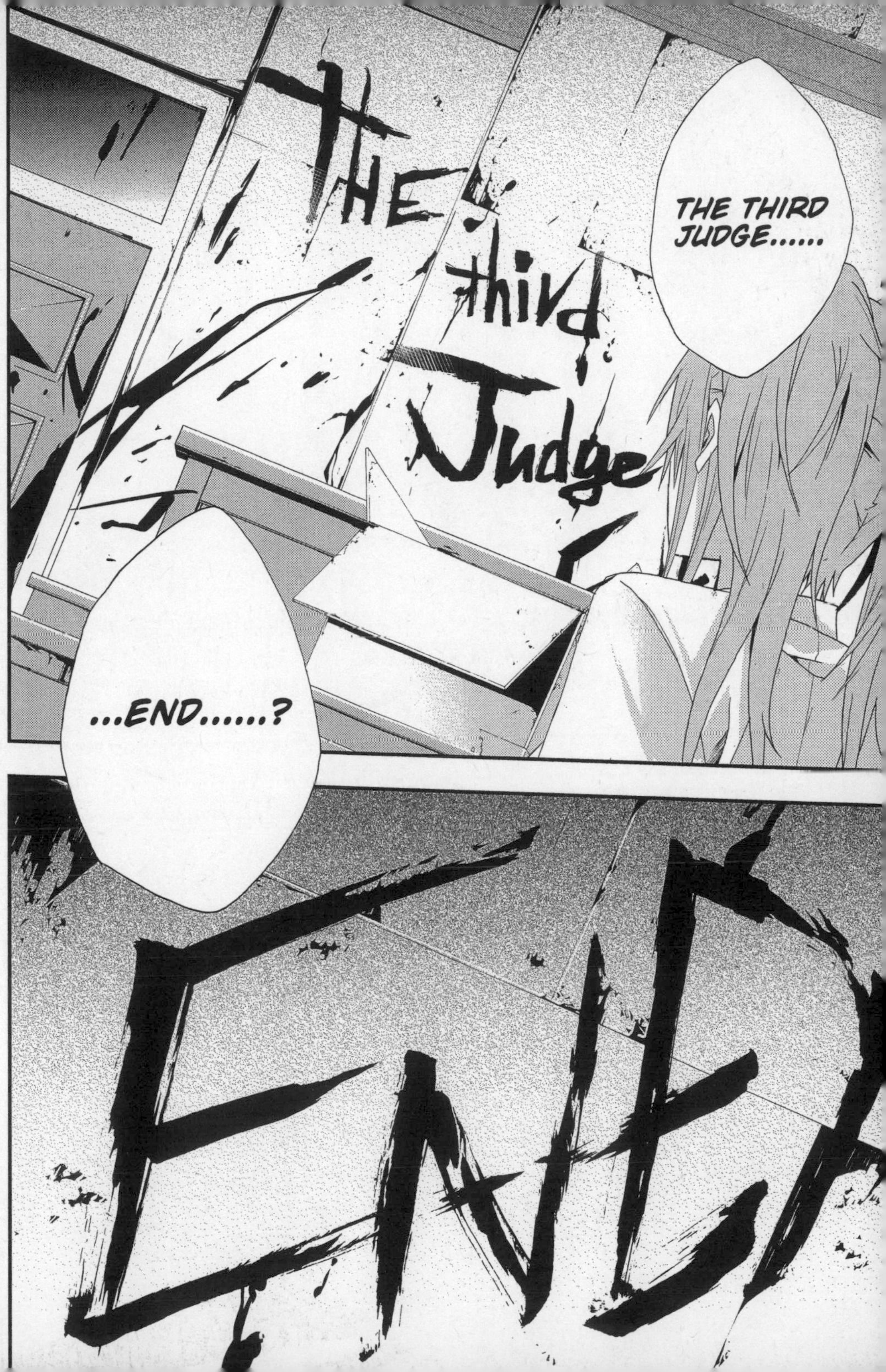
THE THIRD JUDGE......
The third Judge
...END......?
END

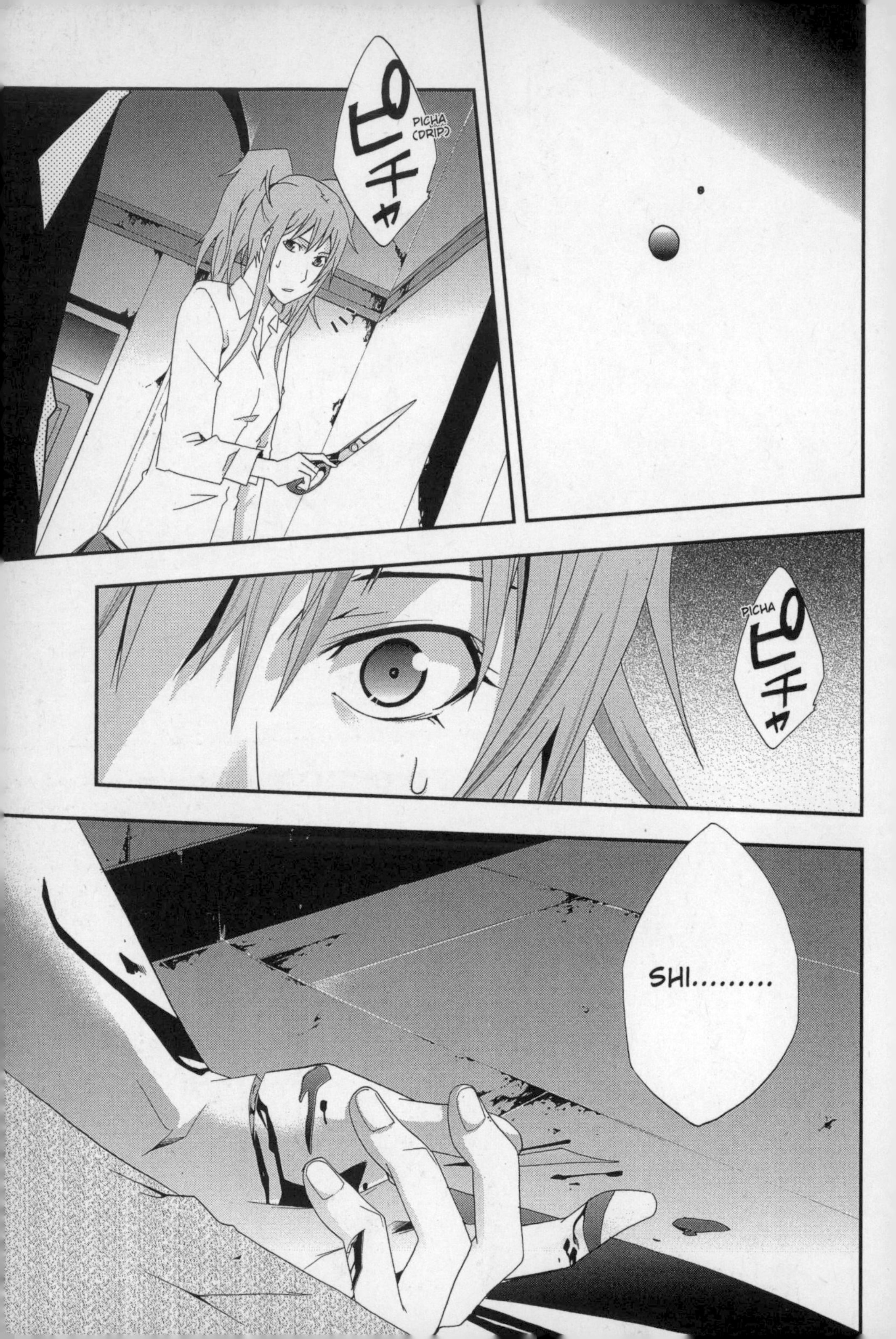

ピチャ
PICHA (DRIP)
ピチャ
PICHA
SHI.........

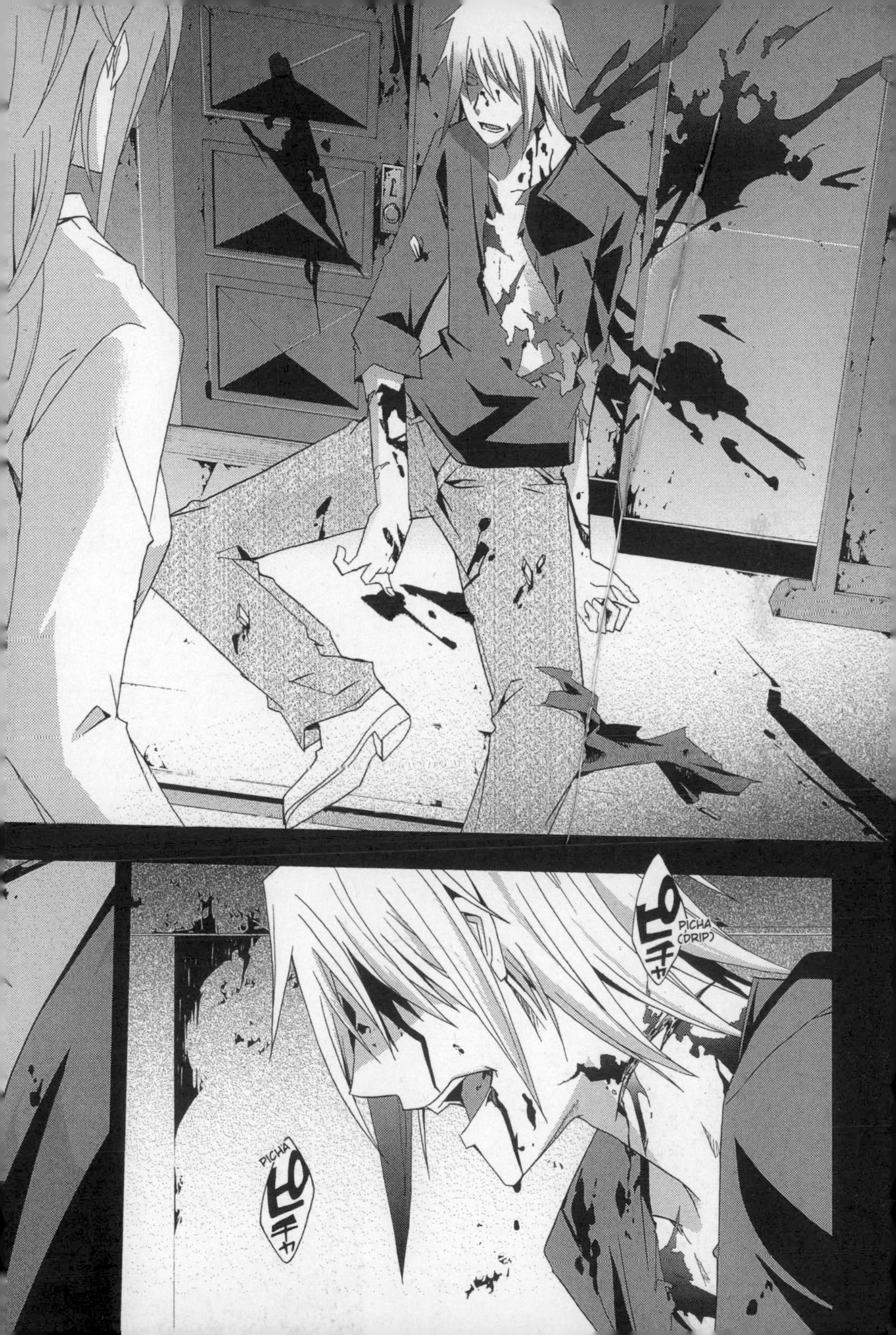
ピチャ
PICHA (DRIP)
ピチャ
PICHA

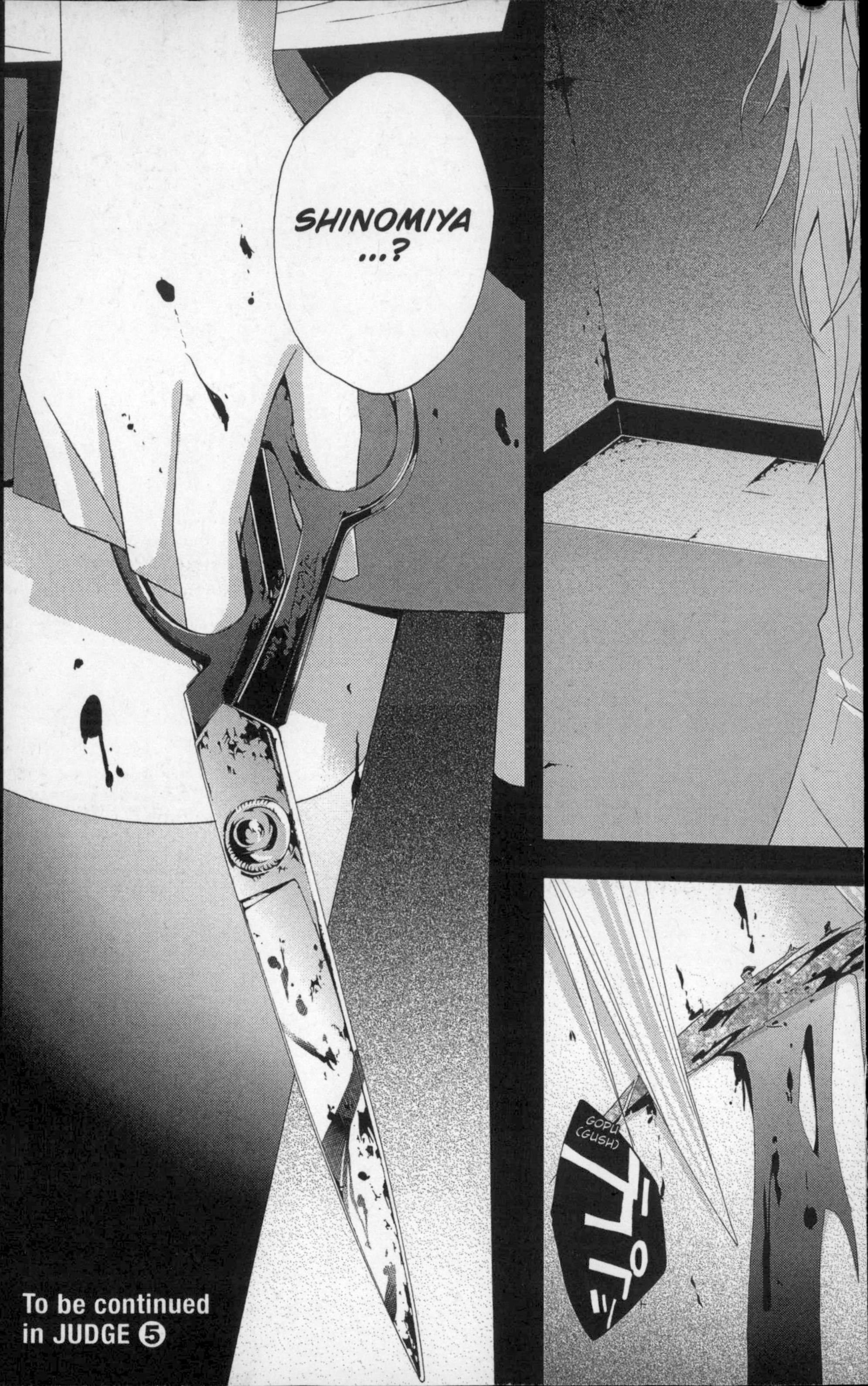
GOPU (GUSH)
ゴプッ
SHINOMIYA ...?

To be continued in JUDGE 5

JUDGE

STAFF

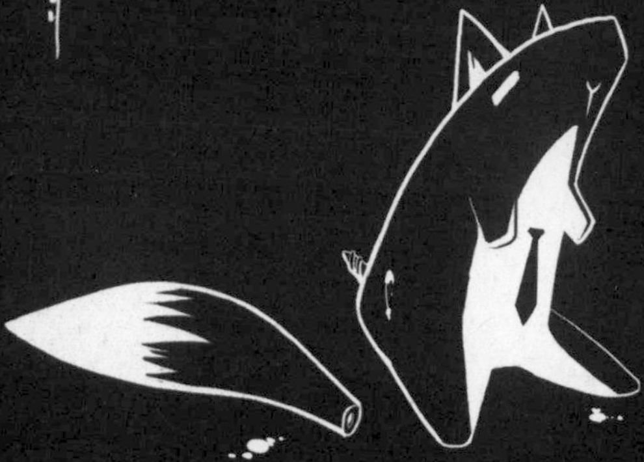

[MANGA]

TONOGAI

NOMURA

OIKAWA

TAKAHASHI

NAGASAWA

SASAI

YOSHIMURA

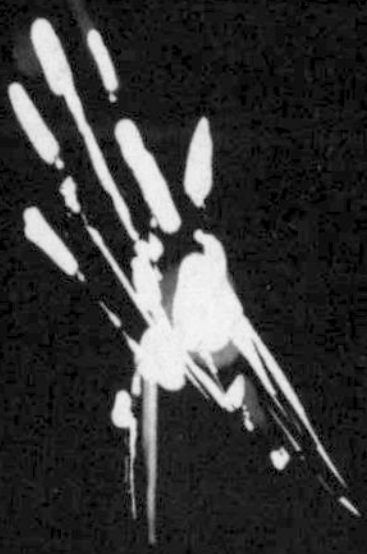

[EDITOR]

NOZAKI

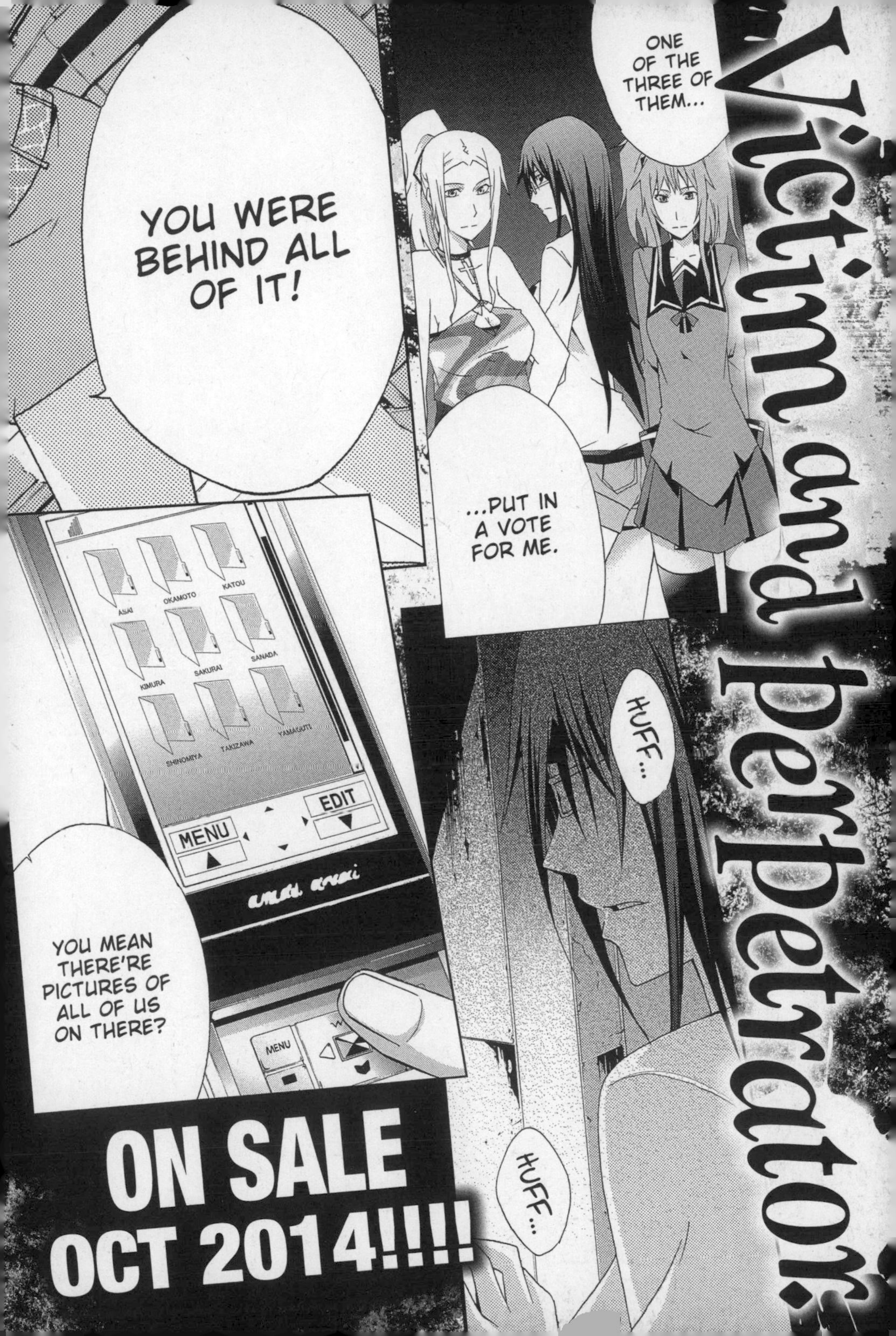
Victim and perpetrator:
ONE OF THE THREE OF THEM...
...PUT IN A VOTE FOR ME.
YOU WERE BEHIND ALL OF IT!
HUFF...
HUFF...
ASAI
OKAMOTO
KATOU
KIMURA
SAKURAI
SANADA
SHINOMIYA
TAKIZAWA
YAMAGUTI
MENU
EDIT
MENU
YOU MEAN THERE'RE PICTURES OF ALL OF US ON THERE?
ON SALE OCT 2014!!!!

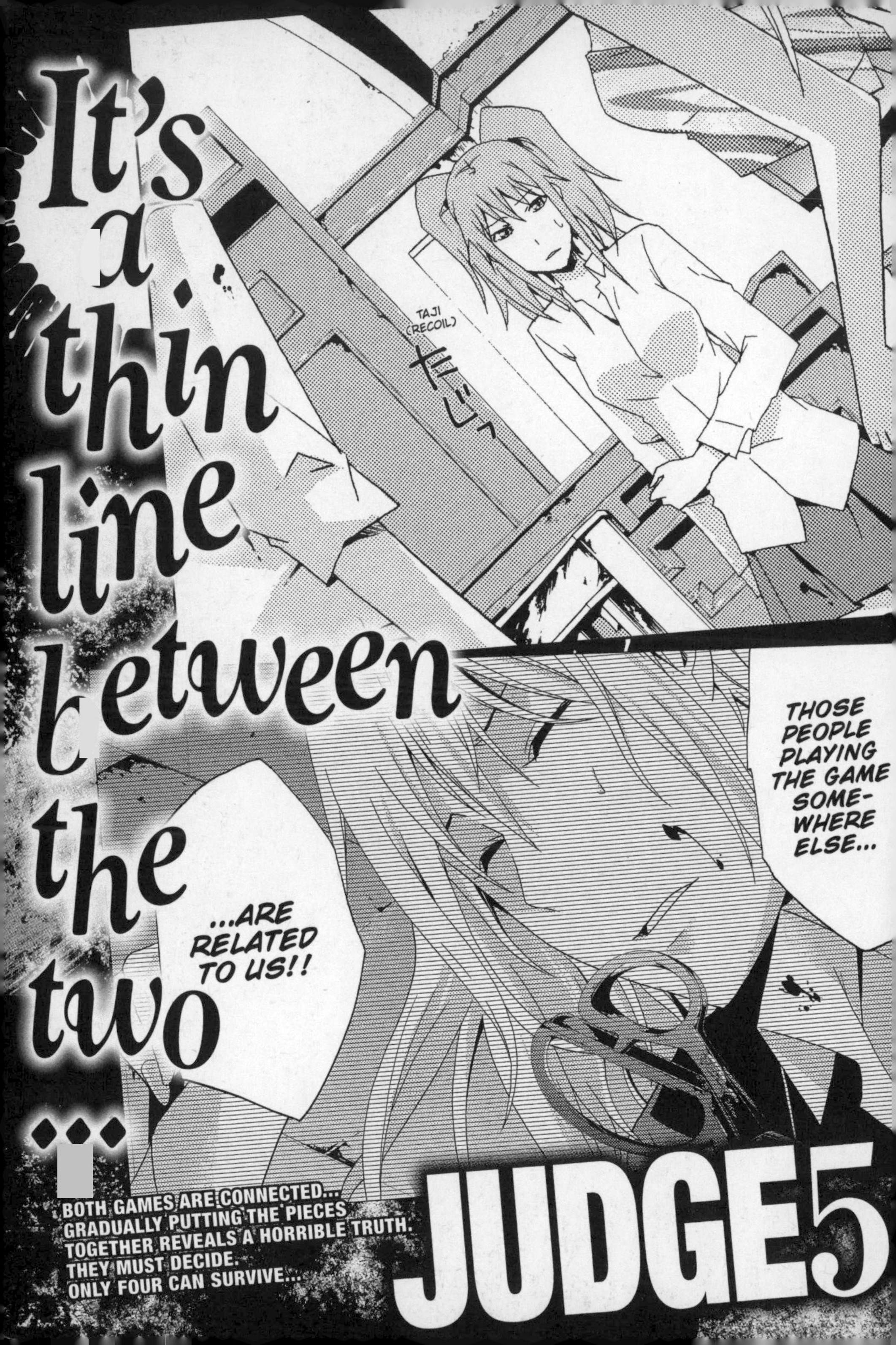
TAJI (RECOIL)
たじっ
THOSE PEOPLE PLAYING THE GAME SOME-WHERE ELSE...
...ARE RELATED TO US!!
It's a thin line between the two...
BOTH GAMES ARE CONNECTED... GRADUALLY PUTTING THE PIECES TOGETHER REVEALS A HORRIBLE TRUTH. THEY MUST DECIDE. ONLY FOUR CAN SURVIVE...
JUDGE5

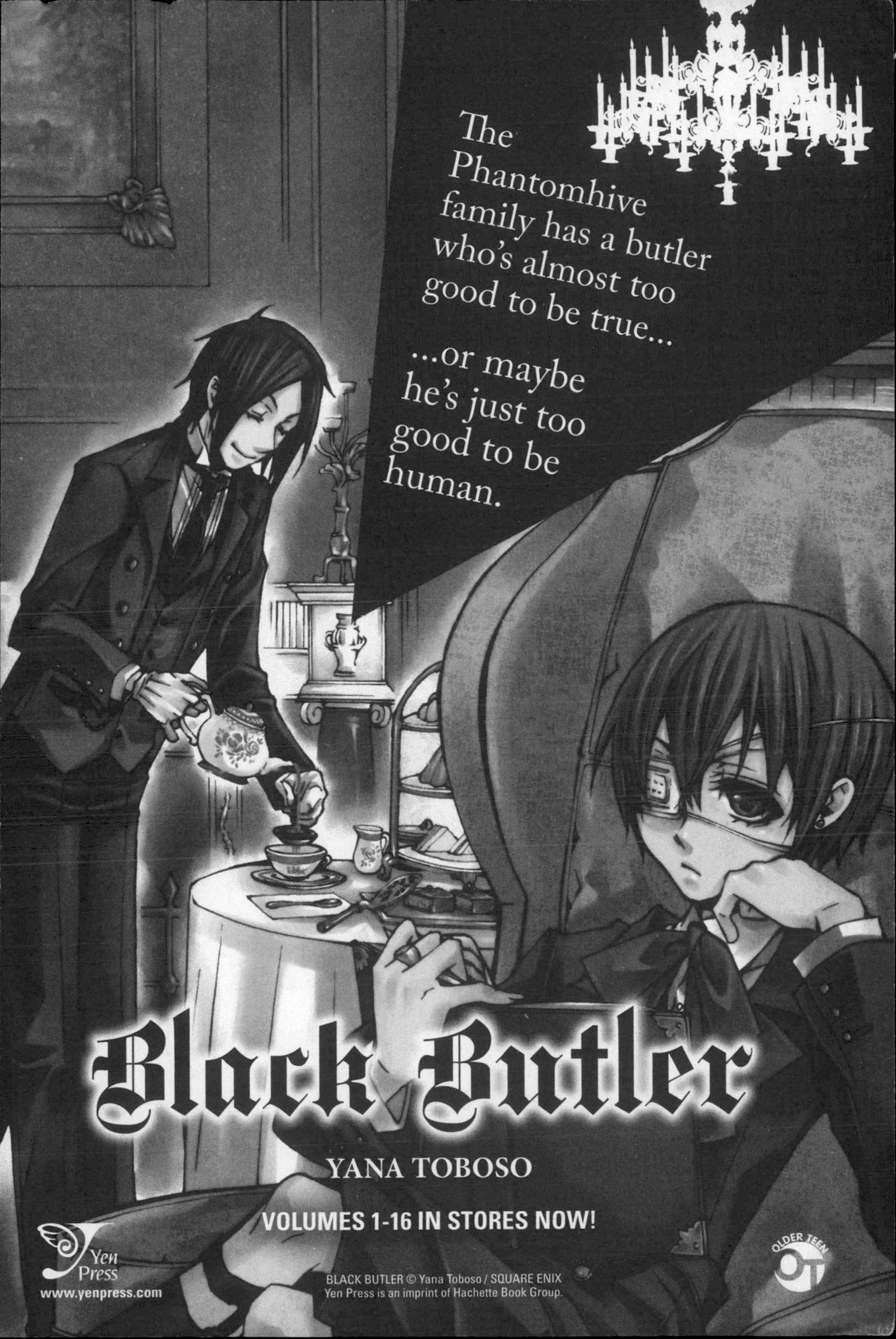
The Phantomhive family has a butler who's almost too good to be true...
...or maybe he's just too good to be human.
Black Butler
YANA TOBOSO
VOLUMES 1-16 IN STORES NOW!
Yen Press
www.yenpress.com
BLACK BUTLER © Yana Toboso / SQUARE ENIX
Yen Press is an imprint of Hachette Book Group.
OLDER TEEN
OT

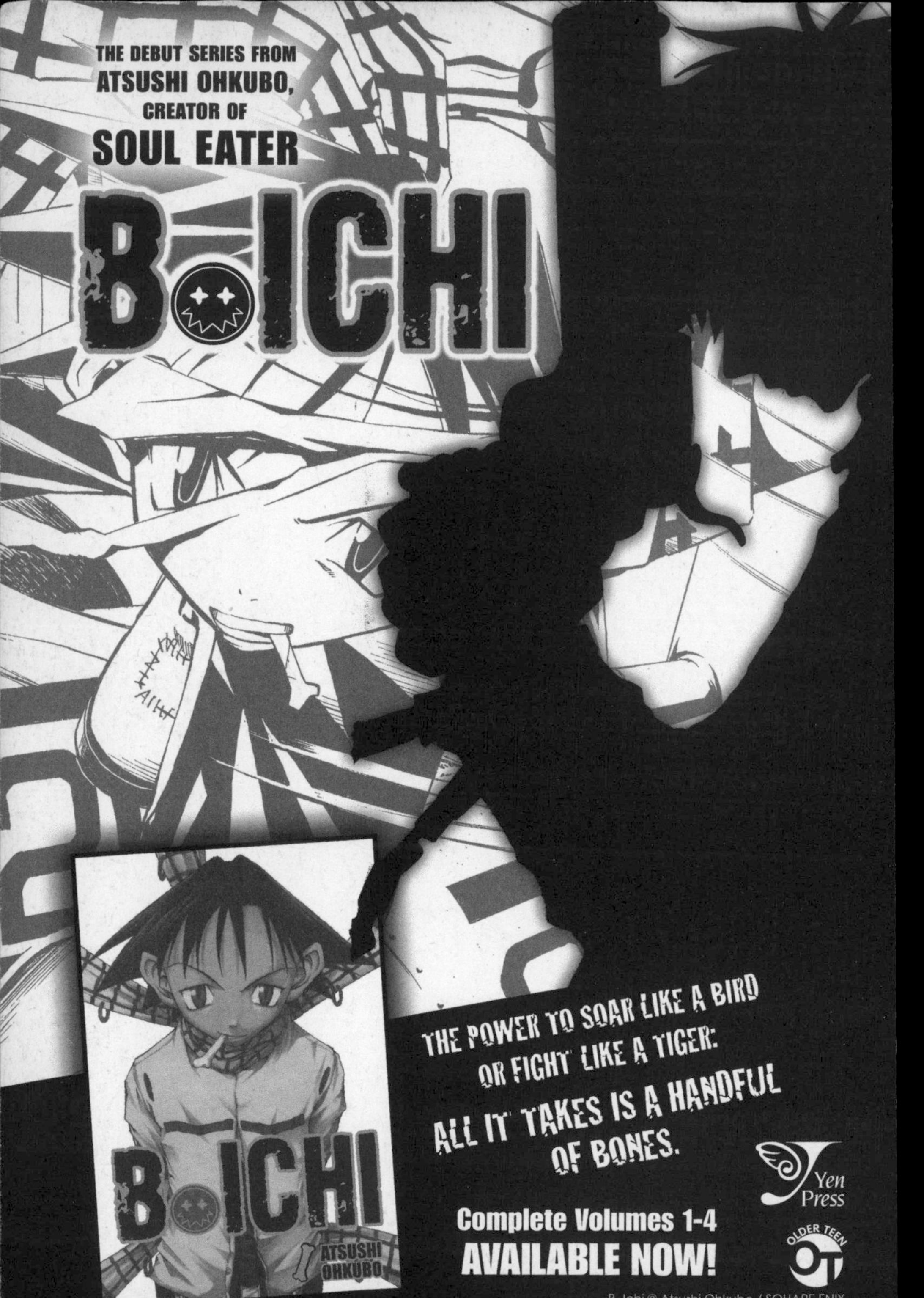
THE DEBUT SERIES FROM
ATSUSHI OHKUBO,
CREATOR OF
SOUL EATER
B. ICHI
THE POWER TO SOAR LIKE A BIRD
OR FIGHT LIKE A TIGER:
ALL IT TAKES IS A HANDFUL
OF BONES.
B. ICHI
ATSUSHI OHKUBO
Yen Press
Complete Volumes 1-4
AVAILABLE NOW!
OLDER TEEN
OT

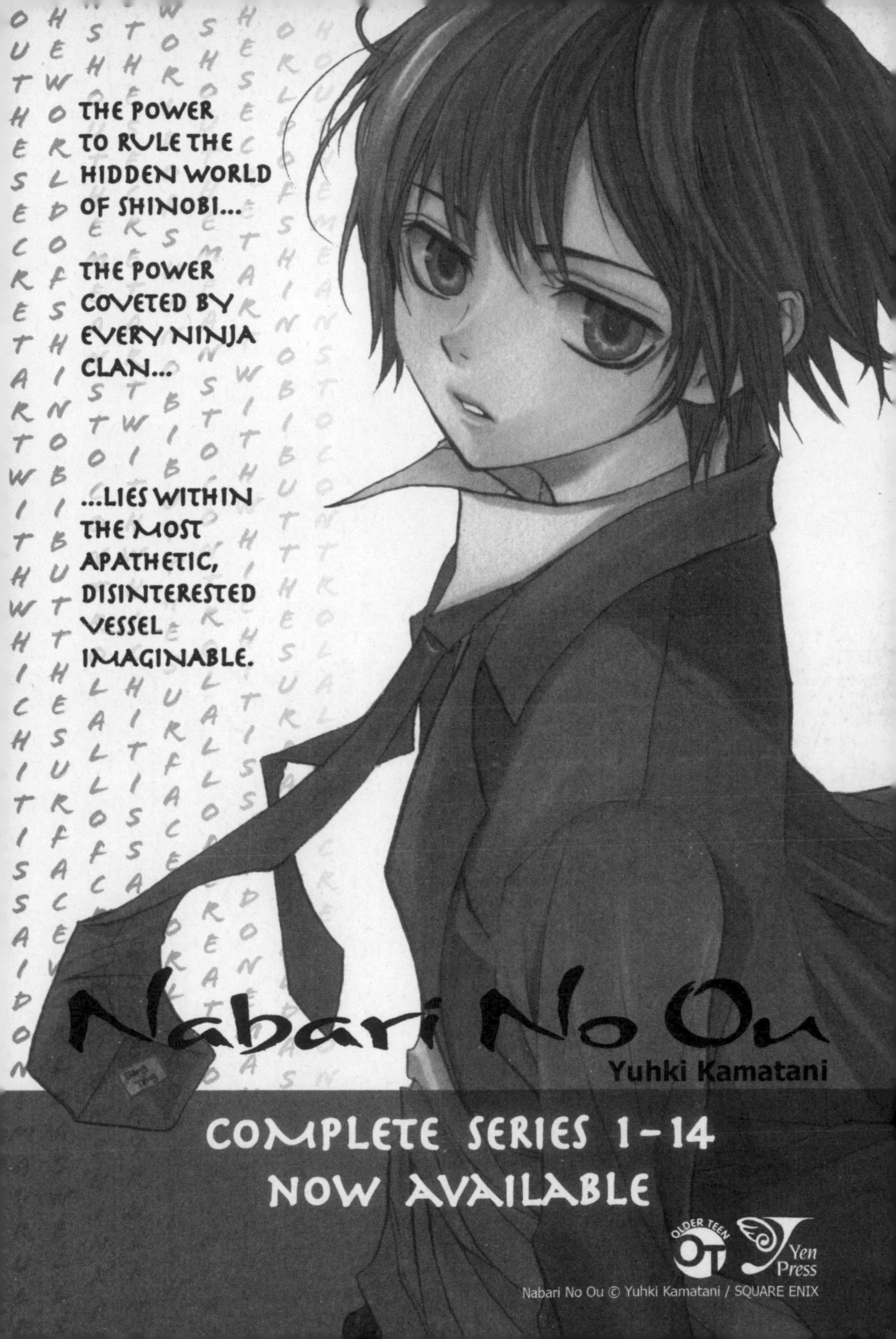
THE POWER TO RULE THE HIDDEN WORLD OF SHINOBI...
THE POWER COVETED BY EVERY NINJA CLAN...
...LIES WITHIN THE MOST APATHETIC, DISINTERESTED VESSEL IMAGINABLE.
Nabari No Ou
Yuhki Kamatani
COMPLETE SERIES 1-14
NOW AVAILABLE
OLDER TEEN OT
Yen Press
Nabari No Ou © Yuhki Kamatani / SQUARE ENIX

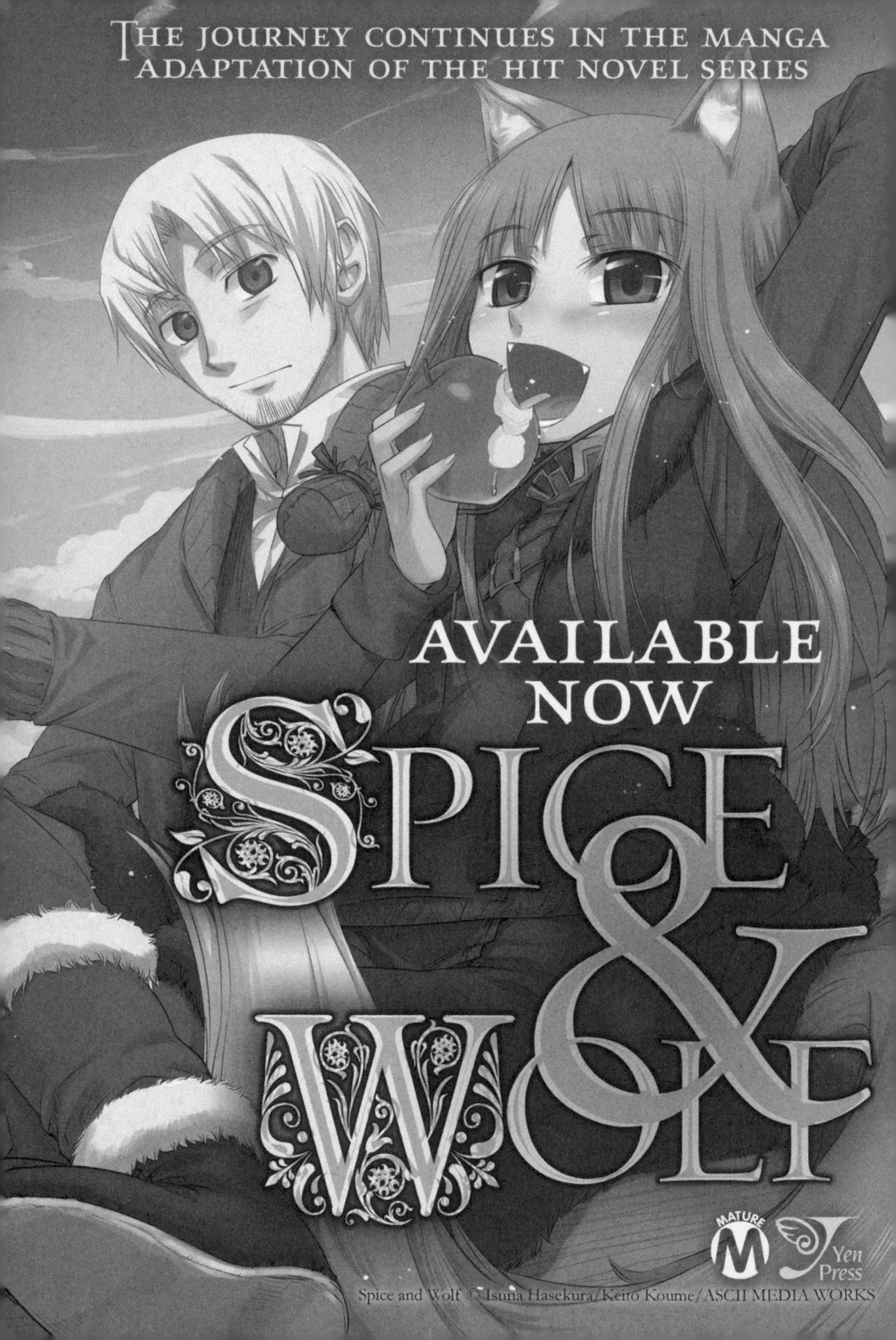
THE JOURNEY CONTINUES IN THE MANGA
ADAPTATION OF THE HIT NOVEL SERIES
AVAILABLE
NOW
SPICE & WOLF
MATURE
M
Yen
Press
Spice and Wolf © Isuna Hasekura/Keito Koume/ASCII MEDIA WORKS

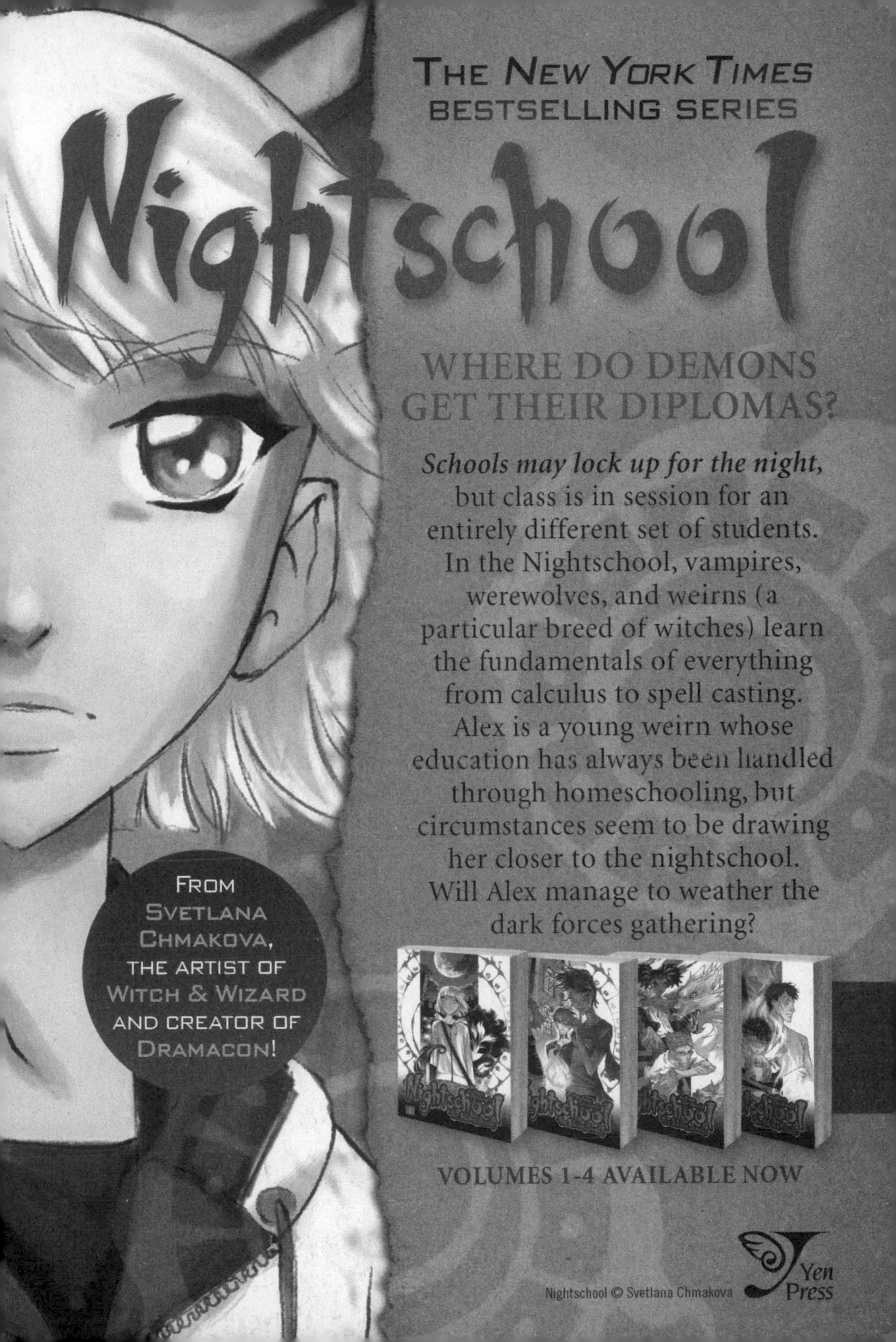
THE NEW YORK TIMES
BESTSELLING SERIES
Nightschool
WHERE DO DEMONS GET THEIR DIPLOMAS?
Schools may lock up for the night, but class is in session for an entirely different set of students. In the Nightschool, vampires, werewolves, and weirns (a particular breed of witches) learn the fundamentals of everything from calculus to spell casting. Alex is a young weirn whose education has always been handled through homeschooling, but circumstances seem to be drawing her closer to the nightschool. Will Alex manage to weather the dark forces gathering?
FROM SVETLANA CHMAKOVA, THE ARTIST OF WITCH & WIZARD AND CREATOR OF DRAMACON!
VOLUMES 1-4 AVAILABLE NOW
Nightschool © Svetlana Chmakova
Yen Press

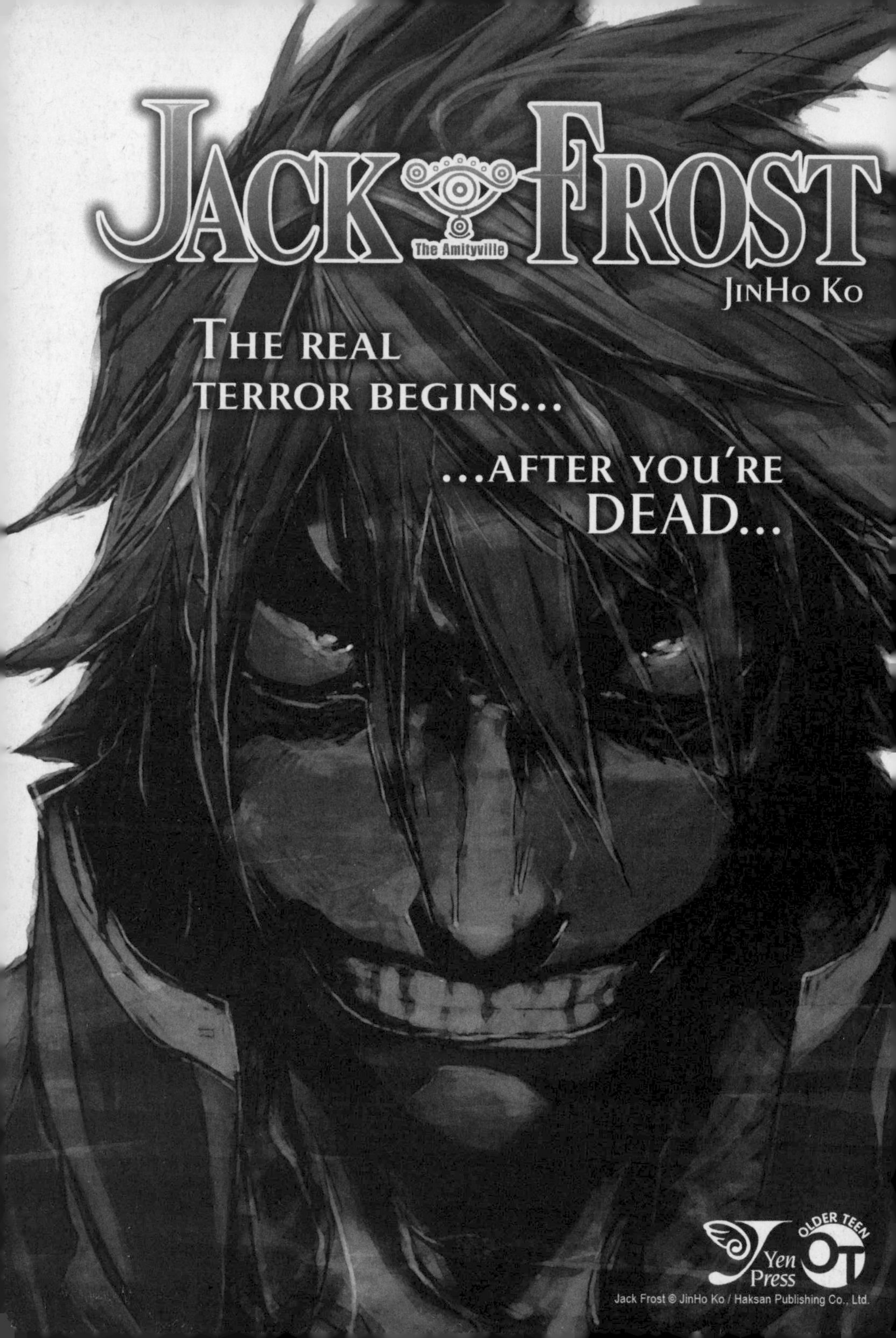
JACK FROST
The Amityville
JINHO KO
THE REAL TERROR BEGINS...
...AFTER YOU'RE DEAD...
Yen Press
OLDER TEEN
OT
Jack Frost © JinHo Ko / Haksan Publishing Co., Ltd.

JUDGE 4

YOSHIKI TONOGAI

Translation and Lettering: Alexis Eckerman

JUDGE Vol. 4 © 2011 Yoshiki Tonogai / SQUARE ENIX. First published in Japan in 2011 by SQUARE ENIX CO., LTD. English translation rights arranged with SQUARE ENIX CO., LTD. and Hachette Book Group through Tuttle-Mori Agency, Inc.

Translation © 2014 by SQUARE ENIX CO., LTD.

Yen Press
Hachette Book Group
237 Park Avenue, New York, NY 10017

www.HachetteBookGroup.com
www.YenPress.com

Yen Press is an imprint of Hachette Book Group, Inc. The Yen Press name and logo are trademarks of Hachette Book Group, Inc.

First Yen Press Edition: June 2014

ISBN: 978-0-316-24034-5

10 9 8 7 6 5 4 3 2 1

BVG

Printed in the United States of America